TREASURE SHIP

ALSO BY DENNIS M. POWERS

The Raging Sea

TREASURE SHIP

The Legend and Legacy of the S.S. *Brother Jonathan*

DENNIS M. POWERS

CITADEL PRESS
Kensington Publishing Corp.
www.kensingtonbooks.com

CITADEL PRESS BOOKS are published by

Kensington Publishing Corp.
850 Third Avenue
New York, NY 10022

All Kensington titles, imprints, and distributed lines are available at special quantity discounts for bulk purchases for sales promotions, premiums, fund-raising, educational, or institutional use. Special book excerpts or customized printings can also be created to fit specific needs. For details, write or phone the office of the Kensington special sales manager: Kensington Publishing Corp., 850 Third Avenue, New York, NY 10022, attn: Special Sales Department; phone 1-800-221-2647.

First printing: September 2006

10 9 8 7 6 5 4 3 2 1

Printed in the United States of America

Library of Congress Control Number: 2006926710

ISBN 0-8065-2747-1

To those who love the sea and its boundless treasures.

CONTENTS

Preface

Over ten years ago, the *San Francisco Chronicle* and other national newspapers ran headlines that salvors discovered a long-lost, ghost ship that sank off Northern California in 1865. The media ran fascinating stories about the gold onboard, the Gold Rush and Civil War personalities, and the era. I was researching a book then on tsunamis (*The Raging Sea*) and filed the articles in an "of great interest file." Three years later, I read about the discovery of gold on the sunken vessel and then of a United States Supreme Court decision that established leading maritime law. The ship was named the *Brother Jonathan.*

I continued researching the ship and its history during summers, vacations, and breaks from my teaching responsibilities. I became enamored by the stories of its owner during the Gold Rush, Cornelius Vanderbilt; its use in ferrying gold and prospectors from both coasts; and the important personalities who were on board. From Abraham Lincoln's closest friend and aide (Governor Anson Henry) to the Commander of the Pacific (General George Wright) and a famous, or infamous, madam (Roseanna Keenan), the rich and powerful mingled with families, prospectors, and businessmen on the ship's fateful journey from San Francisco.

Once again I found myself working in the research stacks of the Del Norte County Historical Society in Crescent City, California, where I researched my book *The Raging Sea,* about the worst tsunami in U.S. history to ravage the West Coast. I was fortunate that this volunteer organization had again taken the lead in gathering as much historical and current information as possible on the disaster and the long search for the lost ship. I had the opportunity to work a second time with the very likeable and knowledgeable Carol Cleveland. She opened up the society's voluminous files about the *Brother Jonathan,* including one-of-a-kind records. From Sandy Nuss and Sean Smith to Linda Cox, Dave Gray, and others, the Historical Society "folks" were helpful in pointing me in the right direction.

The information from Crescent City and Del Norte County was added to microfiche research from Eureka in Humboldt County, California, to Medford and Portland, Oregon. I scrutinized the national accounts on the subject from articles in the *New York Times* on one coast to the *Los Angeles Times* and *San Francisco Chronicle* on the other.

At the same time, I buried myself in wonderful old books dating back to the 1840s and 1850s about travel on the high seas, from *California Gold Rush Voyages, 1848–1849: Three Original Narratives* to Charles Dickens's *American Notes* (1842). Marine historians from the San Francisco Maritime Museum, Puget Sound Maritime Historical Society, the Columbia River Maritime Museum, Vancouver Maritime Museums, and the U.S. Coast Guard Academy proved very helpful. Working with the National Archives in Washington, D.C., and Regional Archives in San Bruno, California, became nearly a pasttime. I was fortunate to inspect copies of records that were nearly two centuries old.

In the exciting world of ancient and old gold coins and ingots, I enjoyed talking with national experts, including Dr. Dick Doty (the Curator of Numismatics for the Smithsonian Institution in Washington, D.C.), Harry Forman, Bob Julian, Jesse Patrick, and Dr. Charles Tumosa. I watched the tapes of the 1999 "Great Debate" between Michael Hodder and Professor Buttrey, thanks to the American Numismatic Association.

I tracked down the people who were involved in the discovery, recovery, and fight over the gold of the long-lost *Jonathan*. As I talked at length with the important salvors—Donald Knight, David Flohr, Mark Hemstreet, Sherman Harris, and others—I found myself marveling at their efforts. Chronically underfunded and having to fight off the legal strikes by the state of California with its unlimited financial and personnel resources, the men who formed Deep Sea Research persevered.

I found myself fascinated by the controversy over the *Brother Jonathan*'s gold bars. Discovered before the ship was even located, the powerful and mighty in the international numismatic (the study and collecting of money, coins, and monetary equivalents) world surged into conflict over the authenticity of the valuable bars. The icons involved in this fight read like a "Who's Who" of numismatics, from the multi-millionaire John J. Ford and the highly regarded Q. David Bowers to Professor Ted Buttrey, who received the highest awards from both U.S. and English numismatic associations.

The courage of the men and divers who plummeted to the bottom of the sea in their search for the gold stood out in a continuing "David versus Goliath," to-the-death legal struggle. Whether in the exploration or monetary world, the successful and famous clashed time and again.

This is a true story about strong men and women, their greed, gold, and egos. It is about their persistence, strength, and courage whether they were among the rich and powerful or not. What we learn about the past is a guide to the future.

Acknowledgments

This book would not have been possible without the support and friendship of the lead salvors in the hunt and recovery of the *Brother Jonathan*'s treasure, Don Knight and David Flohr. Sherman and Rosemary Harris, Mark Hemstreet, Fletcher Alford, and Don Siverts also provided insights, documents, and background information, as did a close friend of mine, Chris Honore. He made various suggestions about the manuscript and is an excellent writer in his own right. Thanks, Chris!

I thank Carol Cleveland at the Del Norte County Historical Society for her help in acquiring photographs and allowing me access to the historical files. My special thanks go to Sandy Nuss who went out of her way on several occasions with research help and suggestions. The director of the Historical Society, Linda Ging, was also very supportive and I thank her, as well.

Regarding the *Brother Jonathan* and the consequential building of the lighthouse, Tricia Brown of the Cannon Beach Historical Society in Oregon, Richard Whitwer of the Oregon Chapter of the U.S. Lighthouse Society, and author Elinor Dewire gave helpful input. Certified genealogist Sandra M. Clunies, who has helped me on different projects, gave appreciated assistance with various biographical information—and thanks, again. Juan Santillan, the dive master at Pacific Quest Diving Center in Crescent City, California, helped explain dive and weather conditions at the site.

The following maritime organizations deserve special recognition for answering questions about steamer travel in the 1850s and 1860s: James P. Delgado, director, Vancouver Maritime Museum; Jeffrey H.

Smith, associate curator, Columbia River Maritime Museum; and Jack Carver, librarian, Puget Sound Maritime Historical Society.

Special thanks also go to Bill Kooiman of the Porter Shaw Library in the San Francisco Maritime Museum and National Historical Park. A longtime mariner and writer in his own right, Bill was especially helpful with maritime history and the design of paddlewheelers such as the *Brother Jonathan.* Colin MacKenzie, of the Nautical Research Centre library in Petaluma, California, was another mariner and researcher who provided needed historical help regarding the St. George Reef Lighthouse—and I appreciated this.

The U.S. Coast Guard provided excellent historical information and assistance. Richard Everett, the head of reference and instruction for the U.S. Coast Guard Academy in New London, Connecticut, deserves special recognition. He located valuable records about the *Brother Jonathan,* along with assistance in tracking down legislative enactments and developments—thank you, Richard. I appreciated, as well, the suggestions of Dr. Robert Browning, the Coast Guard Historian in Washington, D.C., as well as Scott Price, who is in his office.

The inspection of records pertaining to the *Brother Jonathan* was important, and the personnel at the National Archives and Record Administration (NARA) were very helpful. Mr. John Hedger of NARA's San Bruno, California, facility offered invaluable assistance and leads, as did John Fitzgerald of its Seattle, Washington, regional archive and Susan Abbott of the National Archives in Washington, DC.

Another special thanks goes to a fellow Oregonian, Dr. Richard (Dick) G. Doty. From the beginning, Dick offered suggestions and insights on the numismatic aspects of this story that were very helpful. I appreciated the time and assistance of the following individuals for the stories and observations about John J. Ford, Professor Ted Buttrey, and the "Great Debate": Jim Elmen, World Wide Coins of California, Santa Rose, California; Jesse Patrick, the Patrick Mint, Santa Rosa, California; R. W. (Bob) Julian, numismatist, Logansport, Indiana; and Harry Forman, Bauer & Forman, Cheltenham, Pennsylvania. I wish to also thank Scott Mitchell of Stack's Rare Coins, New York

City, New York, for his assistance on information pertaining to the gold bars.

Two librarians provided invaluable help with my research: Jane Colvard is the research librarian for the American Numismatic Association in Colorado Springs, Colorado, and she arranged my review of the complete videotapes of the 1999 ANA's "Great Debate." Working with her on this and other aspects of my research, Anna Beauchamp, the coordinator of interlibrary loans for Southern Oregon University, worked out the details so that I could inspect very old manuscripts dating back to the 1840s. As part of this, Connie Anderson at SOU's library was also helpful in offering suggestions on my research of old statutes and maritime regulations.

No thanks would be appropriate without mentioning the editor-in-chief of Citadel Press, Michaela Hamilton, for her wonderful positive attitude and professional suggestions. I thank and appreciate my literary agent, Jeanne Fredericks. We have worked together for years, Jeanne, and it is always my pleasure.

I so appreciate the loving support of my wife, Judy, who accompanied me again on countless trips involving this book project. I look into the stars and count my blessings—every night.

Part I

The Final Voyage

CHAPTER 1

Steamer Day—Friday, July 28, 1865

Under the warming midmorning sun, the long arm of the Broadway Street Wharf stretched four hundred feet into San Francisco Bay, as the large, black hulk of the sidewheel steamer S.S. *Brother Jonathan* loomed up. Thick black smoke poured from its tall smokestack, as shouting crew members moved steamer trunks, worn carpet bags, and the last of the provisions and mail onboard in organized confusion. Men, women, and children congregated in tight groups on the wharf, by the pilot's cabin, on the ship's main deck, and in staterooms.

A horse and buggy clattered to a quick stop on the dock and deposited one more late passenger and his baggage. A crewman pushed out a handcart, pulled a large steamer trunk with carpet bags on it, and hauled the luggage to a waiting stevedore. Three stories up, people onboard shouted and waved to others below, as several worked their way gingerly up the gangplank, gripping tightly to the hemp rope guidelines as they stared at the nearby bulk of the starboard paddle wheel.

Men in three-piece suits with wide lapels, high-necked collars, and thick bowties conversed with women wearing plumped-sleeved, high-collared dresses with bustles and tight bodices in bright reds, blues, whites, and blacks. Most of the men had beards, muttonchops, or handlebar mustaches, while the women's hairdos were typically parted in the middle and flounced full on the sides. The men wore bowlers and stovepipe hats, while the women carried shawls or held an umbrella high to ward off the sun.

The well-to-do mingled in tight groups of velvet lapels and shiny gold watches, their wives dressed in shiny silks, lace, and frills. Farmers and miners in beaten hats and worn corduroy suits accompanied their wives, dressed less stylishly in plain pioneer cotton dresses of pale blues and checks. Military officers wore their blue formal attire with gold decorations, tassels, and an occasional dress sword; the children wore their own proper attire, girls in open-sleeved dresses and boys in suits or knickers.

Aside from family and business matters, as the Confederate General Robert E. Lee had surrendered to General Ulysses S. Grant, and President Lincoln had been assassinated a short three months before, most conversations were about the Civil War and the South's reconstruction. This was the time of Brigham Young in Salt Lake City, Kit Carson, and Indian raids, along with the unrest, bitterness, and poverty in the war-ravished South. President Andrew Johnson, John Wilkes Booth, and Charles Dickens were household names, as well known then as George Bush, Michael Jordan, and J. K. Rowling of Harry Potter fame are now.

The *Brother Jonathan* at 220 feet long was over a half-city block in length. These sidewheelers, otherwise known as paddleships, were the largest wooden ships ever built. Powered primarily by steam-driven paddle wheels over three-stories high on each side at midship, the vessel had three masts, the largest of which soared nine stories into the sky. Her masts were rigged as a barkentine: A three-masted ship with the foremast square-rigged (the mast closest to the bow had numerous square sails) and the main and mizzen masts were fore- and aft-rigged (the two masts towards the stern flew a large triangular sail over a four-sided one). Held tight by countless spider webs of shrouds and ropes, she carried a full complement of canvas sails that steadied the vessel in bad weather, conserved on coal when needed, and powered the ship if its engine broke down.

The *Jonathan*'s hull was painted in black enamel, the gunwales in deep blue, and the deckhouses a sandy or buff color. Her large paddle wheel boxes were black and red, offset by a large, gleaming brass half-moon in each center. An elevated pilothouse stood immediately forward of the smokestack, adorned by a magnificently carved, five-foot high golden eagle above its front, with one mast set ahead of the stack and the other two located behind it.

Built of redwood and 120-feet long, the dining saloon extended along the main deck towards the stern, while the family suites and cabins, also redwood, surrounded the saloon on both sides towards the stern. In back of the smokestack, a "walking beam" conveyed the powerful engine strokes to move the paddle wheels and was positioned on the deckhouse like a series of large, interconnected grasshoppers pumping oil. The diamond-shaped lever sat atop an A-frame structure and was connected to vertical rods at both ends; these rods caused the crankshaft to move and the paddle wheels to rotate. The steerage and storage compartments were located towards the bow and under the staterooms in the bowels of the ship.

Built in 1851, the vessel sailed the initial New York City to Panama runs on the Atlantic side during the days of the California Gold Rush. When Cornelius Vanderbilt bought the ship, he transferred her to the Pacific Ocean, and she ran from Nicaragua to San Francisco and back. Of the six Vanderbilt steamers that serviced this route, only the *Brother Jonathan* and one other paddleship survived these trips. In 1853, the *Jonathan* sailed from San Francisco with nearly $1 million in gold aboard, now worth multimillions, destined eventually for the East Coast and the U.S. Mint in Philadelphia. In 1854, she arrived in San Francisco on one voyage carrying a record 1,000 passengers.

As California and San Francisco became populated, a new owner in 1857, T. G. Wright, put the vessel into service making West Coast runs that ranged along the coast from San Diego to Victoria, British Columbia. She became the principle coastwise ship, transporting as many as 1,000 gold seekers at a time from California to points north, when prospectors discovered more gold in eastern Oregon, followed by Idaho's Boise and Clearwater basins, and then Montana. Named for the Revolutionary War character—a moralistic Yankee with the tendency to lecture folks about improper behavior—Brother Jonathan was the predecessor to Uncle Sam. From Thomas Nast to Montgomery Flag, gifted illustrators and political cartoonists eventually took over and by the 1880s had created the current Uncle Sam from Brother Jonathan's image. The vessel bearing this name was completely overhauled and refurbished three times during her career.

As there were no propeller ships then, travelers to and from the hub city of San Francisco preferred the sidewheelers. These steamers were vital in transporting people, freight, and the mail from before the Gold Rush until after the Civil War. No railroads connected the Midwest to the West Coast, or the Pacific Northwest, and the transcontinental railroad track wouldn't be complete until 1869. Passage during the 1850s and 1860s, if not by steamer, took weeks to cross over harsh mountain ranges and terrain—depending also on early snows, raging floods, and Indian raids. Sailing by a fast steamship was preferred, and the growing cities of the West and Pacific Northwest needed the goods that steamers like the *Brother Jonathan* could carry on a regular basis.

By the late morning on Friday, July 28, 1865, various dignitaries had already boarded the *Brother Jonathan* for its scheduled noon run northward. Among them was Brigadier General George Wright, the past Commander of the Pacific for the Union forces, en route to Fort Vancouver in the Washington Territory (later, the state of Washington) to take a new command. Governor Anson G. Henry of the Washington Territory, an important figure in the nation's capital, boarded that day and still mourned the recent loss of his close personal friend, President Abraham Lincoln.

Other important people aboard included Mr. William Logan, the newly appointed superintendent of the U.S. Mint in The Dalles, Oregon. He was a friend of Anson Henry and traveling to oversee the mint's construction. Major E. W. Eddy was the U.S. Army paymaster and was assuming similar responsibilities at Fort Vancouver. Captain J.S.S. Chaddock, commander of the U.S. Revenue Service cutter *Joe Lane,* had been placed on a leave of absence due to ill health and was traveling to Oregon to rejoin his ship.

Other well-known personalities onboard the *Brother Jonathan* included non-military personnel. James Nisbet, the widely respected author, editor, and part-owner of the *San Francisco Evening Bulletin*, joined Mrs. Roseanna Hughes Keenan, another well-known San Franciscan. Her standing was due to being a "leading" madam in the city. Mrs. Keenan was leaving the city for Victoria, British Columbia, taking along her seven "soiled doves." Joseph A. Lord, the senior messenger for the Wells Fargo Company, boarded the ship at the last moment to replace a more junior messenger who wasn't able to come and oversee the company's shipments of gold and other valuables.

Military leaders, politicians, prospectors, and husbands and wives looking to rejoin their families joined soldiers returning to their home cities and wealthy passengers on vacation. Card sharks, adventurers, and prostitutes mingled together with newlyweds and families with young children looking for a fresh start, miners searching for gold, and farmers wanting virgin land. A traveling circus was even represented with the owner's wife, child, and animals on board. Rugged men destined for the interior gold corridors of Idaho, Montana, and other territories in search of their fortunes usually bought the cheaper steerage tickets; families did their best to avoid these confined quarters.

The sight of General Wright, dressed in an open sealskin coat over his military attire, his wife in fashionable black-silk lace, followed by a tight group of medal-decorated, smartly dressed, blue-uniformed men, likely created a stir. Along with trunks of luggage and possessions, General Wright also brought along his favorite Newfoundland dog and prized horses.

The image created by Mrs. Keenan's entrance would have been just as striking—but different. Striding up to the purser with seven other perfumed women, all dressed to attract attention in low-cut dresses, she presented the stateroom tickets from diamond-adorned hands. She and her entourage drew the attention of most, including a few leers and at least a whistle or two from the crew. San Franciscans on board certainly knew and greeted Jim Nisbet, but how Roseanna Keenan would have acknowledged Mr. Nisbet can only be speculated. However, anyone in the theater and entertainment business would have welcomed Nisbet warmly, as he reviewed the major attractions in town, his coverage also including circuses.

At least 190 passengers were on this voyage with 54 crew members, ranging from Captain Samuel J. DeWolf and his officers to the engineers, purser, firemen (who stoked the furnaces), coal passers, porters, cooks, waiters, watchmen, cabin boys, and seamen. As passengers would board a ship and then pay afterwards, not to mention stowaways, some were not included on the official passenger list. The official count of 244 people on the *Brother Jonathan,* however, is the generally accepted number.

Although the ship was delayed in its sailing, the times were still festive. "Steamer Day" was an important event, even on coastal voyages with people leaving old friends and looking forward to making new ones. *San Francisco Bulletin* editor James Nisbet had been on the *Brother Jonathan* before. He wrote in *The Annals of San Francisco* (published in 1854) on a previous departure:

> The *Brother Jonathan* is already beginning to be crowded. Above and below, passengers with flushed faces and scarcely steady steps are prowling among the heaps of packages and boxes, searching for their own. The people bustle about, and after some thick speechifying and unnecessary gestures, discover their "bunks" and secure their "traps" as closely as possible. All is confusion.
>
> Something is sure to be forgotten at the last moment; something of the utmost consequence is still to be done. It is neither time nor fit for a person to do the thing needful; and the unhappy passenger dare not leave the ship for an instant, lest she sail without him. There is, however, no danger of that, though there is so much fear. One half of the passengers are still on the wharf, talking fast and hurriedly with friends, and preparing to take the last farewells. On board, a majority of the people are those who have only come to see the emigrant off.
>
> Small groups cluster wherever there is standing room on

> the different decks. The bottle is produced, and the last drop taken; champagne freely flows among the state-cabin nobs, and rum or ready-mixed bottled cocktails among the snobs over all the ship. Among them all, some can and do pay for state cabins; others can, but will not; a considerable number ought not, but do; while the most can not, and consequently do not. All, however, are rejoiced to hold their friends to the last, and seek to show their joy in various ways—in cheerful discourse and in drinks, in a warm shake of the hand, a half-stifled sigh and a heartfelt look.

Captain Samuel J. DeWolf was the Captain of the *Brother Jonathan,* having taken over the vessel that past June. A Southern sympathizer shot the previous captain in an argument just after the end of the Civil War. While on the Columbia River that month, the *Brother Jonathan* then collided with the sailing barkentine *Jane Falkenberg,* cracking the *Jonathan*'s hull. When she returned to San Francisco, Captain DeWolf told the company that she needed to be pulled out of the water and put into a dry dock for repairs to the break, as the weakness was located at and slightly below the waterline. The company decided against his recommendation, ordering its foreman, Mr. Henry Mart, to mend the break from inside as best he could.

The business of hauling freight at this time was good, perhaps too good. Cargo piled up on the docks owing to the demand for non-military, cargo-bearing vessels. The day before the *Brother Jonathan* was set to sail, Captain DeWolf tried to convince the acting company agent to stop receiving goods, warning him the ship was already too deeply laden. Acting in place of the regular agent and executive vice president of the company, Major Samuel Hensley, the substitute agent paid no attention to the warning. He said that he could find another captain to run the ship if need be. The Captain didn't say anything further, but expressed his misgivings to his wife and, afterward, to a friend on the dock. Marie DeWolf later wrote, "In those early days, the captains of the steamers in the Navigation Company had no control over their steamers while in port. From the dropping of the anchor on arrival until raised for departure, the office had full supervision and management."

Consequently, the loading of the freight continued for twelve hours, which included a large quartz-gold ore crusher weighing several tons. The stevedores completed their efforts Friday morning. Three hundred and forty-six barrels of whiskey, fifty cases of cigars, twenty-five barrels of butter, and chests of axe handles, doorknobs, nails, and tools were stowed on board. Men grunted when moving around the ship's holds the crates filled with shipments of playing cards, a billiard table, dry goods with bolts of cloth, rolls of copper sheathing, stacks of restaurant china plates, and farm tools. A fire engine and hoses were destined to be offloaded in Portland and then transported to the eventual destination of Salem, Oregon, the state's capital. The shipping manifest also included machinery headed for a woolen mill being built near Dallas, in Polk County, Oregon. The quartz ore crusher was intended for use in the Owyhee country of southeastern Oregon and Idaho.

"About seven hundred tons of merchandise freight, besides the passengers' baggage, all closely under hatch," was now loaded according to the *Alta California,* one of California's leading newspapers. Although the ship's carrying capacity was nine hundred tons, the particularly heavy items on board and their placement contributed to the vessel's delayed departure.

Ships also carried food and water provisions for the passengers and crew, not to mention the bilge pumps and coal. These ships had the capacity to hold three hundred tons of coal—stowed in the holds beneath the passenger decks but above the bilge—although these voyages would not require a full load of the fuel. Next, the seamen stowed the passengers' trunks and possessions, adding to the weight of what the vessel was carrying.

During the loading of cargo on the evening of July 27 and into the early morning of the 28th, the ship's Purser, John S. Benton, was accepting and signing for monetary and gold transfers from a variety of entities. All were placed in his care for safekeeping, and some amounts were unusually high. Major Eddy brought $200,000 in greenback currency to pay the troops at Fort Vancouver, Walla Walla, and other posts in Oregon and Washington. William Logan, the government's Indian agent for the Northwestern Region, oversaw $25,000 in gold coins for the annual treaty payments to the tribes. This money was paid to the tribal leaders to keep Indians on their reservations, and these payments were nearly always made in gold. Crates of newly minted $20 gold pieces were carried onboard, including private transfers for companies such as Haskins and Company. Wells Fargo and Company was a prime shipper of valuables with a box each of gold, money, valuables, and papers destined for the journey's three ports: Crescent City, Portland, and Vancouver in British Columbia. They were the three prime deep-water ports used on this route from San Francisco at the time.

The passengers themselves were their own banks, as well. They carried gold coins and bars for use at their new destinations; the ability to wire money or make non-physical bank transfers would not be available for decades. Later estimates placed the value of the gold and valuables on board this voyage at greater than $250,000, not including what the passengers were carrying. This amount alone would be worth upwards of $40 million in today's dollars.

Nearing noon, the passengers yelled and waved their goodbyes to loved ones as the anchors were raised, steam increased, word given to "let go of the ropes," and the paddles began turning. Her bottom being firmly embedded in the mud, however, the ship didn't move owing to a combination of low tides and loading issues. Captain DeWolf, the passengers, their families, and the crew waited for the afternoon four o'clock high tide and a steam tug.

Brigadier General George Wright was traveling with his wife, Margaret Foster Wright, to Fort Vancouver on the Columbia River between Oregon and Washington. He was to take command of the Department of Columbia, which encompassed both state territories. A contingent of officers accompanied General Wright, including his Adjutant Lieutenant E. D. Waite and Major E. W. Eddy, the U.S. Army Paymaster (assisted by his clerk), who watched over the troop payroll. Founded in 1825, Fort Vancouver was a central trading depot, which contained sizeable troop barracks, and it was the Army headquarters for the Pacific Northwest.

A graduate of West Point and a career soldier who had spent forty-three years in the U.S. Army, General Wright served in Florida during the Seminole War and in the Mexican War where he was wounded at Molino del Rey in 1847. Wright's most important contribution was his service during the Civil War as commander of the vast Federal Department of the Pacific that included all of the territory west of the Rocky Mountains from Canada to the Mexican border. He was widely credited with keeping San Francisco and the West Coast largely immune from attack during the catastrophic Civil War and extensive deaths and destruction that occurred in less fortunate areas of the country. Sixty-two years old at the time, General Wright received a lesser assignment after President Lincoln's assassination, which allowed his detractors to press their criticisms. The primary one was that he wouldn't commence Union troop attacks from California into faraway states. San Franciscans and most Californians, however, held him in high regard for keeping the state free from bloodshed.

Appointed by Lincoln nine days before John Wilkes Booth shot and killed the president at Ford's Theatre, Anson G. Henry was traveling to take over the leadership of the Washington Territory. He was formerly the U.S. Surveyor General of the Territory, a practicing physician, and an important Oregon political figure. Residing in Illinois as a young man, Anson Henry met and became a lifelong friend of Abraham Lincoln, acting as Lincoln's personal physician. Mr. Lincoln married his wife, Mary Todd, in 1842 in Anson Henry's home. He also served as a fellow editor with Lincoln on a Whig paper named *The Old Soldier*.

When Lincoln once appeared in the Senate with his cabinet, the president walked down the Senate aisle arm in arm with Anson Henry. They were followed by Secretary of State Seward and the remaining members of the cabinet. Henry escorted Mary Todd Lincoln to her seat in the Ambassador's Gallery when the votes were counted in the House of Representatives for the Presidency. The standing joke was that you couldn't see Lincoln without finding Anson close by. Fifty-five years old at the time of his trip on the *Brother Jonathan,* Governor Henry had just returned from Springfield, Illinois, where he was consoling the widow of the slain president.

Dr. Anson Henry and Victor Smith were implacable enemies and ironically both wound up together on this voyage. Henry had previously stated that he would "follow Victor Smith to hell." Two months before Smith sailed from the East Coast back to the West on the ill-fated *Golden Rule,* which wrecked on a reef in the Caribbean. Remaining on the rocks with a gunboat standing by, he salvaged a chest containing government funds that he was bringing to meet payrolls in his capacity as the Collector for Customs for the Puget Sound Territory area. With the aid of a diver on that Caribbean reef, Smith opened the chest containing the gold. Instead of finding "many hundred of thousands" of dollars in gold pieces, the chest was instead empty.

An inquiry ensued and Smith lost his position, in no small part due to Anson Henry's accusations about the missing gold and that Victor Smith was conspiring to set up his own dynasty. Although both men considered themselves spiritualists who could communicate with the dead, any other similarities between the two ended there. After surviving the wreck of the *Golden Rule,* Smith was ironically now on the *Brother Jonathan.* Too ill at the time, presumably from his shipwreck experiences, to walk onto the ship, Victor Smith was carried to his stateroom on a cot. He more than likely stayed there for the length of the voyage.

The editor of the *San Francisco Evening Bulletin,* James Nisbet, boarded the vessel to enjoy vacation time in the Pacific Northwest and then to defend a defamation action in Victoria, British Columbia. A native of Scotland and schooled in the law, Nisbet was a journalist and writer, having lived in England and Australia before immigrating to California in 1853. He loved the written word, having not only been cowriter of *The Annals of San Francisco,* but also authoring the fictional novel, *The Siege of Damascus.* Working in San Francisco on *The Chronicle* as a news editor, Nisbet joined the *Bulletin* in the same position after its editor was murdered. A lifelong bachelor, Nisbet was forty-five years old.

Roseanna Keenan and her "fallen angels" were headed to Victoria, B.C., where Rosanna's husband, John C. Keenan, now ran their newly bought beer saloon. In the 1850s the Keenans owned a similar establishment in Sacramento called the Fashion Saloon, where "liquors and cigars were served in the most proper manner." It ranked with the "very first-class houses of the kind in the country," and lunch was served every day "at 11 o'clock A.M. and 9 o'clock P.M." In 1865, the Keenans owned a liquor saloon in San Francisco at First and Stevenson Streets. They also managed the nearby Oriental Hotel and its restaurant, considered to be one of the city's "finest hotels." Mrs. Keenan and her employees were steaming north to Victoria, British Columbia, ostensibly to profit from the gold-rush activities still running on the neighboring Fraser River.

The seven women were not listed separately in the ship's register. All took berths in cabins under Mrs. Keenan's name and traveled anonymously except for two: a pretty young teenager named Martha E. Wilder and an older Mrs. Martha Stott. Victoria presented an opportunity for the Keenans with its less-lawful environment and gold rush economy. However, the main reason they left the United States for Canada is that they were asked to—and apparently the good citizens of San Francisco didn't leave much room for further discussion. Once John Keenan established the new saloon in Victoria, Roseanna Keenan sold their interests in San Francisco for a reported $5,500. An acquaintance said that Mrs. Keenan traveled carrying "thousands of dollars" worth of jewels, and she wore diamonds that people commented about.

Henry Charles Lee, an Englishman who came to the United States in 1848, founded a circus. After taking various names with different partners, it became known as Lee & Ryland's Circus in 1865, featuring daredevil riders, acrobats, jugglers, and jesters, as well as the "Lee Children, riders and acrobats." The family was well-known in San Francisco for their riding and trooping abilities.

Mrs. Jeannette Lee—H.C.'s second wife and a bareback rider—

came aboard the sidewheeler with their three-week-old baby, booking passage to Portland, Oregon. She would rejoin her husband and the rest of the Lee Family riders there. (H. C. Lee's first wife had died after giving birth to several children.) Not only was Jeannette Lee reportedly carrying the payroll for the circus, but she also brought along two camels and a show horse for the acts.

Daniel and Polina Rowell, age thirty-nine and thirty-three respectively, looked forward to a new life in the Pacific Northwest and herded their four children into their cabin. The couple had decided to leave Iowa, sell their farm, and move back to Oregon to rejoin Polina's father and mother, Elias and Sarah Buell. They hadn't told Elias about their coming back, wanting to surprise everyone with the grandkids.

A SMALLER MAN with a determined manner, Captain DeWolf had a narrow face, manicured beard, long nose, and a strong gaze. At age forty-three, he was already an experienced seaman. Born in Nova Scotia in 1822, DeWolf headed to the sea when he was sixteen years old. He crewed on ships that sailed from Liverpool to New York City and back, working his way up to first officer. He ended in San Francisco in 1849 when the Gold Rush started. DeWolf did have his share of luck in that he was one of two people who survived the fiery sinking of the steamboat *Lexington,* which burned in Long Island Sound in 1840; DeWolf floated ashore on a bale of cotton.

He captained the brig *Fremont,* as one of the first to command a ship in the coastal trade off California. Joining the California Steamship and Navigation Company in 1854, Captain DeWolf was very familiar with the ports of call and approaches up and down the West Coast. With his wife, Marie, the DeWolfs were very active socially and well known in the upper circles of San Francisco society. He was thought of as a thorough sailor ("the forecastle being as familiar to him as the quarterdeck"), strictly moral and temperate, a Christian, and a "kind and indulgent" husband.

DeWolf clearly fretted over what he felt was the overloading of his ship, especially when workmen made less repairs to the vessel than he thought were required. It is puzzling why he succumbed to a junior freight supervisor's demands to continue loading given his concerns. Although the "overloading" of seven-hundred tons was well within the nine-hundred ton limit that his ship could haul, Captain DeWolf was proven correct when his ship stuck in the mud at departure time. He might have had a premonition about the voyage and its loading, in that he said goodbye to his wife not once, but twice—but this could also have been due to the two attempts the *Brother Jonathan* made to leave.

There were no requirements then for loading marks on ships, nor definitions or controls as to what constituted a "fully loaded" ship. Any loading of goods was left to the discretion of the shipping companies. At the time, federal legislation consisted mainly of safeguarding passengers from steam explosions and fires at sea. Inspections and regulations centered on, for example, what steam pressure could be maintained in the boilers.

Another worry for Captain DeWolf was the Confederate raider *Shenandoah* and its captain, Lieutenant Waddell. Although the war had been over for three months, the news hadn't reached this ship. The *Alta California* on July 21 reported the news of the *Shenandoah*'s capturing twenty-five vessels in the Pacific Ocean. Four of the captured sailors—Portuguese seamen who Waddell had returned to San Francisco as proof of his victories—then immediately shipped out on this voyage.

As the tide swept in and the tug took its position, Captain DeWolf could see that his ship would be able to sail, although he was now four hours behind schedule. He knew that he could easily make up time with good steaming conditions, efficient port calls, and closely navigating the channels he knew so well. At DeWolf's signal, two loud blasts shrilled from the smokestack whistle. Families and visitors left the ship a second time, giving once more their farewells and salutations.

James Nisbet in his *Annals of San Francisco* had written before about his leaving on the *Brother Jonathan* from San Francisco:

Leviathan begins to blow and heave uneasily, eager to be off. The escape steam-pipe seems too narrow a throat for the angry breath of the monster, and loudly threatens to burst, as the mighty hulk quivers at the sound. The clamor strengthens on deck. The mate begins to move about and shout, and the men leap to obey his orders. The chief engineer and his aids are at their posts, awaiting the word of command from the captain, who at last condescends to enter on the scene of action. A rapid shuffling of feet is heard, baggage is unceremoniously tumbled aside, sailors handle the hawsers, and laggers rush hastily to the wharf. The last drop has been drunk, the last good-bye given.

The wharf is densely packed with spectators while the voyagers everywhere occupy the different decks of the magnificent ship. There are a few turns ahead of the paddle wheels, and then a few astern; the creature is lazily stretching its gigantic limbs before it begins serious work. The cables are cast loose, and leviathan yawns, and slowly drags its ponderous length half round.

There is meanwhile a general stillness observed by the spectators both on board and on the wharf. Their kind wishes, remembrances, orders, and farewells had all been given; and the heart was too full, or the eye too busily engaged with the ever attractive scene, to permit further active demonstrations.

Slowly and heavily, leviathan splashes and plunges; it moves round the outer end of the pier till its head is clear of the further wharf. Then the great heart ceases for a moment to beat, mustering its energies for the coming race. The excitement among all increases. Now the ponderous iron beams lazily rise and fall. For a moment there is no perceptible motion of the ship. The excitement is intense. Then one sharp eye, and next another, discovers and proclaims loudly that the large hulk is really moving. Onward—slowly, slowly—a little faster, though still but slowly—then moderately—a little more

> quickly—then faster, proudly, triumphantly, with a continuing accelerating speed!
>
> As the loud huzzas die away, and the sullen crash of the paddles is beginning to be heard, smoke is observed near the bow of the ship, and at almost the same instant the boom of a cannon-shot sounds, which thunders and re-thunders among the cliffs of Clark's Point—and the steamer has started. For a few minutes afterwards, the eager crowds can mark the tall masts and the fluttering pennant, till the ship gradually bends oceanward, and Telegraph Hill hides her progress through the Golden Gate.

San Francisco's harbor was considered one of the finest in the world. Landlocked by the surrounding hills and mountains, the bay was large enough as some travellers wrote to "give shelter to all the fleets of the globe." The *Brother Jonathan* steamed through the expansive narrows, which connected the bay with the Pacific Ocean. On the left hand, or port side, was an "amphitheater of hills," covered with fresh green during the spring but now greenish-brown. On the right, or starboard side, were six promontories, or points of land projecting from higher ground. Around the entrance were numerous small islands, or rocks, lifting their "moss-grown heads above water, and beat by the eternal surges of an ocean ten thousand miles wide," according to a passenger on a prior voyage.

Four miles from the city, spectators from the Cliff House point viewed one of the bay's notable features. Scores of huge sea lions, which weighed one ton and up, would rise on their flippers and bark at the passing ships. Passengers reported that they bore a strange resemblance to humans, their barking like that of dogs. Desiring to preserve these tourist attractions, the city deemed it a penal offense to kill or injure them.

As the *Jonathan* powered up, its wake became wider, fanning eventually out to forty feet and stretching far behind. On a previous *Brother Jonathan* Pacific Ocean transit, Elisha Capron wrote in his journal:

> Its wake presents three distinct colors, inimitably intermingled and constantly changing position, proportion, and hues. The ground is deep blue, thickly clouded and waved with a light, bright green. Over the whole floats a delicate pearly white froth, or froth work. Occasionally, the rays of the sun striking upon them burnish all these colors, and tip the white edges of the frost work with sparkling spangles. This gorgeous ocean ribbon is the production of the paddle wheels and action of the steamer.

Dense black smoke poured from her smokestack, trailing behind and curving into a wavy line by the mild wind. The steamer's foaming trail was straight as an arrow and visible for a distance, leading back, seemingly, to the wharf. Occasionally, burning coal would misfire with sparks shooting from the stack in a chute of fiery spray. As the ship rumbled on, flags flying high, its smoke appeared to rest against the sky.

Inside the sidewheeler, first-time passengers gripped to railings or stared from the outside deck at the passing scenery. They watched the coastline become fainter and fainter, hoping to catch sight of a whale or dolphin. In first- or second-class, some were "freshening up" in their rooms, occasionally looking out a port window. Most of the steerage passengers—or the ones paying the least for less—were on the deck enjoying the sunshine and air. Soon enough, they would have to go back below deck to their stacked berths in the long rooms without ventilation, views, or privacy.

Others were inside the large saloon on the main deck. Two long tables were set with "railroad" chairs, the backs reversible so that people could read or write when meals weren't being served. A carpeting of oilcloth with squares of different colors from reds to blacks covered the floor, and chairs and settees with crimson cushions were scattered around the huge room. Travelers sat and talked with their companions, read newspapers such as the *Evening Bulletin* and *Chronicle,* or wrote letters.

People congregated around the bar in the saloon, buying and

drinking glasses of cider, beer, wine, or brandy, cooled with an ice chip or two. They smoked strong cigars and cigarettes, as several started discussing passionately politics or current events. Waiters set the last of the plates, glasses, and utensils down on the elongated tables in the middle, preparing for the dinner meal that would be served in a short hour. The staccato crack of a new card deck being shuffled could be heard and conversations were filling the lengthy room. Those traveling for the first time on a steamer were taking in its grandeur, amenities, and sights. As the ship sailed two- to three-hundred miles per day, many considered this coastal travel to be the best of the day.

The smell of the sea and saltwater was noticeable, however, along with the rocking, rolling, staggering motion of the steamer as it pushed from the bay into the more powerful currents and waves of the ocean. A few unlucky ones began feeling "queasy," hoping that their friends were right when telling them they would get used to the ship's motion "in no time." A light wind blew outside, but this was refreshing, clearing away the heat of the long afternoon.

The summer sun would set in a few hours, leaving time for passengers and crew alike to enjoy the sunlight before it faded. It was a time of contented anticipation.

CHAPTER 2

Gold Rush Days and Cornelius Vanderbilt

The discovery of gold in California started the westward migration to San Francisco and the region, the likes of which has not been seen again in this country. On the afternoon of January 24, 1848, James Marshall, a contractor, discovered a yellow flake of gold about the size of a thumbnail in a recently built mill's tailrace on the American River about fifty miles from San Francisco.

Scouring around the gravel, he found more gold chips and brought two ounces of the glittering metal to the mill's owner, John Sutter. Every morning, the two men rushed to the mill and picked up small chips of golden nuggets at the bottom of the clean washed bedrock. Despite their attempts at secrecy, two weeks later the news was out as it spread as fast as a wild fire. The *Californian* in San Francisco printed the news on March 15: Gold, in "considerable quantity," had been discovered at Sutter's Mill.

Panning for gold in riverbeds or picking away at the banks with a knife uncovered the precious flakes that seemingly were everywhere. As the weeks went by, prospectors brought their gold to San Francisco, and residents now saw firsthand the golden wealth being unearthed. On May 1 the *Californian* was forced to close its doors when the last of its employees left for the Sierra Nevadas. Two thousand prospectors were working the area by June, and the average miner discovered about one ounce of gold daily. A team of eight miners could extract two pounds (or twenty-four troy ounces) of the precious metal each day. By now all of Sutter's employees were prospecting in the hills. Even his flourishing tannery operation quickly came to a complete halt, the unfinished leather left abandoned in the steaming vats.

San Francisco and the towns north and south quickly depopulated. Men from farmhands and cooks to editors and lawyers stampeded into the foothills with their pickaxes and tents. Pioneers from Oregon rode their horses southward to join in the hunt. In a comparatively short time, gold was discovered in nearly every stream and river in the Sierra foothills, from the Mariposa in the south to the Feather River in the north. Miners at rivers north of San Francisco, such as the Trinity, Salmon, and Klamath by the Oregon border shouted, "Eureka, I've found gold!" Discoveries were also made inside southern Oregon around the town of Jacksonville.

In autumn 1848 newspapers across the country ran countless articles about becoming rich overnight—and this *was* happening—although most prospectors weren't that lucky. From Mexico to Chile and Australia to China, gold seekers formed expeditions and raced to charter ships or travel overland by wagon train. The objective was to get to California, then a remote, uncivilized, and sparsely populated wilderness.

The Gold Rush was officially on and people poured into San Francisco, the only transoceanic port that opened into the gold country. Prospectors steamed westward by ship to Panama, crossed overland at the isthmus, and connected with another ship bound for San Francisco. Or, they took the longer journey, rounding the dangerous, wind-whipped ocean off Cape Horn at the tip of South America. This was hard travel.

Journeying to San Francisco by sea was a one-way proposition. Once ashore, entire crews quickly disappeared into the interior to seek their fortunes. The phenomenon started with the first ship in early 1849 when the *California* carrying 365 prospectors lost its entire thirty-six man crew for the hills. Only the captain and one engine-room boy remained to man the ship. Five hundred ships lay derelict in the harbor by July 1850. Some abandoned vessels rotted and sank with their holds full of now useless goods. Men split ships apart for lumber to construct mining sluices and houses, and a number of vessels were left idle, berthed, or later converted into storage warehouses.

Meanwhile, consumer goods became very scarce and commanded high prices. This was also a rough, gun-slinging, no-nonsense, "in-your-face" time. One prospector wrote into his diary:

> There is a good deal of sin & wickedness going on here. Stealing, Lying, Swearing, Drinking, Gambling & Murdering. There is a great deal of Gambling & This appears to be the greatest evil that prevails here. Men make & lose thousands in a night. Flour & pork went for $125 per barrel; molasses for $10 a gallon, cheese at $1.50 pound when room and board in San Francisco went for $5 a week.

The net migration started to slow down in early 1850, as disappointed fortune seekers gave up—broke, sick, demoralized, and wanting to go back home. Franklin Langworthy wrote his account of traveling onboard the *Brother Jonathan* with 564 passengers on an 1853 voyage from San Francisco to Nicaragua, heading eventually to New York City:

> They tell us of the thousands who have made fortunes; all this is correct, but they have not mentioned the tens of thousands who have scarcely made their living. Those who return are in general the fortunate few, and the shiploads of dust have been scraped together by the sweat and toil of countless thousands.

When the easy finds had been scavenged, most miners couldn't find enough gold to pay for the costs of their mining camps and keep. Despite this, new arrivals continued to arrive and offset the numbers who had already left: Becoming wealthy wasn't as easy as the newspapers had so glibly reported.

Men organized themselves into teams, built long wooden chutes into which they fed water and gravel, and then screened out the gold. The cruel use of powerful hydraulics—hoses with intense water pressure directed against stream beds, canyons, and hills—created carnivorous canyons of waste and erosion. By the late 1850s, however, most of the placer deposits in the Sierra foothills were washed out; mining corporations now sunk deep mines to quarry the gold-bearing quartz deposits.

San Francisco grew from a sleepy town of 2,000 in February 1849 to a booming, lawless place of 50,000 in two years. It joined other burgeoning cities and towns in northern and central California whose populations continued to increase each year. Saloons, gambling halls, circuses, and brothels sprang up, only to be quietly replaced with more respectable opera houses and libraries over time as women, families, and the law finally settled into governing San Francisco and its neighboring areas. Fires ravaged in these early years that world of clapboard houses, few firemen, wood construction, and lawlessness, requiring near-constant rebuilding. While the city's debauchery grabbed the headlines into the mid-1850s, most residents tried to live a normal life. By the late 1850s, San Francisco had left most of its tumultuous times behind and was taking on the look of a major cosmopolitan city.

IN 1849 shipping companies pressed into service for California nearly anything that could float—and these made a large profit for their owners. Edward Mills, a successful New Yorker, wanted to profit from this unique opportunity, and he decided to build a sidewheeler that could navigate the oceans. It would use the Panama Isthmus to transport goods and people from the East Coast.

When the first paddleship crossed the Atlantic to England in 1819, these ships continued to combine the benefits of constant speed from steam engines with sails as a second power source. Although clipper ships were also used during the Gold Rush, the ability of steam to move men and ships when no wind blew—and the vessels didn't need to tack one hundred miles to travel ahead a mere thirty—became overriding advantages.

The designers mounted engines in the ship's center and placed the boilers and furnaces forward towards the bow for balance. Huge piles of coal were stored on the last level called the orlop deck, along with the stowed cargo in separate compartments. The passenger or steerage decks were located above, with the first- and second-class staterooms for men and women, dining saloon, and other public facilities placed conveniently on the top level.

With this in mind, Mills contracted with the Perrine, Patterson, and Stack Shipyard in Williamsburg, New York, in 1850, to build the *Brother Jonathan.* The workman laid her keel by late May; after five and a half months of construction, the builders successfully launched her on November 2, 1850. The vessel's interiors were completed by spring 1851. Mills chose the name of Brother Jonathan for his ship, as this "cranky, imperious geezer" was the symbol of the brash young republic.

Thick white oak, live oak, locust, and cedar comprised the massive hull and structure. The floors and decks were built of white oak, fourteen-inches thick; locust and cedar wood were used in the detailing. Iron diagonal braces stitched the hull from bow to stern, and the shipyard attached copper plates to the lower hull below the waterline to further protect her from the corrosive effects of saltwater. The ship had two decks, two masts, a round stern, and an extreme clipper bow. Two seventy-foot saloons were located below the main deck and detailed in white enamel and gold leaf with skylights opening to the deck above. Twelve first-class staterooms were placed on each side of the lounge, and they fronted the main deck and its railings. Designed for the hot Panama run, a ventilation system operated while the boat was in motion. Air was forced into the ship at the bow and then ducted into the cabins.

The ship could carry 1,359 tons of cargo, including 365 passengers, and that number of people carried was greatly exceeded on her first runs. The overall length of the boat was 221 feet with a thirty-six foot beam (or width). It had an extreme draft (or depth in the water) of fourteen feet. The Morgan Iron Works in New York City supplied the *Brother Jonathan*'s large steam engines, which dwarfed the men who shoved the coal into its cavernous furnaces.

This immense equipment consisted of a vertical beam engine with a six-foot diameter piston cylinder and eleven-foot stroke; the two flue-type shell boilers each generated steam from a cylinder twelve feet in diameter and twenty-eight feet long. The engines were coal-fired but could burn wood if necessary. The steam engines and machinery originally powered the Long Island steamer, *Atlantic,* but a hard-blowing Nor'easter wrecked the ship. It blew the stern over the reefs of Fisher's Island off New London, Connecticut, in 1846, creating a total loss. The Morgan Iron Works, however, was able to rebuild the salvaged engines for the new ship.

The installation and use of beam engines in the *Brother Jonathan* and four other steamships at the time was controversial. The objection made was that this approach shifted the center of gravity with its use of a large "walking beam": a ten-ton casting that hovered fifteen feet above the deck and converted the power motion to both paddle wheels. The weight of the boilers and placement of other machinery, however, counterbalanced the walking beam's massive weight-center, and gradually this new design became standard. Its four-hundred horsepower engine drove two, thirty-three foot diameter paddle wheels with a nine-foot face and thirty-inch deep paddles. The total cost to build this vessel was $190,000.

The *Brother Jonathan* started on the New York City to Chagres, Panama, segment of the Isthmus run in March 1851, and its first pilot was Captain Charles Stoddard. Mills was now operating his Independent Opposition Line. As he didn't own any boats on the Pacific side, however, Mills contracted with another company, the Empire City Line, to pick up his passengers at Panama and speed them to San Francisco and the awaiting gold fields. Captain Stoddard left New York at the end of March and steamed down the coast. He stopped at Havana, Cuba, and Kingston, Jamaica, to take on coal, water, and food, before crossing the Gulf of Mexico to Chagres. Arriving in mid-April, Stoddard offloaded his passengers and cargo, and then took on new passengers, treasure, and cargo that had just arrived from San Francisco. The new arrivals traveled forty-five miles by canoe and mule train to reach the *Brother Jonathan* after departing from her contract mate, the *Union,* that had come down the Pacific side.

On the return trip the *Brother Jonathan* stopped only at Kingston, setting at the time a round-trip record of thirty-one days in transit. A new captain replaced Stoddard on the ship's second trip from New York at the end of June. This voyage made up for the uneventful first one and more typically exemplified the risks of traveling by sea during these Gold Rush days.

The ship lost time when a hurricane struck off the Carolinas, but she was able to make this up on the Kingston to Chagres route. Disaster had struck on the Pacific side, however, when the *Union* grounded ashore in early July, a total loss and not a rare occurrence. The *Jonathan*'s passengers were stuck without further transit to the West Coast, as no other steamers were available. The competitive line, the Pacific Mail Steamship Company, refused to honor Mills's lower-cost tickets. His Panama agent refused to refund the unused portion of the tickets, causing much hardship as many passengers had borrowed what they could just to get this far. With a schedule to keep, the *Brother Jonathan* returned to New York, leaving her passengers behind to fend for themselves.

The *Jonathan* on its third trip made excellent time from New York to Chagres, but upon arriving in Panama, the captain discovered that the Empire City's new steamer, the *Monumental City,* hadn't arrived. After a stormy protest meeting, the passengers cornered Mills and finally forced him to give them a refund of $70 on each $100 one-way ticket. They then completed their trip by booking passage on another mail steamer headed to San Francisco.

As this was also the merciful end of Mills's contract with the Empire City Line, he quickly signed a Pacific-transit contract with the

Pacific Mail Steamship Company. This company became the most important American steamship line in the nineteenth century. It inaugurated the first regular steamer service to California when its side-wheel steamer, the *California,* arrived in San Francisco on February 28, 1849. Under the new contractual relationship with Pacific Mail, the *Brother Jonathan* made several successful trips from New York to Chagres and back, its runs becoming near routine with trips of thirty days or less.

THE MAIN COMPETITION for Mills and the Pacific Mail Steamship Line was Cornelius "Commodore" Vanderbilt and his Independent Line. Cornelius Vanderbilt was born on May 27, 1794, on Staten Island, New York, the son of a Dutch ferryman and farmer. He quit school at the age of eleven to help his father in ferrying, and after learning the business, he persuaded his mother five years later to loan him $100 to purchase his own boat. On condition that he plow and sow an eight-acre rocky field for the family within one year—in addition to his working with the family business—she agreed. Vanderbilt not only earned the loan but also paid back the money to his mother by the end of the first year, along with an additional $1,000.

By working extremely long hours and charging very reasonable fares, his ferrying business prospered. When the War of 1812 created even more opportunities, Vanderbilt bid high and surprisingly (by his own admission) won a government contract to supply the forts around New York with their provisions. (It turns out that the other bids were considered to be "unrealistically low.") The profits from this business allowed him to build a schooner and two other vessels for his operations. Vanderbilt acquired the nickname "Commodore" by dressing in a full naval uniform and eventually being in command of the largest schooner on the Hudson River.

Although he was wealthy and controlled the ferry traffic in New York waters in a matter of years, Vanderbilt became convinced that the future belonged to larger steamboats. Against the advice of family and friends, he sold his very lucrative business in 1818 at the age of twenty-six to become a steamboat captain. He learned the trade under Thomas Gibbons, then operating a ferry service between New Brunswick, New Jersey and New York City.

Helped along by a leading U.S. Supreme Court decision *(Gibbons v. Ogden)* that ruled that his competitors' granted monopoly was illegal, Vanderbilt made himself and Gibbons a fortune over the next eleven years. He stayed with Gibbons until 1829, when he left to establish his own service. As he continued to cut rates below that of every competitor, the Hudson River Association was forced to pay Vanderbilt off so that he would move his operations elsewhere. The Commodore then opened service to Long Island Sound, Providence, Boston, and coastal cities in Connecticut. By the 1840s he was running more than one-hundred steamboats and his company, which offered comfort and even luxury at lower fares, had more employees working than any other business in the United States.

During the Gold Rush, Vanderbilt reduced the travel time to California by establishing a new route through Nicaragua. Earlier, people steamed from the East Coast to Panama, crossed the isthmus by canoe and mule, and then transferred to a northbound ship on the Pacific side. Vanderbilt challenged this route by offering a competing service across Nicaragua, which was closer. He arranged an exclusive deal with the Nicaragua government—some say money exchanged hands—to ferry passengers across the Nicaraguan Isthmus from San Juan de Nicaragua to San Juan del Sur on the Pacific Ocean side. Although many said the route was not navigable, Vanderbilt personally piloted a small steamboat up the San Juan River to test it. Vanderbilt's way was six-hundred miles and two days shorter to California than through Panama—and it was cheaper. He immediately slashed the prevailing fair of $600 to $400 for a first-class ticket. Vanderbilt operated two small river steamers and a large pack train of mules to move passengers to his waiting fleet of three steamers on the Pacific side.

On the Atlantic side, Vanderbilt operated only two steamers, and he had been negotiating for months with Mills for an arrangement with the *Brother Jonathan.* Disaster entered and changed his plans when the *North America,* one of his Pacific steamships, grounded seventy miles south of Acapulco and broke into pieces. Vanderbilt needed a third steamer and decided to buy the ship outright, purchasing the *Brother Jonathan* from Mills in March 1852.

Seeing the potential for her use on the Pacific side of the California Gold Rush, Vanderbilt completely refitted the vessel, so she could carry more passengers and be seaworthy for the stormier seas in the Pacific. Workers eliminated the clipper bow in favor of a more suitable, heavy-weather snub nose, and they moved the smokestack back. The forward cabins were removed, and a third deck was added to increase the passenger capacity. The two saloons were combined into one, now eighty-feet long and twenty-feet wide, and built below the main deck towards the stern with the first-class staterooms surrounding it.*

Although her hauling tonnage was reduced to 1,181 tons, her sides and guards were raised, and all of the accommodations were redesigned to carry 750 passengers—double her original capacity. The retrofit added a third mast at the stern, the wheelhouse was elevated for better visibility with the raised guards, and the steam-exhaust and ventilation systems were re-engineered. Evidencing the lack of safety precautions in those days, only six lifeboats were placed on the ship.

Rebuilt, the *Brother Jonathan* left New York in late May. She sailed into San Francisco in early October after a trip of 144 days, which included a rough passage around Cape Horn. Upon the ship's arrival at San Juan del Sur on the Nicaraguan runs, passengers rode carriages or mules over twelve miles of macadamized road to board a lake steamer, sail over 100 miles of Lake Nicaragua, and then ride by mule or horseback to board the steamer on the Atlantic side bound for the East Coast. The *Brother Jonathan* then waited for the passengers dropped off by the Atlantic sidewheeler, who were then traveling across the Isthmus in the opposite direction. When the *Jonathan* steamed under the Commodore's flag on its Pacific runs, hundreds of would-be miners crowded the ship's three decks. The vessel continued on this Pacific run from San Francisco and back for four years.

*In a last major renovation in 1861, workers lengthened the saloon to 120 feet.

Vanderbilt made money quickly and plowed cash back into a fleet of steamers on both coasts. Once he built up the operation, he cashed in by causing the business to be sold to his own company. Vanderbilt sold all of his steamers, in fact, including the *Brother Jonathan,* to the Nicaragua Steamship Company on December 31, 1852, for a cash payment of $1.2 million and $150,000 in bonds. He retained his position as a director in the company since the Nicaragua Steamship Company was a subsidiary of Vanderbilt's Accessory Transit Company. He also retained a 20 percent royalty interest, payable whether the company made a profit or not—an excellent decision but one which would chafe his remaining partners. Vanderbilt then sailed off to England in May 1853 with his family on the *North Star* to take the first vacation in his life.

Cornelius Vanderbilt's personal "yacht," the sidewheeler *North Star,* set the standard for opulence and luxury. Built to his specifications by the spring of 1853, the ship was an exceptionally lavish vessel with berths that contained silk and lace curtains. Satinwood paneling and rosewood trim accentuated the main saloon, furnished with Louis XV rosewood chairs, plush velvet furniture, and a grand piano. The vessel had more than enough room for Vanderbilt, his wife Sophia, and their twelve children, as the ship included ten large private staterooms and numerous smaller ones. Even with its grandeur, the ship's main saloon wasn't the sole attraction. Its reception room was another huge cabin with enough room for a sprawling sofa that seated twenty people. Marble and granite paneled the banquet-sized dining room, its ceiling decorated with medallion portraits of Christopher Columbus, George Washington, and Daniel Webster.

Meanwhile, Mr. Charles Moran in New York City and Cornelius K. Garrison in San Francisco remained to run the steamship company. When the *North Star* arrived back in New York in September 1853, Vanderbilt discovered that Moran, Garrison, and others had double-crossed him by forming their own shipping line to Nicaragua. He reacted by writing: "Gentlemen: You have undertaken to cheat me. I won't sue you, for the law is too slow. I'll ruin you. Yours truly, Cornelius Vanderbilt."

Vanderbilt dissolved the partnership and sold the *North Star* to a newly formed line with Mills, called the Independent Line, and ran it with other steamers under his flag with the Commodore as the majority owner. Using his influence with the Central American governments, Vanderbilt strangled his former partners' line and was responsible in part for putting them out of business. After plunging back into the business world, he never went cruising again for the rest of his life.

After Vanderbilt's departure, the company that owned the *Brother Jonathan* had more coups than most third-world countries, as various bankers, stockholders, operators, and even governments struggled for its control. In February 1856, political unrest caused the Nicaraguan government to cancel the charter which enabled steamship companies to cross the country. Under this cessation, the *Brother Jonathan* was the last steamer to sail from San Juan del Sur, and it was eventually put up for sale. In 1857, however, Captain John T. Wright bought the *Pacific* and *Brother Jonathan* for his Pacific Northwest runs.

Nearing the age of seventy in the 1860s, Vanderbilt decided once again that the wave of transportation for the future was in another direction—this time in railroads. He first acquired the New York and Harlem Railroad, then the dilapidated Hudson River Railroad. He spent large sums of money to improve the railroads' efficiency, and in 1869 merged the Hudson River and the New York Central Railroad. By the early 1870s, Vanderbilt successfully linked New York City to Chicago by acquiring the Lake Shore and Michigan Southern railroads, the Canadian Southern, and the Michigan Central.

Vanderbilt influenced national finances through his power and long-term political savvy. When the panic of 1873 hit hardest, he continued his New York Central Railroad's policy of paying out its millions of dividends, and he issued contracts to build Grand Central Terminal in New York City, creating jobs for thousands. By 1875, his New York Central Railroad controlled the quite lucrative route between New York City and Chicago.

When Cornelius Vanderbilt died in 1877, he left an estate of almost $100 million dollars. This sum in today's dollars is in excess of

$100 billion—a greater monetary worth than Bill Gates and a host of contemporary billionaires. Many of the railways Vanderbilt constructed are still in existence and were critical in the industrial development of the Eastern sector of the United States, not to mention the shipping lines established in moving people and goods to the U.S. West Coast, such as with the *Brother Jonathan.* Although the bulk of his fortune went to his son, William, he did bequeath $1 million to Central University in Nashville, Tennessee, which became Vanderbilt University.

FRANKLIN LANGWORTHY noted in his memoirs that the *Brother Jonathan* was luxurious in its appearance. Staterooms surrounded the central saloon with doors of "ornamented" paneling outlined in gold leaf and washes of gold. When lit up at night, the ship would "fairly vie in splendor with the drawing room of an imperial palace." Large flags flew with the circular-starred United States flag of red, white, and blue at the stern; a second starred, smaller standard was raised at the bow; Vanderbilt's colors flew on the first mast, and a colorful banner with the ship's name was hoisted on the second. Golden diagonal lines slashed down the black smokestack with two black lifeboats hung on her port and starboard side.

Langworthy left San Francisco on the *Brother Jonathan* on April 16, 1853, arriving in San Juan del Sur on April 30. After steaming across Lake Nicaragua to the Atlantic Ocean side, he boarded the *Prometheus* on May 4, which then sailed to the United States, arriving in New York City on May 12—taking a total of twenty-eight days to sail from San Francisco to New York City. His diary indicated that he experienced a fairly smooth voyage.

One month later, Elisha S. Capron took the return voyage, sailing on the steamer *Prometheus* from New York City to San Juan del Sur, crossing over, and then boarding the awaiting *Brother Jonathan* for San Francisco. When at San Juan del Sur, the natives carried the passengers on their backs through the shallow ocean swells to small boats, in which they rowed the people to the awaiting lake steamer. Porters moved their luggage similarly from land and stowed it on board. Capron later found it difficult first to find his baggage among the hundreds of steamer trunks and carpet bags on the lake steamer, and then haul this luggage from there to the beach for loading on the *Jonathan.* The passengers used what was in their carpet bags during the voyage, while their steamer trunks and everything else was stored in a locked room.

Capron later penned into his diary:

> Now we are out to sea, and the same scene is commenced on shipboard that I witnessed on the *Prometheus.* The purser is assigning staterooms and table seats to passengers, and the deck hands are arranging and stowing away luggage. The ship's order is the same, substantially as that of the *Prometheus,* but the *Brother Jonathan* is much the larger vessel.

One time, a live pig escaped from its pen and jumped overboard. As it swam in the vessel's wake, the crew couldn't recover the "rash porker." As the pig rose and sank with the ocean swells, its legs were "flying like the paddle wheels of a steamboat." Although the pig was earmarked for everyone's eventual dinner, Capron knew that the sharks would soon feast on it, unless the pig drowned before they were able to pick up its scent.

The bored passengers stared out at the ocean for any signs of life. Someone soon yelled, "A whale! A whale!" Two miles away, as Capron estimated, he could see the "monster." It blew a large volume of water from its blow hole to a "great height," and as the large whale sounded, his length seemed to be twenty feet. "He remains below a few minutes," Capron wrote, "and again performed the same evolutions, slightly changing his place." The passengers then watched as porpoises entertained them by cavorting with the smaller fish such as blackfish.

On this trip, the *Brother Jonathan* encountered a storm and he scribbled:

> The weather was clear and the ocean calm; but about midnight the wind blew violently, the waves ran high, and the old vessel

> rocked like a cradle. A man sleeping out on deck barely escaped, by the aid of a fellow-traveler, a briny bath over the side of the steamer. The last night was stormy; the rain descended in torrents, the wind was high, fitful, and blustering. I was awakened during the conspiracy of the elements to disturb my slumbers, by the spray cast upon me through the window and the door; but the bath being more grateful than otherwise, I adjusted the curtains to protect my face and pillow.

The ship stopped to anchor off Acapulco in Mexico, one of the coaling, wood fuel, and provision stopovers for these Pacific-roaming ships. Acapulco stretched over a beautiful bay, its "lofty mountains" protecting the harbor from the wind. As the Pacific Ocean experienced stormier weather and "blows" than its Atlantic Ocean counterpart, Elisha Capron noted that Acapulco was within the "Gulf of California" and worried about being in an area where the rough winds and seas would be so common:

> The swells roll heavily. But few of the passengers are able to be on their feet, and all are drooping. We have a revised edition, improved and enlarged, of the comical scenes of the first three days of the voyage: long faces, neglected toilets, and stomach qualms. What a mystery is seasickness! What a medley of contradictions—inexplicable contraries! Now, the voyager is in fine spirits, impatient for dinner. But suddenly a ripple darkens the ocean; in a few minutes the wind rises and the steamer begins to roll and rock. He is prostrate, languid, and pale, disturbed by no word so much as dinner! The blow ceases. It was just a blow. The steamer rocks and rolls no more, and the voyager is well, regretting nothing so much as the loss of the dinner.

The *Brother Jonathan* arrived in San Francisco within thirty days on May 21. Capron wrote that he traveled 2,764 miles from San Juan del Sur for a total 4,982 miles:

> The steamer has now arrived at Pacific Wharf. All is bustle and confusion. The mate is hoarsely giving the order to "make fast," and the sailors, in obedience, are busy with the ropes and cables. The wharf is crowded with the multitude, hand-carts, drays, and hacks. Many persons are pressing their way on board in search of expected friends, and the weary passengers are collecting their valuables, and preparing to bid the good steamer joyful farewell.

Three months later, Capron left San Francisco for home on the paddlewheeler *Winfield Scott,* via the Panama connection. Transiting over the Panama Isthmus by mule through dense jungles, by canoe over the Chagres River to the hamlet of Barbacoa, then by the partially completed Panama railway to Aspinwall, he ended on the Atlantic side. The cost for the three-day transit was seven dollars for two meals and two nights of lodging, plus eight dollars for the twenty-five mile rail trip. Capron left for New York on board the sidewheeler *Illinois* and arrived in New York City in nine days. His last diary notation read, "The time since we left San Francisco is twenty-seven days and two hours; and the length of our track, according to my reckoning, is 5,382 miles."

Seafarers had both good and bad trips on board the *Brother Jonathan.* Many voyages, especially in the first few years of the Gold Rush, were arduous and difficult. Heading to California across Central America could take weeks and weeks of long boredom, heavy seas, scurvy, and dangerous conditions with overloaded boats and scheming men. Food and fresh water could become uniformly bad and progressively worse the longer a vessel was at sea. At the time, owners and their ship captains didn't know how important fresh fruit and vegetables were to keeping their passengers healthy.

Overcrowding was always a problem. Even in 1865, Samuel Bowles complemented the food on his voyage as being "luxurious and nearly equal to first-class hotel fare," but complained about the crowds:

> We are as thick as flies in August; four and five in a stateroom; we must divide into eating battalions, and go twice for our meals. There is no privacy; gamblers jostle preachers; commercial women divide staterooms with fine ladies; honest miners in red flannel sit next to my New York friend in exquisite French broadcloth—and as for the babies, they fairly swarm—the ship is one grand nursery; and like the British drumbeat, the discordant music of their discomfort follows sun, moon, and the stars through every one of every twenty-four hours.

The quality of any trip depended upon whether a passenger could afford a first- or second-class ticket, or the cheapest steerage accommodations. In 1849, passage to San Francisco from Panama originally was set at $250 for first class, $200 for second class, and $100 for steerage. In 1865, the steamers ran three times a month between California and New York and the fares were $350 for first class, $250 for second class, and $125 for steerage. Even fifteen years later, the same basic rates applied with steerage basically set at one-third the cost of first class—and passengers received what they paid for.

First-class passengers enjoyed a larger, ventilated room with portholes on a lower deck or one that opened to the fresh air on the main deck. They enjoyed privacy—not to mention a certain safety with their possessions—and furnishings, such as a double-deck bed, mirror, toilet stand, washbowl, chest of drawers, chairs and/or a sofa, and water bottles plus glasses. First "cabin" included priority access to a "shower" facility where people could bathe. Carpeting covered their cabin floors, and outer damask curtains completely screened their berths. For important first-class passengers, a case of wine or fruits and fine flowers greeted them on arrival. Wine also flowed, either from the voyager's private cache or the ship's own stock.

On board the *Brother Jonathan,* first-class staterooms typically extended down the vessel's midship and along the side of the dining saloon, allowing easy access by closed door to the corridor, as well as to the outside deck. Long tables furnished the saloons at which people sat on their reversible seats. First- and second-class passengers used meal tickets to gain access to their dining times. First-class guests on the *Jonathan* used white tickets, while those in second class showed identifying green ones.

Passengers with white tickets ate at the first table one day, while those with green took precedence the next, and the eating order alternated that way each day. The difference between the two classes was in the assigned staterooms. Second-cabin passengers for their lower price had worse accommodations.

Albert Richardson noted that first-class passengers seemed to embrace "many cultivated, traveled, and agreeable persons," their important goal being to receive a good table-seat assignment for meals. "Nine-tenths" always remained disappointed, however, by being excluded from the especially desired but small captain's table. With breakfast at eight, lunch at one, and dinner at five, first-class passengers seemed to quickly cultivate friendships and social groups within their "class."

Second-cabin passengers had rooms sparsely furnished with open berths. Four to five strangers were assigned to each one. They ate from the same tables as first class but, as noted, at different intervals. Second-class passengers used the same decks as first class, but slept forward, below, or, in both directions, away from those rooms. First-class staterooms were generally located at the stern of a steamer where the noise and vibrations were less of a problem. Second class slept toward the bow at or on a lower deck where the noise, pounding from engines or ocean, and drenching sea sprays would be worse.

A steerage ticket meant no private rooms, often no segregation of the sexes, and being warehoused with many others in a long, rectangular chamber in the bowels of the ship. Accommodations were primitive: smelly bunks, stench, chamber pots, and usually no port holes for ventilation causing terrible conditions where numbers were seasick. These chambers were typically in the vessel's belly, close to the noisy engine room, and towards the bow where the ship "shuddered" more. When separate dormitories were provided for men and women in steerage, the newspapers took notice of this unique fact. Steerage berths were arranged in tiers of three, one above the other, with just two feet of head space.

Workers easily set up "beds" by stretching canvas over wooden bars and fastening the cloth with wood pins. Passengers slept between the canvas bag that was formed. Each berth contained three bags with a traveler expected to occupy just one. Berths could also extend three deep, as well as high, so to find accommodation, the holder of an inner berth had to climb through two outer ones. The ease of constructing these steerage berths made it easy to increase a steamer's capacity when demand was high.

Some steamer lines before the 1850s held a "market" for steerage passengers on the main deck. Seamen brought out and arranged food in rows around the purser, who sat on a cask with his notebook and called out each person's mess number. His assistants then served the biscuits, sugar, butter, raisins, bully beef, rice, split peas, potatoes, tea, and coffee. Some carriers served the food directly to this class, as the people waited in a long line and then ate wherever they could find a place on the ship. As early as 1850, however, the Pacific Mail Steamship Company directed that steerage passengers should have their own table from which to eat with cutlery provided. This approach eventually became the norm.

The long transoceanic trips were romanticized, but boredom, lack of water, lousy food, and weeks of hard accommodations were much more prevalent. Beautiful sunsets, playful dolphins, and large humpback whales did appear, but there were also waterspouts, sharks, and hurricanes. The conditions at sea alternated between no wind, an interminable hot sun, and humid nights, only to be followed by terrifying gales and high seas. Then the winds would die, the sea became like glass, and the sun baked again.

Seasickness was especially prevalent, especially for landlubbers. As one passenger observed in the early 1850s:

> I lay in my bed and am so sick. I can't eat and what I would like, they don't have—just a little coffee. I can't sit up. I am so dizzy. The boat makes such turns to the side. I can't describe how big the waves are.

When someone raced outside for a gasp of fresh air, a large wave could crash over the gunnels and wash the person down the deck. Whether a stiff wind blew or not, passengers could take several days, if not longer, to finally get used to a ship's constant rocking and rolling through the ocean.

Fresh water was at a premium, especially when water needed to be conserved after weeks at sea. When a rain shower fell—not in a storm when everyone was just trying to survive and avoid the mountainous waves—passengers would put out every barrel, tub, bucket, and tin pan around to catch the rainwater for bathing and washing. Fresh water at sea was a luxury beyond imagination, and nearly everyone used seawater to wash with. As one passenger observed: "Saltwater nearly precludes the use of soap: for such a thing as 'good saltwater soap' is not yet invented." If thunderstorms couldn't supplement a ship's diminishing water supply, then people would add a touch of vinegar, molasses, or a few dashes of wine to make the water somewhat palatable, as the quality deteriorated over time into a foul-tasting potion.

Food was another important but highly variable factor on these long ocean voyages. Depending on the ticket price, galley crew, and owner's generosity, the food could range from very acceptable to horribly substandard. Seasoned travelers would bring fresh fruit or their own food in tins or "sundry" little bottles, some "containing the juice of the cane" that could also fermented.

On ships steaming to Central America, the crew brought onboard chickens, pigs, sheep, goats, and cows and penned them in a special room for a ready source of fresh meat. The butcher room was located adjacent to the pens. Passengers who liked these animals would call them by pet names, then plead for their survival, but the need for fresh meat always won out. Taking fresh supplies of fowl, beef, pigs, fresh vegetables, fruit, and water was as important as stocking up on coal at the ports of call. For the shorter coastal voyages, water and food were not as important considerations and were generally excellent.

When a catch was made from the sea, meals would change. Whether a flying fish flipped onboard or someone caught a porpoise, this occasion became a welcomed event. One wrote into his log, "Duff [boiled flour pudding] for dinner—distance about 1700 miles per log book." Several days later, he penned, "We had fried porpoise for breakfast, the passengers generally partook of it, some saying it tasted like moose meat, some like bullocks liver."

The next entry read, "This is Saturday and the cook is preparing a sumptuous dinner of tongues & sounces [tongue steeped in vinegar or pickle], which proved very acceptable, particularly when served up with fried pork and potatoes, pickles, pepper sauce, and a course of pancakes." The next day's entry: "Had chicking [*sic*] pie for dinner & rice soup."

The food was terrible, however, on many voyages. Attorney John N. Stone wrote in his journal while sailing from New York on the *Robert Browne* in 1849:

> We are destitute of the commonest necessaries of life—living (Heaven knows how) on putrid, stinking meats of every kind, including water—without a potato, onion, or any vegetable aboard—without vinegar, mustard, pepper, butter, sugar—or anything to bar off the scurvy, leprosy, or what not, to which the seafarer is exposed in such a strait.

The *Pacific* was a companion steamer with the *Brother Jonathan* on its ocean runs. The passengers rebelled on one 1849 voyage and forced the removal of the Captain, one Mr. H. J. Tibbits, for among other things:

> Inferior food; lack of sufficient quantities of rice, tea, and coffee of the worst quality; no flour puddings, dumplings, or

> pies, while only two meals a day; a degree of filth and negligence in the appurtenances and arrangements of the table calculated to disgust and demoralize us; meals that weren't at regular or normal hours, foul air in the staterooms, lost baggage . . .

One unnamed passenger complained that he had to wait in a long line for the black bread, butter, and coffee that everyone wanted at breakfast. He spent most of his time on deck where the people were promenading, singing, and dancing. But he ended one day's notation with, "Today I have a toothache. If only the whole trip could be as nice as it is now." The weather conditions were then excellent.

To pass away the time, passengers debated the topics of slavery versus abolition, bachelorhood versus marriage, drinking against abstinence, and, of course, national politics, which was always good "for an hour or two of spirited comments." Women would knit, stitch dresses, or crochet patchwork quilts. Passengers would entertain one another with book readings, history lessons, and lectures. Bible classes, singing schools, reading societies, and group exercise classes started up. Others would write or play "different instruments of music, without regard to time or tune." They would sing songs, such as "Home, Sweet Home," "Ben Bolt," "Flow Gently, Sweet Afton," "O, Charlie Is My Darling," "The Arkansas Traveler," and "Auld Lang Syne." In the evening, passengers would stay up until late, playing music, singing, and waltzing.

Franklin Langworthy wrote that if anyone looked closely at the grand saloon after supper, that one would be convinced the company on its Pacific trip consisted only of those who lived in California. "Scores" of well-dressed gentlemen and ladies could be heard exclaiming, "euchre," "right and left bower," and now and then, "high, low, jack, and game." Politely, Langworthy wrote that this was "mere amusement, of course," and that he didn't know of any gambling in the saloon, although there was enough of it being done in steerage.

People became excited when their ship approached another to

exchange newspapers and the latest news. White foam dashing from her prow, the steamer *Cortes* steamed toward the *Brother Jonathan* on Langworthy's voyage. When the ships were within a half mile of each other, their paddle wheels stopped and both saluted the other with an artillery shot. A small boat then exchanged the newspapers and letters between the two sidewheelers. "In a few minutes," Langworthy wrote down, "both ships were under way again, and we soon lost sight of the beautiful *Cortes,* she appearing to skim beneath the unruffled surface of the sea."

Even the captain and crew tried to break the monotony: They would race their steamers against one another, for example, although this activity was usually kept to the coastal rivers and routes. In 1847 the *Oregon* beat the *Atlantic* in a Hudson River race, but not until after Vanderbilt's *Atlantic* rammed into it on the starboard side. The *De Witt Clinton* struck the *Napoleon* in a race on the Hudson River. The *Napoleon*'s captain quickly pulled out his pistol and shot at the pilot of the *De Witt Clinton.*

Unless a terrible storm engulfed the ships, Sundays were nearly always reserved for conducting church services and lessons. Lydia Ridder Nye, a sea captain's wife, wrote down in her diary:

> The Sabbath is reverenced by all together at sea; it wears an aspect different from all other days. After washing the decks in the morning, there is nothing done of the ship's work, and each one is free to do what he wills. Last Sabbath, I handed out to the people hymn books and some religious magazines. It is really pleasant to hear them singing and reading until the time for the services commence. There likewise is a Bible class twice a week in the forecastle. When eight bells strike, everyone on board assembles for prayers. How much like home!

Fellow passengers could be both a boon and a bust on any trip at sea—and making enemies on these long trips was not a wise move.

Habits could also become a disgusting nuisance such as the "American habit" of chewing and spitting tobacco. One passenger wrote about another, "Mrs. Waring is a wicked, vulgar, mischief-making, ugly old maid. We have never before been in such a low and barbarous society as at sea, and, unfortunately, there is no alternative but to bear it."

The same observations—pro and con—held with the crew. Lawyer Stone wrote in his journal:

> Among the sailors, there were special favorites, and easily the first was Little Joe, so named as there was a Bigger Joe. He was of a kindly nature, ready to aid all, carry kids or jelly pots, help the grannies light their pipes, and had a good word for everyone. He was a married man, one of the crew that returned with the ship to her homeport and, I understand, he drowned just before the ship reached home.

Seamen naturally were quite different in their personalities. A passenger steward and a cook were also favorites on this particular voyage. However, the cook didn't know anything about cooking or "of cleanliness, either of person or language." His profanity was "low and dirty and continuous," but not as "blasphemous" as the bosun who cursed everybody, but who then was heartily cursed back by everyone in return.

Another risk on these long voyages was that a crew member or some passenger would go crazy from the hardships especially given the close confining quarters of a grizzled crew and hundreds of passengers. Stone penned:

> Another Irishman named John Dougherty, who for a short time has evidenced symptoms of insanity—hitherto harmless—suddenly became a raving maniac during the storm of last night; he imaged himself captain of the ship, gave orders to the sailors, and drove the man away from the wheel. He

> then cut one of the wheel ropes and attacked a passenger. Dougherty was a Hercules in size and strength—perhaps the strongest man on the ship—and a madman. He was finally secured after a desperate struggle and his attempt to throw the mate overboard. It became necessary for the general safety to iron and confine him.

Across the world, vessels steamed unknowingly into hurricanes, slammed onto rocks and reefs, grounded on beaches, caught fire, and smashed into other ships at sea.

John Stone told the story of one "hazy and dark" evening as the passengers strolled after tea around the deck. The people were alarmed by the captain's hoarse shouting from the top hurricane deck, "Sail ho! Hard down on your helm! Bring a light." As people called up, the captain cried out, "Silence! Or we will all go to Hell together." Heading directly at them and much faster, the lights of a large ship appeared out of the darkness and quickly grew larger. Both ships swerved at the last moment and passed in "rather dangerous proximity," barely missing one another. A collision like this would have been fatal.

On one storm, Albert Richardson wrote:

> At intervals in the darkness would come a tremendous lurch, straining the ship in every joint, and followed by crashing of glass and crockery. I had always longed to see a storm on shipboard; and here it was to my heart's content. The anticipation was a good deal more agreeable than the reality. It was a memorable night—the only one in which I remember to have been kept awake solely by fear. By daylight, it is appalling enough to watch vast waves upon which the ship seems the merest feather—to see every loose article flung across the cabin, and dishes from the tables scattered about like wheat from a sower's hand; but it is far more impressive for one to lie through the slow hours, wondering whether he

> will see the cheerful world again; and remembering that a slight break of machinery would leave him at the mercy of the elements, that only a plank is between him and death.

These horrific storms would be followed almost inevitably by, as Stone recalled, "A calm—lying almost motionless on the bosom of the deep that rocks us gently as a mother does her infant babe."

The danger of being washed overboard was an obvious risk on every trip. One seaman, who couldn't swim, fell from the ship's rigging into the sea. As the sidewheeler swept past him, ropes, planks, and anything that could be grabbed were thrown down at the thrashing man. Finally and at the very last moment, the seaman managed to catch one thrown rope. He was one of the lucky ones.

Elisha Capron on the *Brother Jonathan* noted that one man in steerage couldn't be found, even after a through search was conducted. No one had seen him after dinner several days before, and the presumption was that he had fallen overboard, "either by accident, or with the intention of destroying himself, [he] stepped over the side of the ship."

Boiler and steam explosions on these paddlewheelers were also a danger; consequently, fire drills were held on each oceanic voyage. Nearly every paddlewheel steamer or ship in service collided, grounded, or wrecked more than once. The only questions were when, where, how bad, and how many deaths or injuries came about.

In 1854, the *Brother Jonathan* shipped the surviving passengers back to San Francisco from the ill-fated S.S. *Yankee Blade.* The vessel struck a submerged reef near Santa Barbara, California. Waves breaking over the stern caused extensive damage and broke away several sections of the ship. The captain began transferring people, including the crew, to a nearby beach, and one lifeboat overturned. Seventeen drowned of the twenty-two people in the boat.

With the captain and his assistant on shore, steerage passengers still on the ship broke into the liquor lockers, became drunk, and started a rampage of looting, robbing, and shooting the "snobbish" first-class guests. Passengers weren't allowed into the hold of the ship to reclaim their baggage, and when the "gang of pirates" grabbed the life preservers, they demanded enormous prices for them, including gold watches and $40 for a lifejacket.

By the following morning, the *Yankee Blade* broke apart. Brandishing firearms that day, several of the ship's crew took most of the provisions on the beach for themselves and robbed the passengers of their money and possessions. The loss of life ranged upwards to fifty, mostly women and children. Despite the heavy seas, the S.S. *Goliah* steamed by and picked up six hundred passengers. It took the survivors to several ports where the majority disembarked. The *Brother Jonathan* next brought back to San Francisco most of the passengers the *Goliah* had dropped off.

Over ten years later, the Victor Smiths were aboard the steamer *Golden Rule,* as it sailed from New York City to Panama. This vessel wrecked badly on a reef near the Isthmus. The seven hundred people onboard the ship lived for eleven days on supplies salvaged from the vessel until two gunboats rescued them and took them to Panama. One month later, Victor Smith was back on board the *Brother Jonathan.*

When the seas didn't threaten, the surrounding beauty could be captivating. One anonymous passenger wrote:

> The sun rising from the watery horizon tinges the borders of the clouds with many gorgeous colors, furnished and gilded with light. When sunset came, far down in the west lay long ranges of heavy clouds, piled up in massive grandeur, sometimes assuming the shape of mountains, their peaks reaching high up into the vaulted sky; again you would see towns and castles, and fortresses with steeples and minarets pointing high above; again you see strange shapes of men and monsters, gigantic in their proportions, grotesque in their positions, ever varying, changing, passing away to be succeeded by others still more wonderful, until they and the darkness mingled together in the night.

On board the *Brother Jonathan,* Elisha Capron penned:

Thou boundless, shining, glorious sea!
With ecstasy I gaze on thee;
And, as I gaze, thy billowy roll
Wakes the deep feelings of my soul.

The world can never give
The bliss for which we sigh;
It is not the whole of life to live,
Nor all of death to die!

CHAPTER 3

"Frightful" Winds and Seas of Foam

DeWolf pointed towards the gloomy horizon, as the two men next to him nodded in agreement, then turned around to the stairway leading down to the deck. He could tell by these darkening cloud formations that the *Brother Jonathan,* steaming northward from San Francisco, would soon run into nasty weather, the only questions being how bad and how long the squall would last. He had made one last sextant observation as to the course and it was close to the time when he would leave for dinner.

As DeWolf looked at the black turmoil ahead, he was glad that the rules prohibited his wife being along, although she at times wanted to. Marie E. Knight DeWolf was a strong woman, independent, and well suited to his maritime choosing. Her father was a well-to-do Boston businessman, who was very socially connected but died when Marie was fourteen years old. After attending boarding school, she lived with an aunt for five years, and then opened a successful "millenary [*sic*] goods" business in Pawtucket, Rhode Island. She was "the first to subscribe to new stock each fall and presented the wives and children of each clergyman with new hats."

Selling the business later, she decided to leave for California. A few days prior to her departure, three citizens approached her and offered to refund the money paid for her ticket, if she "could be persuaded to remain." Marie Knight thanked the gentlemen, but declined their offer. "They then hired a hall and invited a large party to bid me bon voyage. It was an event never to be forgotten by the few now living," she wrote later.

After Marie met Captain DeWolf in San Francisco, they soon became engaged. On March 5, 1857, the steamer *Pacific* came into port with Captain DeWolf in command. Major Hensley informed him that a company had chartered the company's steamer, *Surprise,* for a month's trip to various Mexican ports. DeWolf was asked to take command. Although the couple planned to be married during that time, "having been well schooled in disappointment," Marie told the Captain that "the month would soon slip away" and then they could make their plans.

The next morning upon arriving at the *Surprise,* DeWolf found himself asked again to meet with Major Hensley, the company's agent and a later owner of the *Brother Jonathan.* When DeWolf acknowledged the Major's question about the Captain's intentions to marry, Hensley replied, "Well, you can go ashore and remain if you wish, until Saturday at four, the time set for the steamer to sail; also, the charter party kindly invites your *wife* to accompany you on this trip."

"This was Friday at ten in the morning," wrote Marie DeWolf. "We had until Saturday at two, the hour set for our marriage, to perfect our plans." One Captain Fauntleroy (who later commanded the renamed *Brother Jonathan)* escorted them from the "overflowing church" to the steamer, where they found a table "set the entire length of the cabin and loaded with everything that could be had." Every officer connected with the ceremony attended the festivities. Afterward, Captain Fauntleroy told Marie, who was two years older than her husband, that "the mayor is a good friend of your husband" and the effort had been done at his request.

Workers created the bridal suite on board the steamer by taking down a partition, combining two rooms into one, freshly painting all the walls, installing new carpets, and bringing in bridal furniture. The items consisted of an elegant pier glass-and-marble washstand covered with the "choicest" flowers, a high-posted Rosewood bed stand, a yellow-satin damask canopy sofa, and chairs. They even hired a servant to attend to any of their needs.

"In a short time, the anchor was raised, steam started, guns fired, and colors dropped. We were on our way, crossed the bar in safety, and were soon in deep ocean headed for the south coast," wrote Marie DeWolf. After a series of adventures, including civil war, armed insurrections, and unrest, the couple returned weeks later on what turned out to be a very lavish honeymoon and captaincy.

In the eight years since they married, their honeymoon was the one exception to a long-time maritime rule: No captain was allowed to take his spouse with him, even if he paid for her passage. As with the unwritten rule that each master of the ship should inspect every corner of his vessel at least twice a day, another key regulation was that no spouse could come along on a voyage—otherwise he might neglect his passengers to save his family during an emergency.

As Captain DeWolf made his way down from the bridge to clean up for dinner, First Officer W. A. Henry Allen stared at the building storm. Allen was then forty-five years old, having left home at age eleven to follow his wanderlust at sea. He had started as a cabin boy and worked himself up to first officer by the young age of eighteen. Having sailed around the globe twice, Allen had been captain of the ship *Nero* when she burned in the China Sea. He saved every person—even after being at sea for five days without food or water. Ten years ago, Captain Wright hired him as the first officer for the *America,* a steamship that caught fire and burned into a charred hulk one month later in Crescent City harbor. He later captained small vessels for several years and sailed the eighteen-ton steamer *Ranger* up the Fraser River in British Columbia. It was a daring feat at the time, as Allen had to stop often to chop down enough wood from the banks to keep his steamer furnace fueled. Fellow officers and acquaintances considered him to be a man of "generous impulses, kind, courteous, and forbearing." He was a committed family man with four children.

Next to him, Quartermaster Yates tightly gripped the large steering wheel and held to the course. Yates, an African American, was entrusted with various responsibilities, including the piloting of the ship under the direction of an officer. This was a rarity at the time. Yates was also the quartermaster and entitled "Seaman" or "Quartermaster Yates"—in charge of the ship's stores and provisions. He had sailed under Captain DeWolf for several years and followed him to the *Brother Jonathan.* Yates also kept his background to himself, relying on his competency and his relationship with Captain DeWolf to undertake more responsibilities.

Below the bridge, Second Officer James Campbell walked his rounds and stopped by the Purser's Office, which was straight down from the wheelroom on the starboard side. He was thirty-nine years old and—like many of the seamen in these days—headed to the ocean when he was young. Campbell eventually traveled to California by sailing around the Horn. He had married seven years before and was the father of two children: one four years old and the other seven months. Campbell was considered to be a "free-hearted, liberal man, a brave and trusty sailor."

John Benton was the Purser, or the officer in charge of the passenger's baggage, money, and their gold and valuables. These were locked in rooms or held in Benton's large and small safes. He once worked for the California Steam Navigation Company as the purser on riverboats before Major Hensley hired him for his ships. Benton was also married and the father of one child.

These were experienced and very able-bodied seamen. Most had been in the employ of the California Steam Navigation Company for several years and had sailed with Captain DeWolf before, usually on a continuing basis. Down in the bowels of the ship, fireman (and storekeeper) John Hensley worked stoking the furnaces. The huge steam engine needed a continuing supply of coal—and wood if the coal ran out—to keep the large boilers steaming and power the thirty-three foot high paddle wheels. The large room was dark, very hot, steamy, and with poor ventilation. During storms when portholes and vents had to be closed, these working conditions were as if they were out of Dante's *Inferno.*

The nephew of Major Samuel J. Hensley, who bought the *Brother Jonathan* in 1860, was also on the ship. John Hensley was twenty-eight years old. Although a young man by today's standards, John had been in the cattle trade for several years in Napa, California, with profitable government contracts to supply beef. During an economic downturn, however, he lost several thousand dollars and went out of business. A short time after this misfortune, he went to work for his uncle's shipping company and for the last three years, John worked on the California Steam Navigation Company's northern runs. He was considered to be a man of "amiable disposition, and generous to a fault." A single man, his motto was, "Do onto [*sic*] others as you would have them do onto you."

In charge of the steamer's inner workings and engines, Elijah Mott was the chief engineer of the *Brother Jonathan* and monitored the controls deep within the ship. Mott was thirty-eight years old and had sailed to California aboard the steamship *Pacific* (the *Brother Jonathan*'s sister ship) and which was later lost off Cape Flattery. Owing to his past experience as an engineer on steamships on both coasts, Mott was a highly regarded engineer and had served in the employ of the California Steam Navigation Company for "several years." He was married with four children.

As the ship bucked now and then from the growing waves, a gust of wind blew through one of the open dining-room windows hard enough to scatter a few papers over the floor. A steward walked over and closed the porthole as one particularly large wave hissed past. The long dining room on the upper deck was beginning to fill with passengers intent on dining. With its gold leaf trim, crimson-colored settees and chairs, and bright oilcloth floor coverings, the room was still "splendid looking in the bright of day."

One of the first to arrive at the Captain's table, James Nisbet sat at his assigned seating. One of the waiters, William Shields, tidied the table and arranged the settings of ceramic plates, platters, saucers, cups, bowls, and mugs. Condiment bottles, such as Lea & Perrins Worcestershire Sauce in light green glass, graced the dining tables, along with porcelain pitchers, cruets, sugar bowls, utensils, and settings. Porcelain plates by Sedgwick Porcelain in Great Britain were laid out. The settings were recycled after every meal: The cook's staff would clean, wash, and dry everything if possible to be ready in time for the next set-down meal.

Nisbet wrote about the *Brother Jonathan* twelve years before as "a splendid vessel of 2,000 tons" when it left Pacific Wharf in San Francisco on Saturday, April 15, 1853, bound for Nicaragua. The editor noted that the ship was "carrying home the jubilant who had found their fortune and the despairing who had not, beside a treasure in dust and bullion and the people and correspondence of commerce." He was a working newspaperman, first as a staffer on various San Francisco sheets, and then as editor of the *Evening Bulletin,* assuming that post after the *Bulletin*'s founder, the interestingly named James King of William, was assassinated in his crusade against crooked officials and businessmen.

Nisbet was in his middle forties when he took over the *Bulletin.* A bachelor by choice, his personal life was made more solitary by Nisbet's uncompromising honesty and self-sufficiency. Brusque, almost gruff in manner, careless in dress, and giving the impression of unkemptness, his staffers gave him the nickname "The Bear of the Bulletin."

For almost ten years, he made the *Bulletin* the leading San Francisco evening daily with a circulation of 9,000 copies. Hating "vice, corruption, and venality," Nisbet crusaded against any fraud he unearthed. He was quick to react and write about injustice, as he championed human rights. Accordingly, Nisbet made enemies very quickly with his journalistic honesty.

One family in San Francisco, however, knew James Nisbet by another name—and that was Grandpa. Early in 1861, he rented a spare room in the house of Caspar T. Hopkins, a young insurance agent. Slowly, ever so slowly, the solitary, uncompromising Scot became one of the family. He was among people who loved him for himself, and whom he could love for the same reason. Nisbet became an older brother to the parents. To their children of three girls, he became a continuing source of books, toys, candy, and other small indulgences as if a "loving grandfather."

The little girl, Baby Myra, was born in 1864 and literally wrapped

James Nisbet around her little finger. The family saw little of him during the week when he worked long hours with his newspaper; however, the weekends were different. He enjoyed then family picnics, excursions, and even hikes on nearby Mount Diablo overlooking San Francisco.

Inside her stateroom to one side of the saloon, Mrs. Rose Keenan looked forward to rejoining her husband in Victoria. Watching alone over her brood of seven ladies wasn't that easy—especially given her profession—but she accomplished this through a combination of charm, guile, and an indomitable will. With everyone settled in, the unstated rule was that business could be conducted discreetly—but only very discreetly. Only two of the ladies in her entourage were identified by name on the ship's register.

Mrs. Martha Stott, one of the two women identified, said that she was on her way to Victoria to work as a waitress in the saloon of John C. Keenan. She brought along her little son, who was "six or seven years of age." Thought to be very attractive with delicate skin, Martha Wilder was the second so identified as being in Mrs. Keenan's group. Depending on whom she was talking to, she was either on her way to work in the saloon of John C. Keenan, or she was going to Victoria to be a nurse. Only sixteen years old, one of a family of six children who were living with their widowed mother in San Francisco, she was without any real means of survival.

The Rowells settled in for the night. The couple finally rounded up their four young children after an early dinner, and it was now time to read and calm them down. After a long day of getting the family to the dock, the delayed departure, and the excitement of being at sea, the parents and their children were exhausted. Jeannette Lee, the circus owner's wife, was nursing her small three-week-old infant in the cabin where she spent most of the voyage.

AFTER PURCHASING the *Brother Jonathan* with the *Pacific* in 1857, Captain Wright had it cosmetically overhauled with painting and light repairs. He then renamed the *Jonathan* as the S.S. *Commodore.*

The vessel was then pressed into the service run between San Francisco and Vancouver with stopovers at Crescent City, Portland, and Seattle. At the time, the *Jonathan* was the largest steamer to enter the Columbia River. From 1857 to 1858, the *Commodore* was a regular visitor on the North coast. The *Crescent City Herald* reported that she called every week or ten days at Crescent City during good weather. According to ads appearing in the local papers at the time, she was listed at "1500 tons burden" and capable of carrying one thousand tons of freight. The coastal business was very good in 1858 when miners rushed to get to British Columbia and the Fraser River for its gold rush. This migration, however, didn't last as long as the California Gold Rush and the prospects began to filter away over the next few years.

The *Commodore* had several masters during these runs. From June until November 1857, Captain Fauntleroy—for whom the rock at the entrance to Crescent City Harbor was named—commanded her. The sidewheeler was an important visitor, bringing hundreds of tons of freight and supplies for the settlers, prospectors, and miners. It also carried scores of passengers, some of whom were businessmen on trips representing large wholesalers in San Francisco. Other travelers settled and stayed in various nearby areas, but many were enroute to the mines or growing towns on the coast and interior.

From time to time, the vessel underwent repairs. The *Crescent City Herald* reported on July 22, 1857: "The *Commodore* arrived in port and has been much improved by cutting away a portion of her upper work, and receiving fresh paint, and being put in first-rate order for either cabin or steerage passengers."

The next time we learn about renovations, the vessel has a new master, Captain Hanley. The *Crescent City Herald* for January 20, 1858, reported:

> She crossed the bar (at the mouth of the Columbia River) when there was a heavy sea on, and a gale from the southwest stove her galley and carried away her four top masts. We

> learn that since her last trip, she had undergone thorough repairs, and had her hull braced with iron plates and fastenings in such a manner as to make her one of the staunchest steamers on the coast.

Shipping along the Pacific Northwest coast continued to be hazardous. Six months later Captain Staples was her master, and again the *Commodore* found herself in stormy weather. This was almost seven years to the day before her last trip up the coast, when on July 22, 1858, the vessel ran into heavy winds and squalls two days after leaving San Francisco for its run to Victoria. The ship sprang leaks and the sea rushed in to squelch the boiler fires, disabling the vessel. Although in a very precarious position, the ship was able to limp back to port.

The *Commodore* was immediately put into dry dock, and her name was missing from the harbor news for nine months. The *Crescent City Herald* of March 16, 1859, reported:

> The *Brother Jonathan* arrived on Sunday morning under the command of Captain Staples. She has resumed her old name, under which we hope she may be more fortunate than she was as the *Commodore.* She has been for a long time on the dock at Mare Island, where she has been thoroughly overhauled and refitted throughout. Forty thousand ($40,000) dollars, or thereabouts, have been spent on her. She has been strengthened in every possible way and is now, if anything, stauncher than the day she was first launched. She has a Number One certificate and is now worthy of the patronage of the public.

Captain G. H. Staples is still the master after her overhauling, and it is he that is at the helm in the predawn darkness as the *Brother Jonathan* gently noses up to the open wharf in Portland on March 15, 1859. He was bringing wonderful news to the people of the Oregon Territory. Congress had passed and President Buchanan had signed an act giving Oregon statehood. Since Valentine's Day, February 14th, 1859, she has been the 33rd state in the union.

The Senate bill for the admission of Oregon passed the House of Representatives by an eleven-vote majority on February 12. The news was flashed by telegraph from Washington, D.C., to St. Louis at the end of the line. The overland mail route by stagecoach and horseback took another twenty-four days to reach San Francisco. As the newly recommissioned *Brother Jonathan* was the next ship steaming north, she brought the news of statehood to Portland. From there, a rider carried word to nearby Oregon City. The next day, Steven Sender spent thirty hours on horseback riding from Oregon City to Salem—and braving flooded rivers the entire way—to finally tell those in the state capital. By this time Oregon had been a state for one month.

In 1861, Wright sold his steamships to Major Samuel J. Hensley. Now the owner of the Oregon & San Diego Steamship Company (later the Pacific Steam Navigation Company), Hensley had owned and operated several steamer lines before. He was also the agent for the California Steam Navigation Company in San Francisco. When that company decided to concentrate its efforts on the burgeoning river traffic, however, the steamers were sold. Hensley bought the *Brother Jonathan* and *Senator* for a reported price of $200,000. The vessels called at Santa Barbara, San Luis Obispo, and San Pedro (Los Angeles) for the first several months.

The *Brother Jonathan,* however, still needed major repairs. At the time she sailed last, in 1861, she had to turn around and return to San Francisco, leaking so badly that the pumps at the pier had to be operated to keep her afloat. The new owner contracted for a complete rebuilding of the ship, now ten years old. The restoration took place at North's Shipyard, near Mission Rock in San Francisco, where the vessel was completely overhauled. Recommending a horse and buggy ride to the shipyard to see the steamer, the editor of the *Alta California,* wrote on May 4, 1861:

> She looks for all like the skeleton of some antediluvian megatherium [an extinct giant ground sloth] or mastodon raked out from ruins of an extinct creation, for however much like a singed cat she may look now, she will come out gay as a pink [a delicate flower, Dianthus, and also a small sailing vessel] about mid-summer.

The *Brother Jonathan*'s wooden skin was completely removed to the still solid bottom timbers. The workers removed the third deck of the ship, which had been added in 1852, returning the steamer to a two-decked ship. Now it could store and carry more goods. Her old timbers were replaced: Most of the hull was rebuilt with Oregon oak, the spars with Douglas fir, and the cabins were rebuilt in redwood. Two new keelsons were bolted on the ship's bottom and 6,000 new bolts were inserted into her hull.

The reconstruction added more cargo space at the expense of passenger rooms; however, the plans called for double berths and family suites. All of the cabins, regardless of type, were located on the main deck surrounding the rebuilt saloon. The officer's quarters were placed on the upper deck. The old saloon was eliminated and a new 120-foot long dining saloon was built on the upper deck. Space was provided forward to carry up to 900 tons of general cargo. The existing engine was retained. The old boilers were removed and two patented, 21-foot long Martin tubular boilers, hooked to six furnaces each, were installed. This work was the largest overhaul of any steamer completed on the West Coast at the time, and "gay as pink," true to the *Alta California*'s prediction, the *Brother Jonathan* emerged seven months and $100,000 later.

On December 19, 1861, the rebuilt ship left San Francisco on its run to Vancouver. As business boomed in the Pacific Northwest, the *Brother Jonathan* made large sums of money for its owners. Along with its brand-new crimson settees, chairs, and bright oilcloth floor coverings, the cuisine was also first class. Dinners were prepared with the best meat from freshly killed cattle, swine, sheep, and poultry that the vessel carried and kept on ice. White and sweet potatoes, onions, fresh lettuce, dried fruits, and nuts were served, as were fish, crabs, and lobster.

With Captain George W. Staples in command, the vessel carried from 700 to 1,000 passengers on its runs, bringing in 1,000 to Portland in April 1862. The *Jonathan* made the 680 nautical mile distance to Portland in 69 hours, the best time on record. Given the moderate weather and seas, the vessel covered the distance at a speed of 9.86 knots per hour, or nearly 11.5 miles per hour (one knot equals 1.15 mph).

Of note, the ship gained a steady reputation as one of the "staunchest" vessels on the Puget Sound run. The steamer's new coppered bottom caused her to run and steam very efficiently. The ship also did not have the strong drag caused by the heavy growth on her hull so evident when the *Jonathan* was dry-docked in 1861.

The trade conducted by coastal steamers like the *Jonathan* was important and impressive. Everyone from miners to farmers and craftsmen needed tools and supplies. The mills—whether working on gold, wool, flour, or lumber—required ever-increasing amounts of machinery and equipment. Portland became a center for marketing wheat, wool, apples, flour, cattle, sheep, butter, and eggs from its agrarian economy to the ever-growing California market. Cargoes of wool were shipped directly to California's mills, or transshipped back east. Finished consumer goods, in turn, headed up the Pacific Northwest to Portland and on. These consisted of clothing, dry goods, liquors, wines, shoes, tools, and hardware. Meanwhile, millions of dollars of gold continued to flow back and forth from the Pacific Northwest and California through Panama and Nicaragua to the major money centers of both the East and West. As the Civil War dragged on, the Pacific Coast was spared its ravages and the commercial opportunities abounded for growth up the Pacific Coast.

Although not a fast ship, the *Brother Jonathan* maintained a steady pace, which assured her immediate success as a plush, pure-bred coastal workhorse between San Francisco, Crescent City, Portland, Seattle, and Vancouver. Grossly maligned later as an old and tender vessel, the ship was in reality a well-built luxury liner, offering fine passenger accommodations.

However, all did not necessarily go well on its voyages. After the *Brother Jonathan* departed Victoria, British Columbia, one day later on March 18, 1862, one passenger left off in Victoria was confirmed as having smallpox. Two days after that, another passenger came down with the deadly disease. One week later, the steamer *Oregon* from San Francisco delivered another who was infected. A catastrophic epidemic soon broke out in Victoria and British Columbia.

In 1864, Hensley transferred title to the California Steam Navigation Company, an entity formed by the steamer owners to reduce competition when too many ships competed for the same passengers and caused fares to fall to unprofitable levels. This monopolistic enterprise quickly brought fares back up to the levels the owners desired.

Weeks after the close of the Civil War, in the late spring of 1865, the *Brother Jonathan* anchored in Portland as Captain Staples waited out a squall. At a nearby hotel, a gambler named Patterson made insulting remarks about the Federal Government, which in turn ended in a skirmish with pro-North people. The fire bells rang, which summoned there nearly everybody who lived in the area. The crowd collected around the Pioneer Hotel and threatened to hang Patterson. Captain Staples grabbed the rope and ran up the stairs after the man, yelling that he would bring Patterson down by his neck.

As Patterson retreated upstairs, he warned them not to follow. The man fired a warning shot in the air, but Staples kept coming. Before Patterson reached the top, he turned around and shot the man chasing him. Captain Staples died from his wounds. Samuel J. DeWolf was then onboard the ship as First Mate. Upon the ship's return to San Francisco under DeWolf's command, the company confirmed him as the new Master and Captain of the *Brother Jonathan*.

Captain DeWolf and the *Jonathan* left San Francisco again in June of 1865, heading north to Portland. On June 14, the ship collided with the Barkentine *Jane A. Falkenberg* in the Columbia River, sustaining damage to her hull. DeWolf returned to San Francisco without major problem, and "minor" repairs were made to the *Jonathan* while she was at anchor.

A report was made about the collision and damage to the company's office with Captain DeWolf's recommendation to dry-dock the ship, inspect the damage, and repair the break in the hull. The owners decided not to have its repair crew make dry-dock repairs, the break being at the water line and "slightly below," but to instead mend it "as best they could" from the inside. Although this was not satisfactory to DeWolf, the *Brother Jonathan* steamed away on this voyage into the impending storm.

IN THE SALOON, the people drank, smoked, ate, and talked with one another, as the ship powered over its course against the heavier waves and increasing wind. The outside temperature cooled as the black overhead clouds shut out the setting sun. Steward Farrell closed the portholes and lit the oil lamps, as friends and strangers talked about the Civil War, gold and currency, and San Francisco itself. Although the winds and waves picked up, those onboard at first played little attention.

Handwritten in ink with elaborate script, the menu for dinner included a soup, such as barley or ox tail; a choice of entrees such as chicken pie, pig's head, or mutton pies; a main course with a choice of fish with sauce, boiled mutton with capers or an oyster sauce, or roast beef; and vegetables such as potatoes, rice, and string beans. For desert, there were pies, oranges and figs, almonds, or custard pudding. Beverages included coffee, tea, beer, and wine. The choices were usually extensive and the food typically excellent on these competitive coastal voyages. The bill of fare was advertised ahead of time at the shipping company to entice passengers to take one line over another.

As the passengers dined, musicians played the piano or led the people in singing. Songs were played, such as "Tenting on the Old Campground," "Pike's Peak March," "The Fireman's March," "The Dying Californian," and "Tramp, Tramp, Tramp."

Resplendent in dress uniforms and formal attires, Captain DeWolf dined at his table with General Wright who wore his formal Unions. Also present more than likely were Wright's wife and his senior aides; James Nisbet; Joseph A. Lord, the Wells Fargo Senior Messenger who was acquainted with DeWolf; Mr. William Logan, the newly appointed Superintendent of the U.S. Mint in The Dalles, Oregon, and a friend of Governor Anson Henry; and Governor Anson Henry of the Washington Territory. The topics of conversation were Lincoln's death and its effect on Reconstruction, the raider *Shenandoah,* and the war, along with the new responsibilities and tasks of those assembled. The boisterous and evesdroppers were nearby, eating loudly, belching, clinking glasses, and telling lies of the type that everyone does when first meeting someone new.

Mrs. Keenan and her entourage appeared late, stopping conversations and causing hesitation. Dressed provocatively, the group's appearance was a topic changer. How James Nisbet reacted to her—and how well he knew her from his newspaper beat—along with how Anson Henry looked at his archenemy, Victor Smith, can only be speculated.

Due to the building waves and winds, some passengers didn't finish their dinner. Some stayed in their staterooms dealing with seasickness. As the ship skidded or thudded over the large waves, large sofas and chairs rattled. But because they were secured, they didn't shift into a dangerous slide. Tables and benches, likewise, were screwed into the deck, cabinets into the bulkheads. The bunks and compactums (cabinets that folded down with a small sink inside) were also attached to the floor and walls, as were mirrors.

Most everything else was loose from the rattling plates, glasses, and condiments on the tables to personal belongings, carpet bags, and even the stowed luggage below—and they were starting into motion. Navigating the entrance to the steerage compartment toward the bow was a particularly difficult task in stormy weather as it involved maneuvering down steep ladders through the hatch. Owing to the worsening conditions outside, people weren't standing on the covered paddle wheel walkways to watch this night's cruise.

Many of the passengers on board were from or very acquainted with San Francisco due to their trips. By 1865, San Francisco had a population of 103,000 and had made the transition from a rough, shantytown to an icon of wealth with its own moneyed class. New York City in 1865 was populated by a much larger 650,000, but Denver only numbered 5,000 people. Salt Lake City—the largest city between St. Louis and San Francisco—counted 20,000 residents. Males, of course, dominated the Bay City by a three to two margin over women, but this proportion was better than it was during the Gold Rush when the ratio was greater than 10–1.

Traveling from New York City to San Francisco by ship was much longer than the 3,200 land miles between the coasts. Nevertheless, travelers preferred steaming to and from both sides of the Panama Isthmus, including the overland transit, in thirty days versus the months to travel over land through the United States. Rail ended from the East Coast in the Midwest, and then only wagon train and stage coach traversed the harsh prairies. People then traveled generally by horseback over the precipitous mountain passes to finally arrive in San Francisco. However one went, this was hard travel.

San Francisco was then set inside a range of the "purest sand hills"—blown up from the ocean—that were six or seven miles wide. The main business streets were laid out on the flat land carved out by the sweeping sands from the hills. Some of these were cut through to make room for the continued spread of the city, now comprised of multistoried buildings, apartments, and upstanding hotels, as well as stately residences, and homes.

Albert Richardson accompanied Samuel Bowles and others on an 1865 tour. Every morning he looked out upon the "teeming life of a great metropolis with stately blocks of brick and stone, railroads, streetcars, markets, exchanges, elegant residences, costly school houses, imposing churches and generous charities." The men were struck by the magnificent harbor with its miles of steamers and sailing vessels and noted that at one time within its anchorage were more ships than those found in "New York, Liverpool, or London."

By 1865, large farms surrounded the major cities in California, producing large quantities of fruits—from grapes and pears to apples, strawberries, and lemons—as well as large amounts of vegetables, such as tomatoes, lettuce, beets, and potatoes. Since the easy-to-find gold beds in streams and rivers were nearly exhausted, quartz mining took hold in place of panning, sluice boxes, and hydraulic-pressure mining. This entailed digging deep mines to locate the gold-bearing quartz deposits. Mining the gold, crushing it in ore crushers, and then leeching the slurry required massive amounts of capital and men. The industry was in change and required also extensive equipment, such as the heavy ore crushers.

The cost of living in San Francisco in 1865 (in gold) was almost as much as it took to live in Boston and New York, although this was a definite improvement from the supercharged prices of the Gold Rush. Food and lodgings were cheaper than on the East Coast, but dry goods and luxuries cost more, owing to the costs of transporting them to the city.

Bowles observed:

> At the best hotels, the Occidental and Cosmopolitan, the price is three dollars a day in gold, which is the same as the four dollars and fifty cents per diem in greenbacks at your first-class New York and Boston houses. A drink at an aristocratic San Francisco bar is two bits [25 cents], at a more democratic establishment one bit [12½ cents] with butter, seventy-five cents a pound; eggs, seventy cents a pound; potatoes, two cents per pound; turkey, thirty cents per pound; fresh salmon, ten cents a pound; and oranges, four dollars per pound.

As to the women, Bowles penned:

> The ladies generally dress in good taste. Paris is really as near San Francisco as New York, and there are many foreign families here. But the styles are not so subdued as in our eastern cities; a higher or rather louder tone prevails; rich, full colors,

> and sharp contrasts; the startling effects that the Parisian demi-monde seeks—these are seen dominating here. . . . Their point lace is deeper, their moiré antique stiffer, their skirts a trifle longer, their corsage an inch lower, their diamonds more brilliant.

Although hostilities had ended, the controversies of war still hung over the passengers and crew. Loyalties were divided through the entire country during the Civil War, even in California, and they continued for years. Generally, citizens in "Alta California"—or the northern part that included the homeport of the *Brother Jonathan,* San Francisco—were to a great extent pro-Union. In the southern and inland expanses of the state, particularly in the agricultural districts, there was strong support for the Confederate cause. The California state legislature even passed a bill in 1859 separating the state into two parts based on their constituents' preferences. Although the governor signed this act into law, the U.S. Congress rejected the attempted bifurcation.

Despite the West's general opposition to the Confederate cause, Oregon's Governor John Whiteaker, a proslaver, refused to honor President Lincoln's call for troops. In 1862, A. C. Gibbs defeated him at the polls. Oregon immediately raised two troop regiments to replace the regular Army soldiers assigned to aid the Union cause. Oregon's integrity, however, had already been tarnished. The state was classified as an "exception to the Loyalist States." In punishment, the federal government forced Oregon to bear the financial burden of protecting the miners, settlers, and its Oregon Trail, a duty that usually fell to federal troops. The ultimate bill amounted to $1.3 million, which the State of Oregon would still like to collect.

In early 1861, to protect San Francisco and its bay area, the U.S. War Department moved two artillery companies from Fort Vancouver to the hills overlooking the city. After war was declared between the states, the citizens of San Francisco not only generally supported the cause of the North but they would also criticize anyone publicly stating views to the contrary. During the 1861–1865 conflict, Colonel (later Brigadier General) George Wright was placed in charge of military affairs in the West.

Historians usually credit Wright with conducting a commendable job in keeping the state isolated from the blood and gore of a Civil War that resulted in more than one million casualties in the East and Midwest. A West Point graduate, he had a distinguished military career, ranging from fighting in the Seminole Indian wars in Florida in the early 1840s to being wounded in the 1846 war with Mexico. In October 1861, he became the Commander of the Federal Department of the Pacific; Wright remained in command of the federal interests on the West Coast during the Civil War, avoided controversy, and generally received good marks.

From today's perspective, General Wright walked a difficult line. With rumors of impending Confederate attacks, he acted in late 1862 to ban certain newspapers being sent by mail, thus distributing them beyond their initial market. Printing anti-Union, pro-Confederacy editorials and articles, these newspapers were against the policies of Abraham Lincoln's government. Wright eventually lifted the ban, but the academic debate over his ban continues today.

During the early 1860s, the *Brother Jonathan,* and other vessels in the Pacific coast trade, were under constant threat of attack, whether actual or imagined. The risk of raiders off California, however, became very real with the arrival of the Confederate raider, the CSS *Shenandoah.* This iron-hulled, three-masted, propeller-driven steamer carried eight guns. She also had the ability to lower her smokestack, making her look like a peaceful sailing ship, but able to steam suddenly after her prey in calm winds.

While the *Shenandoah* operated in the northern limits of the Pacific under Lieutenant James Waddell, the war was actually coming to a close. On Sunday, April 9, 1865, in a courthouse in Appomattox, the Civil War mercifully ended after a string of Confederate losses when General Robert E. Lee, Commander of the Army of Northern Virginia, surrendered to General Ulysses S. Grant.

On the day that President and Mrs. Lincoln attended a play in Ford's Theatre in Washington on April 14, 1865, the *Shenandoah* steamed toward the Kurile Islands near Russia in the Northern Pacific. The assassination of President Lincoln that night resulted in many lionizing him, including those who hadn't even supported his policies during the war. When the news of his death reached San Francisco by telegraph, angry mobs raged through the streets the next day. The vengeful residents destroyed several newspapers that had published articles defaming or criticizing Lincoln during the war.

On June 22, while Americans still celebrated the peace and began turning their attention towards reconstruction, the *Shenandoah* captured three whalers in the Bering Sea between Russia and Alaska. During the next four days, the raider burned or captured twenty different vessels, keeping one, the *Milo.* It returned the captured sailors to San Francisco with a firsthand report of Waddell's stunning successes. This news reached the city in time for the *Alta California* to run a front-page article on July 21 on its risk to Pacific shipping. At the time Captain Waddell was weighing a decision to attack San Francisco and its coastal shipping lanes. He still hadn't received the news that the war was over.

As the *Brother Jonathan* pitched and yawed, the night had become a leering blackness, and the winds howled with the mounting seas. Just hours after leaving San Francisco, the sidewheeler was bucking heavy ocean waves. One of its paddles occasionally rolled out of water and nearly spinned out of control. The other bit down hard, and the ship suddenly veered or pitched. The strong thuds against the bow shifted people forward, as the waves crashed and the sound of water washing down the sides reverberated inside.

Regardless of its intensity, wind is the movement of air from an area of high pressure to one of low. Caused primarily by the sun heating the earth—which in turn heats up the atmosphere—contrasts in temperature are a basic cause of all wind, such as warm land and cooler offshore waters. When air becomes heated, it expands, occupies a greater volume, starts to rise, and its density decreases. The surrounding cooler air races in and replaces the rising warm air. Although the earth's rotation and the evaporation of water over the ocean can also cause these differentials, the movement of air from cooler (or higher pressure and density) to warmer areas (lower pressure and density) usually creates wind.

Albert Bowles in his 1865 travel diary wrote about the winds:

> What gives San Francisco its harsh summer days is that it is constantly "in the draft." While elsewhere along shore, the coast hills uninterruptedly break the steady north-west breeze of the summer sea, they open here just enough to let the waters of the Sacramento River and San Francisco bay out, and let in like a tide of escape steam the ocean breeze and mists.

Albert Richardson wrote:

> The Golden Gate, the outlet of San Francisco harbor, is a break in the Coast Range Mountains. Through its narrow portals rushes a current of air like a blast furnace, passing up the valley of the Sacramento to supply the basins west of the Sierra Nevadas.

A direct relationship exists between how wickedly a wind blows and the severity of the waves. A wind blowing at 10 knots per hour (11.5 miles per hour) creates waves two feet high. At 20 knots, the winds create whitecaps that are eight feet high. At 40 knots, the waves have well-marked streaks and are twenty feet high. Once the winds hit 50 knots (or 57 miles per hour), the waves are very high with white seas and overhanging crests at twenty to thirty feet. Visibility is reduced considerably. These seas eventually became thirty feet high with winds greater than 50 knots per hour.

Franklin Langworthy's journal entries while on board the *Brother Jonathan* in 1853 mirrors this voyage. Upon passing through the

Golden Gates, the passengers found the sea in "considerable commotion, the wind having raised heavy swells during the night." (The vessel had been at anchor during the night awaiting the proper papers to leave the harbor.) Langworthy noted:

> The ship began to plunge in such a manner that freshwater sailors, like myself, found it quite difficult to maintain our standing. The passengers began to become seized with seasickness, and in a few hours, hundreds were down, and the noise of vomiting resounded from all parts of the vessel. This seemed to be making a bad commencement to our voyage. As to myself, I was not much affected with this sickness. I had eaten sparingly for two days, and I now took to my berth, where I remained a large portion of the time for the next twenty-four hours. The swells rather increased in size as the night set in, and there was no abatement of sickness among the passengers. During the day, several times the sea broke over the bow, pouring a large body of water upon the main forward deck, and drenching a number of steerage passengers.

The night wind shrieked. Charles Dickens wrote in *American Notes:*

> I am awakened out of my sleep by a dismal shriek from my wife, who demands to know whether there's any danger. I rouse myself, and look out of bed. The water jug is plunging and leaping like a lively dolphin; all the smaller articles are afloat, except my shoes, which are stranded on a carpet bag, high and dry, like a couple of coal barges. Suddenly I see them spring into the air, and behold the looking glass, which is nailed to the wall, sticking fast upon the ceiling. At the same time the door entirely disappears, and a new one is opened in the floor.
>
> Then I begin to comprehend that the stateroom is standing on its head. Before it is possible to make any arrange-

> ment that's compatible with this novel state of things, the ship then rights. Before one can say, "Thank Heaven!," she wrongs again. Before one can cry she *is* wrong, she seems to have started forward, and to be a creature actively running of its own accord, with broken knees and failing legs, through every variety of hole and pitfall, and stumbling constantly.

The thunderous waves smacked against the ship, sounding tremendous thumps against the hull that shook the nerves of even the most courageous. As Lucy Hendricks noted, "People and furniture were rolling and tumbling, crockery breaking, doors creaking, and unaccountable noises heard on deck. After much fuming and fussing, we fell into an uneasy doze from which I was awakened by a lurch of the ship that upset a tray of clothes on me and disconcerted me."

THE SEAS RAGED during the night, as the ship tossed myriads of swirling sparks into the air, which the winds quickly extinguished. The smokestacks of the sidewheel steamers at night looked as if fireworks spewed from their insides. With these fiery surrealistic emissions, the sounds of thumping paddle wheels, pops and cracks from burning coal, and smacks of waves against ship, voyages like these were not for the faint-hearted.

On any other night, the *Brother Jonathan* would have looked like a Christmas tree bedecked with jeweled lights. As the ship creaked, moaned, and cracked, the wind whistled outside with spray and foam smacking against, inside, and throughout the ship. Hour after hour, the noises inside and out of the trembling ship echoed with a ghostly effect, unnerving, disheartening the staunchest. The ship moved slower and slower as one monstrous wave after another plowed into it. At times seeming to stand still, the vessel suddenly plunged forward, reeling out of control and heaving from one side to the other.

The ship's dry timbers were still acclimating to their saltwater immersion—and the continued pounding produced even more pressure—as the sea began to seep into the ship's interiors. The cold saltwater leaked through the overhead decks and cracks in the timbers, poured through cracked doorway hatches, and surged through portholes thrown open for untainted air.

Manning the pumps, the crew struggled to keep the ocean at bay; however, their efforts could not keep the sloshing ocean from taking over. Vessels leak as much as one foot of water per hour under these conditions, and the crew was hard pressed to keep up with this flooding. The conditions eventually forced people to leave their cold, smelling, flooded quarters for the relative warmth and dryness of the lounge, braving a rocking, rolling, crashing passage through the ship's interior. Once inside the pitching lounge, passengers found spray pounding against portholes, dishes in small pieces on the carpet, and tired, sunken eyes looking back.

During these frightful times, women sipped from small bottles of Mrs. Winslow's soothing syrup, while the men drank from their flasks of whiskey. The prime ingredient of Mrs. Winslow's thick liquid was laudanum, a "tincture of opium" sweetened with sugar.

EARLY SATURDAY MORNING spray flew from stem to stern, and all hands deserted the decks except for those essential to the ship's working. Lashed by the winds, the whole ocean was wrapped in sheets of foam. The vessel pitched so violently that it was impossible for people to write intelligibly, including James Nisbet. The air was chilly in the morning, and the few curious passengers who ventured outside received a thorough drenching from the spray that whipped over the vessel. The sky at times became unnervingly clear, the waves over the height of the pilothouse, and the bright sunshine sharply illuminating the surrounding, raging seas. Foamy wave crests surged over the gunnels, scattering in drenching sprays down the deck.

The day's experience on board the *Jonathan* continued: high winds, high seas, and little comfort for most. Furniture and personal effects crashed about and daily activities—whether shaving or combing one's hair—were near impossible. Owing to this wild roller-coaster ride, many of the passengers became seasick. This condition isn't a problem of the mind caused by fears or stress. Rather, seasickness is a balance problem that occurs when the inner ear's nerve fibers, eyes, and other senses that detect motion, send conflicting messages to the brain. One part of your balance-sensing system (your inner ear and sensory nerves) screams that your body is moving, while the others don't sense the motion. For example, in the cabin of a moving ship, your inner ear may sense the motion of big waves, but your eyes can't pick up the movement. This leads to a conflict between the senses and results in motion sickness.

Sensory perceptions get out of synch as these nerve fibers try to compensate for the unfamiliar motions of a ship pounding through the sea. Sometimes a few days are needed for the seasickness to dissipate, as the person becomes used to the motion and "earns their sea legs"—or it can take days, even weeks. The symptoms—a general sense of not feeling well or a malaise punctuated with wracking nausea, headaches, and profuse cold sweating—usually go away when the motion stops. In modern times, passengers use the patch and antihistamine drugs, the most common being Dramamine and Bonine. No matter the century, people afflicted by seasickness, or motion sickness, claim that only dying can relieve the problem.

On their own then, people began trying natural cures. Passengers left their cabins to breathe fresher air. They sat on the deck and looked at a fixed point on the horizon in an attempt to stabilize their senses. Some tried bitters (a couple tablespoons of Angostura Bitters mixed in a half glass of water), chewed ginger, consumed saltine crackers and water, drank liquor (but the later hangovers and dehydration were other problems), lay down in a prone position, smelled fresh sea air, avoided food or drink, stopped reading, avoided strong odors, and tried just about anything.

The problem was that in stormy seas like the ones the *Brother Jonathan* was steaming through, no cure really seemed to work. Venturing outside one's cabin wasn't safe. The ship lifted from the ocean, and then pounded down, rolling from side to side like a dog shaking water from a soggy coat after a long swim. This pounding ride continued seemingly forever, and the pungent smell of vomit and sweat pervaded the close confines of the quarters—with no place of refuge.

The seas continued rising into the next night. The winds and waves forcing the majority of the passengers to stay below, many remaining in their bunks. One can only imagine what Daniel and Polina Rowell experienced, if they and one or more of their children were seasick. The two needed to alternate in taking one child or the other to the dining room, if they hadn't brought sufficient snacks and food with them.

Polina was born in Ohio, but her family had moved to Oregon nearly twenty years before. Her family settled around The Dalles, where a new mint was to be built at Oregon's northern tip west of Portland on the Columbia River. When her father, Elias, decided to build a grist and saw mill, he hired Daniel Rowell to work it. Daniel was a miller by trade and had come from England. He met Polina, both fell in love, and they had been now married for nearly fifteen years. They first farmed in Oregon, but the couple left for the Midwest where their four children were born. They were now moving back to be with Polina's family. Taking a precaution, Polina had stitched the gold coins from the Ohio farm's sale into the hem of a dress for her journey home.

At some time during this voyage, it is believed that the young, attractive "waitress" Martha Wilder met up with the kind John Hensley. With seven "doves" on board, a few ventured out and connected with others. Whether or not these two became romantically involved isn't known, but the later actions of Hensley, Wilder, and the crew indicated some familiarity with one another.

Quartermaster Yates was at the helm from time to time, as Captain DeWolf, First Officer Allen, and Second Officer Campbell alternated inside the pilot's cabin. Engineer Mott stayed down at the very bottom of the ship with the firemen running the pumps day and night, as the acrid smell of sweat combined with the pungent odor of the cold seas sloshing inside.

General Wright, seasick or not, ventured up into the saloon to check on his aids, smoke a cigar, swish a brandy, and show leadership. He checked on the condition of his horses, as the ocean crashed and seeped into their stalls, and he or his aid watched over the prized Newfoundland dog. Jeannette Lee checked on her circus's camels when she found someone to hold her baby for a time. In the saloon, James Nisbet read and wrote when he could, observing everything happening around him. Although Mrs. Keennan stayed in her stateroom ill with seasickness, now and then, one of her entourage ventured out.

Only a handful of passengers came to the saloon for lunch and less for dinner that night. Tiny groups of passengers were in tight little groups in the lounge; conversations were less, as tired people stared outside at the sprayed portholes. The lucky ones who didn't have seasickness drank, attempted to play cards, or talked in quiet tones. These few tried to stay in the public quarters, as this was better than being cooped up in tiny quarters, slammed against walls, or drenched by any porthole opened for air. The lit oil lamps gave off surrealistic shades of black and white, as the crashing of furniture, cracks and moaning of the ship's structure, and the overpowering smell of the sea took over one's senses.

Meanwhile, inside the ship's caverns, people lay sick inside their bunks. William Shields, the cabin boy, brought the first-class cabins their French champagne, as some had heard about the "medicinal" value of drinking the bubbly when sick like this. Mrs. Keenan would have had a bottle or two of the unopened champagne as a reserve for herself as well as for her flock. Some tried to have meals brought to their staterooms, but this depended on the elements, who would brave the outside, and how much of a "tip" was expected. Having a bottle of Mrs. Winslow's soothing syrup on hand was as important as bitters, whiskey, or champagne.

Lydia Ridder Nye, the Captain's wife, wrote in her diary, "The first week after my embarkation, I was confined with seasickness; that was a gloomy week to be obliged to keep in one place, and, I might add in one position; for there were five of us sick and our rooms being very small, would not admit the fresh air."

Passenger Albert D. Richardson wrote in his 1865 journal:

> The moment our wheels started, we felt the sharp contrast to the smooth Pacific, and the shining capacity of our steamer

for rolling and pitching. It was difficult to decide which was hardest, to keep in bed through the night, dress in the morning, or eat during the day. The tables were a dreary expanse of empty seats, and our pretext of breakfasting very shallow and ridiculous. Huge waves drenched the upper deck with spray. It is wonderful how steamers ride them, with wheels now entirely submerged, and a moment after, lifted far out of the water.

For two days we staggered about or adhered to our sofas, battling the two difficulties of keeping inside our staterooms and outside our dinners. The third day was a little smoother; and the wretched mortals began to creep out of their hiding places and appear at tables. The women uniformly declared that they had not been seasick, but merely suffering from headache. Why is everybody ashamed of seasickness and innocent of its existence?

However ill you feel, it is far better to try and eat every meal. Iced champagne is the best remedy for this intense nausea. The sea is a relentless leveler, without the slightest regard for personal prejudices. One of our company was a Congressman who advocated prohibition and was a strict adherent. I saw him on a sofa for three days, pale as death, but living and drinking champagne "straight"—and he seemed to like it!

In 1849 Ezekel I. Barra on the *Samson* wrote:

The seas were running mountains high. We were running before a terrific northeaster, and the ship creaked and groaned in every joint, and it seemed as if she could not hold together any longer. Great combers arose as if to engulf us, but the ship would forge ahead. The captain ordered lifelines be placed around the waists of the two men at the helm, and that the ends be well secured. The huge waves with crested heads seemed like living sea monsters, looking at us thirty feet over our heads, as though they would overwhelm and at once engulf us. The ship behaved beautifully and proved herself a fine sea boat, and rose and fell in harmony with each passing wave as it swept past us. All at once an ugly towering wave approached the ship with overwhelming force.

The sea came over the ship and the two men at the helm were carried from their post as if they had been two wisps of straw, but the precautionary measures saved them. The lower cabin skylight was wrenched from its fastenings and the cabin drenched with water. The starboard quarter boat was lifted from its fastenings and wedged between the bulwark and the upper cabin. The ship was waterlogged, and everything that was not well secured on the main deck was floating around. The ship nearly lost her steerageway.

Daylight now began to appear. The ship was rolling and pitching in obedience to the motion of the tumbling waves. Suddenly, there was a blinding flash of lightning that illuminated every part of the ship and masts and rigging as clearly as if it had been high noon on a clear day. There followed a tremendous noise. Just imagine that one thousand railroad steam engines, coming from opposite directions crashed in one instant, the same time exploding the boilers of every one. This would be but a faint comparison to the clap of thunder followed by the lightning's flash.

Then, we discovered the gale had so strained the ship that she had begun to leak quite seriously. Pumping the usual time of fifteen minutes didn't work, so the second mate took the sounding rod and shoved it down into the pump well. He saw that at least fourteen inches of water still remained in the ship. A rotary crank attached to a heavy flywheel worked the ship's pumps, and the two pumps threw water equal in volume to a fire engine's. This worked in two hours.

The seasickness continued and people felt as if a huge swing had captured them—one that never stopped moving back and forth, then up and down. As the towering waves pounded against the boat, the screams of frightened people echoed inside the vessel. Praying was constant.

Sidewheelers worked best on seas not subject to bad storms and high waves, as they often lost control when their paddles rolled in and out of the ocean. These vessels were very maneuverable in calm waters, starting and stopping quite quickly and efficiently. This wasn't the case now. The outside screamed from 60-mile-per-hour winds and thunderous thirty-foot waves, as the *Brother Jonathan* pitched unmercifully on Saturday from early daylight into a second fitful night.

Chapter 4

A Safe Harbor

Through the foreboding night, the beleaguered ship plowed into the angry ocean, bucking badly, with seas crashing over her sides and down her length. The passengers and some of the crew huddled inside their berths and quarters. Other workmen labored inside the engine rooms or peered into the raging darkness from the main deck as if they knew where they were heading. Although the lounge on the main deck was open, it was scarcely populated. Flickering candlelight and whale oil lamps gave scant light inside, and the shadowy features of a few people scattered around tables and couches painted a surrealistic look. Outside, the winds howled and the sea hissed.

The elements denied soul satisfying, peaceful sleep. Cramped inside their narrow berths, seasick passengers could only grip the sides of their beds tight with white knuckles, the air fouled inside, as everything from shoes and clothing to brushes and chamber pots mixed into the seawater sloshing inside. The savage rocking of the ship continued, as the ocean seeped underneath doors, dripped from the overhead deck, and beaded in through the hull. Oaths and prayers sounded out that somehow people would survive.

The ship's pumps barely kept up with the onslaught of saltwater inside the bilge that crept towards the engine room. Inside the fiery room, nervous Elijah Mott kept a wary eye on the sea's progress towards his beloved furnaces and boilers. The ship moaned from its exertions, the steady thump of its paddle wheels nonexistent for hours, replaced by the crashing sounds of ocean and whining sidewheels. As if an exaggerated roll of the ship would be its last, the vessel agonizingly righted itself and plunged downwards, seething and screeching, as fears rose and imaginations ran that the crazed ocean was close to crashing down their doors. The *Brother Jonathan* slalomed uncontrollably, only to slam to a near stop when a large roller swept into it, the crest over the pilot's cabin.

When the goblins of apprehension were at their highest, the winds peaked, then somewhat slackened. The ship's bucking lessened although the creaking continued. Saltwater still ran back and forth inside rooms and down hatches, but the rising waters seemed to have peaked. People at first didn't notice the lessening of the ship's gyrations and the wind's shrieks.

Towards two o'clock in the blackness of early morning, the regular thump of the *Brother Jonathan*'s paddle wheels became noticeable once more, a rhythmic melody that became soothing. The sounds then stopped and only the rocking whumps of waves against the hull were heard. The staccato thumps of the anchor being dropped sounded through the night air. As people tentatively opened their portholes, a few sparkling lights from land greeted them. The quiet quickly became overwhelming.

People heard the garbled sounds of men laughing. After pounding through the ocean for thirty-four hours, at a rate of nearly 8½ knots, the *Brother Jonathan* had finally arrived at its first destination: Crescent City. The day was Sunday, July 30, 1865, and the stevedores worked to offload the cargo onto smaller "taxi-boats," or "lighters" as they were called, for transport to the dock.

Although the harbor had a wharf for boats, its length wasn't long enough to reach the deeper waters required by ships like this one. More importantly, the swells of the waves in harbors could be dangerous. Specific written warnings were in effect in Crescent City Harbor for sailors to be aware of this. Private contractors hauled the merchandise in their owned or rented lighters to land. Once their workers unloaded the goods onto the dock, horse-drawn wagons hauled the merchandise away to their ultimate destinations in the interiors of Northern California and Southern Oregon. As the workmen moved the designated goods from the vessel, the passengers sighed a deep relief at the lack of violent waves and winds. They could certainly find some well-deserved sleep now without uncertain seas getting in the way.

LOCATED SOME FIFTEEN MILES from the Oregon border, the town of Crescent City was nearly fifteen years old when the *Brother Jonathan* nestled in its protective bay. Drawn by pristine forests, bountiful fishing, ample room to live and breathe—and the hopeful allure of finding gold—people began moving into the area. Disappointed in the gold finds elsewhere in the region, other prospectors settled here instead. By the time the city became incorporated in 1854, Crescent City had grown to two hundred houses and eight hundred inhabitants.

Although placer mines and hydraulic operations discovered some gold, this did not become a major part of the city's economy. Its wide bay and approximate equal distance between San Francisco and Portland made the small town a stopover for steamers on the lines' coastal runs. As the population increased, the declines in the small mining operations caused miners and others to leave. By 1865, the population was around one thousand hardy souls with a large number of brick buildings, a few churches, saloons, a newspaper office, hotels, and windblown Victorian-looking houses.

The sea has always been part of the lore and life of Crescent City. Its harbor is one of the oldest on the West Coast, the crescent-shaped bay giving the city its name. Constructed in the same Cape Cod style as the eight original West Coast lighthouses, its Battery Point Lighthouse was located at the northern tip of the harbor and first lit in December 1856.

The area's history was already replete with legends about the wrecks that sank off its coastline. The schooner *Paragon* wrecked at Crescent City in 1850, and the *Gold Beach* wrecked at Klamath—some fifteen miles to the south—six years later. The steamer *America* stopped at the bay in 1855. Shortly after offloading its mail and goods, smoke spiraled from the vessel. Leaping flames soon covered the ship; by the next day, after the captain ran it aground, only the charred skeleton inside its hull remained. A later windstorm off Point Reyes sank the burned-out hull as it was being towed to San Francisco for repairs.

Four years later, the schooner *Exact* loaded barrels of salmon and potatoes in its hull, but soon after leaving the harbor, the vessel ran into a "fierce gale from the southwest." Its captain ordered the ship's two anchors be dropped, so that it could ride out the storm. However, the towering waves snapped the boat from its chains, drove the ship onto shore, and wrecked the *Exact* on the rocks by the Crescent City bar.

Dotted with wood and brick structures, the twelve-mile long curving stretch of beach was hemmed in by towering redwood trees, marshes, and mountain ranges. Despite its small population, the town became a gateway for people and goods heading directly into Northern California and Southern Oregon. As valuable as the freight and passengers were to the area, the ship's commodity that the editor of the weekly *Crescent City Herald* looked for most eagerly was the carried mail and newspapers. These sources enabled him to print a paper read as far north as Jacksonville, Oregon—even though the news would be weeks old.

DRY GOODS and mining equipment were among the merchandise offloaded from the ship early that morning. The men in the hold continued to work the pumps to drain the vessel's interior. Others brought coal on board as the storm had caused higher amounts of fuel to be burned. Joseph A. Lord, the Senior Messenger of Wells Fargo, left the ship that early Sunday morning to visit with his family. He met his wife, Mary Priscilla Magruder, in Crescent City, and the young Mrs. Lord had come to visit her foster parents with their small daughter, Margaret, in mid-July. Her folks, the Theophillis Magruders, were the first appointed lighthouse keepers at Crescent City. This stopover gave Mr. Lord a chance to visit with his family for a few precious hours before the ship would leave.

Thirty-four years old at the time, this was Joseph Lord's first voyage in six months. Previously a partner in a grocery firm in Sacramento and the foreman of a fire department, he joined Wells, Fargo & Co. eleven years earlier. Although seeing his family was a reason why he took over the duties of a junior messenger, it is also true his subordinate was sick and couldn't leave his bed. Joseph Lord was a last minute substitution, along with a steward, pantry man, waiter, and a clerk who also boarded at the last moment for those who couldn't make the trip.

Lord was also guarding a sizeable amount of gold for his company—estimated at upwards of $140,000. Part of it was heading to the Horton Dexter Bank of Seattle and part was being sent to the Northwest Fur Traders Association further north. Some believe that men offloaded one gold box at Crescent City that early morning; the U.S. Army payroll of $200,000 and gold for the Indian treaty obligations would have stayed on board the ship.

It is possible that Joseph Lord could have taken a Wells Fargo strong box off with him for the area, as at least three Fargo boxes of gold were loaded onboard for the three stopovers. However, the prime gold transfers were for the next stops at Portland (the transit point also for neighboring Vancouver, Washington) and Vancouver in British Columbia (a transit center for Seattle).

A substantial amount of gold was onboard the *Brother Jonathan*. In addition to the Indian treaty payments, more crates of $20 gold pieces were on board, some for a private transfer for Haskins and Company. The purser also collected gold dust, gold coins, and other personal valuables from the passengers, storing them in the ship's huge Doblier safe and a smaller one nearby.

The history of money on the West Coast was quite different from that of the East Coast. A fear of the future and lack of confidence in the financial markets and federal government had developed during the Civil War. Given the unrest, the monetary world remained in chaos in the East after the war ended. In California, Oregon, and Washington, however, these problems were very limited. Owing to the quantities of gold discovered and California legislative enactments, gold coins reigned supreme over their Eastern greenback counterparts. No gold or silver coins were even in circulation by 1865 in most major Eastern cities. On the West Coast and San Francisco, however, people valued gold coins more than the inflationary paper money.

Several mints operated before 1848 in Eastern cities from Philadelphia and New Orleans to Charlotte. None, however, were on the West Coast. Once the Gold Rush was underway with its massive discoveries, gold as a medium became plentiful even on world markets—but not on the East Coast. The U.S. government didn't begin to issue federal paper money and gold coins until ten years later. People actually hoarded coins when they were first issued. During the Civil War, no new gold coinage was released into general circulation in the East or Midwest—and nothing was introduced until fourteen years after the war ended. The losing Confederacy had little gold, and its paper currency by then was virtually worthless.

The West Coast, however, had an abundance of the precious metal. In 1850, the California legislature abolished paper money, freeing the state from the monetary crises experienced by the rest of the United States, and the West Coast relied on its gold and silver coins into the 1870s. Eastern paper money traded at a sizeable discount—25 percent or more—when offered in trade for the West Coast's gold coins. Since greenbacks were issued regardless of the gold or assets backing them, an inflationary bias sprang up on the East Coast. As California's gold coins typically were exchangeable at their face value into gold, California and the Pacific Northwest experienced much less fluctuations in monetary values than did the East Coast both during and after the Civil War.

When the California Gold Rush was well underway, the U.S. Mint in Philadelphia became overwhelmed in trying to turn all of that gold into coinage. The San Francisco Mint was consequently built on Commercial Street, striking its first Double Eagles in the federal design in 1854. California soon became and continued to be the dominant source of gold coins and bars, producing 90 percent of the U.S. total gold production through 1865. By that summer, several hundred freshly minted, 1865 Double Eagles were packed in wooden boxes and shipped to northward destinations on the *Brother Jonathan.* At the same time, passengers carried their own gold coins, dust, and bars onboard as their own private banks, not trusting the ship's safe or personnel. Gold bars in two-pound rectangles—manufactured either by private firms or the San Francisco Mint—were very useful when traveling to a new area, as these gold "assayer bars" could be melted down into useful coinage of whatever type once at their new destination, whether that be Canada or the United States.

THE SHIP READIED in the morning for its passage to Portland, a day's journey north. The *Brother Jonathan* and coastal shipping was an important commercial transport for this region. The businesses, farmers, and miners in the area needed tools and supplies. Whether grinding flour, sawing wood, or knitting woolen goods, the mills required equipment and machinery to operate. Portland had become a center for wool, wheat, and agricultural goods that were shipped to San Francisco or Seattle. In addition to the gold and currency shipments, thousands of boxes of apples, sacks of flour, mounds of hides, wool, butter and eggs, cattle and sheep were shipped north and south from Portland. In return, tools, hardware, clothing, shoes, liquors, and other goods were shipped to the city and points north. Among the cases of cigars, barrels of butter, and tobacco destined for Oregon, mining machinery (including the large, heavy quartz ore crusher) and woolen mill equipment were to be delivered there—and overseeing these deliveries were various merchant representatives.

The passengers appeared for breakfast in the saloon, some eating their first meals in nearly two days, while others slept peacefully in their berths, the gentle waves barely felt. A few people chose to take a lighter to the pier and stretch their legs or wander down a nearby dirt street with its crude wooden houses and brick buildings. Third Officer James Patterson watched as the last of the mail and barrels of salmon and potatoes were loaded for Portland. When the engines fired up and a shrill whistle blew, the last of the passengers and crew scrambled onto the sidewheeler from a small boat. Joseph and Mary

Lord hugged each other one last time, looking forward to their reunion in San Francisco; Mr. Lord was one of the last to get back on the ship. The time was 9:30 A.M.

The skies were blue and nearly cloudless. The wind gusted, but most of the voyagers felt content due to the rest and comfort of their short stay. Captain DeWolf gave the order for Elijah Mott's engine room to stand by and then the lines were let go. From his position on the bridge, DeWolf signaled Mott to proceed in reverse, then after the *Brother Jonathan* steamed sufficiently away, he commanded the ship to go ahead slowly. As the vessel turned around in a wide semicircle, the vessel gained steam and proceeded toward the ocean. The steamer quickly left the protective bay and headed northwest past the rocky shoals.

Thirty minutes after leaving the dock, the ship ran into a worse Nor'wester with shrieking winds and a quickly building crashing ocean—although the skies were clear and visibility sharp. The weather was worse now than it was the previous night. This area was prone to terrible windstorms and seas that suddenly rose up, and it was happening again as part of the same front. With the storm more west than north, Captain DeWolf gave orders to steam further west and avoid the strung-out rocks of St. George Reef. Her speed slowed down, however, as the vessel plowed into the face of the winds.

Flowing from high to low pressure, wind acts like a ball rolling down a hill. The greater the difference between the low parts of the hill (or low pressure) and high parts (high pressure), the stronger the winds are. Powerful, high overhead jet streams—moving at 200 miles per hour or more—carry storms along their path with even stronger winds. Pummeling the waves at 60 miles per hour and up, these winds were bad.

The *Brother Jonathan* labored for two hours to make "about fourteen miles northwest of the port," according to Seaman Yates. About noon, she was nearly to the Oregon border and far enough out at sea that no one could see land. The waves were "mountainous," and the howling Nor'wester increased its intensity. Despite full-steam power, the ship was nearly motionless in the crashing sea. Captain DeWolf took a sun reading through a light haze with his sextant. Historians believe this condition was due to smoke being blown from a raging forest fire on the mountains to the northwest. DeWolf then turned the ship's navigation over to his trusted seaman, Quartermaster Jacob Yates, and headed to the charthouse to rethink the ship's course.

Captain DeWolf took out his chart there and marked the ship's position. He was "about four miles north" of Saint George Reef, and the charts had indicated its presence in the St. George Channel since 1850. The waves outside were as high as the charthouse, and their spray shot against the windows with heavy, sharp cracks. The term "mountainous" is a term specific to waves greater than twenty-five feet. The winds producing these monsters are generally greater than 50 knots, or about 60 miles per hour. The waves created under these conditions are defined as being "very high waves with white seas and overhanging crests that are twenty to thirty feet high."

The Captain determined that the ship was several miles offshore and twelve or more miles to the northwest of Crescent City Bay. With the aid of his spyglass, DeWolf watched the breakers to the starboard side crash against the rocks on shore and within the Point St. George area. He considered the possible courses back to the harbor that would allow the ship to avoid the reef and its rocky points. Looking outside at the seas and knowing these conditions, his decision wasn't hard to make.

The *Brother Jonathan* was loaded down, the winds so bad, the waves so ruinous, that the steam boilers weren't generating enough power to keep her heading into the wind. She was unable to keep direction and was nearly standing still, the winds buffeting her about, the rudder almost useless. The passengers, afraid, begged DeWolf to return to Crescent City until the winds let up.

DeWolf laid down a track on the chart south toward Crescent City. According to the maps used at the time, no obstructions stood in the way of that course for a safe transit to the harbor around Battery Point and the lighthouse. He ordered the men to ready the vessel for the run back to Crescent City where they would wait out the storm. Captain DeWolf told James Patterson, the Third Officer, to reset the jib and ordered Seaman Yates to turn the "helm hard aport." Yates worked the wheel around. The *Jonathan*'s bow started swinging, passing west, west by southwest, south, southeast, and then finally settled on a "due east" heading, which steadied the vessel and brought her on a course towards the port. The time was now 12:45 P.M.

Steaming for twenty minutes on her new course, the ship approached Southwest Seal Rock, as shown on the charts. These brown and black rocks had patches of green lichen in the spring, but now were dark from the summer months' sun and streaked with "splotches of white." Owing to the vast numbers of birds, the rocks in the general area were partially or sometimes near covered with white from their droppings. Sea lions, seagulls, and green turtles generally abounded on the various rocky islands, but with these conditions, hardly any were in sight. Charted names such as Great Break Rock, Whale Rock, Hump Rock, Star Rock, and Castle Rock stood in a line from S.W. Seal Rock and led on an angle toward Crescent City. DeWolf's course skirted these rocks to the southwest.

When the *Brother Jonathan* steamed by Seal Rock, Captain DeWolf shouted the orders to Yates to steer, "Southeast by South." The skies were relatively clear near Seal Rock, but "foggy and smoky inshore." Quartermaster Yates changed the ship's course to 135 degrees on the ship's compass direct toward Crescent City on a southeasterly heading outside the known rocks. Two miles from Seal Rock, the ship was safely away from the mapped rocks on its way to port. If all went well, the ship would find the safety of Crescent City within a couple of hours. DeWolf ordered the ship's speed increased to 9.5 knots with the winds now behind it.

This voyage was eerily similar to one seven years before when the heavily loaded *Brother Jonathan* (then called the *Commodore)* tried to buck a Nor'wester and floundered in the troughs of those mountainous waves, her boilers without enough steam power to keep her under control. From the statements of the voyagers and ship's log, the vessel left San Francisco on Thursday, July 8, 1858, with some 250 passengers and nearly 800 tons of freight. On that Friday, the crew stowed the cargo and made the ship snug for the trip. The next day, Saturday, the winds blew more "freshly," and the ship began "leaking badly and showing signs of distress."

On Sunday, the storms "blew a gale, creating a heavy sea, the ship creaking and groaning, and laboring heavily." At midnight, the windstorm was blowing strongly, with a high sea running. The "gunwale was underwater, the ship now unmanageable." By Monday, the ship was lying helpless in the trough of the sea and couldn't proceed.

Captain Staples gave the orders to throw the deck load overboard, and the ship eased a little when this occurred. At five o'clock in the morning, he gave the order to open the cargo hatches and throw everything possible into the sea. Learning that the immense waves had inundated the *Brother Jonathan* to within one foot of its boiler fires, the captain ordered the passengers to work with the crew and help man the pumps.

The ship continued to rock savagely in the ocean. One hour later, Staples gave the order to shoot the twenty horses onboard and throw the bodies into the sea. This scene is truly described as being "most pitiful." The passengers' conduct was "cool, determined, and almost cheerful, each seeming anxious to do something for the general good." When at eleven o'clock in the morning, one of the pumps gave out and the leak increased, the steam engines couldn't move the ship against the crashing seas. A steam pipe cracked and with the ship's side-to-side rolls, the boilers stopped. At noon, the men repaired the pump and were able to "gain on the leak."

At three o'clock in the afternoon, the crew saw another squall approaching, which Captain Staples decided to use by bringing his ship's sails before the wind. Half an hour later, "the *Commodore* answered her helm, and went round, flying before the wind like a race horse, arriving at San Francisco about two o'clock, Wednesday morning, July 14th [1858]." The angry miners and passengers later cornered the owner, Captain John Wright, and threatened him unless he refunded their money. Wright refunded a total of $12,000, although no mention is made of the jettisoned goods and shot horses. The owners later extensively repaired and overhauled the vessel, renaming her once again as the *Brother Jonathan.*

Due to the collision with the *Falkenberg* two weeks before, the waterline crack on the *Brother Jonathan* more than likely began leaking again, as the repairs were made from the inside and couldn't withstand this pounding. The overloading would also have made navigation more difficult. The ship was now in the same general area where a terrible windstorm several years before had forced a captain to turn her about. However, this time the vessel was trying to make a run to the closest port.

CHAPTER 5

Sunday Afternoon—the Uncharted Reef

The *Brother Jonathan* slogged its way through the wind-whipped waves of the "blue Nor'wester"—as the locals called a windstorm under clear skies—with the thirty-foot high, hissing, cresting combers rising high over the hurricane deck and catching the vessel on its sides. The ship bucked down one seething, green roller, then rolled sideways, one paddle wheel digging into the sea, the other spinning helplessly in the spray. The ship's harsh lurching rattled loose items around cabins and scattered broken dishes and glasses across the saloon's floor. As before, the *Brother Jonathan*'s uncontrolled rages scattered people and their possessions around like a giant's game of jacks. Tons of cold seawater washed down the decks, roared into open passageways, and worked its way into every part of the ship, overtaxing the vessel's straining pumps—all under a sharp blue sky and confusingly brilliant sun.

Lawyer John N. Stone wrote in his journal about such a windstorm:

> It is a clear sky with bright sunshine, but the gale rages on with its terrible power, snatching the seawater from the crest of waves and scattering it in a drenching spray over our deck. The ocean dashes and surges and rolls up like mountains around us, lashed to fury by the violence of the winds; and the ship, as insignificant as a cockle shell, madly tempting

> old Neptune in his anger, rolls and pitches like the waves' plaything and sport. Clinging for safety to a rope and gazing out upon the scene, one stands on the vessel's deck and feels that the stoutest ship in such a turmoil is but its plaything and no more; which by some miracle may outride the gale, or at any moment become engulfed and disappear from sight forever, as suddenly as the white snowflake that falls upon the ocean's breast.

Passengers, who enjoyed a brief respite while the ship was anchored in the quiet harbor, now held onto the furniture in their staterooms or the lounge. As some became seasick again, others tried to keep a "stiff upper lip" about the rolling, bucking ride they once more were on. The seas broke over the bow, pouring masses of ocean upon the main forward deck and drenching the steerage passengers below. No matter where one was, keeping one's footing was difficult.

As another large seething wave hissed towards his ship, Captain DeWolf braced himself against the bridge. Seaman Yates peered through the windows and tried to hold the wheel firm on DeWolf's path. First Officer Allen raced below to the engine room and checked on the boilers and pressure. The sea was again inches from shutting down the engines' power. Engineer Mott checked the pumps again, worried that if one gave out, the ocean would soon invade the searing hot furnaces with hissing waves and rending explosions of steam.

Fireman John Hensley checked the steam gauges, then wiped dirty sweat from his brow and shoveled in another heavy mouthful of coal. Third Officer James Patterson had reset the jib at 12:45 that afternoon—a short forty-five minutes before—and then eventually climbed into his bunk in the officer's quarters on the lower deck. Having been on watch from when the ship docked in Crescent City, Patterson had had little sleep and needed the rest.

Waiters Stephen Moran and William Shields cleared off the plates and mugs left from a lunch that most of the passengers thankfully hadn't attended. These responsibilities were a continuing chore:

the cook's crew had just cleaned up and put away the breakfast bowls, dishes, plates, cups, saucers, and utensils, only to have lunch before them under these conditions. The pitchers, cruets, drinking glasses, and even the green-glass Lea & Perrins Worcestershire sauce bottles were placed in the boarded wall racks, designed to hold everything securely—but which didn't always work in severe storms such as this.

In her stateroom on a corridor by the saloon, Rosanna Keenan was still dressed in her nightgown, as were most of her party. She put on an overcoat to get some air, eventually returning back to her room. Becoming "somewhat sick" that Sunday morning, Martha Stott took her seven-year-old son and left Mrs. Keenan's entourage with Martha Wilder also seeking "fresher air" on the hurricane deck.

Mrs. Mary Altrie Tweedale sat on the lower deck. A middle-aged lady whose husband had died, she left Liverpool by steamer in mid-June to visit her son in Oregon. To get this far, she had sailed from England to the Isthmus of Panama, then boarded the sidewheeler *Constitution* on the Pacific side for San Francisco. Mrs. Tweedle was taking this ship to Portland where her son would meet her. Soon she was talking with another woman in the storm, who said she was looking forward to rejoining her husband in Vancouver after a long separation.

Like most of the passengers, Mina Bernhardt was lying in her berth "feeling sick and sad," holding her young son close to her. The Rowell family of six, and Mrs. Lee with her child, were huddled in their tiny second-class rooms. General Wright and his wife were in their more luxurious and spacious first-class rooms. Four hours more of raging winds and sea had taken away some of the people's confidence—but they were heading back to safety.

St. George Reef lies four miles from land off a jutting point called Point St. George. By custom, steamers generally sailed against a Nor'wester by staying close to the shore and inside the reef. The *Brother Jonathan,* however, sailed on a course outside the reef and on a clear path as shown on the charts. Given the lack of control over the vessel and the directions of these winds and waves, Captain DeWolf's decision not to sail around the reef towards the land side wasn't questioned under these circumstances.

One hour had passed since DeWolf ordered the ship turned about for Crescent City. According to the lighthouse keeper's log at Crescent City, the weather there was "foggy and smoky, not being able to see half a mile from shore; wind blowing strong." DeWolf ordered the ship's anchors to be readied when seven miles from shore. The bosun mate worked his way to the bow and sat astride one of the anchors, loosening it for the captain's control, when he stared straight ahead.

To his horror, the crewman saw white-streaked seas foaming over what seemed to be rocks located just under the water. He yelled out a frightened warning. The man had scarcely uttered his first words, when a rolling green wave raised the steamer high towards the skies, then slammed the vessel down in a headlong roller coaster descent toward the base of a shallow trough. Here for millions of years a volcanic peak rose nearly two-hundred feet from the ocean floor, but only visible on the surface at low tide. The *Brother Jonathan* dropped with her full weight and tremendous force upon that hidden spire with a jolting crash, striking her keel on the razor sharp pinnacle between her bow and foremast. The force was so great that it knocked most people down to their knees or onto their backs. The time was 1:50 P.M.

Passengers and crew crashed violently onto the decks in jumbled heaps. Dishes, bottles, furniture, and luggage flew across crumpled planks and shattered against jammed cabin doors. Screaming passengers tumbled down passageways in horror, as terror-struck horses and camels bellowed, losing their footing and crashing onto the spray-covered decks. The cries of children and shrieks of babies mingled with the frightened yells of men, panicked cries of women, sounds of rendering timbers, and hissing winds and sea.

The collision hurled Third Officer Patterson to the floor, and he immediately tried to get topside—but the door was jammed from the force of the blow. Patterson worked feverishly to get out. Finally, he was able to crash the door open and raced to the main deck. Steward Farrell and Jim Nisbet were thrown headfirst against the lounge's carpeted floor, as the bone-jarring hammer impact raced through its copper hull and reverberated inside the vessel. People were thrown against the interiors or headlong into the terrifying, frothing seas.

When Martha Stott looked around, she noticed that everything about the deck appeared to be loose and the whole vessel was "apparently shattered." A moment afterwards, she watched in amazement as planks floated up from the steamer's bottom. She couldn't see what happened to her companion, Ms. Wilder, who had by then disappeared.

The shock threw Mary Tweedale "violently" under the huge feet of General Wright's horse, which had been tied in a "partly secluded space" off the main deck. The scene was one of "wild confusion." After she escaped from under the flying hooves of the frightened beast, Tweedale couldn't focus on what she was doing until she found herself "hanging to the captain's ladder." As Mrs. Tweedale climbed to a cabin window, she watched in horror as huge cold waves surged over the ship and swept screaming, horror-struck people overboard, including the woman she had just been talking with.

Far below deck, the savage shock jarred the sweating and cursing firemen and crew face first into the bilge-inundated water, as the broken bunkers poured out tons of coal in a virtual avalanche. The brown-black, thick pinnacle, strewn with seaweed and barnacle-like mussels, thrust through the splintered timbers just forward of the fireboxes, as a flood of cold saltwater surged inside. A geyser of chilling sea erupted through the hull, upwards through the deck, and high into the air.

The rocky spire impaled the ship, as huge waves crashed over its stationary stern—one by one. Hissing rivers sloshing down the decks washed people away. The pinned bow pointed in the general direction of land. Captain DeWolf hurriedly picked himself off the pilothouse floor and signaled the engine room by ship's telegraph. He wanted the paddle wheels to come to a full stop and then reverse to wrench the vessel from the hidden reef.

When he received the orders, Elijah Mott inside the engine room grabbed the working bar, forced it down into its position with frightened strength, and wrestled it down. A heavy iron bar, approximately six-feet long, the working bar was used to turn a floor-level shaft which, when moved, simultaneously opened an intake valve on one side of the huge steam cylinder and an exhaust valve on the other. With a roar of released steam, the piston begins to move. When reaching the top of its stroke, the engineer reverses the bar's direction. This up-and-down "hand-valving action" can bring about a rocking motion of the paddle wheels in the desired direction.

Mott forced the bar up, manhandled it down, and then heaved it up and down. Slowly, ponderously the mammoth paddle wheels reversed their direction. The sweating engineer cracked open the mainstream valve. The plunging wheel buckets lifted tons of foaming water in large waterfalls through the wheel boxes, as the sharp sounds of cracking timbers answered back. Despite all of these efforts, however, the *Brother Jonathan* remained impaled.

The next wave struck and carried the ship farther up the rock, shattering more of her hull. Tons of seawater rushed in and swept more screaming people into the heaving waters. As Mott worked below with the working bar, another surge cascaded over the vessel and drove her further up the reef, ripping out more of her underbelly. Cold saltwater surged around the fire hold.

After about three minutes, large fragments of the ship's bottom, keel, planking, and parts of the rudder floated up alongside it. The vessel continued to roll in the seas, and, slowly, the ocean's power twisted her around until her head was pointed away from land, the waves pounding against her port side.

As Third Officer Patterson reached the deck, he watched one large wave in particular raise the ship from the rock and come down with a "terrific force," tearing a "tremendous hole" where the foremast rested on the keel. The keel and hull beneath the foremast gave way, and the huge mast plunged into the ocean until the lower yard slammed against the guardrails, just above the main deck. Patterson was shocked, but he still ran to his position by a small wooden lifeboat.

The cabin boy, William Shields, watched with horror as the thick, tall mast dropped sharply. He heard the "terrible crashing" when the foremast ripped through her bottom and its yardarm lay draped over the sides. Five minutes had gone by since the *Brother Jonathan* struck the reef, and Captain DeWolf knew beyond any doubt that his ship was mortally wounded.

Mina Bernhardt had been lying in her berth, feeling quite seasick when she was suddenly startled by a "fearful shock, followed by a labored rolling of the ship, a creaking of her timbers, and the distinct sound of rushing waters." Reportedly, a woman came screaming from steerage and yelled to her, "Get up. The vessel is sinking." Bernhardt answered, "I don't care if it is. I am too sick to get up." When she looked out of her porthole, she saw a piece of the ship's timber floating by. She then saw a man running to the upper deck with a life preserver on, convincing her that they were in "great danger." Bernhardt hurriedly dressed, seized her child with one hand, grabbed a life preserver with the other, and raced up on the deck to find "great confusion." On the way, she met ladies "rushing from rooms in their nightclothes, their hair hanging loosely about them and their faces pallid as death. Owing to the heavy sea, many were sick in their berths when the disaster occurred."

Mary Ann Tweedale said "in the uproar of rushing, shouting, and praying, it was hard to make out anything clearly except the terrible fact that the vessel was lost." She watched spellbound as numbers of passengers rushed to the life preservers and began to struggle to put them over their coats and bulky jackets. As she reached for a preserver, the ship careened so badly that she was thrown away to another side.

Through all of this, most of the passengers were in their bunks below the decks. As people gathered their wits, many took the time and precious minutes required to put their clothes on, and then wrap or stuff their gold coins and bars onto their person. Some numbly raced topside with only their nightclothes on; others wrapped an overcoat over them as they stumbled upwards. Numbers would stay in their cabins forever, unable to break through doors jammed against frames or buckled inward, able only to stare and scream as the cold saltwater surged in through portholes, underneath doors, or through ruptured walls, filling up their trapped rooms: As chilling water swirled around them, a horrifying death was mere moments away. Passengers that were already on deck, and most of the crew members, could only think about survival. Captain DeWolf walked coolly forward on the deck and yelled, "All hands aft and try to save yourselves."

The impaling was so sudden, so unexpected, and so terrible that those aboard had barely recovered their senses, when the cry was given to "Abandon Ship!" Some women fainted, others cried for help, and strong-willed men who had faced death before paled as they looked into its face. All looked to Captain DeWolf for "the means of safety and delivery," but he was too busy overseeing the first lowering of the lifeboats. The crew passed out life preservers, two guns were fired in quick succession as the signal of distress, and the command was shouted to "Lower Life boats!"

Panicked passengers and crew milled around the lifeboats and station. Jim Nisbet watched the pandemonium with coolness and a reporter's detachment to the extent that was humanly possible. Watching the calamity in progress, he walked to the lounge of the ship, sat down at a table, and took out a pen and parchment. He started to write. Interrupted by the cries of people who scrambled through the lounge in a variety of states of dress, Nisbet would look up and then go back to his parchment. As a crewman pointed the way, Rosanna Keenan herded some of her women through the saloon toward the port side of the ship.

Six lifeboats were onboard the *Brother Jonathan:* Four were large Francis Patent iron lifeboats, and two were much smaller wooden surfboats. Each of the large iron lifeboats had a carrying capacity of fifty people, and all six boats could together carry two hundred and fifty. Everyone, including the crew, rushed to where the boats were stationed on the different sides.

First Officer Henry Allen was in charge of one of the iron lifeboats; Second Officer James Campbell was in charge of a second; and Third Officer Patterson was at the side of a wooden surfboat. Officer Allen directed the forward boat on the port side, and he filled that boat mainly with woman and children and only a few crew members. Seamen escorted Mrs. Keenan—clad only in an overcoat over her nightgown—and most of her entourage onto that first boat.

Captain DeWolf helped General Wright lead his wife, Margaret, to the closer wooden surfboat of Officer Patterson. Taking one look at the small boat and the people milling into it, DeWolf took her arm and led Margaret to the other side of the vessel where the larger iron lifeboat of Officer Allen was being readied. General Wright helped his wife into that same boat with Mrs. Keenan and the other ladies, then withdrew gallantly into the crowd.

As this first boat was being lowered, one terrified woman leaped at the last moment from the deck into the boat. As she landed inside, the steamer careened from a powerful ocean surge, which upset the boat, "engulfing all in that merciless wave." Everyone was tossed into the seething seas, including Margaret Wright, Rosanna Keenan, and her women. Clutching an infant with one hand, one young woman grabbed at a rope thrown over the side. As she swung with the rope against the swaying ship, then thrown airborne when the vessel rolled back, a roller hissed in and inundated mother and child. As another wave rolled against the wreck, both disappeared forever when the ship and its living freight bobbed down into the sea.

When the two-story wave engulfed Officer Allen's Francis Patent lifeboat, Captain DeWolf threw a plank overboard towards one woman. She reached for it and pulled herself onto it, just as a rolling wave drove her against the ship's side. Struck unconscious against the vessel, she sank into the ocean's depths, "pressing her head with one hand." She was never seen again. Others onboard the ship tried to save those tossed into the ocean from the lifeboat. Officer Allen threw a rope to General Wright's wife and pulled her back onto the

Brother Jonathan. There is a discrepancy from the accounts as to whether Margaret Wright was in the first or second lifeboat; regardless of this, she was pulled back from the ocean onto the vessel to rejoin her husband.

Fireman John Hensley raced to the ship's side and lowered himself toward the frothing ocean while holding his hand out. Martha Wilder—one of the "fallen angels" that was still close to the ship and struggling to survive—desperately tried to reach out to him. As a wave pitched the ship over toward the sea, Hensley was able to grab Wilder. Crewmen pulled him onto the ship, as the near-hysterical woman was brought safely back. Nearly naked, she was wearing only a soaked, clinging slip. Hensley took his coat off and gently wrapped it around her trembling shoulders. He immediately escorted Martha Wilder to Patterson's surfboat.

Others were trying to keep their heads above water around the swamped boat, and people stared at one man sitting astride the overturned hull. While these rescue operations were underway, the second iron boat was readied for lowering on the starboard side and directly astern of the wheel. This boat also contained a "large number of ladies" and few crew members. As the boat was being lowered, the crew had "great difficulties" in releasing the lifeboat into the water from its davits, the curved arms of timber or iron over a ship's side that raised or lowered a boat. A large comber suddenly smashed the ship on her port side, causing the second lifeboat to slam against the vessel's side. Passengers spilled out into the ocean from the impact and the heaving waters that quickly swamped the boat, once it finally broke clear of the davit lines.

Second Officer James Campbell's actions at this time on his boat were also heroic. When his lifeboat smashed against the side as the steamer careened, Campbell found himself underwater. He swam back to the surface, dodging people and debris. Then with the aid of a rope, Campbell pulled himself up onto the anchor chains. From that precarious point, he pulled several of the women back on board. First Officer Allen also helped in hauling passengers back from this overturned lifeboat.

Arms outstretched with dresses billowing in the seas, the tiny dots of heads and silhouettes of drowning bodies now littered the ocean alongside the wreckage. Inside the ship's belly, Engineer Mott turned on the bilge injection valve, but the pumps weren't responding. Seawater had flooded the fireboxes, and all of the reserve steam was lost through the wrenched, cracked pipes. The rising ocean waves that cascaded into the searing hot furnace and boilers caused metal to sizzle apart and dense vaporized clouds of hissing steam to envelope the engine room.

Mr. Mott stood by his post, ordering everyone else to save themselves, then at the last moment raced to the upper deck. Fireman William Lowry also fought his way up and out of the fast-flooding engine room and thick clouds of steam. He and Mott were the last to escape the inky-black maelstrom swiftly welling up from below. Everyone else drowned inside that mass of wreckage-filled holds.

Buffeted by winds and waves, the *Brother Jonathan* slowly slewed around the rock, its bow coming to the wind. Slamming against the pinnacle, the ship's bow began breaking up, as it bounced down the rock's south side and the vessel began sinking by its destroyed bow.

Numbers of people never left their rooms. Mrs. Jeannette Lee and her infant son were never seen again. William Logan, the Superintendent of the U.S. Mint at The Dalles in Oregon, also disappeared. The bodies of Victor Smith and Anson Henry were not discovered. Daniel and Polina Rowell with their four children made it to the deck, but Polina and the children did not get into the first lifeboats.

Paymaster Major Eddy's clerk, Mr. Belden, offered a life preserver to a young lady who refused to wear it. Concerned about his shipments of gold, Joseph Lord raced to the Purser's Office to confer with John Benton. By this time, Mott had worked his way through the confusion and joined the men there.

Watching the death and destruction from above, Captain DeWolf stood fixed on the hurricane deck. Fifteen minutes had gone by since the ship hit the rock, and she was quickly breaking up. He shouted to Steward David Farrell to put the plugs into the surfboat swinging at the starboard davits, just astern of the last boat that had swamped.

After Farrell did so, DeWolf ordered him to remain in the boat and keep the men out, while assisting Officer Patterson.

Watching the lifeboats capsize from where she clung to a railing, Mary Ann Tweedale knew that her situation was desperate. People were drowning in front of their loved ones, wives in front of husbands, children in front of mothers, brothers in front of sisters. As she saw another lifeboat about to be launched, she left her perch and made a "great effort" to reach the boat. She succeeded and scrambled into the surfboat of Officer Patterson and several other women. Martha Stott and her son ran to this lifeboat, along with the wet, shivering Martha Wilder whom Fireman Hensley was escorting.

The men gathered about this wooden boat were mainly the ship's crew. As they helped a "Chinese woman" with her child into the surfboat, her husband begged to get in and join his family. The man's cries were "piteous." The crewmen refused, and he begged harder, but the men were firm. This parting between the husband and wife "wrung even the hearts of those whose only emotion was that of self-preservation."

The last one to leave the bow—now awash with waves and sinking next to the reef—was Quartermaster Yates. He walked over towards the surfboat. As he headed aft to the stern, Yates came across a "lady and a gentleman" standing close by the lifeboat. Asking them why they weren't getting in, as the boat was about to be lowered, they said, with a "toss of their heads," that they were going to get in a larger boat. Yates took their place inside the small surfboat.

Fireman Hensley then brought two women to the small lifeboat and tried to get them into it. They refused, however, having seen what had happened to the previous boats. Already safely onboard and holding to his position, Steward David Farrell yelled to Hensley, "John, you had better get in yourself." Hensley told everyone that he would be better to stay back and help others live. Even in these dire times, he held to his philosophy of "Do onto others," putting their interests above his own.

The men told Hensley that they needed a bucket. The crewman leaped from the hurricane deck to the higher pilot's deck and found the fire buckets that lined one rack on the wheelhouse. He grabbed one, and raced back to hand it to Farrell.

Rushing to the boat, Mina Bernhardt and her child arrived "seeing the boat fall and ready to be lowered." She called out to them, "Save my child!" When a hand reached out to her, she took it, and then buckled her life preserver because she had no "expectation" that they would take her in. One of the men said, "Don't you want to come, too?" Mina "joyfully" accepted the offer. Martha Stott's version was that "As we went down, we noticed a German woman (Mina Bernhardt) crawling up from the lower deck with her child tied to her neck. One of the crew took hold of her neck and dragged her into the boat, saving them both."

As two men dragged Bernhardt over the guardrails, a man with a "red jacket on" jumped into the boat, one foot landing on the shoulder of the Chinese woman and the other upon a child. Neither one of them cried out when he landed on them. Seeing this, Captain DeWolf shouted, "Stay back! You'll all be drowned!" A dripping wet woman then ran up from below and rushed for the boat. But the "barkeeper" grabbed her around the waist and pulled her back, telling her that she would surely drown if she got into that lifeboat.

First Officer Allen assisted in the lowering of the larger metal lifeboats, including this smaller wooden one. When Patterson asked Allen to get into his boat, the First Officer replied, "No, no! Get away and God bless you." Turning down an offer again to go with the crew in this lifeboat, Hensley's last words were "Keep cool, and save yourselves. Good-bye!"

As a crewman loosened the boat to lower it down, the surfboat plunged down at a "frightful" angle on its lower end and threatened to spill everyone again into the sea. The nineteen people on board, including eleven crew members, somehow held onto the boat, the other passengers, and their seats to stay inside. Their condition was precarious at best. As Mina Bernhardt observed:

> Here danger still threatened us—the rolling steamer to engulf us in her dark whirlpool, the angry waves to dash our frail

> boat to atoms, and a shoal of drowning people struggling to catch at any hope of rescue, to clutch at our boat and drag it down with them.

The crew lowered the boat with jerks towards the seething ocean. Looking up, Mina Bernhardt noticed a woman standing with her husband and two children, looking wistfully down at her. She had seen the woman before, characterizing her as a "beautiful woman" and would long remember that "sweet face" as she looked down at the lowering surfboat.

The sinking vessel, however, lurched against the overfilled boat just before it hit the rolling sea. As soon as the surfboat hit the ocean, a wave pushed the lifeboat upwards as the huge *Brother Jonathan* rolled over on top of it, nearly pushing the tiny boat underwater. The surfboat miraculously stayed on top of the frothing ocean and eddying whirlpools, its only damage being the loss of a starboard oarlock.

Patterson yelled at the crew to pull away with the boatload. When the first strokes were made, Captain DeWolf gave his last order: "Tell them," he shouted over the din of the wind and water, "that if they had not overloaded us, we would have got through all right, and this would never have happened."

As the huge mother ship rocked violently back and forth, the tiny surfboat below had to navigate around its very shadows. The lifeboat moved to the stern, and then around its back toward the dubious safety of the open sea. Patterson's boat had a great amount of difficulty in clearing the ship with the swirling ocean currents ripping it around. Although people wanted to get away from the huge vessel as soon as possible, the men had to move cautiously, taking their time to be sure that the savage currents and waves didn't upend the tiny boat. The oarsmen rowed the surfboat behind the steamer, as its stern loomed higher and higher above them.

While the lifeboat worked around the pitching vessel and crashing seas, the sight of the flotsam of wrecked lifeboats and drowned people startled even the strongest. Held up by their life preservers, women floated in the sea, face down, their hair loose and outspread, arms stretched outward, soaked clothing coated with frothy spray. Yates watched silently as a third boat was lowered and swamped—this one also "full of women"—when the boat rounded the stern towards the other side. He also saw the first capsized iron boat with the man still clinging to its overturned bottom and the second one, which had been "stove into pieces." The men thought for a moment about trying to rescue the new boatload of victims tossed into the seas, but with an overloaded wooden boat in these raging waters, they quickly decided against it.

After the surfboat cleared the vessel's stern, Martha Stott saw Mrs. Keenan struggling to keep her head above water. Keenan was "partially dressed" and wore two life preservers tied around her. It isn't known if Roseanna Keenan was the woman whom the wave smashed into the vessel or that Mary Tweedale was talking to on the lower deck. She was on at least one of the iron lifeboats that capsized; and if on the third iron lifeboat that the ocean claimed, then she had been rescued from the sea once before.

Passengers and crew stood on the steamer's deck. Everyone was cold and wet. The pounding waves and blasts of wind, ill-fated lifeboat attempts, and drenchings had reduced those onboard to shivering masses. Others bobbed up and down in the ocean. In these seas, no one knew if any lifeboat would escape from the wreck. Then the towering smokestack crashed down and smashed another lifeboat with rending sounds into crumpled metal.

General Wright tenderly placed his military cloak around the shivering shoulders of his wife. Captain DeWolf stood to one side of General Wright, his arm intertwined with that of his wife, Margaret. His aide, Major Eddy, was by her side. The group stood on the hurricane deck and waited bravely and calmly with as much dignity as possible as the white ocean began rolling toward them.

The wooden boat was loaded down with arms and legs hanging over the sides; it moved just six inches above the angry seas. As fast as they could, the crew took turns bailing out the water sloshing in side with Hensley's bucket and their hands. One huge wave quickly hissed up and seemed to hang over the boat, its dark green and white bulk towering over them. The mass broke over the insignificant surfboat and swamped it. With the violent ocean mere inches below the gunnels, people prayed that they could bail out the water before another surge overwhelmed them.

PART II

FINDING THE *JONATHAN*

CHAPTER 6

The Lucky Few

The remaining passengers and crew held to railings, portholes, and door jams as the vessel's bow slipped further beneath the ocean, its stern pitching toward the sky. Whipped by the winds, the rolling waves surged up and onto the ship, the brackish ocean washing over frigid bodies. By now, the swirling ocean had engulfed most of the steerage and several staterooms, claiming unmercifully those who were imprisoned. Victor Smith probably never left his room. Jim Nisbet put down his pencil as the ship sank deeper into the ocean at a steeper angle by its bow. He carefully wrapped his writings inside a waterproof oil cloth and wrapped two life preservers around himself. The seas then crashed over him.

The stern surged up faster, as its angle forced people to lose their grip and fall screaming into the sea. The waters had already taken Colonel Wright, his wife, Captain DeWolf, and Major Eddy from the hurricane deck, as the *Brother Jonathan* headed down.

When the boat struck the rock, the Rowells emptied their chest of its contents and Polina quickly put on the dress she had hemmed with the gold coins. Daniel strapped the chest to her back. She held two of their four children, while he clutched the others. Daniel held onto the chest, as the ocean poured over the boat and those congregated at its stern. The ocean surged over the family with its chilling blanket.

Two by two, one by one, people clutched to the pitching vessel, then slipped into the cold swells and were swept away, heads bobbing up and down, nearly all with life jackets on, some struggling to stay on top of the swells, others giving up. Nearly everyone was now in the sea, clutching to floating objects or lifejackets with their cries growing fainter, overcome by the hissing seas and shrieking winds.

Meanwhile, the overloaded, tiny wooden surfboat sloshed mere inches above the cold brackish water. So far these people had been fortunate, as the crew was able to bucket, splash, cup their hands, kick their legs, and use everything imaginable to remove enough killing seawater before another larger roller surged to push them up and then down into the ocean valleys.

When one swell swept the boat down, people couldn't see anything except for the surrounding green-white sea. The ocean constantly swept into the boat, the female passengers cupping their hands and joining the crew to help bail the water out. The bucket given by fireman John Hensley proved the difference in keeping the ocean at bay, as one crew member after another took turns bailing out bucketfuls of the water until his arms were spent.

The surfboat carried nineteen passengers in its cramped interior: Third Officer James Patterson; Steerage Steward David Farrell; Henry Miller, baker; Patrick Lynn, fireman; William Lowry, fireman; Edward Shields, waiter; Mr. Sevener, crewman and comedian; Quartermaster Jacob Yates; three Portuguese seamen; Miss Martha Wilder; Mrs. Mary Ann Tweedale; Mrs. Mina Bernhardt and child; Mrs. Martha Stott and child; and Mrs. Lee and child. The tiny surfboat headed for shore as it ran quartering with the waves, which broke over the people at higher crests, at times filling the boat to near its gunnels. The odds were strongly against their survival.

They were ten miles from Crescent City, as Yates headed the lifeboat in that direction. He continued on the basic course set by Captain DeWolf when the vessel turned back. Another hissing comber washed over the people, causing them to gasp for air and cough up seawater. The soaking-wet passengers hunkered down inside the boat's middle in a near panic, as the crew tried to keep their wits and continue bailing out the water.

Officer Patterson took off his vest and put it around one of the women "who seemed more thinly clad than the rest," said Mrs. Tweedale. "Some men rowed and others bailed the water out of the bottom. The women huddled, shivering, in the bottom of the boat."

When the surfboat had moved one mile from the stricken vessel, the people heard a two-gun report. They saw that the ship's flag was hanging at distress with the Union flag down. The boat members kept looking back toward the sinking ship. When they were on top of a wave, they could still see the *Brother Jonathan,* although the ship was pointing up into the air by her stern. Surrounded by the green and white seas, the surfboat then plunged down into a trough between waves. When the lifeboat came back up, no one saw the vessel. Twenty-five minutes after the lifeboat left, the large ship had disappeared.

The *Brother Jonathan* sank beneath the surface, carrying inside her people still alive inside air pockets, but trapped within staterooms or passageways. Others were already drowned or had died of hypothermia. Those still alive clung precariously to debris, wreckage, and their lives.

The surfboat had three oar-locks on each side, but the collision with the *Brother Jonathan* sheared one away. The men took turns rowing, bailing out water, and steering, as they battled for their survival. Mary Tweedale said,

> The sea was exceedingly rough, but the boat was staunch, the crew capable, and we seemed to have a fair prospect of making land. Besides the cold and the sad discomfort of body and mind, my most graphic recollection is of a large Negro sailor [Quartermaster Yates], who was pulling at an oar, and who hardly took his eye off me during our awful four-hour journey to land. I think his actions and his scrutiny did much to drive from my mind a sense of the late horror and the imminent danger we were still experiencing.

The lifeboat carried eleven crew members, five women, and three children. Of the crew, three were the Portuguese sailors who had just shipped out on the *Brother Jonathan:* The same ones whose whaling ship had been destroyed by the Confederate raider *Shenandoah* and sent them back over the ocean with other prisoners to San Francisco on the whale ship *Milo.* According to Mina Berhhardt:

> At last we heard the joyful news that half an hour would take us into Crescent City, but as we neared the land, other dangers awaited us. Those frightful breakers rolling against us, and frowning cliffs towering above us, looked dangerous and dismayed our anxious hearts. The many-voiced waters dashing on the beach seemed to murmur a low, deep funeral dirge.

Mrs. Bernhardt said they were afraid to land below the cliffs because the Indians were above that point, and the survivors feared such an attack. They rowed past a small outcropping called Bird Rock and toward the harbor. However, with their emotions at a razor's edge, the people saw immediate danger again. The first persons they spotted on the beach were Indians "gaily decked in feathers," and their first thoughts were that they had "landed among savages." The irony hit them of having been saved from the wreck, only to be "devoured," right then and there.

The surfboat rounded Battery Point and ran into the bay at Crescent City. Ben West, owner of Ben West's Saloon, watched through his telescope with mild interest as the lifeboat came into his sight. He wondered why such a small boat was so crowded with one man having to dangle his feet in the ocean as he straddled and held precariously to the bow. The residents began to arrive at the beach, having heard about the boat's approach or curious after hearing the two guns fired a few hours before.

One man was picking blackberries when he heard the cannon firing. As a "blue Nor'wester" was blowing, he felt there had been trouble and walked back to town. A crowd had already congregated inside one building, when a person outside yelled loudly, "Hello! See that boatload of people coming around the point." Everyone rushed from the store and down to the beach to help. The boat was

James Bard painted this picture of the original *Brother Jonathan* in 1851 before the major retrofit by Cornelius Vanderbilt the following year. (San Francisco Maritime National Historical Park)

After the overhaul, among other changes, the ship had three masts (instead of two), the clipper-ship bow was eliminated, and the stack was moved back. (San Francisco Maritime National Historical Park)

Cornelius Vanderbilt's ventures made him a multi-millionaire (his fortune was over $100 billion in today's dollars). He owned the *Brother Jonathan* during Gold Rush days, using it on the Nicaragua route. (University of Michigan Making of America)

This historic 1863 San Francisco photograph is the only one known to exist of the ship and shows the *Brother Jonathan* anchored offshore (*top center*) to the right of Broadway Wharf, which extends toward the left from the center of the picture. (San Francisco Maritime National Historical Park)

An enlarged image of the vessel anchored in San Francisco Harbor. (San Francisco Maritime National Historical Park)

A portrait of Captain Samuel J. DeWolf of the *Brother Jonathan* (San Francisco Maritime National Historical Park)

Steamer Day was an important occasion, when family and friends saw their loved ones off on a new venture.

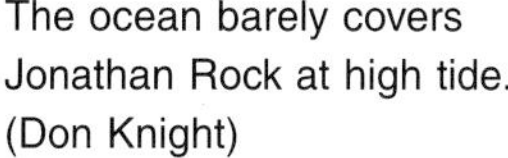

The ocean barely covers Jonathan Rock at high tide. (Don Knight)

This rare photograph shows Crescent City residents gathered around the wrecked ship's wheel, after pieces began washing up on the coast. (Del Norte County Historical Society)

Two carved golden eagles adorned each paddlewheel; after a retrofit, one eagle remained, affixed to the bridge. It is now on display at the San Francisco Maritime Museum. (San Francisco Maritime National Historical Park; Del Norte County Historical Society)

Donald Knight stands by a replacement ore crusher, identical to the one on the ship and built months later after the vessel's loss. (Betsy Knight)

Over time, countless expeditions searched for the fabled lost gold inside the wreck, including this intrepid 1915 diver and his crew. (Del Norte County Historical Society)

Undaunted by crude equipment, savage underwater currents, and the darkness at the depths where the ship lay, the divers showed remarkable courage. (Del Norte County Historical Society)

One of the eleven gold bars said to have been recovered from the *Brother Jonathan* and the subject of much controversy later. The granular markings and erosion on the sides are due to the effects of the long immersion in saltwater.

The ship's sinking tragically emphasized the need for a warning lighthouse around St. George reef, and the structure became operational in 1892. (Del Norte County Historical Society; U.S. Coast Guard Service)

Due to unpredictable gales and towering waves, including frightening "rogue" waves, transporting men, supplies, and equipment to the lighthouse was always risky. (Del Norte County Historical Society; U.S. Coast Guard Service)

Captained by Barry Sutton, the *Top Cat* was used in the early searches by Sea Epics Research and Don Knight. (Mary L. Barnes)

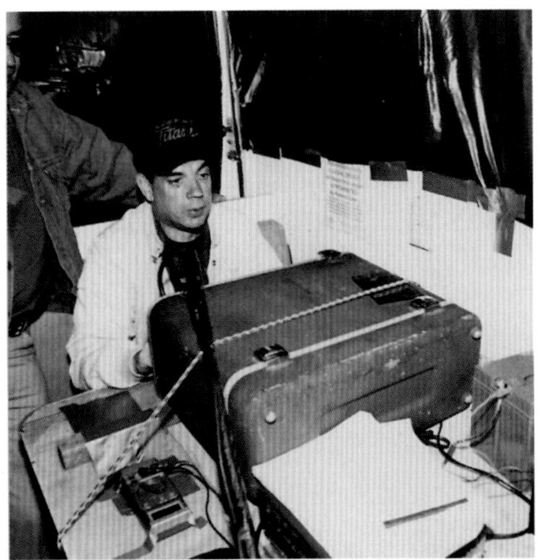

Don Knight operates the Phantom 500 ROV (remote operating vehicle) in his search for the lost vessel. (Barry Sutton)

At the *Cavalier*'s stern, the operation's center is to the left, while the *Snooper* and *Delta* are piggybacked to the right. (Mary L. Barnes)

Don Knight spent twenty years searching both archival records and the oceans off Crescent City to find the ship's location. (Petra Kellers)

Another important figure in the discovery, Harvey Harrington, is in the foreground, while Don Knight talks to the captain in the background. (Petra Kellers)

Joining the venture in 1991 as an investor, David Flohr was key to the operations and management of DSR and to their successful recovery of the lost gold. (Mary Flohr)

Sherman Harris was another key person in the successful running of DSR. (David F. Flohr, son)

The founder and owner of Shilo Inns, Mark Hemstreet was another important member of the inner management team. (Mark and Shannon Hemstreet)

The two-person submersible, *Delta*, was the "jeep" of the mini-subs. Here the salvors prepare to lower it overboard on October 1, 1993, just after the discovery of the wreck. (Petra Kellers)

The one-person mini-sub, *Snooper*, approaches the mother ship after completing an exploration. (David F. Flohr)

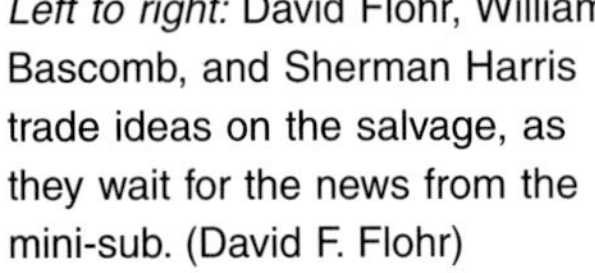

Left to right: David Flohr, William Bascomb, and Sherman Harris trade ideas on the salvage, as they wait for the news from the mini-sub. (David F. Flohr)

Don Knight (*center, on one knee*) views the first six artifacts retrieved from the deep on October 1, 1993—two porcelain plates, a wine flask, a black champagne bottle, a medicine bottle, and a spike—as Jim Wadsley (*left*), Mark Barnum (*center left*), and Doug Privitt (*right*) group around him. (Barry Sutton)

Don Siverts (*left*) was the first to spot the sunken ship in 1993 from his mini-sub, *Snooper*; his son, Curt, is to the right. (David F. Flohr, son)

The overhead crane has hooked the *Snooper* and is raising it back on board the mother ship. (David F. Flohr)

Porcelain platters and dishware recovered from the wreck, on display at the Del Norte County Historical Museum. (Del Norte County Historical Museum)

Gold coins from the first recovery expedition. (David F. Flohr)

A variety of different colored glassware, bottles, cruets, and stoneware discovered at the site. (Del Norte County Historical Society)

The divers lived for weeks in this "habitat" on board the mother ship, only leaving to enter the attached diving bell that was then lowered into the ocean. (*The Daily Triplicate*)

The extensive search in September 2000 involved the *American Salvor.* After the wreck's discovery, raising needed funds from investors was much easier and in turn allowed for more extensive recovery operations. (*The Daily Triplicate*)

A diver adjusts his air tank by the diving bell during the last expedition. (*The Daily Triplicate*)

Bob Evans was Dwight Manley's representative, the onboard curator, and ROV operator, as well as the coordinator, with Harvey Harrington, of the explorations in 2000. (*The Daily Triplicate*)

The ROV used in the final explorations. (*The Daily Triplicate*)

Marine archaeologist Mike Reedy carefully probes at an iron-crusted box that has been recovered. (*The Daily Triplicate*)

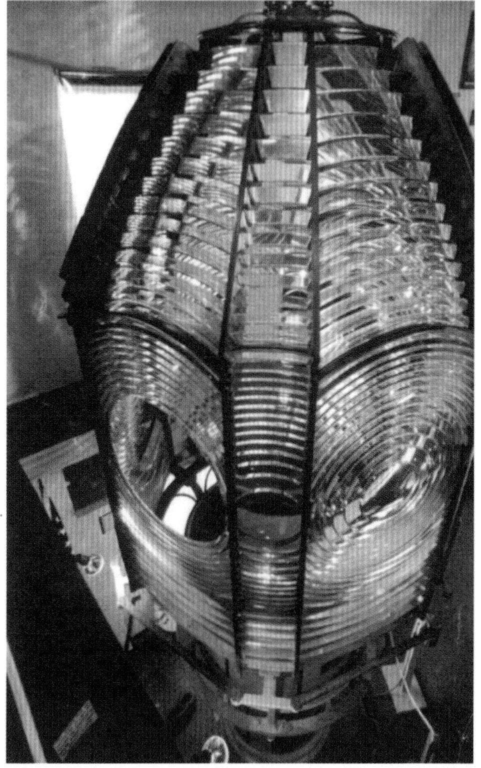

Formerly operating at the Point St. George Lighthouse, the first-order Fresnel lens was later removed and put on display at the Del Norte County Historical Museum. (Del Norte County Historical Society)

Some of the recovered gold coins on display after initial restoration work. (David F. Flohr)

One of the gold coins recovered from the last exploration of the sunken ship. (*The Daily Triplicate*)

The site of the *Brother Jonathan*, where the safe, gold boxes, and priceless artifacts still remain at the bottom of the ocean. The wake from a supply ship leads away from the site where the mother ship remains in position. (David F. Flohr, son)

so crowded, the men on the bow were forced to hang their feet out into the water.

The surging waves drove the low-riding surfboat closer to the beach. A few hardy residents battled the surging waves to grab the surfboat and drag it to the beach. The people left the boat "cold and chilled" with their "few rags dripping and clinging to our shivering forms." After a dangerous and seemingly impossible journey—and a three-hour voyage through terrible waters for miles—Patterson's boat landed on shore at 5:05 P.M. As Mina Bernhardt said, "By almost superhuman efforts, and through the mercies of God, we land and are saved." Left behind were two hundred and twenty-five passengers and crew members.

Greenleaf Curtis sat inside the Del Norte Hotel and had no idea about the wreck or the survivors. Then he saw one resident walking along the street while holding a baby in his arms and the mother, dripping wet, slowly following behind him. The people of Crescent City gave their homes and hospitality to the survivors. "We were nearly naked," said Mrs. Bernhardt, "and we were cold and hungry, but thanks to the generous hearts and diligent hands of the Crescent City people—even the poorest—we were soon clothed, fed, and warm." One man, a partner in a merchandising business in Crescent City, took Mrs. Bernhardt and her son to his home, where she remained for about a month.

Disregarding his fatigue, Officer Patterson headed out that evening to guide rescue boats to the scene of the wreck. Men launched four boats (including the wooden surfboat) into the waters to head for the site and search for more survivors. Outside the harbor waters after a short distance, however, the high seas and gale-force winds forced these boats to turn back. Once back on shore, the men in those boats were amazed that any wooden surfboat had been able to navigate those horrible conditions and reach the harbor, especially with the ocean nearly at its gunwales.

Men and women walked back and forth over the beach looking for any signs that people and other lifeboats had made their way back to safety. The residents lit huge bonfires to guide anyone from the ill-fated ship that might be trying to find shore. From south of Crescent City to Point St. George, these large fiery beacons raged into the skies for one week.

EARLY THE NEXT DAY, July 31, Ben West commanded one of two boats sent out to look for survivors. The boats returned that evening, and the men reported that they had not seen any wreckage or bodies. Given that this boat didn't turn back, the presumption is that it rowed close to shore and northward. On that same Monday evening, a boat manned by Third Officer Patterson and others sailed south for Eureka to ask for assistance in the rescue operations. Although the still-heavy seas forced it to turn back, Patterson did report sighting wreckage from the *Brother Jonathan*'s hurricane deck, including beds and trunks. Again, no bodies were reported as being seen. One of the iron lifeboats that had swamped when being lowered from the side-wheeler then drifted ashore on the Crescent City beach. At the same time, a "portion of the upper work" of the ship floated onshore at Point St. George, along with a "twenty to thirty foot long" piece of the heel of the foremast.

On Tuesday, August 1, the *Brother Jonathan*'s surfboat again headed out with "Indians and two of the saved Portuguese seamen," per the diary of Curtis Greenleaf. Greenleaf was at the time a soldier at Camp Lincoln near Crescent City. Although the seas were still rough with headwinds, the boat came "within a distance of Seal Rock," where DeWolf ordered Quartermaster Yates to make the "Southeast by South" heading back to Crescent City. The men spotted three shapes on Seal Rock—and then two of the indistinguishable figures moved. The men shouted, "People were still alive," and tried to approach the outcropping. The waterlogged surfboat still ran deep in the ocean, however, and the rough seas forced the crew to turn back and row quickly for the harbor's safety.

Once the surfboat returned with the happy news, three boats pulled from the harbor back towards the rock, including one boat that Curtis Greenleaf manned. They left a "little after three P.M." and had to row through the continuing heavy surf, rolling seas, and strong winds. Hours later, the boats came close to Seal Rock. As they approached the rock cropping, however, they found to their disappointment that the moving shapes were sea lions. Survivors had yet to be found.

The boats turned around. Once underway, the winds suddenly calmed "sound dead ahead." The storms had quickly ended and only the sounds of the sea were heard. Greenleaf and the crews made Crescent City at 1:00 A.M. in the dead of night. The men were tired and "thoroughly wet" because the surfboat still "shipped a lot of water" in its passing due to its low rise and high waves. Curtis Greenleaf's last diary notation was: "Went to bed without any supper." The following day, he wrote: "August 2. Very lame, hands blistered—completely done up."

Meanwhile, relatives waited for their loved ones to arrive at Portland. When the vessel didn't dock on time, those waiting knew that something had happened. Jeremiah Luckey waited at the Columbia River landing for his wife, children, brother, and family. Even after receiving the news of the vessel's sinking, he still waited for the ship's return. Hoping against the odds, Jeremiah stayed there, but his wife, two children, brother, brother's wife, and their two infant children had died at sea.

News of the *Brother Jonathan*'s loss did not reach the citizens of San Francisco until Wednesday, August 2. No direct telegraph line connected Crescent City with San Francisco, so a soldier from Camp Lincoln early Tuesday rode up the plank road over the surrounding mountains from Crescent City to Jacksonville, Oregon—which had a telegraph that linked the town with larger cities—with a message addressed by its commanding officer. Although this was usually a full day and night ride, the soldier arrived late Tuesday evening on August 1. The dispatch read:

> At 2 P.M. yesterday, the steamer *Brother Jonathan* struck a sunken rock, and sank in less than an hour, with all on board,

> except sixteen [*sic*] persons, who escaped in a small boat, the only survivors of the ill-fated ship. No trace of the vessel is left. General Wright, family, and staff are supposed to be lost.

This message was received at San Francisco at 10 P.M. on August 1, and the next morning, when the *Alta California* published the news, the city plunged into mourning. Bells tolled and buildings were draped in black crepe. Flags hung at half-mast in San Francisco and all of the major port cities, from Los Angeles to Victoria, British Columbia.

The steamship *Del Norte* left San Francisco on Friday, August 4 with a "great many people" who were coming to search for their missing loved ones. The passage was very smooth and nothing occurred to "make the occasion unpleasant." When the ship reached Crescent City on August 6, a boat came alongside with Joe Wall, the Wells Fargo messenger. He told them that there was no word yet about the ship or any survivors, other than the surfboat with its nineteen people. He explained that no bodies had yet been discovered, although there were patrols on the beach "night and day."

Mrs. John Benton, the wife of the purser, burst into tears upon hearing this news, as did many others at the railing who were listening to the report. Upon reaching shore, the family members talked with the surviving crew and passengers who had reached land. Mrs. Benton then learned that the last time anyone had seen her husband alive was when he, Chief Engineer Mott, and Senior Messenger Joseph Lord were seen standing in the doorway of the Purser's room. Not finding any survivors, the *Del Norte* returned later with those that did survive. It also returned with filled coffins, including one with the body of Mr. Benton who had washed ashore.

Several days after the disaster, Quartermaster Yates led boatmen out into the ocean and tried to pinpoint the site of the rock and the ship's sinking. He began back-tracking the course he remembered taking. By now, the winds had passed and the ocean was smooth as glass, as the men pulled hard on the oars past the smaller rock outcroppings toward the open sea. Yates scanned the horizon with his sextant. After some hours, he pointed out a rocky ledge—only a small portion of which was visible at low tide—as the one that the *Brother Jonathan* struck. Not on any charts issued by the U.S. Coast Survey at the time, this barely visible outcropping was later named "Jonathan Rock."

A patrol of soldiers from nearby Camp Lincoln watched the beaches near Crescent City, while troops from Fort Humboldt patrolled the coast north to Trinidad. One week after the wreck, the first body discovered was that of a woman, which surfaced on the beachfront of the town. Every day afterward boatmen picked three to four bodies from the sea, as numbers washed ashore on the beaches above and below Crescent City. As fast as the bodies could be loaded up and moved by wagon to the city, they were taken to Dugan & Wall's warehouse in Crescent City, where an inquest was held.

The coroner hired men to make coffins for the dead. Bodies began coming in so fast, however, that the workers couldn't make enough wooden coffins to keep up—even when working night and day. An estimated thirty bodies were in the morgue at all times and eighty-two bodies were ultimately brought there. Forty-five identified bodies were buried in the old Crescent City cemetery, near Pebble Beach. Some sixty unidentified corpses were buried in a common grave. Those that could be identified were put in marked graves. Friends and relatives later took most to family burial plots, and residents scattered the ashes of others over the ocean.

Bodies began to drift ashore as far south as Humboldt Bay in California and north to the Rogue River's mouth in Gold Beach, Oregon—a distance of nearly 125 miles; Crescent City was roughly in the middle. Pieces of the ship's superstructure, cabin doors, a boom, and other flotsam floated onto the beaches, as well as trunks, personal possessions, and more bodies. Corpses discovered south of Trinidad were laid to rest at Dows Prairie or taken to Eureka. Searchers discovered the remains of General Wright's horse and a circus camel on a beach, eight miles north of Trinidad. Survivors maintained that

Captain DeWolf's Newfoundland dog, a superb swimmer, would certainly reach shore, but the angry seas were unfortunately too strong. Searchers later discovered the dead dog's body.

An estimated one hundred and seventy bodies in total were recovered. Most drifted into Pelican Bay, north of Crescent City; many of these bodies could not be identified owing to the deterioration and lack of identification on the person. Some seventy-five bodies were never recovered, being either entombed within the ship or alone at the ocean's bottom.

Thirteen years before, Miss Mary Berry and her father had traveled on the *Brother Jonathan* from New York around the Horn to San Francisco when Cornelius Vanderbilt moved the ship to the Pacific Coast. She was also on this trip. The remains of Miss Berry, also the niece of the popular Portland hotel owners, the Arrigonis, drifted an incredible ninety miles south before washing onto a beach. Discovered on the peninsula three miles north of the entrance to Humboldt Bay, her body still had a life preserver attached, a Virgin Mary medal around her neck, and her name stitched on her clothes. Ironically, Confederate sympathizer Ford Patterson had killed the *Brother Jonathan*'s previous captain (Mr. Spires) at Arrigoni's Pioneer Hotel in Portland, and this act had brought DeWolf to take the ship's helm and make the decisions as its captain. The hotel's owner, H. Arrigoni, and ex-U.S. Senator Ben Stark posted the $10,000 bail for the killer. The man was never brought to trial. A special policeman, who had been in Portland at the time of the shooting, later shot and killed Patterson while he sat in a barber chair.

Mr. Arrigoni and Captain Brooks then arrived in Brooks's ship, the *Cambridge,* to search for their loved ones. When the explorations weren't successful, the ship continued on to Honolulu. The bodies of the captain's wife, Mrs. A. C. Brooks, and sister-in-law, Mary Place, who had sailed on the *Brother Jonathan* in anticipation of an exciting holiday, were never recovered.

The August 19, 1865, issue of *The Oregon Reporter* in Jacksonville, Oregon, reported:

> The body of a young girl was found on August 9, about four miles from the lighthouse off Eureka by the beach patrol. (It had drifted some seventy miles from where the ship went down.) Her hair was auburn, eyebrows fair and heavy. The only clothes she had on were a chemise, a nightgown, and a red blanket. The body was delivered to Father Thomas Creiman, and was buried at Bucksport, today. She looked very natural when she came ashore, but soon after changed very much. The life preserver, which she wore, can be obtained at Eureka. A large number of citizens followed her remains to the grave. She was seventeen of age [*sic*], and had been very pretty indeed.

Various bodies were weighted down with currency and gold coins. For example, an unidentified person, "Body #45, a man" had $420 in coins and $8,500 in currency on his person. Another unidentified woman had the following tucked in her blouse: a common breast pin, a thimble, seven plated spoons, three ivory handle knives, a $1,000 note, five $20s, seven $10s, two $100s, five $50s, and one $5 note on the Bank of Poughkeepsie. A Mr. Mathewson was discovered with a $21,000 note in his pocket. One distraught family arrived a year later to exhume the body of their beloved husband and father; they recovered $4,000 from the clothing.

THE NINE-HUNDRED TONS of freight, mail, baggage, animals, and 225 people were lost forever. The entire Purser's inventory in the strong room and ship's safe disappeared into the ocean—nearly half a million dollars at 1865 valuations went down with the ship. This included the gold, payrolls, and valuables in the safe, on the ship, and carried by the passengers. It was the worst nonmilitary shipwreck that ever took place on the West Coast. Aside from the loss of the *Pacific* off Cape Flattery, Washington, in 1875, this disaster off Crescent City is still considered the nation's greatest peacetime shipwreck on our Western shores.

The bodies of many passengers weren't recovered. Numbers of people didn't leave their staterooms, either because they were ill or didn't want to face the shrieking winds and waves. Some stoically awaited their fates; others screamed behind jammed doors and wreckage, as the ocean spilled inside what became their tombs. Weighted down by their strapped-on gold bars and coins, some sank to the bottom of the sea. Fish scavanged on the remains of the rest.

Drowning is the obvious danger in any shipwreck. When someone continuously inhales water, the red blood cells are destroyed. The blood becomes diluted, and the resulting lack of oxygen causes death. Fluid can also accumulate in the lungs (pulmonary edema), which is fatal. Most of the people who died on the *Brother Jonathan*, however, died from hypothermia in the enveloping frigid conditions. Hypothermia is a decrease in the core body temperature (37°C/98.6°F) through exposure to continuing cold and wet circumstances to a level at which normal body functions become impaired. The lowering of the body temperature occurs as the surroundings rob the body of its heat. In fact, water conducts heat away from the body up to twenty-five times faster than air exposure at the same temperature.

As the body starts to shut down, there is a continuing mental and physical collapse. The symptoms include loss of coordination, slurred speech, irrationality, decrease in heart and respiratory rates, extreme weakness, and uncontrolled shivering. Abnormally slow breathing, cold and pale skin, dizziness, and lethargy are also present. This collapse can come on slowly, and a person may not even be aware that one is in danger.

Once a person is in hypothermia, a prolonged low oxygen level occurs in the blood. Depending upon the degree of this oxygen insufficiency, the victim can develop cardiac arrest and central nervous system disabilities. This can also lead to the mouth and air passages relaxing, which allows the lungs to fill with water, otherwise known as "wet drowning." Or cardiac arrest occurs first and water isn't inhaled into the lungs, which is known as "dry drowning." The victim's body completely shuts down into death.

Hypothermia can occur at temperatures well above freezing as easily as at colder ones. For example, many of the passengers died with their lifejackets on. It is evident that they died from hypothermia, even though it was the summertime and ten miles from land. The same conditions are as deadly in warmer waters, especially when there's a chilling wind, mountainous waves, panic, and frantic swimming to try and stay above the foamy seas (causing more body heat loss). And this was the case.

The average ocean temperature off Crescent City is fifty degrees with a range of forty-six to fifty-four degrees. People can die from hypothermia within an hour at these temperatures in even better conditions. As soon as the ship began to sink, those onboard the vessel were doomed.

Albert Richardson was a passenger on the steamer S.S. *Sierra Nevada*. The ship was scheduled to meet the *Brother Jonathan* that Sunday outside of Crescent City. He wrote:

> From Victoria we returned to San Francisco by ocean steamer. We threaded Saint George's Reef—a series of dangerous rocks near the land—some rising two or three hundred feet, others entirely under water. Here we hoped to meet the *Brother Jonathan*, with papers from San Francisco only twenty-four hours old. The swell was very high, and our captain's face wrinkled with anxiety until the perilous point was passed. Meanwhile, we were discussing the chances for life that one would have had if shipwrecked in that heavy sea.
>
> We missed the *Brother Jonathan*. Two hours after we passed the reef she reached it, struck a rock, and in forty-five minutes went to the bottom. All of those people with their human hopes and fears, their loves and longings and ambitions were engulfed in that repository which keeps all its treasures and all its secrets till the sea shall give up its dead.

Offshore Crescent City searchers discovered the body of James Nisbet floating in the sea. Carefully wrapped in oil paper in his breast pocket, the seamen came upon his last will and testament. Realizing the hopelessness of the situation but with incredible coolness, he sat down in the saloon—as the ocean crashed over the fracturing ship with the shrieks of wind and people—and in pencil wrote out his last bequeaths and a note to a loved one.

His will read:

> At Sea on Board Brother Jonathan
> July 30, 1865
>
> In view of death, I hereby grant my brother, Thomas Nisbet, at present engaged on the Pacific Railroad, near Clipper Cap, California, my sole executor, with instructions to wind up my sole estate, real and personal, and convert the same into cash with all convenient speed but so as not to sacrifice same, and to pay over and divide the same equally between himself and my sole sister, Margaret Nisbet, now residing in England; and under burden of the payment of a legacy of five thousand dollars in gold to Almira Hopkins, wife of Casper Hopkins, insurance agent, San Francisco, California. And I desire that my brother, said Thomas Nisbet, shall not be asked to give security for his missions with my estate.

He attached a note to Hopkins' wife:

> My dear Almira, a thousand affectionate adieus. You spoke of my sailing on Friday—Hangman's Day—and the unlucky Jonathan. Well here I am with death before me. My love to you all—to Caspar, to Dita, to Belle, to Mellie and little Myra—kiss her for me. Never forget Grandpa.

Wrapped in oil cloth, he placed the documents inside a breast pocket. After his body was discovered two days later, the searchers removed the papers, dried them, made a copy, and gave the originals to a policeman who took them to the brother in San Francisco. The will eventually came before a California court, but it was refused probate on the grounds of lack of witnesses. Allegations were later made that the brother had taken undue personal advantage of his position as executor, which brought to an unhappy end a gallant gentleman's effort to make people happy. The act of this writing, however, is still remembered, as is the affection he felt for his friend's wife, Almira.

Among other newspapers, the *Sacramento Union* wrote an impressive eulogy about one of the West's great newspapermen. A large number of persons, including many of the old and well-known citizens of San Francisco, attended Nisbet's funeral later in that city. When Nisbet, years before, wrote about the experiences of Steamer Day aboard the *Brother Jonathan,* no one could ever have imagined that he some years later would be on its last voyage.

In addition to James Nisbet, the bodies of Captain DeWolf, General Wright, Margaret Wright (his wife), Natalie Shirpser, Daniel and Polina Rowell (and their four children), John Benton, and others were recovered. The bodies of First Office Allen, Second Officer Campbell, Engineer Elijah Mott, Major Eddy, William Logan, Anson G. Henry, Fireman John Hensley, Roseanna Keenan, Mrs. Henry Lee, William Logan, Victor Smith, and others were never recovered—or able to be identified. The majority of the passengers and crew who were lost on this ship were never found or identified.

Most of the survivors left Crescent City within days, choosing to board the steamer *Del Norte* when it returned to San Francisco. Mina (Sarah) Bernhardt and her son stayed for one month before continuing north. She gave Paul, her two-year-old son, a ten-cent piece to play with in his berth. When he was rescued, his hand was pried open and the dime was discovered still held in the palm of his hand. At Crescent City, ladies gave Martha Wilder clothing and she returned to San Francisco onboard the *Del Norte.*

In the following three weeks, a song was written about the disaster entitled, "The Sunken Rock: The Wreck of the Brother Jonathan," and the lyrics swept across the country. As the word spread about the tragedy, newspapers from the *San Francisco Examiner* to the *New York Times* published front-page extras about the disaster. As a national telegraph didn't yet exist, the news didn't reach the East Coast until August 25. That next day, the *New York Times* and *Daily National Intel-*

ligencer blared the news about the great loss. The *Intelligencer* reported:

> The steamship *Ocean Queen* brings San Francisco papers of August third. The steamship *Brother Jonathan,* from San Francisco, July 28th, bound for Portland, Oregon, and Victoria, and between two and three hundred passengers, was totally lost near Cape Lincoln, Oregon.

The newspapers soon published calls for an immediate investigation into the circumstances of this calamity, especially given that "many prominent families from the East and Middle western states went down with the ship," as the *Alta California* reported. From speculation over why so many of the crew had made safe passage aboard the one small surfboat to whether the life preservers were defective, the papers called for the federal government to conduct an immediate inquiry.

Suspicion quickly centered on the high number of crewmen on that one surviving surfboat. Why were eleven of the nineteen people on board the one lifeboat crew members, especially when they denied access to others just before the boat was lowered? Quartermaster Yates stated that Captain DeWolf had admonished the passengers to allow more crew members to be on board the first lifeboats, and that if more crew had been there, that those boats wouldn't have capsized. Critics argued there was no evidence of these remarks ever being made and that the argument was self serving: The need was not proven that eleven crew members had to be present to save five women and three children.

Yates later recalled that people preferred to stay on board the bucking vessel, primarily because they already had seen what had happened to those who tried to escape in the first lifeboats that capsized or were crushed. He stated that he would have switched with any other passengers had they asked and testified about the couple that refused to enter the surfboat—whose place he had taken. The rest of the crew didn't say much as to why they were on board, other than that Steerage Steward

David Farrell insisted that DeWolf had ordered him to remain in the boat and "keep the men out, assisting Third Officer Patterson." He didn't do a very good job in keeping them out.

Although Mina Bernhardt questioned why there were so many crewmen on board, Martha Stott's statements ended the possibility of a specific investigation into the crew's conduct. Given what had happened to the previous iron lifeboats, she made a point. She stated:

> I am positive that Yates, the quartermaster, did all in his power to get others into this boat, and the reason that so many of the crew were saved was that this being the smallest boat, the officers and gentlemen on board considered it the least safe, and sent all the ladies into the larger ones.

The newspapers lauded the heroism of the men on board, including Captain DeWolf, First Officer Allen, and Second Officer Campbell—all lost at sea. Little was known of Fireman John Hensley, other than he worked as a ranch-hand in Napa, California. Even as a lowly fireman aboard the *Brother Jonathan,* however, the newspapers lauded him as a "giant among men, when on that tragic day he had declared, 'There are others to help,' and declined to save himself." First Officer Allen's refusal to get into another boat also brought praise. The comments from the survivors were laudatory about the crew in general. Another paper reported:

> The diversity amongst the crew of the *Brother Jonathan* existed as it does aboard all ships. Mexicans Diaz and Gonzales, newly arrived from the south, free Negroes G. W. Hill, Jacob Yates, and John Clinton, along with Germans, Irish, Portuguese, and others men were thrown together in an uncommon situation; yet all became equal by their heroic actions toward their ship and her passengers.

These newspapers and their accounts were right: The men were heroic in their actions, especially those who gave up their lives for the sake of others. They showed the courage of common people who reached uncommon levels of bravery.

Speculation centered about Mrs. Keenan and her entourage of "fallen angels." Although Mrs. Martha Stott and Ms. Wilder were the only two of that group who survived, the way the other ladies were included in lifeboats created this possibility: A few crew members knew these women better than the typical passenger. All of this party except for Mrs. Stott were escorted into the first lifeboat that overturned. Ms. Wilder was on two of the lifeboats, and at least a couple of the women in the first were placed on others. William Shields, the cabin boy and waiter, fueled more controversy when he said that three women in the Keenan group had been saved in the one surfboat. Other than Mrs. Stott and Ms. Wilder, only three other ladies were onboard: the unidentified Chinese woman, "Mrs. Lee," along with Mary Ann Tweedale and Mina Bernhardt. Mrs. Tweedale was from England and journeying to see her son in Oregon. Could this third person identified by Shields have been Mina Bernhardt?

None of the bodies from Mrs. Keenan's group were discovered—or if found, they couldn't be identified. The only person who identified Mrs. Keenan as struggling in the water was Martha Stott. Ms. Bernhardt was on her way to Victoria and not on the passenger list. Some argue that Bernhardt was actually Roseanna Keenan, her gold able to buy the secret. Historians generally accept the newspapers' conclusion that Mina Bernhardt was not part of the Keenan entourage—but the mystery still continues.

Another of the folk stories that emanated from the tragedy concerned a small boy, little Charles Brooks. His mother was the wife of Captain N. C. Brooks, the skipper of the bark *Cambridge.* She and her sister left San Francisco for Portland on the *Brother Jonathan,* the mother leaving little Charlie with her parents at their well-furnished ranch house in Napa in Northern California. At approximately 2:15 on the afternoon of July 30, 1865, Charles Brooks started crying uncontrollably. The little boy sobbed that he had just seen "My Ma and Aunt Mary go down into the water in a ship." Turning away after delivering this chilling message of doom, the child buried his face in his grandmother's blouse and continued his sobbing. Late the next night, Charles's grandfather and a wealthy Napa Valley rancher returned home.

His anxious wife had stayed up waiting for his return while the exhausted child lay fast asleep. Taking one look at her husband's ashen face, she asked what had happened.

"The *Brother Jonathan* has gone down. It came over the wire," he answered sadly. She then told him what his grandson had said and done. At the exact moment that little Charles broke down about his mother and aunt, the two sisters were dying in the ocean three hundred miles away on the *Brother Jonathan*. The bodies of the little boy's mother and aunt were never found.

When the Oregon newspapers first carried the names of the dead passengers and crew, they listed the "Rowell" family as "Powell"—so Elias and Sarah Buell, Polina's parents, still thought that their daughter was on her way to see them with her family. When the papers corrected the list to read the "Rowell" family, Elias hitched up his team of horses and drove his wagon from The Dalles in Oregon to Northern California. After days of traveling, he finally arrived in Crescent City and asked if there had been any survivors. When he heard the story of the one surviving surfboat with who was on board, the distraught Buell drove his team northward along the coast and searched for the bodies of his daughter, son-in-law, and four grandchildren.

After days of looking closely along the coast, he discovered two Native Americans picking at something from the skirt of a dead body. As he clucked his horses toward the scene, the people ran away. Buell stopped the wagon and dropped down onto the sands. He discovered that the scavengers had been trying to work out the gold coins that had been stitched into the skirt of the deceased. The body was underneath a strapped chest. When he turned the chest over, Elias was staring into the bloated and bleached face of his dead daughter. Buell fell to his knees.

After he was able to regain some composure, the father loaded Polina's body into the wagon and stared for a time at the beach.

Buell then slowly drove his horses away, heading north. "Some distance from that point," he discovered the dead body of his friend and son-in-law, Daniel Rowell. Understandably deeply grieving over his discoveries, he drove his wagon further with the dead couple together in the back.

Buell drove up to a small clump of clothing on the beach and discovered another but much smaller body. Bleached and decomposed by the sun and its immersion in the sea, this body was about the size and sex of one of his grandchildren. Elias Buell hadn't seen any of his grandchildren yet, as they were born in the Midwest after Polina and Daniel moved away, but his daughter had written him about each "blessed event." Buell put this small body next to the other two in the wagon.

He decided to bury his family on the Mesa in Crescent City in the plot where the other *Brother Jonathan* dead were buried. However, he didn't want the Rowells to be separated. The grandfather found three other bodies in the morgue that were the size and gender of his remaining grandchildren. He said that they were his daughter's and buried all six together in the plot. Tearfully and despondently, the father slowly drove his horses back to Oregon. He died six months later of a broken heart.

Workmen much later moved the Rowells' headstones to the Brother Jonathan Memorial Park by the sea, although prior to then, relatives had interred the bodies to another site. Polina's headstone was not chiseled correctly, as the marker misstated her age by ten years and misspelled her first name. If her age was twenty-two as noted at her death, she would have had to meet Daniel at the gristmill and married while she was a pre-teenager.

After the *Brother Jonathan*, the *Del Norte* became the workhorse for the voyages between San Francisco and northbound cities, including Crescent City. This steamer carried people searching for missing loved ones and stacks of empty metal caskets. The *Del Norte* continued to return with filled coffins and grieving family members. On August 9, the ship brought back to San Francisco all of the survivors, except for Mina Bernhardt and her son, who returned later.

Many of the victims did not have funerals, as their bodies were never found or identified. These people were buried in little-noticed proceedings where the corpses were discovered or in Crescent City. More publicized and extensive memorial services were held for Victor Smith, William Logan, Major Eddy, First Officer Allen, Second Officer Campbell, and Dr. Anson Henry, among others.

The proceedings for General Wright and his wife, however, were as magnificent as his position commanded. Ironically, workmen had started tearing apart an old steamer named for the man, the *Colonel Wright,* on the day after the *Brother Jonathan* sank. On August 20, a thirteen-gun salute was fired in San Francisco, and the American flag was lowered at all public buildings. One day later, the same gun salute echoed in Sacramento. The bodies of General and Mrs. Wright arrived in San Francisco on the *Del Norte* in mid-October. Their son traveled with the bodies from Crescent City.

After a funeral procession and services in San Francisco, an honor guard accompanied the remains as they were placed aboard the steamer *Sacramento* and transported to that city. Church bells peeled, fire bells rang, and all the flags in Sacramento were lowered to half-mast. In the procession, soldiers marched sharply in unison with the two coffins into the California Senate Chamber. The caskets lay in state inside those chambers during the afternoon. The guards later accompanied the caskets as they were moved to a church for services. "Large numbers" of Sacramento residents and visitors alike filed past the coffins in the chambers and at the church. "Hundreds" of those unable to get into the church for those services milled about outside. The funeral procession was one-mile long, taking half an hour to pass a given point. At the Sacramento City Cemetery, after the internment of General and Mrs. Wright, an Army battalion fired three long volleys over the graves, as their son (Colonel T. F. Wright) and two other adult children stood by. The U.S. Government erected a monument over the site some years later.

The *Del Norte* brought back Captain DeWolf's body in mid-September to San Francisco. In honor of this man, the flag of the Association of Pioneers at Pioneer Hall was dropped to half-mast, and the membership passed a resolution in honor of their lost member. Seafarers and the socially prominent attended his service. DeWolf was buried at "Lone Mountain," which was later named Laurel Hill Cemetery.

Until her death, the socially prominent Maria DeWolf strenuously maintained that the ship had never struck a rock, but that its sinking had been due to being overloaded. It also had insufficient repairs, she believed, from its collision with the *Jane Falkenberg* at the rough Columbia River mouth. She argued continuously that her husband and his officers were well aware of the condition of the vessel, but that the owners refused to send the ship to the needed dry dock. Her husband had no recourse but to follow those "wretched orders," as he was otherwise threatened with termination. Mrs. DeWolf's theory was that the heavy ore crusher on board had somehow become loose and plunged through the weak part of the hull, causing the massive destruction that brought about the loss of the ship.

For several weeks after the disaster, bodies and bits of wreckage floated onto shore from Northern California to Southern Oregon. Debris and much of the passenger's luggage washed up on the beaches, leading to the conclusion that the ship had broken up. The huge, gilded wooden eagle (once on the wheel box, then attached to the front of the pilothouse) was retrieved and later placed on display in the San Francisco Maritime Museum.

The ship's wheel and forty feet of its upper deck, with the bell still attached, had come to rest on a beach, grinding onto the shoreline at Gold Bluff, California. Rigid in death, one man was still snared on its top. The long, high cliff at Gold Bluff overlooks the coast and is some twenty-five miles south of Crescent City toward Trinidad. Although the dead young man wasn't on the passenger list, he was later identified as Edward Cardiff by a "memorandum book" in one pocket and another holding a $20 Confederate note and "photographs of ladies and others."

The large steering wheel later graced Henry Saville's Saloon in Crescent City for years. Today it resides at the Oyster House in Portland. After floating back to land, the ship's piano keyboard was also kept in the city. It was displayed in a "conspicuous place in the bar-room of a hotel." The *Brother Jonathan*'s bell hung on display at the old lighthouse near the entrance to the harbor until a burglar stole it over one-hundred years later.

CHAPTER 7

Lifetimes and the Lighthouse

After the news of the wreck became known and the tragedy fully reported, newspapers began to condemn the ship owners, status of current laws, and alleged improper motives of profit as the reason for the high loss of life. One newspaper account called the sinking an act of murder. *The Oregon Reporter* in Jacksonville, Oregon, on August 5, 1865, wrote:

> Thus, another wanton sacrifice of hundreds of valuable lives has been made to the cool-blooded avarice of steamship companies. Her owners knew the *Brother Jonathan* to be an old, unsafe hulk. She is probably insured for twice her value, and her loss was coolly calculated during one of her trips, when her insurance would fill their pockets, although the lives of hundreds of innocent men, women, and children might be lost in the operation. This is no better than cool-blooded, diabolical murder, and the perpetrators of it should be hung high as Haman.

The papers crusaded for improved maritime safety laws. Reporters wrote stories about why the first survivor reports were so optimistically far off. Stories in newspapers from the *Alta California* and *San Francisco Evening Bulletin* to *The Oregonian* alleged improprieties by the ship owners and crew as the reason for the high death counts.

With the breakdown of the telegraph line between San Francisco and New York City delaying the East Coast's receipt of the tragic news, over one month expired before those newspapers first reported the *Brother Jonathan*'s demise.

The Steamboat Inspection Service held an inquiry and made a "Report of Casualties and Violations of Steamboat Laws." The Board of Inquiry reported its findings in the 1865 *Annual Report of the Steamboat Inspection Service, First District.* The Bureau of Marine Inspection and Navigation records of this inquiry in the National Archives make clear that the investigation absolved everyone from responsibility for the collision, loss of the ship, and large fatalities. The investigators concluded:

> The *Brother Jonathan* was rebuilt four years since, and was a very staunch vessel, and was very fully supplied with boats and all other equipments required by law; she also had very able and experienced officers and a full crew. The public was very deeply impressed by this sad calamity; the ship and her officers having the fullest confidence of the people—there has not been heard, in the public press or elsewhere, the least complaint against either.

The press also roundly criticized the quality of the life preservers and concluded that since so many people died with their life jackets on, the preservers must have been defective. The newspapers, of course, had failed to recognize the effects of hypothermia and "dry" or "wet" drowning. However, the cries about the deaths—despite the findings of the Steamboat Inspection Service—led to Congressional investigations and eventual changes in maritime safety laws.

Three areas seemed more significant than others: the alleged "overloading" of the ship; the lack of lifeboat carrying capacity, especially since the vessel carried more boats than the law required; and the crew's inability to quickly free a lifeboat from its lines, which brought about the swamping of three boats. *The Annual Report of the*

Steamboat Inspection Service in its investigation included recommended changes in the maritime safety laws in light of the *Brother Jonathan* disaster.

The Superintendent of the Steamboat Inspection Service called on Congress to investigate and pass a new law requiring that a "boat may be instantly relieved at will from the tackles by which she is lowered into the water." He also called for increases in the salary of the ship investigators whose responsibility it was to oversee that all vessels were in good condition with equipment maintained in good order and the ship "properly managed." The Superintendent stated outright in his printed report that without such increases in compensation, these investigators would continue to seek support "mainly or partially in some private occupation," all to the disadvantage of passenger safety.

Congress enacted these recommendations into laws. The Congressional Act of July 25, 1866, as one example, provided:

> That all sea-going vessels carrying passengers, and those navigating any of the northern and northwestern lakes, shall have the lifeboats required by law, provided with suitable boat dispensing apparatus, so arranged as to allow such boats to be safely launched with their complements of passengers while such vessels are under speed or otherwise not moving, so as to allow such disengaging apparatus to be operated by one person, disengaging both ends of the boat simultaneously from the tackles by which it may be lowered to the water.

The salaries of the local steamboat inspectors were significantly increased. Further, given the problems of steamship collisions—and which the *Brother Jonathan* had its own, such as with the *Jane Falkenberg* just weeks before—this law required that all vessels had to display operable and specific white, red, and green lights at prescribed locations.

The records of the House of Representatives in the National Archives in Washington, D.C., include a file on H.R. 394. It was approved on April 12, 1866, for the relief of the estate of Major E. W. Eddy. Transferring with General Wright to Fort Vancouver, Eddy was overseeing the Army payroll. Among the documents supporting this bill were copies of three sworn affidavits indicating that the "$200,000 in the hands of Major E. W. Eddy as paymaster in the army on board the *Brother Jonathan* were U.S. Treasury notes packed in an iron box." The resolution also indicates that this payroll money was never found and was presumed lost in the tragedy.

The steamer was equipped with four Francis Patent iron lifeboats, although the U.S. Steamboat regulations at the time required only one. The ship carried two wooden surfboats, as well as 397 "lifebelts" for the passengers and crew on board. The six lifeboats on the vessel could save approximately 250 passengers and crew—or the total then onboard. Legislation and administrative regulations were subsequently enacted to provide for more carrying protection and flexibility in case of loss.

Although the "overloading" of the *Jonathan* wasn't a prime cause of its loss (but did cause a lack of maneuverability), the U.S. Government took another look at the maritime laws on overloading. The ship's experience was not as important to this issue, however, as it was in others. Further, Congress had enacted legislation dealing with this subject prior to this time.

THOSE WHO SURVIVED the *Brother Jonathan*'s loss went on living their lives, including a few who had died in the ocean. Third Engineer G. W. Hill, for example, is listed as being a member of the crew, but no significant accounts credit this person with having survived and being on the one surfboat. The accounts of Third Officer Patterson and Greenleaf Curtis, which appear to be most accurate, don't include this man's name as having survived. In any event, one "G. W. Hill" haunted the San Francisco waterfront for many years, telling and retelling the story of his survival. He sold the "location" of the wreck to various treasure seekers, once for $200 (worth well over $10,000 today).

Miss Martha Wilder reportedly by one newspaper account gave

birth nine and a half months later to her first baby. However, the actual occurrence of this blessed event—although very interesting from a romantic account, especially given the deceased Fireman John Hensley's heroic saving of her—cannot be substantiated.

For those who lost loved ones, the situation was very different. The quarters of Miss Natalie Shirpser was the bridal stateroom, although she was not married. This indicates that either the first-class staterooms were all reserved then or that she liked to travel in style. Miss Shirpser was said to be seventeen years old, a very attractive woman of "great beauty and accomplishments." Her grieving mother and father cut up bolts of the same cloth used in her dresses into small bits and distributed them to the Indian tribes along the coast for miles up and down Crescent City, telling them they would pay a reward for any information about the "woman wearing that cloth." The family reportedly paid Indians to patrol the coast and cruise in their canoes around the wreck site. Her photographs were widely distributed. The family finally and reluctantly concluded that their beautiful daughter had to have died inside her cabin with her body dragged down to the bottom of the sea.

Major Samuel J. Hensley, who bought the vessel in the early 1860s, lost his courageous nephew John Hensley in the disaster. At the time of the sinking, Major Hensley was the ship's agent and the company's executive vice president. Six months later, Major Hensley died of a "disease of the liver and a general debility," leaving his wife and two children to inherit a large estate.

Mary Priscilla Macgruder Lord received the news of her husband's probable death before anyone else did. Shocked and understandably incapacitated by the news, she had tenderly embraced her husband that early Sunday morning, only to learn mere hours later of the ship's loss. Her husband, Joseph, had taken the place of his junior messenger, who had become ill prior to the ship's departure. A few days later, Sergeant Greenleaf Curtis and others went looking for survivors, but found instead sea lions on Seal Rock. He married Joseph Lord's widow, Mary, seven years later in 1872, and they remained in Crescent City. The couple had three children by their marriage. Joseph Lord's surviving daughter, Margaret, grew up, married, and lived for many years in Crescent City, then died in the early 1950s in San Jose.

Mrs. Martha Stott did not continue to Victoria to be a waitress in John C. Keenan's saloon. While staying at the home of Dr. Edward Mason in Crescent City, she turned to Dr. Mason and said, "Daddy Mason, it seems I wasn't born to be drowned." However, six months after returning to what was said to be her home in Sacramento, she committed suicide by leaping from the bridge into the swollen Sacramento River. Short years before, the operations of Mr. and Mrs. Keenan had been based in Sacramento.

General and Mrs. Wright's son, Colonel T. F. Wright, accompanied the bodies of his parents from Crescent City to San Francisco on board the *Del Norte.* Colonel Wright died ten years later in the Modoc War, and his body is interred besides his father and mother in the same plot in Sacramento. The Wrights had two other children, a daughter who married an Army officer and a younger son who became a lawyer.

On board the *Shenandoah,* Captain Waddell captured numbers of fishing and whaling ships and set them on fire. He saved one now and then to send the captured sailors back to land. As Waddell weighed a decision to attack San Francisco, he finally learned from a British ship on August 2, that the war had ended four months earlier. He sailed his ship and crew to Liverpool, England, and surrendered to British officials, who immediately released them. (England was responsible for arming the *Shenandoah* in the first place.)

England later turned the vessel over to the United States consul, and, later, the ship was sold at auction. During the vessel's one-year attack on shipping off the Pacific Coast, the *Shenandoah* captured or destroyed a total of seventy-two ships. Captain Waddell eventually returned to the United States in 1875 and worked for the Pacific Mail Steamship Company—the same company on his prime list of Union targets. He then captained the S.S. *San Francisco,* which steamed between San Francisco and Melbourne, Australia.

The son of the late Victor Smith, Norman Smith, attended school in Ohio, learned surveying, and later became the elected Mayor of Port Angeles on the Olympic Peninsula in Washington—the same area that his father oversaw previously as Collector of Customs for the Puget Sound district. His father had tried to move the headquarters of the customs house from Port Townsend to Port Angeles. Victor's actions in trying to move the headquarters to a place where he owned real estate, among other situations, ultimately brought about his downfall.

Biographers credit Norman with showing his father's charm and energy, but also exhibiting the same impatience and judgment. Convinced that the Union Pacific railroad would approach Port Angeles from the west, he bought one iron rail, cut it in half, hauled it up to the pass, and spiked in the ties; at the time it was the shortest railroad in the world. His efforts did not make a difference in his fortunes, which later soured. Smith moved back to California, settling in Crescent City, where he died in the 1950s, but he was able to look over the horizon where his father had died so many years before.

A prominent worker for fifty years with San Francisco charities, the destitute Mrs. Marie DeWolf was placed in the home of the San Francisco Ladies' Relief and Protection Society, which she founded in 1868. At one time, Mrs. DeWolf was worth $1,000,000 in round figures—an immense sum in those days. She spent one-half of this sum "doing good" as a prominent charity worker. The other half was stolen from the elderly lady, by one whom she had trusted as a son. A descendant of one of the families of the Revolutionary War, she was an active member of the Daughters of the Revolution, among other civic and social organizations. She died shortly after moving into the home in 1906 at the age of eighty-six. The services were held in the chapel of the old people's home with a private internment—a far cry from what her station had once called for.

THE TRAGEDY also clearly showed the need for a light and fog signal on St. George Reef. The rock struck by the *Brother Jonathan* was named "Jonathan Rock"—or at least Quartermaster Yates pointed out this one as being the deadly culprit when he returned to the area. Public outcry over the disaster soon spurred the Lighthouse Board into action, and it requested funds to start the process of such a construction project.

Owing to the costs of Reconstruction after the Civil War, however, Congress for several years was unwilling to allocate the large sums required to construct a lighthouse on that dangerous, exposed reef. As the wave-swept outcropping was deemed too difficult to build on, the board looked at alternate sites in the area.

In 1875 it decided to build the light on the coastal land bluff at Point St. George. However, members then reconsidered and rejected that idea because it was located too far from the hazardous reef. Six years after that the board finally settled on building the protecting light six miles off the coast on Northwest Seal Rock off Point Saint George. It was over fifteen years since the *Brother Jonathan* crashed on the uncharted rock.

Although there were some misgivings about the chosen site, the board felt it had no other choice. The frequent coastal fogs blanketed the protective lights and foghorns on land and the sidewheeler had been lost even further away. This lighthouse had to be constructed on a faraway site to be effective—and modern warning buoys would not be developed until decades later.

The Lighthouse Board hired Albert Ballantyne, the engineer who built Oregon's Tillamook Rock Lighthouse in 1881. His construction there proved that a lighthouse could be built on a dangerous, exposed rock. The following year Congress granted a $50,000 appropriation that allowed Ballantyne to visit St. George Reef and survey Northwest Seal Rock, which was confirmed as the lighthouse site. The initial surveyors were only able to land on that reef three times in four weeks due to the difficult and treacherous weather conditions. In 1883 Congress authorized an additional sum of $100,000 to start major construction.

Because the rough seas continuously washed over the 54-foot cliff selected as the location, Ballantyne decided to use a former lightship, *La Ninfa,* as the barracks for the workers. He arranged for the steamer *Whitelaw* to leave San Francisco and tow the *La Ninfa,* men, tools, freshwater, and provisions to the reef area. After several misadventures, his crew was finally able to tether the *La Ninfa* to the ocean bottom with large chains tied to larger mooring buoys—350 feet away from the reef. The ship could then serve as the quartering and mess hall for the workers.

One of Ballantyne's important steps in the construction was to build a solid foundation on Northwest Seal Rock. As the mother ship tugged at her moorings off the reef, his team swarmed over the rock and began to chisel out the foundation's outlines. However, the unpredictable savage seas always created the risk of large waves suddenly sweeping over the tiny reef, forcing Ballantyne to use a boat-to-island aerial tramway that he also employed on a smaller scale when building Tillamook Rock. His workers rigged a cable with an attached cage between the *La Ninfa* and the rocks. This served as a means of transporting workers to the point—and quickly back if a storm suddenly blew in. When the seas threatened to wash over the reef, the men lashed their tools to iron rings set into the rocks and quickly rode back to the ship's safety.

The crew used powerful explosives to blast away large chunks of the rock in carving out the foundation outline. After lighting the fuse to the explosives, the men would "hunt holes like crabs" and dive inside them to protect themselves from the flying rock fragments that showered the area, even occasionally striking the schooner moored over 100 yards away. As the daily blasting continued, large pieces of rock flew about like shrapnel in a grenade battle. Given the constant dangers from sudden winds, high seas, and the blasting on a small rocky point, it is remarkable that only one worker died during the entire construction process.

In September 1883, the sea surged over the rock and swept two workers away. As the crew scrambled from their handholds and higher ground, they were able to rescue the men, who nearly died in the frothing waters. As the crew had nearly leveled an area deep enough to start construction, Ballantyne immediately suspended all further activities for the duration of the reef's "winter season." This decision limited the work period on the dangerous outcropping to the spring and summer months when the seas weren't as risky.

In December of that year, Ballantyne learned about a granite deposit along the Mad River near Humboldt Bay, some eighty miles to the south. The granite proved to be of excellent quality, so he contracted for a local railroad to transport the rough blocks to the North Spit of Humboldt Bay, where his workers built a depot to cut and finish the granite stones. His men then loaded the granite blocks onto waiting ships that then transported them to the reef.

Work on the rock started again in June of 1884. His men spent the first weeks building a construction derrick with a fifty-foot boom. Ballantyne then learned that Congress had appropriated a scant $30,000 for the 1884 work season instead of the requested $150,000. Funding was a disappointingly small $40,000 in 1885, and totally lacking in 1886. A financial panic changed congressional priorities, and the project's escalating costs contributed to the lack of funding during this time. During this period, work was limited to preparing the granite blocks at the depot and performing minimal maintenance at the site.

Congress then approved a sum of $120,000 for construction in 1887 and even more was granted for the subsequent two work seasons. Each spring, the workmen scurried around the rock to reset the moorings for the mother ship and repair the site damage from the preceding winter; the huge waves continually smashed the heavy rocks from their set positions and ripped away the concrete. Once these repairs were completed, ships could again start hauling in the large blocks. During 1887, the workers built the first nine levels of the elliptical pier, which contained the engine room, coal room, cistern, and tower base. With some of the stones for the base weighing as much as six tons, the pier was raised during the next year to its thirteenth block level.

By the end of 1888, the walls of the lighthouse pier were thirty-two feet high. Workers constructed temporary wooden quarters against the pier to house the men and end the need for the costly work ship, but bad weather prevented further site work from being completed until the following year. One night in May, a series of huge waves struck the quarters, blew in the doors, and washed the men out of their bunks.

Although no one was injured, the workers didn't get any sleep that night; they kept a wary eye and ear for the ocean's return.

With the hundreds and hundreds of huge interlocking stones finally set in place, the hardworking men completed nearly all of the dangerous work on the pier in 1889. Funding came late in 1890, and the holdup prevented further work that year. The crew returned to the rock the next spring. On arrival the men discovered further repairs needed to be done. Huge storms as in the past blew the mooring buoys away and badly damaged the living quarters again. When the seven-story high pier and pad were firmly in place, the lighthouse tower's first stone was set in May of 1891. With continual good weather, and the men working virtually around the clock, the tower structure was completed by the end of August. It was built with over 1,300 granite blocks, some weighing two tons or more. These were fit with no more than three sixteenths of an inch gap away from each other. The squared stones were set in place with metal dowels, cement, and stones shoved into the crevices.

Ballantyne's crews spent the rest of the season removing the scaffolding around the tower and completing the lighthouse's interior, including the kitchen, bunks, work stations, storage, and communication facilities. Although the work was finished in 1891, another year passed before the "First-Order" Fresnel lens (its largest light classification size) arrived from France.

Augustin Fresnel was a French physicist specializing in optics who invented this lens in the early 1820s. Looking like a giant glass beehive with multi-colored lights trapped inside, the superior eight-foot high lens had concentric rings of glass prisms that bent the internal light into a narrow beam. Fresnel shaped the lens like a magnifying glass at its center, so that the concentrated beam became even stronger. While an open flame lost nearly 97 percent of its light, the Fresnel lens captured all except 17 percent and radiated the light's beam over twenty miles to the horizon.

When the lighthouse structure was finally complete in 1891, the total construction costs were $705,000—taking eleven years and making this the most remote, expensive, and dangerous lighthouse ever built in the United States. This cost was an incredible amount of money for a nineteenth-century lighthouse. The expenditure was double that of constructing the Minot's Ledge Lighthouse in Massachusetts and $100,000 more than building the base and erecting the Statute of Liberty (also constructed at the same time). In today's dollars, the cost would be in the high multimillions of dollars.

The construction used more than 175,000 cubic feet of granite, 14,000 tons of stone, and 325 tons of brick, all of which had to be transported to the reef and hauled to the site in some of the worst possible weather. The entire 146-foot high structure is massive and imposing, with a 76-foot tower (including the lantern room) sitting on a 70-foot base. Lit for the first time on October 20, 1892, the light station was named the St. George Reef Light House.

The St. George Lighthouse is different from the Crescent City Lighthouse, built on the seaward side of an island just off Battery Point on the westerly side of Crescent City harbor. This site became operational thirty-six years before in 1856, did not figure in the wreck of the *Brother Jonathan,* and was a much safer place for lighthouse keepers to work and live.

THE COMMISSIONER OF LIGHTHOUSES believed that only St. George Reef and Tillamook Rock in Oregon (which cost one-fifth of St. George Reef's construction) were so difficult to operate that they warranted a crew of five lighthouse keepers. Although both were rare wave-washed rocks—where the ocean hit the lighthouse from all four sides—St. George was located five times farther away from land. With a crane used to lift small surfboats with supplies and relief crews from stormy seas on a stories-high lift, just bringing in needed provisions and food was dangerous, especially when large rollers unexplicably surged in.

Owing to the hazards of this duty, families were not allowed to live on site, and they resided in houses on the point or mainland. As the only way to land on or leave the St. George Lighthouse was by its risky derrick and sixty-foot boom, the only time families were permitted was on visitor's day. As distinct from the myriad lighthouses on land, on this rock, conditions made it impossible to grow vegetables or tend sheep, and pets just didn't seem to last very long.

Duty on St. George Reef was isolated and extremely hard. The savage surrounding waters and ocean crashing on its rocks—as different from inland rivers and generally quiet bays where other lighthouses were located—marooned these keepers, even when essential medical help was needed. During the early years, several keepers died and others became seriously ill. Among the eighty men who served over a forty-year period from 1891, thirty-seven resigned and twenty-six transferred to other stations due to this hard duty.

The first keeper who operated the station was John Olson. He started his duty on November 1, 1891, with two helpers. One drowned nearly two years later, and the other assistant resigned six months after that. Olson spent twelve long years at St. George before transferring to different duty, and then returning later. George Roux set the record, however, when he served as the head lighthouse keeper for twenty straight years from 1918 to 1938. These men were the exceptions.

One year before his stay ended, Roux and his crew experienced some of the harshest and stormiest weather in the lighthouse's history. Since the conditions cut off all contact with land for over one month, no supplies could be delivered or connection made with the outside world. Although the crew had worked with each other for years, they came down with bad cases of "cabin fever." Men stopped speaking to one another and saying "Good Morning" became a personal affront. Altercations broke out, men threatened one another, and it was a miracle that no one was murdered. After several weeks, a supply ship was able to finally venture out and bring in relief crews and needed provisions.

Not only was it near impossible for people to have any semblance of a normal life at the station, the storms themselves were so threatening. During the savage winter of 1952, one wave swelled to over sixteen stories high as it surged over the reef. This immense mass of ocean smashed into the lighthouse and hurled debris against the top windows, causing the lantern-room windows at the highest levels to shatter.

The St. George Reef Lighthouse was understandably one of the least sought after assignments. Duty at the station was inhospitable at best and hazardous at worst. The tower was cold and foreboding with frequent storms. Relief only arrived when weather allowed, and lighthouse keepers could be stranded during rough weather for mind-numbing periods of time. Logbooks recorded an average of only five visitors each year from 1892 through 1939, when the Coast Guard took over all lighthouse operations, and these visitors included the inspectors and boat supply crewmen.

The lighthouse personnel worked in shifts of three months each at the station, which then was followed by two months with their families. In the early 1970s, keepers stayed at the lighthouse for four weeks at a stretch and then had two weeks of liberty on shore, until the next four-week stretch. Later, these shifts would be shortened. As always, the rotation depended on whether boats could go out and safely transfer people.

Service at the lighthouse taxed the mental health of many and claimed lives. During construction, one worker holding a tag line to the derrick's boom was pulled off the pier and fell to his death. Several keepers lost their lives while serving at the station. In addition to the 1893 disappearance of the assistant and the station's boat in heavy seas, keeper George Roux died of injuries and exhaustion after unsuccessfully attempting to reach the lighthouse by launch during a storm. The worst tragedy occurred in 1951, when a rogue wave roared in and inundated a surfboat as the derrick lowered it to the sea. Three young Coast Guardsmen died.

Despite all the risks from unexpected gales, storms, undersea currents, and towering sneaker waves, expeditions kept searching over time for the missing *Brother Jonathan.* Whether constructing the lighthouse or operating it, crews watched as treasure seekers steamed around the area in their search for the fabled treasure. The newspaper reports stoked the public's interest and salvors' desire to find the gold—and this started before they recovered most of the bodies.

Chapter 8

The Search over Time

Just two weeks after the disaster, the tug *Mary Ann* steamed from San Francisco to explore the seas around Crescent City. It made the first search for the lost ship. The men found nothing, except for the rusted anchor of an old sailing ship, which sank to the south. Two years later, the William Ireland expedition tried and failed to locate the *Brother Jonathan.* Four years after the sinking, the schooner *Charles Hare* appeared. It searched for several weeks without success, the hearty explorers spending "several thousands" of dollars in town on needed equipment and supplies. The much-touted Brother Jonathan Treasure Company ended in failure in 1872, when its new steamer and an overabundance of faith in two "new-fangled diving bells" was not successful in locating the sunken ship.

Silas White and others mounted multiple attempts to find the fabled vessel. He arrived at Crescent City about ten years after the *Brother Jonathan* went down. Trying various ways to locate the wreck, White lost his boat, equipment, and nearly his life in a stormy wreck. Prior to that calamity, he announced that his men had succeeded in "grappling a plank" identified as being from the ship's paddle boxes.

Another consortium hired the wrecking schooner, *Phantom,* to explore off Point St. George in 1879. The newspapers reported:

> With the expert divers, Mr. Dan McGlade and Mr. Peebles, who are acknowledged to be the two best on the coast, if not in the world, there is little doubt of their success. Mr. McGlade and Peebles promise to give us their experiences for publica-

tion, one hundred and thirty feet under the sea after their work is completed.

Again, nothing was found and successors to this group experienced the same fate. Notwithstanding the risk and lack of success so far, the allure of finding sunken treasures of gold, currency, and valuables motivated divers, salvage groups, and adventurers across the country to raise money and plan different approaches to finding the remains. When someone reported a find from the ship—regardless of the lack of authentication—the announcement whetted the appetites of reporters, the public, and those who wanted to strike it rich at the bottom of the sea.

Despite the initial optimism at the start of each salvage expedition, afterward treasure hunters were left scratching their heads at their lack of success. They questioned one another, "Just where is that wreck?" No one had a clue. Expecting to meet the *Brother Jonathan* on Sunday to exchange papers, the captain of the *Sierra Nevada* placed the scene as being twenty-five miles north of Crescent City. A popularly accepted location was Jonathan Rock—the one that Quartermaster Yates pointed out several days afterwards—and an outermost projection of the Saint George chain of reefs. Other points and rocks were also candidates in the St. George Reef area, not to mention that the expansive ocean swept away in every direction. Some argued that the rock named "Jonathan Rock" wasn't even the one that Quartermaster Yates had pointed out.

Despite Ballantyne's experiences when building his lighthouse, promoters typically organized their expeditions when they believed the weather was less of a risky factor in the late summer and fall. These attempts relied on Indian eyewitness accounts, fishermen's stories, the direction from which kegs of whiskey washed up, survivor accounts, and anything that seemed to be different from what everyone else had relied on. The question to all was: which story or fact was the one that held the key to the sunken chests of gold.

In 1880 explorers reported that they had "good grounds" for their belief in announcing a discovery. They had discovered the wreck in eighteen fathoms of water (one hundred and eight feet down), and the salvage boat had come across the wreck by dragging a "sounding iron" or heavy steel-pointed bar. However, the divers couldn't descend to investigate as the seas were then too heavy. One Mr. Jackson gave directions for this group, promising that from land he had seen where the ill-fated steamer sunk. This group gave no further details or later announcements of success.

Between August 1865 and 1894, salvage groups made no less than twelve organized attempts to locate the ship, and this number doesn't include the multiple attempts made by people such as Captain Peter Gee and Silas White. An old San Francisco sea captain, Captain Gee started making annual summer expeditions to Crescent City in 1877 to search for the wreck. He hired boats and their crews for these explorations, preferring to search by trolling long, weighted lines with grappling hooks behind the vessels.

Gee said that he had located the *Brother Jonathan* eight years later, but that since the weather was "thick," he lost his bearings and couldn't find the location again—that is, until the tenth year of his search. With great fanfare, in 1887 Gee reported to the press that he had discovered the ship again. He stated that the vessel was sunk precisely at 33.5 fathoms, or about 200 feet down. To Gee, it was "about a mile to the westward and two miles south of Northwest Seal Rock, where the new lighthouse is being built." The location was established as being "some miles northwest of Jonathan Rock around the hidden rock known as Saddle Rock." Captain Gee announced that the treasure was worth two million dollars, mostly in gold coin and currency. He continued his search even after this announcement with divers who wore a "complete diving apparatus," but, ultimately, he never found anything.

"C. W. Hill"—or the man who said he was the assistant engineer who survived—told people in saloons that he knew where the vessel sank. He sold his story one time for $200 to John F. Ryan, who boasted that he was the world's "Champion Deep Sea Diver." In 1894 Ryan proudly told a *San Francisco Chronicle* reporter that he held the diving record for deep-sea divers, having descended "hundreds of feet using "submarine armor." He produced a certificate from the Divers Union of New York certifying that he had descended to a depth of 640 feet for three hours. The man told a reporter that he had discovered the famous wreck, even walked in the murky depths across the deck and around the ship. He had retrieved a bucket with the name *Brother Jonathan,* three brass buttons with the same name from the uniform of a drowned sailor, and a piece of cloth from one of the military passengers.

Ryan showed the items off to an eager media. He told a newspaperman that a large shark had attacked him, but that the sharp teeth couldn't rip through his specially designed diving suit with armored plating. The diver stated that when he fell about half his length into a hole, he decided that it was time to leave due to the new danger of "twisting out his air tubes." Ryan then announced he had figured out how to retrieve the valuables: Once he raised the necessary money, his exploration crew would attach four huge air bags to the sunken ship, inflate them from the surface with air pumps, and secure the "$1,000,000 treasure." "Of course," he added, "the precise location of the wreck is my secret."

One year later, newspapers ran Ryan's account again of the discovery, adding that the wreck was at the bottom of the ocean "a few miles from Crescent City." He was confident that it would be "but a few months until the *Brother Jonathan,* and particularly her treasure, would be in some other place than at the bottom of the Pacific Ocean." Ryan apparently was not able to raise the money, however, and there were no further follow-up reports. Although some researchers discount his tales, especially since a fire bucket and brass buttons with the name of the ship weren't unique objects, his tale added to the mystique of the whereabouts of the lost *Jonathan.*

In every decade after the sinking, salvage attempts with extensive public interest took place. In September 1897, after sixteen years of effort, the Klamath Brother Jonathan Searching Company announced its success "in bringing to light such evidence as may with safety be regarded as conclusive that the location of the ship was a little southerly from Point St. George and about a half-mile off shore."

Nothing further transpired. In 1914, another salvage company formed, based on the story of an Indian eyewitness who had kept the location secret for half a century. No further news about a discovery was issued.

Diving is dangerous work, especially during those times, as the men used antiquated diving suits, screwed-on lead helmets, and descending ropes. One aged photograph taken in 1915 shows a *Brother Jonathan* diver, a large man for the times with strong facial features and a determined look. He holds an antiquated diving helmet in one hand, his other draped down to the side. He wears heavy weighted boots with heavy ropes wrapped around his body with which to be dragged back to the surface. Another image from the same year shows six men on a large surfboat, the diver on the side, ready to descend once more into the depths. Although these men were courageous to say the least, their expeditions weren't successful.

Along with the risks of these explorations, the intrepidness of the people stands out. Weighted down with heavy, inflexible gear, divers depended on the crew above. After intense effort just to position the boat over a dive site, the men started their explorations even when the waters were choppy or a windstorm approached. Relying on his crewmen to keep a crucial mechanical air pump running, the diver plunged feet-first into the depths. He then quickly plummeted toward the bottom and a cold, lightless, inhospitable environment.

Curious sharks followed or swam around as the diver headed down, his lifesaving tie-rope secured above. The filtered sunlight quickly gave way to darkness, as the water became colder and colder and the water pressure increased. At times, strong currents swept a man in a curve away from the designated spot, or even caught him on the bottom and pushed him off his feet. Although the crew had measured the depths by dropping a weighted line, no assurances existed that they had measured the correct depth due to underground ledges, small canyons, and overhanging rocks.

When a diver landed in the depths, he couldn't see five feet ahead. Walking around on the bottom in these conditions was extremely dangerous, especially if the wreckage of a sunken ship snagged a diver. No rescue was possible. With the underwater currents and murkiness, the fact that a diver found something didn't mean he could ever find that particular spot again. It is quite likely that some divers had retrieved a piece of the *Brother Jonathan,* but they never again could find that exact place.

Regardless how fast a diver wanted to surface, he had to ascend very slowly to avoid the dreaded "bends"—or nitrogen bubbling through his body due to rising too fast from the extreme depths. Those bringing the man up by ropes had to use good judgment as to how fast they hauled him up. If someone made a mistake in this regard, the likelihood of being crippled for life or dragged up dead were definite possibilities. The diver would also not know what the conditions would be like at the surface upon a return. One explorer left a sunny day only to discover a howling storm and large waves breaking over his diving barge when he surfaced. This man was lucky as his ship was able to weather the crashing rollers.

Despite such risks, the anticipated wealth and recognition drove more explorations forward. Following in the footsteps of John F. Ryan, other "world-renowned" divers announced findings. In 1916 Martin Lund, of the Lund and Freese expedition, reported that he had discovered the wreck in forty-five feet of water. An acclaimed diver, Lund found financing and equipment from J. C. Freese, a San Francisco marine contractor. Lund reported they had located the vessel one year before, "fifty years to the day after it had sunk, finding an air chamber from a deck pump, pieces of copper contained in the cargo and other parts of the ship, all encrusted with marine growth." Lund attempted his expeditions twice more, and then another salvage group tried five years later, all seeking the one million dollars in gold lost at sea.

During the 1920s Chicago businessmen hired deep-sea divers who were lowered from barges to find the ship, but found nothing. Two years later, another diver descended in a diving bell to search. The weather frustrated his attempts, as the man discovered that calm weather in Crescent City Harbor could be windswept and stormy in the area off Point St. George—as Captain DeWolf and others before him had found out. Other attempts followed during this decade.

Even the U.S. Navy considered joining in the hunt. In 1927, Frank L. Moorman, a Pacific Coast investor, and the Navy began discussing a diving exploration for the wreck. Moorman was interested in finding the gold, while the Navy wanted the payroll and Civil-War records on board to help clear up "many pension cases that have come before Congress in years gone by." This didn't happen.

In the summer of 1931, two expeditions from Los Angeles (the Ennis-Turnbull and Schlaudaman-Parks explorations) appeared with salvage ships and divers. The only problem was that they came to the same place in the ocean. When the Parks group arrived on the scene with their boat, the other (Ennis-Turnbull) left in a huff, the men angrily yelling back that they would return after the late-arrivers left. Although neither exploration reported that they discovered the wreck or artifacts, two local Crescent City residents later said that one of the salvage groups had discovered the famous wreck but was keeping it a secret. This information later supported how the ship's gold bars might have been found.

Attempt after attempt generated greater amounts of publicity and public fanfare. The Marine Division of the U.S. Customs Service in the Treasury Department received so many inquiries that it issued a bulletin stating that the *Brother Jonathan* did not carry large amounts of gold bullion. Copying the *San Francisco Bulletin* of August 2, 1865, the bulletin stated: "The cargo was insured for $46,490 (corrected to $48,490 by the U.S. Supreme Court) and probably two-thirds of the cargo was uninsured."

An experienced Navy diver, Robert Thompson, announced why he wouldn't join the search:

> I was approached, in 1935, by a man who asked me to dive for the treasure of the *Brother Jonathan.* I was an experienced deep-sea diver, having been in the Navy in World War I. The man's first idea was to use a boat from which he would

watch while I dived. I decided that the currents near Star Rock, where it was thought the ship rested, would just beat me around, so I didn't want to do this. Then the man built a large derrick, which he evidently hoped to locate near the site. I remember seeing the derrick being taken on the ocean toward the point. Evidently the man gave up his project for some reason, because I didn't hear any more about it.

OVER TIME, twisted spars, whiskey kegs, soggy old planks, and other wooden debris washed to shore. On February 16, 1934, the *Crescent City American* reported that a plank, "well covered with barnacles" had recently floated ashore and was identified as being from the ship. "No doubt a company will soon be organized to search for other portions of the wreck on the rocky reef, twelve miles northwest of this point." Barrels of whiskey continued to wash ashore now and then from the hundreds of kegs lost at sea. In 1942, thirty-five to forty of the ship's barrels washed on the beach around Point St. George and as far south as Battery Point off Crescent City Harbor. As one resident observed, "The *Brother Jonathan* kept reminding us that it still rested offshore and was waiting to be found."

Sailors and salvors alike sailed around Jonathan Rock in the hopes of finding one of the famous kegs, as the decaying holds released the buoyant containers to the surface. In the 1930s, rumors abounded that a fisherman had hauled up gold bars from the *Brother Jonathan,* but no one owned up to that fact. The residents knew that if someone had found something that valuable, the worst thing would be to tell anyone else and attract attention. These rumors continued to stoke the gold fever of residents and explorers alike.

The would-be salvors searched at the same time on land for an "old paper" or aged account that would lead them to the fabled riches. Archival research centered in Crescent City. Fishermen were interviewed, files were searched at the Del Norte County Historical Society, old newspaper accounts reviewed, and the last moments of the dying ship recreated. The research expanded, as people poured over old papers and microfilm from the Bancroft Library in Berkeley, San

Francisco Library, and the State of California Library in Sacramento to the Library of Congress, California Historical Society, San Francisco Maritime Museum, and national and regional archives. The work was long and tedious, but the potential riches drove people on.

Newspapers later reported that a young woman named Mary Cable lived on a ranch at Point Saint George and saw the *Brother Jonathan* sink. She told a friend in Smith River that she felt sure she could point out the exact spot. Salvors rushed to see if the woman was still alive, had descendants, or left something to lead them in the right direction—but this lead also didn't pan out.

Fishermen drank and told tales, taller than the beers or whiskey and water that they drank. Every so often a howling Nor'wester swept in and debris washed up on the beaches, the underwater currents sweeping in different directions to loosen old timbers, spars, or parts of decking. The area newspapers dutifully took pictures of the unidentified barnacled-covered wood and reported that a particular image "could very well be" from the long-lost *Jonathan.* And some were. The fishermen roared their toasts and solemnly told their stories to whomever was interested—especially if that stranger picked up the tab.

Local scuba divers and diving clubs mounted explorations on and around Jonathan Rock, as commercial fishermen dragged their nets for fish and dropped heavy hooks to try and retrieve what the sea snagged underwater. Locals knew several sites for years where they lost gear but were good for fishing. The fishermen said they sometimes rigged their old, worn-out nets and gear, and made a few passes around the sites, hoping for a good catch. Sometimes this worked; at other times they lost their nets. For miles around the reefs, fishermen told about hooked debris, netted pieces of ships, and lost rigs. Given the numbers of wrecks in the area, however, it was difficult to put all of this information together and pinpoint just one ship.

The problem was that divers could work at depths of two hundred feet or more for only about twenty minutes due to the water pressure and cold. Their equipment also wasn't sophisticated enough, not to mention that the murky waters limited visibility to one arm's length. At the depths that the ship sunk, light was insufficient—"it is really dark down there", the divers commented. The strong bottom currents could also rip divers around suddenly and swirl the sands to destroy any visibility.

Over the first one-hundred years, the attempts with antiquated equipment were indeed amateurish. This lack of success, however, was not due to lack of effort. Sophisticated scanning devices needed to be developed in place of "hit and miss" murky underwater inspections. Also no one knew precisely where the ship sank. It wasn't clear that the rock struck was even the one Yates pointed out as "Jonathan Rock." Another unknown key was whether the ship broke up in pieces around one place or if it basically sank intact.

Additionally, an important uncertainty was in what direction the ship drifted after the impact. Locals know that the currents offshore Crescent City and Point Saint George are uncertain and treacherous. Major ocean currents that sweep down from Alaska along the U.S. West Coast and northward from Mexico actually meet off Crescent City, converging at the surface to fifty feet below. When these ocean streams collide, strong flows can spin in a different direction from what's indicated on the surface. Currents that carried debris northward could enter this convergence and swirl around to sweep the objects south. This is why wreckage and bodies were scattered north and south from the impact point, regardless of where the ship ultimately settled.

A further contributing factor is that the waters off Crescent City are a virtual minefield of wrecks and sunken ships. It was entirely possible that divers and expeditions could find something on the bottom but these remains would be of anything but the *Brother Jonathan.* The area's history is replete with stories about the wrecks that litter the coastline.

A savage storm pared the moorings off the schooner *J. W. Wall* in 1881 and blew her ashore at Crescent City; five years later, the schooner *Restless* wrecked there. Seven vessels, including the *California, Wall,* and *Elvenia,* were stranded near Crescent City during the years 1878–1881. The *Queen Christina,* a British 360-foot steamer, met thick fog and grounded off Point St. George in 1907. When the steel ship could not be towed off the rocks, it became a total loss.

In 1911, the schooner *Mandalay* was steaming from San Francisco to Crescent City when a violent storm overtook it. A huge wave crashed over the boat washing one man overboard with his two dogs. Five minutes later, the man—complete with the two dogs gripping his trousers tightly by their jaws—was washed back onto the ship by another towering wave. The vessel managed to turn around, make it back to San Francisco, and ran aground to avoid sinking from the extensive damage incurred.

In 1924, another storm caught the 122-ton steamship *Shark* while crewmen were trying to unload its cargo in Crescent City Harbor; the winds and waves pounded it mercilessly until the vessel broke apart. A Japanese submarine torpedoed the oil tanker *Emidio* some eighty miles south of Crescent City, two weeks after Japan attacked Pearl Harbor. The surviving members of the crew abandoned the ship, and the boat drifted onto Steamboat Rock at the entrance to the harbor. Another winter storm blew in and broke the ship in two, washing one part ashore while sinking the other.

CHAPTER 9

The Numismatic Genius

The time was the 1930s. Flights of seagulls with their sharp, melodic cries mingled with the dull thumps of rumpled water smacking against the sides of a small fishing boat. A late afternoon sun still warmed the neck of the lone fisherman. As the story goes, he started the motor to winch in his webbed brown nets, white buoys bobbing behind in the surrounding sea of green-blue rippled glass. Off toward the horizon, the squat cement base and massive lighthouse at Point St. George stood guard over the collection of exposed rocks and covered ledges. Feeling the wind gust up now and then, the man looked up into the cloudy skies, sensing that a storm would sweep in during the night.

The rhythmic appearance of wet nets and dripping saltwater stopped with a sudden jerk downwards of the cable. The winch motor strained, its gears grinding slower with deep growls. The line on the nets tightened and pointed at an angle into the sea. "Damn," the man thought, he had passed into that "no man's land" of lost nets and equipment. "Those damn underwater rocks again."

As he reached to disengage the motor, the line lost its tension. The boat lifted up before dropping back down. The motor strained further, but the winch continued with its work. Something thudded against the boat's side, and as the man peered down, he saw an object trapped in the net. Chalky, rusty particles and leeching sand inked away into the darker ocean. As the boat rocked in the swells, the man worked his boom over the net, attached it, and pulled on the lines.

The seagulls swept overhead, calling down while keeping a watchful eye. As the net swung over the boat, the fisherman heard only the wind at his back and seawater splattering against the deck. He stared at the orange-red water spilling from the strange shape, looking like someone had crushed a dark beer can in a fit of anger. The man released the net and the strange thing thudded onto the deck, blood-like condensation still running out. He pulled the net away and stared at the object in the direct sunlight.

It was an old, iron Francis Patent lifeboat, the type used decades ago, snub-nosed with iron rivets. The hulks of ships caught by the winds, rocks, or man's negligence fairly littered these waters. This was another one. It had been in the sea for years, the fisherman concluded, as he eyed the greens and browns of marine growth encrusting the relic, eaten away by undersea organisms and corroding saltwater.

He watched the sea trickle from the sprung, rusted seams and picked at the barnacles, which had attached themselves to feed. They were hard to his touch. The man pried open part of the collapsed hull and peered inside, spotting a rotted leather satchel tightly wedged underneath one crumpled seat.

The man lost track of time, as he began to dismantle what was left of the lifeboat to get at the strange moldy valise. Finally he was able to grab it with both hands, pulling it carefully from the wreckage. The fisherman placed the soggy mass down on the stained deck.

It had indistinguishable etchings on it. Due to the frills on the top and the look, he thought that it must have belonged to a woman. Pulling the grip apart, he found another moldy leather wrapping and pulled that away. Inside, he discovered different pint-sized bricks, each wrapped separately in wet but still oily paper. The fisherman unwrapped each one and laid them down against one another, discovering that some blocks were golden and others slightly discolored with a matte-like appearance.

Holding one to the sunlight, then another, the man saw that each one had the same year "1865" scored inside a circle with the wording "U.S. Mint San Francisco." Each bar was marked with the imprint, some slightly larger than others. He estimated that each weighed about two pounds. Starting to feel an excitement growing inside, he searched for his fishing knife. Locating it, the fisherman scratched at the thin bars, but his knife couldn't cut into the metal.

These were bars—gold bars—and the man knew what to do. He tied a rope around the crumpled, thin heap, then winched it up with the boom. Pushing the remains of the lifeboat back over the ocean, he quickly sliced the rope and let everything slide back into the sea. The fisherman watched the twisted shape swiftly disappear, trailing rope, white sand, and red-rust trails into the murky depths.

Looking around, the man saw that he was much closer to shore now than before. A few lights of nearby Crescent City started winking back at him as the twilight faded into darkness. The lighthouse was now at least a mile farther away, and higher seas and stronger winds gusting from the northwest pitched his boat from side to side. Knowing that these winds would soon whip the ocean into a hissing froth, he quickly started his engine and motored to the nearby harbor and its safety.

For years, the fisherman would never tell anyone about what he had found or its approximate location. He was no fool. Needing Americans to use paper money, and stop hoarding gold during the Great Depression, the Roosevelt Administration declared any holding of gold by private citizens to be illegal. The man decided that these eleven bars would be his secret until he had the chance to cash them into money and wouldn't have to look over his shoulder.

He didn't know precisely where he had discovered the rusted lifeboat and never again came across anything old from the deep, no matter how hard he tried. He would wonder about who had owned that gold, however, and who had lived and died on that day.

John J. Ford is an icon in the field of numismatics. He was unquestionably a genius and a multimillionaire—but also controversial. Success breeds controversy. Ford had different jobs while working his way through high school. In 1938, when he was fourteen, he had a paper route where he earned three dollars a week, including tips. He would travel to New York City on Saturdays and see coin dealers. When the dealers came to know him, they gave him coins "on memo" to take to other coin collectors and sell. By Ford's own admission, he became like a "bee going from flower to flower" and in the process made "some money."

His first coin deals took place as a teenager. An antique-shop owner owned a box of United States patterns. When the U.S. Mint, or any other monetary agency, considers implementing new designs for the coins in circulation, it will produce patterns. As the Mint works through the selection process, it produces sample coins of the various designs being decided on. These "pattern" coins allow Mint officials to see how the proposed designs would look in three-dimensional relief, test for production problems, and try out new alloys.

Ford would look at the dealer's coin patterns and then "sneak over to the New York Public Library, which was right around the corner, and look them up in the Adams-Woodin textbook." He discovered that some coins weren't even mentioned in that text, but Ford believed that they were authentic. At age fourteen, John Ford made his first deal by agreeing to buy those patterns for two dollars a piece. He would buy one, take it to Stack's, a prestigious coin collection and auction house, and sell it to that dealer for five dollars. The next week he would buy another one and sell the pattern to another dealer for five or six dollars. He alternated where he sold the proofs. After this, as he said, "Stack's decided it would be better to get this kid off the streets and working for them." The firm had numbers of coins that needed to be researched, and it hired John J. Ford for the summer to do this.

Money went a long way after the Great Depression and before World War II bailed out the U.S. economy. At age seventeen, in 1941, Ford quit his job as a theater usher. Although still in high school, but hungry for success, he decided to sell coins as his primary source of income. Noticing a tiny classified ad in the *New York Times* coin section that read, "Have J. J. Conway Quarter Eagle, Reasonable," Ford went to his friend, an assistant bank cashier. Ford then sent a telegram to the owner in Minnesota that read, "Send coin for examination to my bank." He put down the name of the bank where he had about eighteen dollars in his checking account and the name of his teller-friend as a reference. Although his total capital was forty dollars, Ford wanted to play with a "big-league coin."

The man sent the coin with a price of $500, which was market price. Ford's cashier friend let him take the coin out of the bank "to schlep" around New York City. If he lost the coin, the teller would be looking for another job and Ford would be in jail. The coin was shopped at various places, until Ford found someone to buy it. He offered the Quarter Eagle at $700. Unfortunately, the expert knew the value and would only buy it for $550. As the coin's owner was sending telegrams asking about its whereabouts—not to mention that the bank wanted to know what was going on—Ford took the deal. After paying off the bank for handling the coin and the "teller for his trouble," Ford made $25. This transaction was typical of his moxie at even a very young age.

John J. Ford Jr. stood out as a wonder kid in the late 1930s and early 1940s due to his instincts and amazing memory for the tiniest of details. His reputation was increasing even before he had completely memorized the Adams-Woodin text. Then he decided that coin patterns were low priced. This realization allowed him to deal very successfully with the New York City dealers in the area, following the commonsense rule of buying low and selling higher.

He would spot trends, work a decent profit, and collect at the same time. World War II slowed his activities down because he joined the U.S. Army and spent his time reading intelligence dossiers. Afterward, he worked for Stacks again, and then began doing business with Charles Wormser who ran New Netherlands, which was the coin department of the Scott Stamp and Coin Company.

Wormser was very impressed with how this young man understood the different aspects of coinage and numismatics, their basic value, and the art of making a deal. Within months he "basically" offered Ford a 50/50 deal. The two men ran New Netherlands Coin Company from the 1950s into the 1960s—a long time for numismatic partnerships. At night, Ford would retire and read coin books while others partied or took time off.

Another numismatic "legend in the making" joined their operations early on when Walter Breen came to their firm. After he graduated from Johns Hopkins in one year, Breen joined New Netherlands in the spring of 1952. In an interview with Mark Van Winkle for Heritage Galleries in 1990, Ford described his approach:

> The philosophy of putting all this information in auction catalogues was mine. The philosophy of an unconditional guarantee was mine. And the philosophy of describing every nick, blemish, cut, and defect was mine. The theory was that if you tell them about the flaws, they can't easily return the item. This resulted in our getting the highest prices in the coin business, because my "Very Fine" would be everybody else's "Extremely Fine," so I would get a much higher price for "Very Fine" than anybody else.

John J. Ford Jr.'s approach of "undergrading" coins was controversial, to say the least. He liked it, did it, and didn't care what anyone else in the industry thought. This approach was certainly better, however, than "overgrading" coins where people paid more for less.

The industry is known for its wheeling and dealing. One day, a bank teller called Ford and said that he had these "funny-looking" half dollars and asked about Ford's interest when he was at New Netherlands. These coins were rare fifty-cent pieces called "Long Islands," and they had been sitting in a bank vault since 1936. Once a month for three months, Ford bought a bag of the coins from $2,500 to $3,500 per bag. He then resold each coin wholesale at five dollars and made a fine profit.

In another 1957 deal, the wife of an ambassador wanted to buy a very rare doubloon. Ford found the owner of the piece and told him that he'd pay $12,000 for the coin, apparently discovered in

1899 by workmen who were digging a sewer in Philadelphia. At this time, the sum of $12,000 would buy six new cars. After Walter Breem briefed Ford on all of the details of the doubloon, the woman came to the office. After answering her questions for thirty minutes, she momentarily inspected the coin, said it was fine, and dropped it into her purse. Ford earned $2,500 on the one deal, selling it for his cost and fee.

In 1971, Ford left his association with New Netherlands Coin Company and worked as an independent dealer. His career continued to flourish as he worked with others as a consultant (including with Christie's on the *S.S. Central America*'s gold bars). He also bought and sold valuable collectibles. For over fifty years, Ford assembled the most complete collections ever attempted in areas ranging from Confederate bonds and gold bars to merchant tokens, territorial gold, and numismatic manuscripts. As Mark Van Winkle observed in his interviews with John Ford, "The man followed a pattern in which he centered on the less traveled areas of the U.S. numismatic world." He treasured history and collected historical pieces, ranging from an original Confederate half dollar and Continental dollar to assay ingots.

To say that John J. Ford Jr. was unique is an understatement. In 1986, *Coin World* published an article entitled "Ford Has Special Shelter for Sale" and told the world about the fallout shelter he had in his New York home that was now his "numismatic vault." Since he was moving from the New York area to Arizona, Ford's old house and the 187-ton nuclear blast shelter—designed to survive a ten-megaton and five-mile surface blast—was put up for sale. Ford had converted it into "a quiet, comfortable place to sort and list coins and things." The structure by itself was massive.

In the fall of 1952, Ford met up with Paul Franklin, a brilliant engineer with an addiction to finding old gold coins and bars. Ford later wrote that no single event triggered his exploration of the unknown areas of the "pioneer gold field" more than his meeting with Franklin at the Brooklyn Coin Club. Franklin was "a specialist in odd and unusual numismatic items, and he also resided in New York with a comparable keen interest in the American West." Franklin had discovered two mixed (gold and silver) assay ingots,* and Ford purchased them from him. These discoveries were the famous (or infamous) 1860 Parsons & Company twenty-dollar monetary ingots. Ford in turn sold them and, eventually, these gold bars worked their way via Stack's into the Lilly Collection. Later, Ford even gave Paul Franklin a bonus for finding the 1860 Parsons piece.

As he studied the first gold ingots, Ford became "more and more interested." He asked Franklin if he could find others. Franklin liked Ford and their mutual interests, so he agreed and started to search for more ingots. For several years prior to their meeting, Franklin traveled throughout the West on vacations with his family. He had friends from his Army days in the Southwest and an ability to easily meet and make new ones.

From his World War II service, Paul Franklin knew one man who was in charge of the linemen for local Southwestern Bell telephone companies. During the early 1950s, the men worked in small towns in New Mexico, Arizona, and Nevada. Franklin set up a network of these telephone field men, friends, ex-Army buddies, and others who sought out old or promising coins or ingots. They found them in jewelry shops, pawn shops, banks, antique stores, and assay offices, located anywhere from the smallest of ghost towns to cities the size of El Paso and Phoenix. When someone located something, Franklin routed the information to John Ford, and if the piece looked promising enough, Franklin flew from his Long Island home to the town and purchased the piece. He wired the money at other times to Franklin's friends or agents, who then acquired the gold coins or ingots for Ford's account. Through the New Netherlands Coin Company, John Ford supplied the needed capital, coin and ingot assessments, and marketing expertise.

Franklin joined the Arizona Small Mine Owners Association and

*Assay ingots were bars made by assayers from the miner's melted gold or silver and generally stamped with the weight in ounces, a serial number, and fineness.

advertised in the available mining trade magazines, papers, and journals. By the mid-1950s, the venture printed circulars with pictures and descriptions of gold coins and assay ingots. The elaborate handout explained what numismatic bars and ingots were, and it illustrated the various pioneer gold coins, Western paper currencies, and assay bars. The venture printed thousands of these flyers with Paul Franklin's name and address, and he distributed them throughout the Western states. People with items of possible importance were asked to tell Franklin what they had, or, preferably, to send him a pencil rubbing. After a wide distribution of these circulars, Ford spent weeks in 1956 and 1957 visiting Western ghost towns and out-of-the-way places as he appraised the items.

Basically, Franklin was finding the unique pieces and Ford was researching and selling them. John Ford also kept items for himself that had a "particular personal interest." Their working relationship was simple: Each kept their contacts—whether acquisition or resale—to themselves. Franklin wouldn't tell Ford where he found the objects, but he did agree to tell Ford the original source names whenever possible for the needed research. In turn, Ford wouldn't reveal to Franklin the names of his contacts or customers when reselling the items. He wrote:

> Since a great many of the items he (Franklin) unearthed were unknown or not previously published, it was my responsibility to find out exactly what they were, and why and when they were made. In instance after instance, Franklin argued with me, always taking the conservative position.

The project lasted "twelve or fifteen" years and then fewer and fewer ingots were located. Ford bought the last gold assay ingot in 1981 from Franklin.

Paul Franklin worked from the 1960s as an antique gun dealer in Phoenix, Arizona, and he made the rounds of all the gun shows in the Southwest, coming across more prized pieces. John J. Ford commented: "Over the years, he (Franklin) located some really fabulous material, some of which is in the Lilly Collection (at the Smithsonian). Some items ended up in the Norweb and Clifford Collections, and I still own some interesting pieces that Franklin unearthed."

An example of Franklin's working relationship with John Ford is seen in what is called the "golden spoon" incident. Ford told Franklin that he wanted a very rare, particular gold spoon (created in 1849 by Broderick and Kohler, a private San Francisco gold-coin mint and jeweler). Paul told him the owner didn't want to sell the item, and that he didn't know how to get it. At the next coin show, Ford, Franklin, and others headed out to grab a bite to eat. Since everyone ordered soup, Ford joined in. As he looked over at Franklin, he saw that his venture-partner was eating the soup with a gold spoon, just as if he always ate with one. Ford couldn't believe what he was seeing, so he reached over, grabbed the spoon, and cleaned it off. Inspecting it closely, he saw that the spoon was stamped Broderick and Kohler. At the time, there were only two known Broderick and Kohler gold spoons in existence. Franklin had found one of them for Ford.

THE STORY of the alleged counterfeit U.S. Assay Office gold pieces shows how Ford and Franklin made finds that were controversial. According to Ford, Paul Franklin in 1956 to 1957 "stumbled into a spectacular find of 1852 to 1853 United States Assay Office gold coins, alloy assays, patterns, lead trials, proofing pieces, and ingots. Practically everything was new and unpublished. There was even a rusted steel die."

On one of his trips west, Paul Franklin found an Arizona bank employee who had an assay office $20 gold piece. He bought it for one hundred dollars, a price that was then well below wholesale. Every time Franklin visited the bank, the teller would have two or three additional pieces. According to Ford, the coins were "proof-like, well handled, 1853, '.900 Fine' Double Eagles, and some of them were a lot better than others." When John Ford concluded that these and the other pieces were genuine, they decided to find out where all of this was coming from and to try and purchase all of them.

Franklin investigated and later discovered that the bank teller at the Phoenix, Arizona, area bank was getting his coins from the bank president. In 1934, he had been a teller there, when all of the coins had to be turned in as gold bullion. This was due to the the federal legislation that declared any such public holdings illegal. The senior bank officer apparently kept much of what was turned in twenty-three years earlier, and he was handing them out to the young teller, who was a relative. The bank president then directed Franklin to an elderly man in his eighties who lived on an Arizona ranch with the bulk of the hoard. However, the owner didn't want his relatives to know what he had or was selling. The following year, Franklin purchased most of what was left for the venture.

The items included seven perfect, proof-like 1853 U.S.A.O.G. ".900 Fine" $20 gold pieces, which Franklin acquired direct from the rancher on one of his Phoenix trips. With three other "impaired impressions," the coins were wrapped in "three or four old, yellow linen handkerchiefs." Eight of the pieces had their weight marked on the handkerchiefs in lead pencil, and a few of the coins also had the alloys and the precise fineness similarly inscribed. Franklin and Ford worked out a price and bought all of the pieces. Concerned that his family might find out he was selling the coins for a lot of money, however, the old man insisted on keeping the handkerchiefs. In spite of the man's reluctance to give out information, Franklin became convinced that the seven perfect specimens, along with the impaired ones, were "experimental alloy strikings." As with other deals, Ford personally purchased two of the assays for his collections and New Netherlands resold the other five. Ford recorded the gold-piece weights, but he didn't have any metallic analyses conducted.

One of the "perfect proof" pieces sold progressively through several dealers and collectors. Four or five years later, someone told the latest owner that the piece couldn't be genuine. When John Ford heard about these allegations, he offered to refund what he had received for selling the item. All the other dealers offered to give up their profits and refund money up the line—except for one—and this killed the rescission that everyone was agreeing to do. The last owner of the proof went ballistic, and he wrote angry articles to the media and congressmen about being defrauded. The entire matter wound up in a 1966 Professional Numismatists Guild (PNG) arbitration, whose members are considered to be some of the world's leading rare coin and paper money experts. The arbitration was held between the last two dealer/collectors in the chain, the last one arguing the proof was a fraud, and the seller arguing that it was genuine.

As with most of these situations, the people who questioned the authenticity of the coin hired their own expert to make their case. At the first PNG arbitration meeting held at the 1966 American Numismatic Association (ANA) Convention in Chicago, their expert concluded that the coins were false (modern counterfeits struck from cast dies), that Franklin was a forger, and that Ford had been duped. As the defender of the gold piece, Ford was given one year to prepare a reply to those claims. A maxim in the numismatic world is that it's always more difficult to prove that an item is authentic than to make the charge that it's false. Although determining authenticity in the field of numismatics is always difficult and complex, Ford presented his defense at the next year's ANA Convention in Miami.

After hearing Ford's presentation that the piece was genuine, the PNG arbitration panel met in the following year and declared that the twenty dollar gold coin was not a proof, but, according to Ford, "Said nothing either way concerning its authenticity. The U.S.A.O.G. twenty-dollar gold piece went back to the last seller. I bought it from him in 1971 and sold it to Stack's."

Although many of the "Franklin Hoard" pieces were sold to Ford and his New Netherlands Coin Company, Paul Franklin placed various pieces privately that Ford didn't have an interest in. Franklin also was a skilled metallurgist; the criticisms of his and Ford's work was that he could have created some of the pieces sold to Ford. A number of expert numismatics discount these allegations arguing that Ford's reputation was worth considerably more than what he could have obtained by dealing in fakes. Also, they maintain that these allegations were based on professional jealousies and that numismatics is an art—never an exact science.

The easiest certification of a gold ingot is that one not only has the design, markings, and alloy composition of that era, but that it has a "pedigree"—or is discovered in some way that indicates it's genuine. For example, a bank locates a deposit of 1858 gold coins in its vaults, recorded as being deposited there in 1858. This doesn't happen very often. The challenges start when these collections are in the hands of people who hoarded them and never kept records. Many finds have this problem.

The presence of pedigree, or a documented history, isn't conclusive evidence as to whether a coin is genuine or not. On the other hand, this can be helpful and supportive. Technical evidence, such as the metallic composition, weight, die characteristics, surface anomalies, and other factors, however, combined with pedigree can become near-conclusive evidence of authenticity. There is always a problem in determining the genuineness of unique pieces, and experts can always disagree among themselves on any particular piece.

To understand why gold bars and coins were hoarded privately and sold secretly without pedigree—as they were from the 1930s to 1970s—one needs to look at the Great Depression. By the spring of 1932, hundreds and hundreds of banks across the entire United States were folding, and millions of depositors had lost some or all of their hard-earned deposits and savings. Federally mandated insured deposits in banks, thrifts, and savings and loan institutions had not yet come into existence. As people waited in long lines to close their accounts and pull their money out, to the extent any bank funds were left, the others ahead of them cashed in their deposits for gold and gold certificates. Depositors sucked out gold at the rate of $20 million per day and there was substantially less cash to support the much greater amounts of deposits on record.

President-elect Franklin Roosevelt was inaugurated on March 4 of that year; in the two days before his inauguration, Americans cleaned out one-half billion dollars from the nation's banks. With the U.S. dollar now virtually worthless, the country's citizens were using scrip, stamps, credit, barter, and even streetcar tokens as money. In five days, Congress rushed through legislation, which Roosevelt quickly signed into law.

Among other provisions, this law prohibited the ownership of gold. The names of everyone who withdrew gold were published. The act was designed to force people to bring their gold back to the government in return for paper money. Paper currency was now legal, gold was not, and inflation as an official government policy was born. As an exception to this law, people could own historical gold objects, provided these were not used for monetary transactions in any way.

Not wishing to declare his illegally held discovery, and understandably wanting to keep them, the lucky finder of the eleven *Brother Jonathan* gold bars secretly stowed away his treasure for years. At the same time, Franklin and his cadre of men started to comb the small towns, curios shops, antique stores, and coin dealers for what Ford would want to buy or resell. It was only a matter of time before Franklin and his legionnaires ran into the story about the fisherman's gold bars.

In the mid- to late-1950s, they came across the fisherman's family. From there, the *Brother Jonathan* and Western assay gold bars made their way into the hands of John J. Ford, a wealthy Californian, Clark Clifford, and other collectors—including one Josiah Lilly.

THE FIRM OF ELI LILLY and Company grew from humble beginnings to one of the world's largest pharmaceutical companies. Born in 1893, Josiah Kirby Lilly, Jr., was the grandson of the founder. He collected things from the time he was a child, beginning with his first movie theater ticket stubs. After finishing college in 1914, he joined the family firm. He served in France during WWI where he continued to collect things for fifty years. After the war he returned to work in the family business and in 1948 succeeded his brother as president. Later he became Lilly's chairman of the board, a position he held until his death.

Josiah Lilly collected coins, bars, and ingots from every era and realm, whether it was from ancient Greece, Rome, Byzantium, Mexico, or even modern Western America. Lilly created a huge coin and stamp room with special desks, cabinets, and tables just to accommodate these extraordinary acquisitions. He also collected stamps, gems, guns, eighteenth-century paintings, rare books, and marine memorabilia. He owned a seven-thousand piece miniature toy soldier exhibit. His book collection numbered twenty-thousand acquisitions and his rare manuscripts alone came to seventeen-thousand items.

He kept many of his collections in museums at his private estate, Eagle Crest, on 3,469 acres in Indianapolis. The mansion was built in a French-country home style as seen in old Victorian England, and the grounds included a variety of exquisite formal gardens, tennis court, cottages, barn, large greenhouse, fruit and vegetable gardens, orchards, recreational building with a large indoor pool, and other structures. The television program *American Castles* featured his mansion and grounds on one of its shows.

He was a distinguished-looking man with a thin mustache and a "British look and air" about him, preferring to be well dressed in a proper suit. A highly secretive person with a Midas-like love of gold, Josiah had the money and the compulsion to purchase whatever he wanted or drew his attention. When a particularly good "find" came along, the premier dealers would instantly contact him. Harvey Stack of Stack's Coin Company—one of the country's most respected coin dealers with offices on West 57 Street in Manhattan—was one of his favorites. At least twice a year, Harvey would meet with Josiah and the two men at lunch would pore over Lilly's gold interests. "He (Josiah Lilly) had a pirate's chest and put some of the coins in it," Harvey Stack stated in one interview.

Lilly bought about forty gold ingot and assay bars, including several of the *Brother Jonathan* gold bars, numbers of which John Ford turned over to Stack. According to John Ford, the bars carried an illustrious history of colonial Mexico and of colorful Gold Rush miners who had dug the metal from the earth. Ford had acquired these bars from his venture with the treasure hunter, Paul Franklin.

The Western gold bars primarily included assay bars from the private assayers who melted down the miners' gold, removed impurities, and forged the precious metal into bars. These bars were then used as currency or converted into coins at a U.S. Mint. Gold coins were also melted down into ingots, stamped by the assayer, and then carried to a new place to be reconverted into gold coins as useful currency there.

When Lilly died in 1967, the Smithsonian Museum in Washington wanted his collection of coins and gold bars so badly that Congress passed special legislation one year later to grant a $5.5 million tax break to Lilly's estate in return for receiving the artifacts. The exquisite collection dates back to the earliest of Grecian and Roman times and is comprised of 6,115 numismatic objects and fifty gold ingots and bars. However, the public holding or ability to transfer gold still wouldn't be legalized for another six years. Now known as the Lilly Collection at the Smithsonian's National Museum of American History, the exhibit includes some of the items that Paul Franklin and his men discovered.

The Lilly Collection held a large number of the assay ingots and gold bars that originated with Franklin, as well as its pioneer gold-coin section including a number of rarities that Ford had authenticated. When the U.S. Government was deciding on its acquisition of the Lilly numismatic material by granting a tax credit, it consulted with the Bureau of the Mint, Bureau of Standards, and Treasury Department, as well as the Secret Service, FBI, congressional staffers, and others with information about this collection and its items. The museum's curator also vouched for the collection, and once the authentication was completed, the Smithsonian acquired the Lilly Collection. This exquisite collection is today worth over one hundred million dollars.

MEANWHILE, JOHN FORD continued to acquire and resell the various gold bars and coins located by Paul Franklin, the self-taught mechanical engineer. Ford sold at least three 1853 $20 gold coins that were part of the wide assortment of collectibles moving through Stack's to Lilly. During the late 1960s and early 1970s, the Museum of American Money at Union Bank in San Francisco obtained twenty assay gold bars from Ford, of which he had authenticated most as being from the Gold Rush days.

Ford began his search for the original owner of the fisherman's gold bars and what was the history or story behind them. All the while no one even knew where the ghost ship of the *Brother Jonathan* was. All was quiet until 1973 when Professor Ted Buttrey gave a talk entitled "False Mexican Colonial Gold Bars," at the International Numismatic Congress in New York. He argued that the bars dated with the years 1741 and 1746 had a stamped design that was not in use at that time. Another bar from the 1740s, he alleged, contained assayer's initials that were used only in 1770 and 1771. Buttrey associated John Ford and Paul Franklin with these acquisitions.

Like John J. Ford and everyone else associated with this continuing controversy, Buttrey is an established and well-respected numismatist, although depending on whom one talks to now, he also is controversial. Mr. Buttrey's biography also reads like a "Who's Who" of coin and numismatic experts. During his career, he was the president of the Royal Numismatic Society in England, a chairman of the department of Classics at the University of Michigan, and the "keeper of the coins" at the Fitzwilliam Museum of Cambridge University in England.

Prior to the 1973 allegations by Professor Buttrey, John Ford had visited the National Archives and San Francisco Mint. This resulted in the discovery of information concerning the found *Brother Jonathan* bars, although Ford said that it was "incomplete." The first public offering of the *Jonathan*'s gold bars, an ingot stamped number 2186, was at a 1974 Stack's auction known as the Gibson sale. The heading read, "Allegedly from the Wreck of the Side-Wheel Steamer *Brother Jonathan*," and the text stated:

> It is strongly believed that all eleven ingots were indirectly obtained from the wreck of the *Brother Jonathan*. The ingots could well have represented the personal property of one of the cabin passengers. It is probable that these eleven ingots

> were salvaged adjacent to the wreck. Another probability is that they could have been looted from trunks or other luggage of the victims as the flotsam drifted ashore. Failing that, they could have long been held by people who originally obtained them from contemporary looters. The source of these ingots apparently had them in his family for many years and seemed well acquainted with the story of the *Brother Jonathan.*

The ship's gold bars had moved from Paul Franklin to John J. Ford, then to private collectors. After five gold bars on display at the Bank of California were subsequently returned to Ford, three were in the hands of different collectors and eight were in the Ford collection. The bar brought $19,000 at the auction versus its bullion value at the time of $2,750.

Even though the ship's gold bars were in the hands of collectors, the *Brother Jonathan* itself remained undiscovered and a mystery. No one knew where it was, although the search continued.

CHAPTER 10

The City, a Psychologist, and the Ghost Ship

Commercial fishing craft operate along with an ever-increasing number of pleasure and sports-fishing boats in Crescent City Harbor. Ancillary businesses such as boat repair and maintenance, marine supplies, and equipment repair have grown around the industry. The commercial boats catch shrimp, Dungeness crab, salmon, swordfish, and bottom fish such as flounder, sole, rockfish, and albacore dating back to its settlement days. Crescent City was and is still a leading port for crab and shrimp tonnage in California. This business is cold, grueling, dangerous work given the raging winds and pounding seas that can so swiftly rear up. Sudden windstorms and crashing waves capsize fishing vessels and drown men every year along this coastline.

Blessed with a seemingly endless supply of redwood and pine trees, since the 1850s the area has been a center for logging, milling, and manufacturing lumber and plywood. However, the industry has had its economic fluctuations, and the people have learned to live with them. Living on the coast, the residents also aren't strangers to the hurricane-force winter storms and high tides that surge over their beaches.

There always had been a sense of community in Crescent City, due in part to the isolation and dependence on one another, as well as living in a small town. It was then and still is an older town with mainly wood-frame houses and one-and two-story buildings. For years, the local timber industry, commercial fishing, tourism, and the local shops and services accounted for most of its economy.

By the 1960s, the town was a mixture of quaint curio shops, small museums, woodcarving stores, fishing and bait shops, bars, and restaurants that catered to the summer tourist trade. Welding shops, timber supply, boat repair, and local department stores serviced the locals. Some seventy-five lumber mills and seven plywood and veneer plants were located in and around the surrounding Del Norte County, which supplied employment for Crescent City people—although this industry has declined dramatically since then.

On Good Friday, March 27, 1964, a watershed calamity changed the face of Crescent City. An 8.4 Richter-scale earthquake off Alaska created local tsunamis, including a trans-Pacific tsunami that coursed down the entire U.S. West Coast, centering its destructive powers on the city. Within the space of two hours, four surges decimated the downtown section, inundating sixty blocks, destroying thirty city blocks, destroying or damaging 289 structures and businesses, and officially killing eleven people. Seventy-five more were injured while others were missing and are presumed dead. The seas had crashed in, as documented in the book, *The Raging Sea,* by this author, and struck at the town's economic viability.

Bolstered by the renewed dollars flowing in during the tsunami reconstruction, the building of its Tsunami Landing Mall, and other redevelopment projects, however, Crescent City enjoyed somewhat better economic times for three years. The Army Engineers eventually built Beachfront Park by filling a two-block by ten-block area with landfill to bring the area fifteen feet above sea level and act as a protection against another tsunami. The engineers composed the fill from the material dredged up from Crescent City Harbor in the wave's aftermath, along with the rubble of the ripped-up gutters, streets, and sidewalks left behind in the destruction.

When a national building slump in 1967 particularly affected California, the local economy skidded once again. The initial boost to the economy from the rebuilding of the tsunami-ravaged parts of the town had fallen off. As lumbering and milling businesses closed their doors, residents left Del Norte County and Crescent City in numbers. The decline of the timber industry in Northern California and Southern Oregon continued to be especially hard over the following years, followed by more recent declines in the fishing industries due to state and federal environmental regulations and worldwide competitive trends.

Fortunately, diving and salvage expeditions for the *Brother Jonathan* allowed Crescent City residents to enjoy the money that these operations provided. They were a boon to local motels, cafes, dive shops, boat operators, and bars, especially since these explorations again and again were unsuccessful. Although the people were friendly and worked with whomever needed help, there was a secret hope that the vessel wouldn't be found—it was after all their ghost ship—or that one of their own would discover it. The *Brother Jonathan* had taken on a life of its own, along with the 1964 tsunami, as a prime tourist attraction.

Arriving during the summer months, tourists were drawn by the legends of the *Jonathan*. They took tours to the Point St. George Lighthouse, walked to see the Crescent City Lighthouse during low tide, and paid for charter boats to see or dive where the vessel might be. The lost vessel became part of the town's folklore, just as the tsunami was with its "Tsunami Landing" shopping mall, "Tsunami Lanes" (bowling alley), and other places such as the "Tsunami Bar."

As one expedition after another proved unsuccessful, the *Brother Jonathan* became a ghost ship. People were sure that it had existed—but then again—did it really? As salvors announced that they found the ship's remains, a later report followed that explained—due to inclement weather, bad currents, or some equipment malfunction—that the precise point couldn't be located again. From being drunk or unable to take a reading in bad weather, the reasons varied. After the excitement died down, residents simply shrugged their shoulders and went about their lives. From diving bells and deep-sea divers in antiquated equipment to more sophisticated sonar readings in later years, air surveys, and mini-submarines, the *Brother Jonathan* stayed elusive.

DR. LARRY HOLCOMB, a psychologist for the Del Norte County Unified School District during the week, was an adventurer during the weekends. He left his mother's and stepfather's house in 1952 when he was fourteen years old to escape their battles. Convincing the owners of a fishing camp to hire him as a guide in return for bed and board, Holcomb showed his ability to handle difficult situations at an early age. When the fishing season ended that late summer, Holcomb next secured a job as a pond hand at one of Crescent City's lumber mills. He worked his way through school with no financial support and earned his doctorate from the University of Oregon.

A lifelong resident of Crescent City, Holcomb spent twenty years collecting what information he could about the *Brother Jonathan* and where it could have disappeared. He was a close friend of John Fraser, who was also a Del Norte County supervisor, and the two discussed at length how they could locate the missing vessel. As Fraser commented later in an interview,

> Growing up in Crescent City, you can't help but be attracted to the sea and the *Brother Jonathan.* You stand on the rocky cliffs overlooking the ocean knowing that somewhere on the bottom, not too far offshore, lie the remains of that ship.

Larry told the story that he and John Fraser had an old history teacher in high school, whose father had been ten years old when the *Brother Jonathan* sank. He told about walking the beach with other residents looking for bodies. The connection between the past and the present with the ship and Crescent City remained strong over time.

Holcomb searched the National Archives in Washington, D.C., corresponded with the relatives of those who had perished, and scoured the reports of those who survived. Dr. Holcomb even contacted the Canadian government, when he discovered that it had sent a salvage ship to Crescent City in 1914 to search for the gold. Canada's interest was when it received unverified reports that the vessel had been carrying in excess of one million dollars of gold bullion for delivery to the Canadian government.

Holcomb and seven others formed the Brother Jonathan Company in the early 1970s. Each member brought along a special skill—which was important when capital was limited and skills in short supply. Three divers, an undersea photographer, a metal-detector operator, and an electrical engineer joined Holcomb and Fraser. One member, Lorin Bosch, was from a family that had hunted for the *Brother Jonathan* in the nineteenth century; his grandfather was a diver who had searched during the 1880s and 1890s for the downed ship.

The California State Lands Commission (CSLC) also entered the picture and told Holcomb that it flatly would not approve the usual permits for offshore exploration in its "coastal waters." The CSLC felt that it had the sole right "to determine who did what and at what cost." Rather than fighting an uncooperative city hall, the group decided to accept a one-sided, exorbitant deal. In return for the permit, and not having to fight them in court as the CSLC threatened, California would receive 25 percent of anything discovered up to $25,000 and one-half of everything found above that amount. For not putting up one dime of capital, nor giving any assistance in finding the wreck other than supervising any eventual recovery, the CSLC did very well indeed—although its heavy-handed approach to the deal eventually pressed later entrepreneurs to enter the courts and reverse the state's inequitable approach.

The State of California and its commission said that they wanted to protect the public from the "unscrupulous" recovery efforts of salvors and safeguard precious artifacts. Rather than work with the groups in that regard, however, they took total control of all activities and one-half of all proceeds ($25,000 was an unreasonably low amount for cost reimbursement)—a position quite different from the much less punitive approach of most other states described later in this book. The CSLC also took the stance that it owned *any* sunken wreck within three miles of the coastline (and as measured from any reef or outcropping in the sea), a view that clashed with longtime federal maritime law.

In the early to mid-1970s, Holcomb and his group started with their recovery efforts using divers and support ships. They raised capital to pay for the work of Intersea Research and General Oceanographics, two major La Jolla firms specializing in high-tech underwater research. The Brother Jonathan Company would now use proton magnetometers, side-scan sonars, and computers that could create instantaneous printouts of the ocean floor. The salvors also contracted to use a two-man submarine with cramped quarters. The pilot's upper body completely fills the conning tower while the observer, lying prone under the pilot's feet, looks out a lower front-port window.

The group contracted for a four and one-half square mile survey of the ocean floor around Jonathan Rock. It also arranged for the use of sophisticated rangefinders, which can pinpoint any given spot on the ocean floor within three yards. On the successful discovery of the ship and its treasure, Dr. Holcomb even considered raising the hull in one piece, either by using a giant crane from an overhead barge or with "air-escape" (floatation) balls. Holcomb, additionally, signed a contract with a film company to document the search.

Receiving a listing of forty-five "hot spots" where Intersea Research's equipment indicated that a man-made object of "sizable proportions" rested, the group brought in the mini-sub to investigate. One afternoon in June 1975, the two-man crew of the leased mini-sub slowly motored at the bottom of the ocean some two hundred and fifty feet below the surface. John Fraser observed:

> This is one of the most treacherous areas along the Pacific Coast. We know of eleven other ships at the bottom off our shores, ships that crashed into huge rocks that litter the bay. There's seldom a calm day in the waters off Crescent City. Most of the time, white caps slam into shore.

The visibility at that depth and conditions was two to three feet. Despite their use of a strong light for illumination, the men had to be very careful in their navigation. The underwater turbulence rocked the submarine back and forth as the crewmen looked for any signs of a sunken ship. Cruising at one- to two-miles-per-hour, the mini-sub poked along the bottom.

The crewmen suddenly felt a strong bump, and the electric motor whined. Immediately cutting the battery-powered engine, the two crewmen peered outside the port windows. They were speechless and felt a chill at the sight. An arched doorway loomed close to the sub's "bubble view port," and its barnacled timbers seemed to be from a very large, old wooden ship. As they stared at what they had run into, the men saw that the sub's longer protruding cylinder was under what appeared to be a submerged bow.

The men immediately radioed the mother ship that they had located what looked to be the *Brother Jonathan* and had started videotaping what seemed to be an arched doorway. On the surface, Holcomb listened elatedly to the initial radio statement. It had to be the long-missing ghost ship. He then heard the excited voice exclaim, "But we're under the bow of the wreck and timbers are on top of the sub. Do you read me?"

In the space of ten seconds, the feelings of elation changed to the apprehension heard in the crewman's voice. Both Holcomb and the crew agreed that the sub should pull in reverse, but slowly at first. A minute ticked by, then another. The operator radioed that this didn't seem to work, quickly adding "Any other thoughts other than the ballast tanks?"

The expedition didn't have another mini-sub or divers handy that could descend and free the submarine. To be trapped under debris that deep could be a death sentence, and everyone above and below the ocean knew it. These mini-subs didn't carry batteries with long lives for power and had a limited air supply. The one piece of good news was that the propeller wasn't fouled, as this would have ended nearly any chance of the crew's survival.

"Do you read me?" said the nervous voice. "We seem to be trapped." Everyone's concern was now on saving the men.

The best solution was to let the water in the ballast tanks out, replace that space with air, and at the same time push the propeller into a hard reverse. The mini-sub crew and those on the mother ship quickly agreed.

The radio went silent. The minutes ticked by. Finally, the report came, "We are free. We're floating upwards to the surface." Holcomb again felt jubilation, but this time for the crewmen. He then realized and yelled into the radio, "Did you release the marker buoy, so that we can position the wreck?"

"Negative," the crewman replied. Without the buoy to mark the site, finding that spot again would be very difficult. The expedition didn't have positioning coordinates at this spot, nor did the exploration have a precise way to find the ship again. All they could do was send the sub down to cruise around the same site, with the same poor visibility, at a future time.

On the other hand, Larry knew that the video would show the long-lost ship, and he could secure more investment funds for continued exploration. Although the mini-sub centered on that area for the duration of the scheduled time, the men were not able to find the spot again. The submarine could be five feet from the ship and the observer could just miss seeing it, not to mention that the ocean currents at those depths had kicked up with the underwater turbulence becoming "unbelievable." The divers would hit these currents and be diving blind under those conditions.

After the last dive, the sub reported that a huge ling cod swam lazily by, a half-devoured octopus hanging from its mouth. Other than observing large sea life mere feet away from the observation bubble, the crewmen didn't find anything resembling what they had run into before. When Dr. Holcomb looked at his copy of the videotape, he discovered that due to mechanical failure the tape didn't cover the important parts of that dive, including the time when the mini-sub entered the archway. They never could find that specific location again.

* * *

ONE YEAR LATER, in 1976, thirty-eight-year-old Holcomb announced that his group had discovered the long-lost treasure ship at a depth of 132 feet. He said that their divers had located the "completely encrusted hull" of a wooden ship the size of the *Brother Jonathan* and had set foot on the hull "a half dozen times" in recent weeks. Conceding the difficulty of identifying "anything specific," the age-old problems of lack of visibility and the inability of divers to stay down for any length of time rose again. The technology to send down a remote-controlled vehicle with robot arms and a TV monitor was not yet available, nor would it have been affordable for this group.

Dr. Holcomb tried to raise more funds to find the wreck. Once again the newspapers published great descriptions of the lost ship's wealth from the provided information:

> Twenty-five cases of gold coins bound for the Pacific Northwest; a safe filled with $200,000 of still-negotiable greenbacks; possible gold bullion and bars, of which eleven pieces were recovered back in 1935; some $3 million being transported by Vincent Smith to a government post; and thirty kegs of whiskey now worth $30,000 a barrel.

He then decided to make a movie and raise the necessary exploration capital from that venture. Finding ten new backers to invest the money for a script, Larry created Bro-Jon Productions in 1976. From friends at the University of Oregon, Holcomb secured Ken Kesey's phone number and called him for advice. Kesey, the author of *One Flew over the Cuckoo's Nest,* said that he would be interested. That following weekend, Kesey drove a 1960s group bus down from Oregon to Crescent City to talk with him. According to Holcomb, "Everybody had been partying pretty hard on the way down, and it took us about four days to get down to business." Accompanied by his wife, a "long-haired" film director, and a few others, the deal started looking good. However, Kesey's agent entered the discussions and, according to Holcomb, demanded large sums of money upfront for Kesey's screenplay development and participation. That ended the discussions.

Still looking for money to finance the Brother Jonathan Company after its mid-1970 expeditions, Holcomb decided seven years later, to partner a commercial fishing venture for shrimp in southeastern Alaska. Holcomb slipped and fell during that first season, however, and pulled his back muscles. Just before he was to be released from the hospital, the attendants dropped the stretcher carrying him and the impact shattered one of his discs when he hit the hard floor. He needed immediate back surgery.

Back in Crescent City, Holcomb's financial affairs became worse. His partner in the shrimping business died, leaving him with large unpaid bills on his fishing boat, the *Double Eagle,* along with the hospital bills. Holcomb had to sell most of his shares in the Brother Jonathan Company to pay off those debts.

However, what sets Larry Holcomb apart is his attitude. He said later:

> I'm always going to have three "hots and a cot." Look life's the vacation. You can take it in Crescent City looking for the *Brother Jonathan* or you can take it in southeast Alaska. I don't want to give up what share I have left in the *Brother Jonathan.* But, by the same token, if it came down to having to give up some of that in order to enhance my southeast Alaskan vacation, I'd do that in a second. I can't just sit around and wait for someday, because we don't have any control over those somedays, do we?

Searches continued through the 1980s aided by scuba divers and more side-scan sonar and magnetometers. In 1985, Hal Dryer formed a joint venture with the Brother Jonathan Company to try and find the wreck, "once and for all." Another company and experienced diver, Phil Holt, arrived from Anchorage, Alaska, to invest $50,000 and become part of this group. In 1987, the venture arranged for a jacked-up barge to hover over the designated site while divers in wetsuits searched from an adjacent boat, the *Lin-Dee.* This venture wasn't successful. Holcomb later said that his first announcement that they had located the ship was mistaken. By the end of the 1980s, divers had visited the wrecks of hundreds of sunken ships off the California coast—but the missing *Brother Jonathan* wasn't one of them.

Under Larry Holcomb and then its venture with Hal Dryer, the Brother Jonathan Company scoured the entire area north of Jonathan Rock. They looked for technical signs of something large sunk on the bottom. Although the group didn't find the ship, future salvors now knew where they didn't have to search in great detail.

One man had been quietly tracking the unsuccessful ventures of everyone else, however, while he studied the old records. He would have the persistence to continually face the overwhelming odds—and that man was Don Knight.

CHAPTER 11

Deep Sea Research

Donald G. Knight was born in 1942 in Medford, Oregon, a small rural place located forty miles from the California border. The area's prime industries then were logging, lumber manufacturing, and agriculture. Another employment base centered on tourism with salmon fishing on the Rogue River of Zane Gray fame, white-water kayaking, and elk hunting. The Rogue River courses its way around the city and eventually ends at the Pacific Ocean at Gold Beach, Oregon. Medford is a two-hour drive from Crescent City, mostly over Highway 199, a winding, narrow two-lane highway that still passes through towering forests and mountainous terrain.

Known by his family as Gerald, his middle name, Don attended local schools, before he dropped out in 1959 to join the U.S. Navy. Six feet tall with an athletic build, Knight was on Medford Senior High School's track and football teams, playing right offensive end in football.

Enlisting in the Navy, he served over ten years as a radar operator and radar technician, among other responsibilities. He was involved in the Bay of Pigs invasion (April 1961), the Cuban missile crisis (October 1962), and he spent three years in Vietnam (1964–1967). Knight experienced combat on the high seas, being on board the U.S.S. *Turner Joy* in the Gulf of Tonkin. The U.S. sank two torpedo boats and damaged a third from the North Vietnam naval base at Hon Me Island, which battle catapulted the United States into the Vietnam War.

After an honorable discharge in 1970, Don decided to complete his education. After receiving his Associate of Arts degree, Knight earned his B.A. from California State University-Fullerton with graduate studies in anthropology and an emphasis in archaeology. Degree in hand, Don worked on digs at three Southern California campsites that the Juaneno Native Americans lived on as early as 1000 B.C. While working as a salvage archaelogist in Orange County, his responsibility was to try and save historic artifacts before the developers began their earthmoving and building operations. After several negative experiences in this regard, in 1980, Knight decided to leave land operations and head out to sea to do a line of work where "there would be no developers' bulldozers." His approach was one of undersea historical and cultural preservation, and this orientation continued through to his involvement with the *Brother Jonathan.*

His father, Richard, worked most of his life as a skilled machinist, but changed occupation later to be a fireman. When his dad was seriously injured while fighting a large building fire, after his recuperation, Don's grandfather asked Richard to join him in his fishing business off Crescent City. After his grandfather purchased a forty-two-foot long commercial fishing boat in 1946, the *Roxy,* Richard commuted between Medford and Crescent City. His father did this for four years as part of its operation, until they sold the boat and he went back to working as a machinist.

When Don was thirteen, his father told him the story that changed his life. His dad had just read an article in the *Oregonian* about the *Brother Jonathan.* It triggered something in his mind about an experience he had on the high seas. While at the kitchen table with his son, Richard said to Don, "The *Brother Jonathan,* I know where it's at." For the first time, his father told him about the time he was fishing in the *Roxy* with Don's grandfather around Jonathan Rock. When they lost one of their crab pots, his dad threw out a five-pronged grappling hook on a weighted line to probe the bottom. When his father felt a strong downward tug, he started the boat's winch and pulled the grappling hook back to the surface. As the object broke the surface close to their boat, the men saw seaweed and sand sink from what was a "long piece of wood." When the seamen hoisted it up, they could tell that the wood was very old and "pliable like cardboard." It was part of an old ship's decking.

Several months later, his father was talking with several of the local fishermen about the old piece of wood that he had recovered. The men in turn told his dad that they had also pulled up debris from the same general place and that he had pulled up a piece of the *Brother Jonathan.* Up to that time, his dad had no idea about the ship or its history. His father didn't remember where the exact location was, except that the fishing was good around the area, and that fishermen lost their nets fairly easily in that location. His father bought a Morse diver's suit and apparatus, complete with lead boots and helmet.

After reading the book, *I Dive for Treasure,* by Lieutenant Harry E. Rieseberg, Richard bought the story about the *Brother Jonathan* "hook, line, and sinker." He told his son "We'll be rich." However, when Don's father tried the diver's suit in the ocean, he found that the suit leaked like a sieve. Richard put it away and never tried searching for the sunken ship again.

Don Knight greatly respected his father, and his love of the sea dated back to when his dad fished off Crescent City. Don joined the Navy, rather than "waste any more time in high school, opting to see the world and live it." In 1974, he read the same book and began his archival and library research on the *Brother Jonathan* that lasted twelve years. He spent considerable time in the archives of the National Archives, Library of Congress, San Francisco Maritime Museum, California Historical Society, and numbers of other depositories, compiling a five-foot high pile of documentation. His dad's death accelerated his passion to find the lost wreck. While spending his free time researching, Knight worked in fiberglass manufacturing.

He became certified during the same period as a scuba diver and gained the time to qualify in advanced scuba work. Between 1982 and 1984, Knight constructed a mock-up of a shallow water submersible for offshore surveying. Lying ahead of him, however, would be seven seasons of exploring the seas off Crescent City. His sister and brother-in-law resided there so he could stay without incurring expensive motel bills.

Tall with dark hair and eyes, Knight is a very detailed, bright, and charismatic person. He takes people at face value and, by his own admission, is the "most tenacious person that anybody will ever meet." He would need to rely on this characteristic during the years ahead.

CRESCENT CITY is a relatively isolated place even now. Its prime connection with the outside world is still through Highway 101's north and southbound coastal artery. The small Oregon beach town of Brookings is located some 15 miles to the north, while the tiny towns of Requa and Klamath are 20 miles to the south. The closest major town to the south is Eureka—a one-and-a-half-hour drive or 90 miles away by car, while San Francisco lies 375 miles away. Inland mountain ranges form a natural barricade sealing the coast from any other real highway access.

The nearby Redwood National and State Parks, Smith River National Recreation Area and Scenic Byway, and other wilderness areas surround the city. Jedediah Smith State Park with its massive trunks of old-growth redwood trees lies minutes from downtown. Crescent City was built on a level part of the lowlands by the sea and its slope gradually increases toward the mountains. It is a quaint and rugged city—attractive but not hit with the "cutes" like a Santa Barbara or Carmel.

The local economy showed small but discouraging growth during the seventies, then declined during the general boom times of the eighties. Owing to extensive declines in the area's timber and fishing industries, Del Norte County's unemployment was 25 percent before Pelican Bay State Prison was built. It changed both the economy and Crescent City.

Located to the northwest, the prison was built on 275 acres of land and opened in 1989. It imprisons California's most serious criminal offenders, who are habitual criminals, problem cases, prison gang members, and violence-oriented inmates. The facilities employ some 1,400 people, nearly 1,000 who are guards. Its fully staffed capacity is 3,500 and currently there are 3,300 incarcerated inmates. Even given the employment and revenue base of Pelican Bay to the locality, the psychological impact on any area having a maximum-security prison like this one clearly isn't the same as building a deep-sea harbor, a theater complex, or an international airport.

Crescent City's population is still just 5,000 (not including the prison population). Del Norte County's population numbers a low 26,000, and the area is still considered to be a small, basically rural area with average-per-capita income lower than the California state average. As retirees locate to this area with its relatively inexpensive housing and ocean location, however, this trend is definitely reversing.

BY 1986, Don Knight was ready to start search operations for the *Brother Jonathan*, relying on the testimony of Quartermaster Jacob Yates and his considerable research, as well as the experiences of the local fishermen and others whom he had talked to. Knight used a magnetometer at first, which is a big, floating metal detector that reads the earth's magnetic field for distortions created by the presence of iron. This equipment is only sensitive to iron objects, and it will not pick up the wood debris from a sunken wreck. The magnetometer then relays the data to the surface for viewing. His first attempts with this equipment yielded only data about scattered underwater debris that couldn't have been from the ship.

He also brought in a side-scan sonar apparatus. Side-scan sonar is a torpedo-like device that the mother ship tows behind it on a long cable. The equipment's sonar emits timed sound pulses that are reflected back by hard objects on the ocean floor. These return echoes are recorded, digitized, and transmitted by the cable to monitors on board the mother ship. The computer's software creates the acoustic images on the screen, which can be positioned within the given coordinates.

Knight then formed an underwater research firm, Sea-Epics Research, in 1986 to conduct specific searches for the *Brother Jonathan*.

Don made eight different undersea investigations for the ship prior to 1993. He conducted two searches each in 1986, 1987, 1989, and 1991. Every time something promising stood out, however, later searches at that spot with a remote operating vehicle (ROV), mini-sub, or further side-scan passes indicated that the image wasn't anything like the long sought-after ship.

The particular ROV in use then was a 42-inch long, 28-inch wide, and 26-inch deep projectile, otherwise known as a Phantom 500, which two-horsepower motors powered underneath the sea. The mother ship generally anchored or stayed in the basic target area, while the operator controlled the ROV and its closed-circuit television camera by a long cable. If the bottom being investigated was two-hundred feet deep, then the men needed to have at least four-hundred feet of cable out with which to maneuver the ninety-pound object. Although twin motors powered the "flying eyeball," controlling the projectile and long cable over the bottom with limited visibility was hard, tedious work.

Knight headed out in June 1986 with "mag and side-scan" on different boats, from "a twenty-two-footer to a thirty-foot-plus long one." The objective was to try and locate targets that he could investigate later in greater detail. Knight's crew stayed out sweeping the ocean waters for seven days from June 18 on, although the expedition lost three days due to stormy weather, which confined him to port.

On July 15, he headed out for another week, using side-scan sonar and finding three potential targets from the *Flow,* a thirty-eight-foot fiberglass commercial fishing boat. He funded his 1986 operations with $20,000 from investors. One of the men who invested a portion of the capital that year then disappeared and later called him from Haiti. It appeared to Knight that the investor was "on the run from somebody."

One of the most difficult jobs in undersea explorations is not only finding people who believe in what one's doing and understand the high risks, but that these investors are a good personality match with the right motives. The same challenge exists in locating the right partners to work with the organizer—and who also have the right "fit" and intentions.

Don Knight traveled to Crescent City the following year and continued searching for the lost ship. He needed to find another boat to operate from, as the present one had a problem with engine fumes pouring over the decks. This led him to work with Barry Sutton and the forty-foot boat *Top Cat.* Sutton was an ex-Highway Patrolman, who once stopped a drunk driver and was attacked by the man with a tire iron. In the savage fighting that ensued, the struggling men rolled down a steep incline, and Barry broke his back. Now on permanent disability from the California Highway Patrol, he chartered his boat for day trips, commercial fishing, and explorations such as this one.

In April, Knight operated an ROV from the *Top Cat* for eight days on a gamble that the weather would work out. This time luck was with him, as the "seas were as smooth as glass." He searched with the ROV in September 1987 and as the weather worsened, located "some interesting objects" for later investigation. Then the men were caught on the high seas.

Although the marine weather stations had warned about rain and some waves, this weather suddenly changed to an extreme. An atmospheric cooler high-pressure system raced into the region and increased the winds and waves to where a Nor'wester windstorm suddenly howled. The *Top Cat* was a decent, working-order boat, but like most vessels around, it was not designed for these types of conditions.

The winds gusted to 60 knots with an average of 45 to 50 knots (almost 60 miles per hour). The storm whipped the ocean into white-caps that were eighteen- to twenty-feet high. At the same time, Don Knight was trying to operate the search equipment. The conditions became so dangerous that one-half of the six seasoned maritime explorers onboard soon became terribly seasick (but not Knight or Sutton), as the *Top Cat* pitched violently in the heavy seas.

When two wind-whipped waves combined into a "rogue" or

much larger one, the stories-high hissing comber began rolling down onto the quite a bit smaller boat. Sutton needed to maneuver the *Top Cat* so that the boat headed into the apparition. The *Top Cat* slammed up its side and then bucked down on the wave's back side, skidding over the unusually high roller. Although this combination was thankfully rare, Sutton kept a wary eye on everything around him. If anything was loose on the boat by then, it slid into a wall—or into a person. The boat's harsh lurching rattled the equipment and people on board.

Sutton turned the *Top Cat* around and motored back toward the harbor's safety, all the while looking for another bad wave. Aside from the obvious danger of the seas, the seasick crew was also handicapped. According to Don Knight, "People would run to the fantail and barf, then head back inside to work, and then run back again to the fantail to barf." Finally, the boat arrived safely at Crescent City Harbor with minimal damage to its equipment.

Although the storm was bad, it wasn't the meterological bomb that explodes once each century, such as the unexpected 1962 Columbus Day storm. In that, winds powered through the Willamette Valley in Oregon with 100-mile-per-hour gusts slamming into downtown Portland—the *Brother Jonathan*'s next scheduled destination years ago. The October 12, 1962, storm was as close to a hurricane as anything that develops in the eastern Pacific Ocean north of the equator. On that day, the St. George Reef Lighthouse off Crescent City recorded a 104-mile-per-hour blast in this "Storm of the Century," which ravaged the Pacific Northwest. Twenty years later, another windstorm hit 63 miles per hour, and in 1995, St. George Reef recorded a storm with a high wind of 80 miles per hour.

As Don Knight contended with the vagaries of the elements, and his constant funding needs, his time was always at a premium. While Knight tried to locate the *Brother Jonathan,* he also worked to earn a living. He worked in fiberglass manufacturing until 1988, and then became a high school teacher in San Dimas, Walnut, and Diamond

Bar, California, teaching chemistry, geometry, and algebra for ten years. Knight took part in the explorations during the vacations and leaves allowed by his employment.

With his passionate commitment to finding the lost ship, Don Knight not only had to line up investor funds, he also had to manage operations, contract for the equipment and boats, schedule the men, and maintain the ROVs. The problem with even the best of plans, however, is that they don't always work out as first intended. As Knight observed, "When you're finally ready to go, there would be fog, or heavy seas, not to mention the considerable time required to double-check the side-scan targets. The work is and has always been exacting, hard, and long—and full of surprises."

His approach was to first chart the quadrant that he wanted to investigate. The boat in use would make several passes within that prescribed area with side-scan sonar. When the sonar pinpointed an underwater object, then he and the others would determine its likelihood of being the *Jonathan.* Based on its shape or identification with another ship, if the sighting was a low probability, then this fact would be logged. A high priority target would be marked with a buoy for later investigation by the ROV. Knight generally worked with Barry Sutton and the *Top Cat* during these times in the later 1980s. The boat piggybacked the ROV on it, so that the salvors could explore a really promising object as soon as possible. This exploration was painstaking, exacting, and long work where the fog, bad weather, heavy seas, and money were always key constraints.

It was also risky and dangerous work, as Knight and the others were constantly in the sea, exploring, and searching for signs. One time, Don and another crewman were on an inflatable raft around Jonathan Rock, attempting to determine if the marine maps' pinpointed location of the reef was correct. It was apparently off by 150 yards. As others on board the *Top Cat* watched incredulously, the seas unexpectedly carried the raft toward the "Fang"—or the uppermost point of that wash rock, which looked like the upper teeth in a jaw. If the raft ripped on those jagged edges, the currents would quickly sweep both men over the rock's coarse edges, back and forth, and then away. A large wave caught the raft and surfed it over the teeth. Knight punched in the electronic positioning coordinates, as the man at the tiller tried to maneuver the craft. Luckily, the raft actually slid over the rock, without puncturing, to the other side. Knight then determined that the stated location was off by that 150 yards.

Don didn't make any trips around Jonathan Rock or in the channel during 1988. He was too busy trying to line up investment funds and obtain the necessary salvage permit. This permitting process required numbers of trips to Sacramento and various meetings with California's State Lands Commission. The California legislature delegated the authority over California's lands to this commission, which included the coastal lands stretching three miles off its coast.

Up to then, he had worked hard and long, conducting the explorations through his company, Sea-Epics Research. Anyone can search for a lost ship, but the problem is who owns it when the salvor does find the vessel. Depending on the governmental entity involved, the exploration group needs an appropriate permit to salvage the wreck if it is within the agency's jurisdiction.

In September 1988, the California State Lands Commission (CSLC) granted a permit to Sea-Epics for its search and recovery operations on the *Brother Jonathan*—but limited it to finding the large Doblier safe. According to the State of California, his searches from that point on would be legal. Although Knight believed from the permit's "loose language" that he had given up a straight 20 percent interest to the state in whatever was recovered, there were numerous strong conditions that California required before Sea-Epics could rely on that percentage interest. The State had actually made a conditional interim grant of this permit—subject to further negotiation and hearings—as Knight to his dismay later learned.

Don was back in business the following year, when he explored the offshore areas for five days from December 14. This search went well, as the sea was "like glass." Harvey Harrington, a new salvage operator and partner, had arrived two months before and searched for nine days in October. This operation, however, wasn't successful due to "lousy weather." The 1989 log indicated that for most of the time the weather was "foggy, visibility little, and stormy." The *Top Cat* was not available for the operation because Sutton was having the boat hulled.

That same year, Knight talked at length with Mel Fisher about making an investment in Sea-Epics Research. Fisher had discovered and claimed millions of dollars in Spanish gold and silver coins when he discovered the wreck of the Spanish galleon *Atocha*, which sank off the Florida Keys. The two discussed Fisher making a sizeable dollar investment in the company for a share of the profits, most of the funds dependent on the ship's discovery. An agreement was drafted up by the attorneys. At the very last moment, Fisher changed his mind and decided not to go further with the investment. Had Mel Fisher decided to become involved, it is very possible that the results down the road would have been different.

Soon after granting the permit, the CSLC decided that it needed more information with additional conditions met, otherwise they would cancel the permit. Knight then started trying to meet the demands, as the commission also began reviewing the profit percentage that it really wanted. It turns out that the state wanted one-half of all of the gold and valuables that were discovered. In January 1990, the CSLC sent a letter to Knight demanding that Sea-Epics give adequate assurances as to its continued financial condition and solvency; that the Doblier safe would be kept "safe and conserved," if found; and that the company would hold the State of California harmless from any potential liability from its operations, among other conditions.

In other words, when Sea-Epics discovered the valuable safe with its millions of dollars in gold coins and bullion, the safe's contents weren't really part of the deal. During the real hearings over the permit, the CSLC then demanded that Sea-Epics Research procure a $1,000,000 on-site insurance liability policy, safeguarding the State of California for 365 days of every year—when the salvors could only work a few weeks during that time for their operations. A big difference in premium cost exists between insuring operations for one month, let's say, as opposed to twelve months.

Three people were then on the voting board of the CSLC, including Leo McCarthy and Gray Davis. The Commission then told Knight that without these conditions being met, he couldn't even turn on his boat's sonar when he motored into the Crescent City area. Don couldn't believe that every fisherman in the area could use their side-scan sonar for any purpose, but that the "State of California would control my use as soon as I crossed through the ocean into Crescent City."

A big problem surfaced in that the state actually wanted the same deal from Sea-Epics that it had exacted from Larry Holcomb: 25 percent up to the first $25,000 and then one-half of everything from there on. After checking, Knight determined that "nearly every state in the Union was at the twenty percent to twenty-five percent level." California stood out like a sore thumb with its one-half without any regard to the salvor's costs or investor's funds.

Knight argued strenuously with Leo McCarthy, then lieutenant governor of California. He believed these conditions were not needed, not specifically discussed before, and weren't appropriate. The angry salvor told the startled state officials, "If you want your salvage license back, then you'll get it back, and I'll march over to Federal Court and sue you right afterward." Gray Davis, who was then the state's controller (he was later elected governor of California, but recalled by the electorate in favor of Arnold Schwarzenegger), sharply gaveled down his answer that the permit was now gone. Knight recalled later that "Davis couldn't get to the gavel fast enough to give the commission's response and say in a tight-lipped way, 'Mr. Knight, your salvage permit is revoked.' "

The CSLC notified him of the revocation of the permit to search for the Doblier safe in a March 27, 1990 letter. Sea-Epics now had neither a permit nor investor funds. He had learned now what it was like to deal with the State of California and its State Lands Commission, as others had before and would again.

WITHIN A SHORT PERIOD OF TIME, however, Don Knight attracted new, experienced people to come on board, and a different organization entitled Deep Sea Research, Inc., (DSR) emerged. These people were: Harvey Harrington, James Wadsley, Sherman Harris, David Flohr, Willard Bascom, and later Mark Hemstreet. All shared a love for the sea and adventure—and discovering a long-lost gold treasure.

Already on the scene with Sea-Epics, the first new person with a reputation was Harvey Harrington. A charismatic, handsome man, who had years ago "caught the bug of diving for treasure," Harrington was an experienced diver who had worked on different projects over the years. According to Don Knight, Harrington called up Don's wife, Betsy, and told her that he had heard where Knight and Sea-Epics had obtained a salvage permit. He said that he lived in Southern California and had "one more shipwreck project" left in him. At the time, Knight was driving back to his home after obtaining the Sea-Epics exploration permit, and the radio newscasts were announcing the news of this development.

Harvey Harrington is ten years older than Knight, but he became interested in diving when he started inspecting and repairing the work on bridge piers for Rhode Island municipal and state authorities. By the early 1980s, Harvey had worked in Panama as a superintendent and diver on a communication cable salvage project, served in the U.S. Navy and Coast Guard on undersea inspections and repairs of shoreline installations, recovered submerged railroad cars, and investigated a number of wrecks.

Harrington had even traveled to Northern California in the early 1980s and researched the *Brother Jonathan,* but the salvor decided to put that project on hold when he discovered how tough it was to gain a salvage permit from the state. He then traveled to Delaware to look at another ship on his list of "best salvage sites," this one being the lost British privateer *DeBraak.*

A small, 110-foot long brig, the H.M.S. *DeBraak* was fitted with two masts and armed with sixteen cannons. It began its Royal Navy service in 1797, and one year later, a violent squall slammed into the ship as she headed into the Delaware Bay for repairs. Sinking in eighty feet of water, the brig gradually became part of the archaeological record and maritime lore of Delaware's Atlantic coast—just as the *Brother Jonathan* had become on the Pacific coast. The *DeBraak* was said to have sunk with silver and gold coins seized from Spanish vessels in the Caribbean, and it was also carrying British gold. When the ship capsized, its captain, thirty-seven crew members, and many captured Spanish prisoners in the holds drowned. Its location over time was forgotten.

Harvey Harrington had dreamed of recovering lost treasure for years. His ambition dated back years ago to a trip to Central America when turtle fishermen showed him jewels they said they'd discovered in a sunken Spanish galleon off Panama. Harrington decided to center on the wreck *DeBraak* and later put together an investment group with an initial $75,000 in available funds. Before he commenced exploration operations, he applied to the State of Delaware for a permit in 1984. He was approved. The fee was $1,500, and Delaware required $27,500 in security bonds (not the million-dollar policies later required by California for the *Brother Jonathan*). The state asked for and received a 25 percent interest (as opposed to California's 50 percent) in the value of any goods recovered within its coastal waters.

British records stated that the ship had sunk in thirteen fathoms of water (or about eighty feet). Therefore, Harrington focused on areas where the contours of the Delaware Bay's channels were of such depth. Using side-scan sonar, he began to map the ocean's underbelly.

By the end of April, Harrington had discovered thirteen wrecks, which he then narrowed down to three prime targets. After securing the salvage permit from the state based on his assumption that one of these was the *DeBraak,* he secured more investment funds. He also started looking in earnest at those images on the bottom. One proved to be a barge, the next a schooner, and the last was confirmed as the *DeBraak.* The proof was a bottle, a small anchor, and a bell from the lost brig. Among other objects, divers then brought up a thirty-eight-pound mass of silver coins and doubloons, fused together by the saltwater's "electrolytic" actions.

In his 1993 book, *The Hunt for the HMS DeBraak,* Donald G.

Shomette charged that although Harrington wasn't allowed to remove any artifacts from the site under the permit terms, he nevertheless returned "only the anchor to the bottom, keeping the coins, cannon, bell, and chalice." The author stated that the salvor had apparently sequestered the cannon in twenty feet of water in a riverbed some distance from the wreck site.

Harrington's salvage company Sub-Sal had to prove, however, that what he had found was indeed the *DeBraak* before salvage operations could legally proceed. According to Shomette, Harrington invited the supervisor of Delaware's Wetlands and Underwater Lands division to the wreck and raised a second cannon. Schomette wrote:

> With the state official looking on and entirely unaware that a carronade had already been recovered, the treasure hunter raised a second one. The piece was still packed with hemp and a charge, ready to fire. Harrington solemnly pretended that it was the first artifact to come up.

Armed with his salvage permit (the ship was well within Delaware's three-mile coastal limit), Harrington filed his legal action to "arrest" the ship as the salvor. The court quickly granted him the order decreeing that Sub-Sal was the wreck's legal custodian. After telling the public about his find and raising more investment capital, Harrington continued salvaging the wreck. The exploration was difficult at the site—as all such operations are for one reason or another—due this time to the strong underwater tides that raced back and forth at speeds up to 10 miles per hour. This created difficulties for movement as well as visibility.

Sub-Sal decided to use teams of divers with surface air feeds from a mother craft, the *Mariner,* which anchored over the wreck with a four-point mooring system. Another line supplied electricity for the diver's helmet light, and a communication line provided voice contact. As the *DeBraak* had settled in relatively shallow waters, its divers only spent thirty minutes in a decompression chamber for each one-hundred minutes spent getting to the bottom and back.

From pistols and cannonballs to shoes, rum bottles, and bowls, the divers brought up hundreds of artifacts—but no treasure. The lease with Delaware provided that a state representative be on board the mother ship at all times during operations. As an ever increasing number of the artifacts were catalogued, the quantities began to tax the ability of the state to properly oversee their conservation.

In his book, Shomette charged that the divers inappropriately "disturbed" the bones of the dead. Soon thereafter, they brought up some one hundred coins, mostly Spanish gold doubloons from the mid-1790s that the English had looted from the Spanish ships they had stopped. Without any cash flow allowed from the discovered artifacts, coins, and jewelry, however, the costs of the continuing operations outstripped Harrington's ability to pay his bills.

He was forced to lay off employees. Shomette alleged that "a thirty-pound clump of oxidized silver coins of nearly two hundred Spanish pieces of eight were taken back down and 'rediscovered.' " Later, after several anonymous telephone calls, the Delaware State Police searched the storage premises and a safe deposit box, discovering that Harrington (according to Shomette's research) had sent "more than one hundred coins" plus jewelry for appraisal and sale by an out-of-state company. As the state had permitted only coins and jewelry "deemed not historical" to be sold, the author charged Harrington was in violation of Sub-Sal's lease.

After five months of salvage work, the operators discovered and brought up over one thousand artifacts, but limited treasure that was marketable. As his company's cash flow deteriorated, two investors finally sued Harrington for breach of contract over the amount of treasure to be received. The State of Delaware refused to renew Sub-Sal's salvage lease. A New Hampshire businessman, L. John Davidson, then came to the rescue of Sub-Sal. He invested additional funds and took financial control of the salvage company as its chief executive officer. He later renegotiated the lease with the state, and, in September 1985, exploration operations began once more. A new system of sucking up sediment from the bottom was used, but the blockage by debris and rocks caused the system to shut down too frequently.

Divers still located and placed heavy objects into baskets. These were then hauled to the surface. These three-month operations netted nearly 3,750 different artifacts, but they only found again limited amounts of recoverable gold and silver coins. The conservators placed the objects in plastic trash cans with circulating fresh seawater that was rechanged. This started the leaching out process of the invasive sea minerals absorbed by the artifacts.

Whether the operations had been profitable or not, with his stature from the discovery of the *DeBraak* and its treasure, Harrington raised over $100,000 in November 1985 to form a new company. He intended to salvage more wrecks located off the Delaware and New Jersey coasts. As Davidson and Harrington battled over the diving operations and "who controlled what," Harrington spent less time on the *DeBraak* project. Claims and counterclaims followed, ending in Davidson firing Harrington in December. Having invested nearly $1,000,000 in the operations, Davidson is estimated to have recovered only fifty-seven coins. Treasure hunting is a risky business.

With Harrington away from the salvage—and soon to come into contact with Don Knight—Davidson decided to look somewhere else for the gold and silver. He devised a plan to excavate under the *DeBraak*'s hull, cover it with a screen to keep the artifacts on board, wrap cables and block and tackle from the mother ship, lift the hull from the bottom, and place it safely onto a waiting barge. A large wood-and-steel cradle was set on the bottom near one side of the hull. The plan was to use an onboard crane to lift the hull onto the cradle. Then both would be raised onto the barge. Already costing over two million dollars, the plan was put into operation on August 11, 1986. Nearly 15,000 people watched from nearby Cape Henlopen State Park. Unfortunately, high winds and seas began to build unexpectedly.

The divers told Davidson that the cradle was in the wrong place, but the decision was made to go ahead without it. They also decided not to attach any wire netting to the hull, although this would create a risk of the artifacts sliding away as the ship lifted. In the evening with harsh floodlights lighting the barge and surrounding ocean, the crane began to raise the hull. When it slipped through the ocean's surface, a simultaneous celebration broke out, as people cheered, boat horns blared, and bullhorns sounded. The crane's friction brake failed, however, and the operations stopped for repairs. When the crane resumed its lifting, the seventy-foot long, twenty-two-foot wide piece of old wood broke clean from the water.

To the horror of the onlookers, the wreck hung as artifacts spilled from it into the sea. The timbers used to protect the hull from the cutting cables failed, as the thick wires started slicing into the ship. The hull was lifted toward the sky by one end while the artifacts and oozing mud slid back into the ocean. When the hull finally made the barge, its keel cracked from the landing. Although it yielded incredible artifacts—from gun flints and musket pieces to a brass belt buckle and shot locker—the operation was a financial loss. Over 2.5 million dollars had been spent to recover 40 pieces of jewelry and 650 assorted coins, basically Spanish and Portuguese escuados and British guineas, pennies, and half-pennies. However, Drew and Associates (Davidson's firm) and Sub-Sal had discovered over 25,000 artifacts, nearly all of them stored in warehouses and as yet unseen by the public.

Donald G. Shomette's book, *The Hunt for the HMS DeBraak,* claims that Harrington and others violated Delaware laws, destroyed artifacts, damaged the ship's hull, and carelessly handled human remains in their quest for a treasure that never materialized. While crediting Harrington for finding the ship, Shomette writes that he brought up wreck artifacts that included silver coins and doubloons without the required state permit, but then kept the hoard from authorities while using it to raise money from investors.

Eventually Delaware stepped in and budgeted money to try and save the hull and artifacts, ranging from china plates to cannons that were not being properly preserved, charged Shomette, who worked on the *DeBraak* as a consultant to the state. Harrington dismissed the allegations. "He was inaccurate almost 100 percent," Harrington stated publicly. "We recovered 35,000 artifacts and they all went into preservation. I have stacks and stacks of recommendations from people that worked on the project, and they don't say the same thing as the book."

Harrington also states that he left the *DeBraak* project before the damage to the ship and its artifacts was done. "It was a hell of a mess after I left," he said. The *DeBraak* wreck was one of three salvage operations that resulted in the passage of the federal Abandoned Shipwrecks Act (ASA) in 1987—ironically, the same legislative act that became the center of the maritime litigation between DSR and the State of California. Shomette won a national archaeological society award for his book on the salvaging of the *DeBraak.*

One fact is clear: Harrington didn't make money on his venture, even though he located the ship and started its exploration. After Delaware and the *DeBraak,* he made his way back to California and contacted Don Knight, ending up working with Knight on his explorations starting in October 1989.

DON KNIGHT was still the proverbial optimist. At the same time he was searching for the *Brother Jonathan* and earning money to pay his bills by teaching and consulting, he found the time to write a book about another steamer that had wrecked on rocks off California. In May 1990, Pathfinder Publishing published his book entitled *Agony and Death on a Gold Rush Steamer: The Disastrous Sinking of the Side-Wheeler Yankee Blade.*

This book centered on the life and destruction of the S.S. *Yankee Blade,* a sidewheeler that struck a submerged reef in 1854 near Santa Barbara, California, causing the deaths of some fifty people. Ironically, the *Brother Jonathan* steamed by the wreck and transported the surviving passengers back to San Francisco after a series of harrowing experiences. Later the grateful survivors gave a gold watch to the *Jonathan*'s skipper, Captain Seabury, for what he had done to save them.

Several months after publication, in December, Knight traveled to San Pedro, California. At the California Wreck Divers Club, he made a presentation on both the *Yankee Blade* and the *Brother Jonathan.* According to Don, Jim Wadsley came up after his lecture and said he would be interested in working further with Knight on the *Jonathan*.

Wadsley was another highly trained, experienced scuba diver, who was known for his diverse underwater experiences. Jim's self-taught engineering skills and passion for shipwrecks led him into the field of undersea wreck surveying. His specialty was side-scan sonar operations. He had run his own diving and machine shop companies and worked on a number of salvage operations, including searching for ancient antiquities in the Mediterranean with Willard Bascom. It was this relationship that brought Bascom into contact with Deep Sea Research.

Wadsley was a private man: He would go out of his way not to sign documents, according to his partners in DSR, in a desire to keep his life private. Knight said that Jim Wadsley promised to bring along much needed side-sonar search and other equipment, a fact that came into later dispute. In recognition of his diving career exploits, and as a longtime member, the California Wreck Divers Club voted Wadsley into its Hall of Fame in 2002, along with director James Cameron of the movie *Titanic* fame and three others.

The third important member of the new group was Sherman Harris. He had a friend who was a doctor and also knew Don Knight. The physician, Cliff Cummins, sometimes spent weekends in Palm Springs, California, where he met Harris. It wasn't long before Don and Sherman met, and he became an investor in the search for the *Brother Jonathan*. Knight recalled that Harris was always very generous when he came to Palm Springs. "My money wasn't good with Sherman when it came to meals; he was a very gracious person." Harris then brought in his brother-in-law, David Flohr, who was also a very experienced businessman.

Sherman Harris was born in Superior, Wisconsin, in 1923 and graduated from high school as its student-body president. After a stint with the U.S. Army during World War II, he returned to his hometown to open his first business, a coffee shop. He then moved west to manage Laurye's Steak Ranch in Palm Springs, California, until the late-1950s. Then opening his own dinner house in Palm Springs, he formed the nucleus of an enterprise that eventually included five restaurants. In 1968, Sherman was invited to take over the management of the Palm Springs Aerial Tramway restaurant, gift shop, and other public facilities, a multimillion dollar operation that he managed for over thirty years. Sherman invested $21,000 for a 6 percent interest in the *Jonathan* venture by the end of 1991.

Sherman Harris is known as "Mr. Palm Springs" at times and is a compassionate, well-liked person. The community honored him in 1998 by awarding him a "star" on the main-street sidewalk with other known and famous people, and he and his wife, Rosemary, still reside there.

Another very important member of the new team was David Flohr, the brother-in-law of Sherman Harris. He and Sherman were investors in the project and brought in management expertise. At the time Flohr was usually identified as "a retired Navy pilot from Southern California who is a member of Deep Sea Research"—but his role would be much greater.

Born in 1925, David Flohr spent his youth growing up in Southern California. He joined the U.S. Navy and served as a pilot flying carrier-based TBM "Avengers" just after World War II. As Don Knight did later, David Flohr went back to school after his tours of duty in the Navy were over, leaving as a Commander. He graduated from the University of Redlands in 1951 with his BA in Business Administration. He then earned his MBA two years later from Stanford. After graduation he worked as a financial analyst for Kaiser Steel until 1965, managing its computer systems and procedures.

David founded an automobile repair company and then sold it to work with D. W. Phillips in Brussels, Belgium, overseeing its manufacturing and distribution functions. He resigned to open a chain of franchised specialty food stores (Hickory Farms of Ohio), which grew to being a multimillion dollar operation with seventeen outlets and five hundred employees. Thirteen years later, in 1984, Flohr sold the business to the franchisor.

In the same year, he headed to Israel to assist in a diving and underwater exploration as part of the Caesarea Ancient Harbor Excavation project. He discovered an ancient Roman oil lamp from the last quarter of the first century B.C. at the bottom of the Caesarea Harbor. In 1993, he joined with others to eventually bring the U.S.S. *Midway* out of mothballs and tow it to San Diego, where it became a major museum ten years later. The *Midway* was a U.S. aircraft carrier whose career spanned from the surrender of Japan in WWII, the Cold War, and Vietnam, to the Gulf War and Operation Desert Storm. It is one of the historical ships of our navy.

Flohr also had extensive diving experience and sailed his own eighty-foot, gaff-rigged, two-masted schooner *Jade Dragon* from Florida to San Diego through the Panama Canal. When he left Fort Lauderdale on that voyage, a storm howled in that first night. The waves pulled the ship's stove away, dumping food on the deck and hot coffee over his hand. When he stepped into the engine room, he found himself in ankle-deep water from the seawater that had seeped in through the dry planks. He needed to operate all seven onboard pumps to keep the boat afloat.

Having known Sherman Harris from the 1970s, Mark Hemstreet also became an investor in DSR. As a teenager, his family owned and managed lodging properties in Oregon and Nevada. When he was sixteen years old, Mark was managing a family motel site at Rockaway on the Oregon coast. After graduating from high school, he attended Portland State University for two years. His goal since his youth, however, was to own his own hotel. He realized that in 1974 when he negotiated a bank loan and purchased his first motel near Gresham, Oregon, a town close to Portland. With hard work and a strong plan, Hemstreet built the Shilo Inns into the largest independently owned hotel chain on the U.S. West Coast with forty-nine hotels now dotting nine states.

WILLARD BASCOM was the last person to join the team. People viewed him as the consummate professional in the diving community. He was a highly respected individual in a variety of occupations. Bascom had been an ocean engineer, diver, and an ocean adventurer. He had wide-ranging interests, was described as a "maverick" innovator, and was quite passionate about the arts and sciences. He studied poetry, music, painting (an avid oil painter with an affinity for seascapes and landscapes), photography, cinematography, and underwater archaeology.

Born in New York City (Bronxville) in 1916, Bascom studied mining at the Colorado School of Mines. A disagreement with the school president prompted him to leave before graduating. According to David Flohr and Donald Knight: "Bascom was kicked out of the Colorado School of Mines because he slugged a professor with whom he disagreed with greatly. After all his accomplishments, the school later sent him an honorary degree, but he returned it." When recounting this experience, they said that Willard would "break out in gales of laughter and say it was a product of his errant youth."

Although he didn't have a college degree, Willard worked as a mining engineer in Arizona, Idaho, and Colorado, and he taught college classes. His career in ocean science began in 1945 when he conducted advanced studies of waves and beaches first at U.C. Berkeley and later at the Scripps Institution of Oceanography. He lived in Monterey after World War II, and his friends included John Steinbeck (who he befriended while at Berkeley) and Ed Ricketts. He was a member of a scientific party that observed the Bikini Atoll atomic bomb test.

Bascom joined the staff at the National Science Foundation in 1954, where he organized and directed the initial phase of Project Mohole, the first effort to drill through the earth's crust in very deep ocean water. In 1962, he founded Ocean Science and Engineering, Inc., and worked as the president of the oceanographic consulting firm. He pioneered in undersea explorations for diamonds, discovering twenty million carats of gem diamonds for the De Beers Diamond Company in the ocean off the coasts of South Africa and Namibia. While with Ocean Science, he founded Seafinders, Inc., in

1972 and discovered the longlost wreck of a Spanish galleon, the *Nuestra Señora de la Maravillas.*

Over time, Willard Bascom was involved in numbers of environmental projects. In 1980, the venerable Explorer's Club of New York gave him its honoring medal for his work in deep-water archaeology and ocean geophysics. In 1992, the University of Genoa awarded him an honorary doctorate on the five hundred year anniversary of Columbus's first landing in the Americas—a rare award, if ever, for an American. He authored several widely respected books on deep-sea archaeology, salvaging, oceanography, and many scientific papers (including numerous articles published in *Scientific American).* His work on the team became invaluable as the crisis with the State of California escalated.

In May 1991, the entrepreneurs incorporated their activities into their new entity, DSR. Just prior to that act, Sherman Harris invested his monies in the new venture. He was soon joined by others such as David Flohr and Marc Hemstreet. The new investors raised $55,000 by mid-June for DSR's upcoming explorations, a modest sum by most salvage standards, but not bad when compared against where the venture stood short months ago.

Don Knight was DSR's CEO, director of research, and project director. Jim Wadsley was its vice president and director in charge of equipment development; Harvey Harrington was the vice president, director of offshore operations, and diving superintendent; Sherman Harris was a vice president and the investor representative. Don Knight, James Wadsley, and Harvey Harrington were the three members of DSR's board of directors.

Their search techniques involved GPS, side-scan sonar, magnetometers, and mini-subs. The GPS, or global positioning system, is based on a ship's receiver that captures satellite signals providing precise coordinates to define an exploration's search grids or positions on a seafloor. The salvors would use more refined ROVs. This underwater search equipment developed over time to house powerful lights, TV cameras, and video links. Controlled by a computer on board the mother ship, very sophisticated ones included mechanical arms to pick up artifacts and coins. Their expeditions, however, would not have this ROV attribute.

DSR planned two searches in late July and September of 1991. The explorations would involve the new team and organization in a revived search for the lost ship. Don Knight was upbeat.

Chapter 12

The Search Around the Rock

When the ship disappeared in 1865, searchers concentrated their efforts around Jonathan Rock, located seven miles from Crescent City Harbor. This reef seemed an ideal candidate, as it was low lying, just underneath the surface, covered by high tides, and had a pinnacle that rose two hundred feet from the bottom of the sea. Deep Sea Research was no different. For years Don Knight's assumption was that the large safe, and its hoard of gold and valuables, had sunk into the deep when the ship broke up around the rock.

Without results in previous searches, boats had dragged side-scan sonar equipment for undersea images and magnometers looking for iron concentrations around the rock and other locations. In 1991, DSR again hired Barry Sutton and the charter boat *Top Cat* to conduct the same recovery techniques.

American Underwater Search and Survey in Massachusetts arrived with sophisticated side-scan sonar equipment, and Sutton headed "due west" from port on the *Top Cat,* eventually working a northerly direction for Jonathan Rock. He turned the boat and steadied it, as the crew dropped the tow fish with its side-scan sonar into the water, and the operator calibrated its onboard instrumentation.

By this time, the *Top Cat* was cruising inside "Dragger Lane"—the term for the broad course heading out to the open sea. This is where the shrimp and deep-sea fishing boats drag their seventy-five-foot long nets. Dragger Lane (also called "Dragger Channel") is not marked on any charts or official navigation maps. It is the fishermen's description of a course for fishing areas, which are away from the main shipping lanes. Some people have confused it with "Dragon Channel," which is a different course designation that cuts through St. George Reef.

Not more than five minutes after Barry Sutton wheeled the *Top Cat* under clear skies into Dragger Lane—attempting to duplicate the course that the *Brother Jonathan* would have been on—a target appeared "right in the middle of Dragger land," as Don Knight said later. The image passed by without a defined shape and, at first, it was just a question mark.

The sonar man yelled back to Sutton and Knight, "Damn, I had this set on the wrong frequency." He had apparently put the sonar frequency at 600 kilohertz, when the setting for this particular run should have been on a much lower 100 kilohertz. At 100 kilohertz, the sonar image would have been clearly defined—not "smudgy" as it then showed. Otherwise, everything was in order. It was a fine, beautiful day, and the tow fish ran "straight and true." The men continued on to Jonathan Rock and made several passes around the reef, trying to recreate the *Brother Jonathan*'s course again, sweeping the tow fish behind.

The salvors sailed back the next day to the coordinates where the shady image appeared. Jim Wadsley pointed his magnometer into the depths. From the iron reading and side-scan image, the men decided that below them rested a fifty-foot target, more than likely a barge that had broken in two some years before. Knight, Wadsley, and the others disregarded this image, or the "smudge," as it was then called.

The boat continued "mowing the lawn"—the explorer's term for making continued passes over an ocean grid in a search. In between these sweeps, Barry Sutton told the men about meeting an old fisherman. He had been drinking in a smoky bar a few years before with some friends. The older man stopped by and chatted with them over drinks, finally telling Barry that he had pulled up an old brass railing from a ship that had gone down in Dragger Channel. The fisherman wrote down the location where he had netted the railing and gave the coordinates to Sutton.

Barry disregarded the story then, as fishermen for years had told a number of tales over stiff drinks about where some "old ship with souls" was waiting to be discovered. The local newspapers also ran stories periodically about a fisherman who netted debris from a long-lost sunken ship or wood spars that had washed ashore in a storm. Such news could be maddening for salvors because the wreck was relatively close to shore. The problem was figuring out which story gave the real clue to its location.

Knight and Harrington believed that their searches were knocking out area after area, and that they would eventually get back to this spot—primarily because the point was located some distance from Jonathan Rock. Then their sophisticated scanning equipment broke down. As replacement parts wouldn't be available for two days, Sutton and Knight headed again to this "area of curiosity." When they arrived at the smudgy image's location, the men discovered that the place matched the fisherman's coordinates and the old brass railing's location. The *Top Cat* worked the area with several passes, but the less-sophisticated equipment in use that day couldn't sharpen the undersea image.

Again they concluded it might be a broken barge, especially since the wreck was so far away from the shipping lanes shown on old charts. They put the smudge's coordinates to a lower search position on their exploration priorities.

The funds available for the search, meanwhile, ebbed and flowed, just like the tides. For 1993, the budget for their proposed undersea operations was set at $125,000. It took a strenuous effort to raise the money but eventually they succeeded. Without a large exploration investment angel, the company relied on its public investment seminars and private pitches to anyone who had a potential interest. Neighbors, policemen, doctors, podiatrists, secretaries, and individuals from every walk of life invested in the endeavor. From the very beginning, this was a blue-collar expedition when contrasted against those with millions of dollars for their investigations.

The months of August and September were the best times to search offshore, as weather conditions then were usually best. Windstorms still blew in and high seas stormed around, but did so less frequently. In the summer of 1993 DSR contracted with Buccaneer Marine, headquartered in Ventura, California, for the use of its large salvage ship, *Cavalier.* They also signed with Doug Privitt and Rick Slater of Delta Oceanographics for use of its two-man mini-submarine, *Delta.* Previously, Knight met with Don Siverts of Undersea Graphics of Redondo Beach, California, who owned a one-man mini-submarine named the *Snooper,* which would also be employed in the search. Both Siverts and David Slater, one of the operators of the *Delta,* were highly recommended and experienced in operating their subs.

The *Cavalier* was a one hundred and fifteen-foot long utility vessel with quarters for the divers and salvors, space for their sophisticated sonar and communication apparatus, and areas to store the mini-sub and diving support equipment. The ship's pilot cabin and radar equipment were located at the bow, its high prow and sides cut down toward an open stern, which allowed easier loading and offloading of the subs and equipment.

Fifteen men worked on board full-time. The crew included cook, mini-sub operators, and DSR's recovery team of Don Knight, Jim Wadsley, Harvey Harrington, and others. This mother ship contained bunks, a galley, showers, and support facilities for the operations. Two long compartments were set behind one another at the stern: One stored spare parts and the diver's equipment, while the other functioned as the expedition's control shack with sophisticated monitoring equipment.

To the starboard side of the compartments, the two mini-submarines were positioned, each looking like a large yellow propane tank with a hatch and portholes. A bubble with small circular windows protruded from the middle of the one-man submersible

Snooper; its operator entered from the hatch on top. The *Delta* was wider, squatter, and made room for a second man, its portholes ringing the front, back, and sides. Protected by a screen and enclosing metal, a battery-driven propeller moved each submersible around the bottom. A crane on the mother ship attached to eyehooks, deposited the subs into the sea, and plucked them back once their operations were completed.

The *Delta* was longer at fifteen and one-half feet with a height of six feet. Its cruising speed was 1.5 knots, and as one knot equals 1.15 miles, this meant 1.75 miles per hour. The mini-sub had a maximum hourly speed of 3.5 knots, or about four miles per hour. The *Delta* had nineteen view ports, its weight was 2.5 tons, and eight six-volt lead-acid batteries powered it.

The *Snooper* was quite similar to the *Delta,* although somewhat smaller at twelve feet in length. The one-man sub would be used in exploring and mapping the ocean bottom, as two dedicated bow portholes at 45 degree angles had video cameras for recording whatever came into sight. This submersible could make a pass on one side with one camera, then turn around and take videos with the other—with no need to change film. It had the same approximate speed as the *Delta.* The two-man submersible was also useful in searching the bottom, but it had an outside mechanical arm and attached "goodie bag." The second crewman could operate the arm to explore and recover objects while the operator maneuvered the sub.

The *Delta* was conveniently in use off Alaska on board the *Cavalier* during DSR's window of diving opportunity. Therefore, arrangements were made to have the mother ship with its submarine swing by Crescent City on the way back to its home port in Southern California. The salvors spent months arranging and coordinating the different operators, ship personnel, equipment, and support necessary for the operations.

Although prior salvage approaches had been unsuccessful, all the attempts since 1865 now assisted DSR's efforts—especially Larry Holcomb's attempts to the north, northeast, and east of Jonathan Rock.

As the team knew they had discovered nothing there resembling the *Jonathan,* the crew members could concentrate their efforts to the south and southwest of Jonathan Rock.

The group and its investors were upbeat, so optimistic, in fact, that several traveled to Crescent City and stayed onshore in a local motel, so they could directly hear the news of any discovery. Lincoln Gray captained the *Cavalier,* and he sailed a few days before from Coos Bay, Oregon, with members of the recovery team. As the explorers awaited the arrival of other members of the dive team, the mother ship cruised outside the search area for two days. On Sunday, September 26, 1993, the search for the *Brother Jonathan* started again in earnest. The set goal was to find the huge safe with its mother lode of valuables; their working assumption was that the ship had broken up in pieces, its bow and safe of gold close to the base of Jonathan Rock, the stern and engine settling elsewhere, but near the reef.

From Sunday to Tuesday, the men ran *Delta* and the *Snooper* around selected areas and targets by Jonathan Rock. Nothing resembling the ship was found. As the top targets on their list hadn't worked out, the salvors and their investors were disappointed and morale dropped. On Wednesday, September 29, the recovery team sent down their mini-subs to investigate another site with coordinates closer to Dragger Channel.

Deep Sea Research hosted a hamburger barbeque that day on the *Cavalier*'s stern for its investors, including the principal representatives: David Flohr (the now elected Investor Representative), Sherman Harris, and Mark Hemstreet. The salvors answered their undersea recovery questions, but the investors were still uncomfortable as to whether there was enough money available to meet the salvage goals.

David Flohr accepted Knight's offer of a mini-sub ride around Jonathan Rock in the *Delta.* He described the reef as being barely visible that day even at low tide. The pinnacle had a "clear break," sheared clean as if a ship had struck the surface, and its steep sides and irregular shape then angled down to the bottom, about one hundred and fifty feet below. At high tide, the ocean completely covered the reef. It had existed "undiscovered" during the nineteenth century until a commissioned 1869 U.S. Coast Survey was made.

As Don Knight observed later:

> For five hours the operators and recovery team were down at the different coordinates away from Jonathan Rock, and they found nothing that was helpful. The next day, Thursday, we were around the rock, but again came up empty-handed. At 1700 (or five o'clock in the evening), I convened a meeting in the galley and said, if we didn't find the wreck within the next two days, we wouldn't be having any operations the following year.

On board the *Cavalier*, Harrington, Wadsley, and Knight debated long into the night. Each new day proved again unsuccessful and their list of targets was growing thin and less likely. There had to be an answer somewhere.

Just what would Captain DeWolf have done when he knew his ship was fatally grounded on the uncharted reef? Why had everyone else—including this group—met such lack of success in finding a treasure ship that had sunk so close to shore? Did the sidewheeler actually strike the reef identified as Jonathan Rock, as everyone had assumed? The *Brother Jonathan* was two days away from staying a ghost ship with only eleven controversial gold bars as the proof of its having ever existed.

The searchers realized that spending one more day around Jonathan Rock would be a complete loss. They had done that at great expense. The treasure seekers knew that searching above or north of the rock was another waste of precious time, given the experiences of Dr. Holcomb and others. For decades and decades, everyone believed that the safe and its valuables had sunk around Jonathan Rock. "Well, it wasn't there," concluded one member, "and after all of the sub trips, we still hadn't discovered any debris trail that led away from the rock to some other place."

For years, would-be salvors simply assumed the vessel had broken up after hitting the uncharted reef due to the wreckage that had washed onto the beaches later. Debris, steamer trunks, and goods had floated ashore, along with its huge, gilded wooden eagle. The ship's wheel and forty feet of its upper deck with the bell attached had grinded to rest on another beach. Wreckage was scattered over a wide part of the coastline.

If the *Brother Jonathan* had broken up on the reef, then why wasn't more wreckage spotted on the ocean floor by or nearby the base of the rocky peak? As the group argued among themselves, yelling at one another from sheer frustration, the men debated whether the assumptions made over the years were, in fact, wrong. For example, the effects of the collision, winds, and waves could have carved away large chunks of the vessel, which then floated away, as forty feet of the upper deck had. And since over one hundred and twenty-five years had elapsed since the ship disappeared into the deep ocean, could it be possible that saltwater and marine worms had eaten away most of what would have been a debris trail anyway?

The key to finding any sunken wreck is to do extensive research on land in libraries and archives, test those conclusions in the sea, and then make new assumptions if the first approaches don't work out. Discovering sunken treasure is an art—not a science—especially given the depths of the ocean, currents at the bottom, and lack of visibility as this one involved. During the first days of the 1993 search, Knight, Flohr, and others were struck by the testimony of Quartermaster Jacob Yates. When the *Jonathan* smashed onto the rocks, he was at the helm.

Yates was an African-American. His testimony had to be reliable, they concluded, because in order for him to be a petty officer, as well as be given the duty to "man the helm," then he must have been an exceptionally good sailor—at that time, blacks weren't typically placed in such positions of responsibility on the high seas. Yates also had given very detailed testimony at the government inquest on the incident, including an excellent description of the ship's location when Captain DeWolf tried so desperately to get the ship safely back to the harbor.

Yates testified:

> Her course was then due east. The time was about a quarter to one P.M. I kept her on that course until we made Seal Rock, and the captain ordered me to keep her southeast by south. It was clear where we were, but foggy and smoky on shore. Then we ran along until ten minutes of two o'clock P.M., when she struck the unknown sunken rock, and with such force that it felled the passengers who were standing on the deck.

The salvors argued over how true the ship had proceeded in those heavy seas on its easterly heading. When the *Brother Jonathan* proceeded as far as Seal Rock, Captain DeWolf shouted the orders to the helm, "Southeast by south," and they plotted this course again on their 1869 U.S. Coast Survey and other maritime charts.

DeWolf made his decision to run for Crescent City's safe harbor on a southerly course outside St. George Reef. He lined the ship's track on a chart that showed no obstructions to the harbor, as the vessel's course skirted the known reefs of Whale Rock, Hump Rock, and Star Rock. Quartermaster Yates put the wheel over to starboard and steadied her on that southeast by south heading. One hour and five minutes had gone by since Captain DeWolf had ordered her about. The salvors estimated she had returned about seven miles when DeWolf instructed that the anchors be readied. The bosun had made his way to the bow and was loosening one of the anchors. Suddenly he suddenly saw the hissing reef below as the ship plunged down, and he yelled out the warning, too late.

DSR had taken numerous readings on its global positioning system. There were lots of rocks and reefs that the *Brother Jonathan* could have struck under the course Yates had described. They, finally, centered on one: When the ocean ebbed at low tide, part of the reef was above the ocean. The formation was a total sixty feet long, close to the surface, but the only usual evidence of its existence was by a foam trail.

Divers confirmed that there was a right-angled chunk or gouge out of its top. Rocky debris was strewn around its very broad base at the ocean's bottom, as if a ship had sheared part off the top. Basically a small spire with teeth at its top, but an "ugly, broad pyramid" at its base, this rock—Jonathan Rock—was most likely the one.

Yates ventured out after the tragedy and pointed out a rocky point that he believed the vessel struck; the U.S. Coast Survey in 1869 identified the reef in that proximity as Brother Jonathan Rock, shortened to Jonathan Rock. The salvors continued on that working assumption. Yates had to be right, they concluded. But where was the ship? Their time was running out.

The recovery team debated, "Would Captain DeWolf do nothing as huge rollers pounded over his ship, beating its bow apart, and sweeping terrified people overboard to their deaths?" No, they concluded. He would have ordered everything thrown overboard to lighten the ship. The *Brother Jonathan*'s previous pilot, Captain George W. Staples, ran into similar high winds and seas seven years before on a voyage two days north of San Francisco. When the same ship with dead boilers lost its ability to navigate, Staples ordered everyone to throw as much of the cargo as possible into the ocean and form a bucket brigade to bail the water from the ship's holds. These actions worked. The crew restarted the boiler fires and the ship limped safely back.

None of the testimony, however, indicated that DeWolf had given such an order, others argued. Regardless of the commands, some of the crew could have thrown goods over. The winds, waves, and sinking ship might have spilled everything into the ocean without such actions. If people weren't already paralyzed by fear, how could they have avoided the huge rollers crashing over the boat and throw heavy items overboard?

Regardless of the reasoning, the old assumption wasn't working. The men decided on a different one: The *Brother Jonathan* didn't break into pieces around the reef, but instead stayed basically intact except for the large bow section and parts that the impaling eventually broke off. The ship started to sink by her destroyed bow end, but trapped air inside buoyed her stern and mid-ship up, as the sinking bow dragged the vessel down into the sea. Perhaps the ship bobbed a long distance in the ocean with her stern pointing up in the air, or sank quicker bow first, semi-buoyant with trapped air inside. Caught by underwater currents, the *Brother Jonathan* could be farther south than anyone had ever imagined. Where else could she be?

Recorded several miles offshore, the 1991 strip of sonar tape had indicated two curious shapes still unexplored and on the seafloor. They decided that one was a sunken, split barge, the other very much like a "tall box." DSR concentrated its efforts on the box with the outline of a large safe, but these efforts had not found anything extraordinary. The "smudge" image was left. The salvors provided the coordinates to Captain Grey, as they had nothing else to lose. DSR's disappointed investors had already packed up and left. By Thursday night, September 30, Deep Sea Research and its backers were down to their last day of searching for the treasure.

Late Thursday night, the *Cavalier* positioned itself in Dragger Channel and moved towards the unclear image's position. The channel was not more than 300 yards wide and known only to the fishermen and locals; their boats motored through it to head outside the harbor and fish. In the very early morning darkness of Friday, October 1, the mother ship cruised south of Jonathan Rock, towing its side-scan sonar behind through calm seas.

On board the *Cavalier*, Jim Wadsley, Harvey Harrington, and Don Knight monitored the operations in an array of green-lit monitors and subdued light inside the war room of the stern compartment. Mark Barnum, the project navigator on board, was defining the relative position of the mother ship to the target through his GPS positional data and calling this to the attention of the team. At two o'clock in the morning, the image appeared on the side-scan monitor, and Wadsley asked how big the target was. The large object stood out in an area otherwise devoid of rocks, as Harvey Harrington's eyes fixed on the screen.

Knight recalled, "I got the readings from Jim Wadsley, calculated its size, and told him that the target was 'one hundred and eighty-nine feet by fifty-five feet.' We just looked at one another. This was a much bigger ship than we first had thought." At the exact coordinates, the *Cavalier* stopped and its crew members marked the spot with a buoy. Although the target now looked very good, several team members were exhausted, as they had been searching nonstop for hours. The recovery team agreed to search later, short hours away, and Don Siverts told the men that he could be ready to dive at 7:30 A.M.

Siverts is a thin, short man who was well-liked, affable, and considered to be very professional. Although he was raised in the Montana badlands, attended art school, and was a gifted illustrator, Siverts had a love of the ocean that he said dated back to his ancestors. His grandfather was a Norwegian sea captain who immigrated to Montana in the 1880s, and Don himself lived on a boat when he was young. While working as a graphic artist, illustrator, and in other positions for defense contractors, Don's dream was to live an adventurous life while exploring the ocean in his own one-man submersible.

Saving his money and working different jobs, Siverts realized his dream when he designed and built the *Snooper.* He started his career with the mini-submersible by inspecting the undersea sewer lines of California municipalities for corrosion and leaks. His job performance was so good that his firm of Undersea Graphics still continues in this capacity. Even though Siverts had no prior experience in searching for undersea wrecks, Don Knight felt that his previous performance and professionalism was so good—with sufficiently reasonable fees—to take the chance and use him in the *Brother Jonathan* explorations. Like everyone else on this project, Siverts was relatively inexperienced and underfinanced, but his professionalism and determination stood out in trying to overcome the high odds that existed against this group.

As the sun rose over the horizon with its flashing colors, the crane on the mother ship lowered Don Siverts and his *Snooper* quickly into the ocean depths. He flicked on the mini-sub's outside lights with their 150-watt and 250-watt lamps. Even with these strong lights, visibility at those depths was typically five to six feet at best.

Once down on the bottom, Siverts stared intently outside his front porthole. He saw that the ocean bottom in front was flat and sandy, very different from the rocks and boulders at the base near Jonathan Rock. Darkness hid everything else. Siverts maneuvered the mini-sub over the ocean floor, as the sub's propeller left circular marks on the soft bottom.

Some two hundred and seventy-five feet above on the *Cavalier*, the men feverishly worked out positioning coordinates with respect to the sub's placement towards the target, as the mini-sub didn't have onboard directional sonar. Curt Siverts relayed another course change in directing his father towards the object. At the time, Don Siverts didn't want his one son to be underwater in any of the mini-subs, as he didn't want Curt to face the dangers that he knew existed.

Don received a different bearing every ten to fifteen minutes from on top. Although the object of interest was so close, the currents, lack of visibility, and impreciseness as to location continued to bedevil the search—as they had everyone before. The bottom was "very monotonous" with wavy sand and very little else. A few curious fish swirled around but the hazy light in front kept any unusual visual sightings to a minimum.

As the minutes ticked by, Siverts looked around trying to find the wreck. As one course correction after another didn't work out, whether on topside or under the sea, men became impatient, even doubtful again. Back in the operations shack, Don Knight peered at the monitors and gave orders to Curt Siverts for his father to continue looping around the coordinates at which the mother ship hovered. The continual adjusting was necessary both under the sea and on its surface. Owing to the delicacy of the operations, the *Cavalier* wasn't anchored, relying instead to maneuver over the target by its twin engines. Siverts meanwhile continued navigating the *Snooper* below in its meanderings over the sparse, foreboding bottom. Despite everyone's hopes, the long-sought-after wreck still stayed elusive.

As he watched through the porthole, Siverts became curious about the colorful rockfish that started to appear in more numbers. Various red, copper, and gold-colored rockfish, one to two feet in length, swirled in front of the mini-sub. The fish seemed to be concentrating to one side. Don steered the mini-sub in the direction of the rockfish. He followed them, knowing that a "tell-tale sign" of a larger wreck, deposit, or habitat was where they could be living.

He noticed that the sand waves had become spotted now with scattered debris. Siverts at first couldn't tell what these were, but dark, smaller objects dotted the white sand outlined in front. The rockfish began to multiply in schools, and they danced around as he continued on. Seeing the sand kicking up and dispersing into the undersea currents, Don reduced *Snooper*'s speed and adjusted its buoyancy to minimize the disturbance.

The flash of white against the darkness stood out, and he made out what appeared to be the outline of a dish. Depending on the mini-sub's position, it bounced in the currents that at times moved faster than the sub did. Siverts peered out and saw a darkness in front of him that was different from the haze he had become accustomed to. Motoring slowly along the bottom, he concentrated on what seemed to be a large shape that was materializing and becoming larger.

The visibility improved, and Don Siverts could see eight to ten feet outside his port windows. He maneuvered the submersible closer towards the ominous shape, covered with darker shadows and then pitched into total blackness. Looming directly in front, Siverts couldn't believe his eyes when crockery in the sand and the outline of a large paddlewheel hub magically appeared. A fisherman's net surrealistically rose high up from the hub, still held up by its buoys but tightly snagged to the grounded wreck. Illuminated by the lights, an extensive black belt of once-colored copper hull plating swept away below the paddlewheel. Covered with "bumpy" marine organisms and corrosion, the large main shaft that connected the paddlewheel assembly became visible in the shadowy currents.

At 8:44 A.M. on October 1, 1993, Siverts radioed, "Eureka . . . I've found the target. I think I've found the ship." Cheering, yelling, and loud claps filled the air of the *Cavalier*'s control room, as men jumped up and gave "high fives." "To say the least, this was a very exciting moment," one observed later.

Under the ocean by the length of a football field, Siverts had to be careful of the draping net, as its strands could easily foul his propeller and rudder, jamming them until someone could get down and free the sub—a very difficult task at best. Several months before, the *Delta* fouled on a net when diving down on the *Lusitania*. The salvors had anticipated this, and the mini-sub was forced to jettison its rudder and propeller before it could surface. *Snooper* couldn't do this.

Due to his concentration on navigating safely, Siverts's sub motored past the wreck. He had "run out of ship" and what he first saw in that moment, now seemed to be an illusion. With limited visibility, he couldn't find the wreck again in the darkness, despite the outside lights and monitoring directions from the mother ship.

This lack of visibility was an important reason why divers couldn't find the ship over the years. Or locate it again, if they had. David Flohr observed from his later experiences:

> It was very dark down there. There were times when we were right next to the ship and didn't even know that. It was too dark. The mother ship was above the mini-sub with an antenna in the water on the starboard side. The operator would direct a submersible with 'you're five feet due west of us,' or 'you're ten feet south of us.' The area was so dark that we once went around that ship for one hour and didn't even know it, even while having the precise coordinates.

After fifteen more minutes of searching Don Knight gave the reluctant order for Siverts to "come on up." All was not lost, however, because Siverts had turned *Snooper*'s onboard video taping system on. Anticipation ran high as the yellow submersible motored through the fog to the large mother ship. Meanwhile, Mark Barnum was writing down the positional data regarding the relative positions of the *Cavalier* and the target, an important task in finding the wreck again.

The mini-sub slowly moved to the *Cavalier,* where crewmen attached the cables and brought the submersible up.

Once at the side of the ship, Siverts opened the hatch and emerged. As soon as he appeared, Don Knight started talking with him and confirmed what had been seen. Siverts handed the videotape to Knight, as they discussed more about the undersea conditions. Don Knight then took the videotape to the monitoring room with the rest of the salvors and crew crowding around. Everyone kept their fingers crossed that their fate wouldn't duplicate that of Larry Holcomb's crew, when that tape mysteriously ended due to a "mechanical failure."

As the video played the scenes of continuing flat sands, the men commented, "Different than we've seen before." Although the mood was somber, when the red rockfish began to appear, the men talked about the sea life of sand dabs, large halibut, and petrale sole that might also be found around shipwrecks at these depths. The outline of the paddleship hub then became distinct, a draping net in the background. Everyone became silent. On screen, the whites of dishes, browns of bottles, and the occasional blackish remains of crates contrasted against the flat seafloor. Dark barnacles, white coral-like growths, and greenish marine organisms dotted the corroded iron of the ship's shaft and engines.

Then cheers broke out. Knight said loudly, "I'm ninety-nine percent convinced that we've found the target." He quickly assembled everyone outside on the main deck and admonished all to keep everything quiet. They could lose the entire project if someone weren't careful, as other salvors would race to the site, work the location, and try to beat them to court for the salvaging rights. After all of their work, this would be a very unpleasant scenario. "Make one wrong move and she will be lost forever," he concluded. The men also knew that keeping such an important secret, however, for any length of time would be hard.

That noon, David Slater and Don Knight took the two-man *Delta* with its mechanical arm down to retrieve artifacts, particularly the white porcelain objects that *Snooper*'s video had identified by the paddleship hub—a necessity in making the required legal claim. The conditions were still foggy in the distance, but the seas were calm when they left. Slater put the mini-sub into a dive by the buoy marking the wreck's spot. He followed the buoy line as the submersible slowly descended.

Once at the bottom, the men discovered the wreck was nowhere in sight, as the currents had swirled the buoy and its line away. They turned to head in the direction where the men felt that the *Jonathan* lay. As the mini-sub slowly cruised that way, the underwater currents swirled particles past it like flurries of driven white snow. The metallic-sounding communications from above gave course directions over the sub's intercom, and the high pitch of the battery-driven engine, blasts of ballast, and loud sound bursts of the lateral thrusters (or propulsion units) enveloped the interior.

The submersible's lights reflected against lighter objects with a dark surrounding background. A specific dark spot grew larger and the hub of the ship suddenly loomed up "with all its magnificence." Although the water was never clear due to the flowing particles, the playful, colorful rockfish and *Metridium senelle* (also known as cauliflower sea anemones) abounded at the wreck site. Metridium are filter feeders that attach to all wrecked ships and leech out the iron. Spotted "white" in the sub's lights, and with a cauliflower appearance, these mushroom-like anemones have a long and wide base.

Don Knight observed:

> When we were at the *BJ*, we thought that we were on the bow section, but we were actually instead on the stern, ran out of ship again, and had to button back once more to see it. We came to rest above the main deck and sand sediments. I soon saw a small champagne bottle lying in the sand, and I then understood the significance of all of this. There was the celebration and elation, but there was also so much more. I told David Slater, "Let's have five to six minutes of silence and just

> watch everything out there." After nineteen years of effort, twelve of research and seven of searching, I now found myself staring at the wreck of the *Brother Jonathan* and its bow section.
>
> But then I started hearing inside me the multiple voices of the dead of the *Brother Jonathan.* They were saying to me, "Now that you found us, we will give you all that we have, if you will protect us." The voices became louder, "We will give you all that we have, if you will protect us," and then louder, "If you will protect us."

AFTER THREE HOURS of inspecting the site and retrieving artifacts, Slater brought *Delta* to the surface. The men discovered that the wind had kicked up, blown away the fog, and created choppy water. As the submersible bounced around in increasing seas, the crew found that it was a tricky business to attach cables to the guy loops and wench up the sub. Once they were successful, the two men left the mini-sub one by one, as Harvey Harrington raced over and grabbed the goodie-bag from the sub's exterior. When he opened the netted canvas bag, the men found the champagne bottle, ale crockery, a salad plate, pieces of a cereal bowl, and other objects.

Inside *Delta* that day, Knight videotaped the wreck, then used the mechanical arm from inside the mini-sub to snare debris to support DSR's legal claim to the *Jonathan.* This was the next important step to accomplish. They plucked up six intact artifacts overall for proof, recovering two old porcelain plates (manufactured in Great Britain by Sedgwick Porcelain), a wine flask, the black champagne bottle with the cork intact, a medicine bottle with a "sampling" of the contents, and a spike with part of the hull still attached.

These efforts took time, as not all of the recovery attempts were successful. Don's work to recover one plate ended when he became concerned that the efforts would break the artifact. The task of operating the arm was also difficult, because the outside water pressure of well over one hundred pounds per square inch pressed against their efforts to move it toward the artifacts lying on the bottom. When the sub surfaced and Knight was back on the ship, he was tired and exhausted from the hard work in the recovery.

In a later inspection, Don Siverts hovered close to the wreck, when the currents forced *Snooper* against part of the wood. The minisub, however, bounced back from the material as it was flexible like cardboard, according to Siverts. In the limited visibility at the site, the submersibles would operate mere feet from the wreckage, making sweeps around and over the ship slower than "walking speed."

Nothing directly proved, however, that this hulk was the *Brother Jonathan*. They hadn't located an insignia, bell, or some object with the ship's identifying name. On the other hand, although vessels disappeared around this general area, there were no other paddleship steamers that had gone down to the ocean's bottom in the area. Also no ships of this size had sunk around this location. By changing their assumptions, Deep Sea Research had located the wreck in forty-five minutes, after a search that had started 128 years ago. Interestingly enough, when the salvors mapped the wreck's site, they discovered that for all those years, several fishermen had marked the site as a "hazard" spot on their charts, due to their lost fishing nets and equipment.

If prior salvors had drawn a map and charted where fishermen were losing their rigs, searchers arguably could have found earlier success. David Flohr felt later that if they had started doing "lazy-eight" search patterns south of the rock, they would have come across the ship sooner. All of the past expeditions had underestimated the strength of the 1865 storm. Winds blew from the northwest, the ocean current swept southeast, and the conditions drove the ship underwater two miles south of Jonathan Rock to its final resting place. This was a remarkable distance from where the ship had first struck the deadly reef.

The "California current" in that general location is like the Gulf Stream—although the Gulf currents are generally stronger. The California underwater flow sweeps from Asia, Japan, around the Aleutians and Alaska, and then down the U.S. West Coast to Crescent City. After the vessel impaled itself on the rocky spire, then loosened to start sinking, its bow drove the ship downwards into the ocean. The *Brother Jonathan* then swung around when it hit the bottom stern first, so that its bow was pointing north by northeast and the stern, south by southwest. It finally settled pointing in the opposite direction from land.

With the salvors confident that they had finally discovered the ship, their next move would be to hire legal counsel to represent them. The next move would be to file an actual legal proceeding against the wreck of the *Brother Jonathan*. They'd request the judge award Deep Sea Research with full title to the sunken ship and whatever was of value. Little did they know that this battle would take them from hundreds of feet under the sea to the hallowed halls of the United States Supreme Court.

Part III

LAWYERS AND TREASURE

CHAPTER 13

A Time of Dispute

Although Deep Sea Research discovered the S.S. *Brother Jonathan,* a rift was developing between the salvors. As the men discussed how to best explore the wreck, and finally to gain the requisite permits from the State of California, tensions were surfacing. Don Knight felt that the problem originated well before the discovery. On the second day of the 1993 explorations—just days before the sighting—two of Knight's friends drove to nearby Brookings, Oregon. The investors were staying there to avoid attracting attention to the harbor. Knight recalled:

> On Monday night, friends of mine headed to Brookings to see the investors. David Flohr, Sherman Harris, and others were staying at this particular motel, waiting for what they hoped would be our announcement of finding the *Jonathan.* Jim Wadsley was also there, as well as Harvey Harrington, I believe. I had stayed on board the *Cavalier* to work out our exploration passes that next morning.
>
> Wadsley, as I recall, told me that he couldn't be on board because he had to "reset some equipment." As these friends came to the door of a room, one overheard someone say, "If the guys find the *Brother Jonathan,* then we should take over the project as this is the only way we're going to get our money back."
>
> They reported back to me, of course, what they had heard.

> Two days later on Wednesday—as we were getting closer again to coming back home empty-handed—as a precaution, I told this to the *Cavalier*'s skipper. He answered, "We have guns and we'll be able to repel all boarders." Both of us felt that if any steps were made to physically take over the ship, that this would have been an act of piracy. However, by then most of the investors were leaving and the problem didn't materialize.

The major problem that did surface, however, was just how DSR should explore the downed vessel. Salvors and investors, who wanted a quicker return of their capital and profits, clashed head-on with Knight's concern about protecting "this graveyard of lost souls." He saw the need for painstaking detail to preserve the site's archaeology. Given Deep Sea Research's tight budget and its continued need for cash, this conflict put even more pressure on everyone.

Don Knight already felt that Jim Wadsley directly opposed his decisions. The report (whether correct or not) that Wadsley had been with the investors that Monday night was unnerving. Given the egos and achievements of the three operational heads—Wadsley, Harvey Harrington, and Knight—it is not surprising that they would run into conflict with one another. Since the three were also the only directors on the board, Knight decided to try and work out an accommodation with Harrington. Unfortunately for him, Wadsley was apparently doing the same thing.

According to Knight, he talked at length with Harvey Harrington about the cost and time necessary to do the recovery the "right way." After these conversations, Don believed that Harvey would support him on his recovery plans. This "politicking" between the DSR members and investors took time away from deciding how best to secure the legal rights to the wreck and raise more investment funds. Knight also assumed that he had effective control of the operations, and he counted on the investors backing him.

The investors, however, were already nervous. David Flohr worried how their scarce funds would be parceled out, as he understood Don's plans were more expensive than first thought. Flohr was a tough-minded, financially oriented businessman, and he knew the value of strong financial planning and controls. The problem was that large unknowns existed as to what had to be done in finding the gold treasure at 300 feet below the ocean—not to mention that the State of California was not being cooperative in its preliminary permit discussions.

David Flohr and Sherman Harris said afterward that they would have preferred seeing Knight save the money for exploration rather than spend it that September on the investors for his "fantail" barbeque and undersea submarine trips. This was a classic conflict between the free-flow, optimistic world of risk-taking divers and the business-oriented investors who were putting up the money. When one adds the personality and operational differences between the lead officers, the situation was best described as being "volatile."

One month later in November 1993, Knight held an investors' meeting at the Spa Hotel in Palm Springs. He had worked up an elaborate presentation from a public relation's viewpoint that unfortunately fell flat from some of the major investors' perspective. It was a classic case again of differing motivations.

When the investors walked into the hotel lobby, they came upon a large announcement board that read in large letters, "Brother Jonathan Treasure Project—Meeting Room One." Some of the investors were upset when seeing this, as they felt the company should be working in total secrecy. As David Flohr said, "We hadn't secured the rights to the wreck and at that time anyone could have found the ship and beaten us to court to acquire the rights to explore it." Whether one agreed or not with this assessment, the gulf between people was ever widening.

Once inside the meeting room, three persons sat at the head table, being Don Knight, the company's accountant, and Deborah Brazeal. Ms. Brazeal, an attractive, younger blonde, had been elected to the board as its secretary. She had earned her doctorate from the University of Alabama, was then a professor at California State Polytechnic University (Pomona), and an expert in small business entrepreneurship. There were about thirty people in the room, including Sherman Harris, Jim Wadsley, Harvey Harrington, and David Flohr. Most knew everybody else.

Knight started the meeting by announcing proudly, "We, the directors of Deep Sea Research, are pleased to announce that we've found the *Brother Jonathan.*" He then played a video of the wreck that Don Siverts had made, including that which showed the 180 feet left of the "elongated saucer shape" of the ship. When the tape finished playing, Knight held his two hands together and said, "We're giving you the *Brother Jonathan* on a silver platter."

Don then announced to the group, "We will need five million dollars and five years to recover the gold." According to David Flohr, "The investors nearly fell onto the floor at this statement of the cost and time required." Although the meeting ended on apparently good terms, the investors were very concerned about what was said.

Sherman Harris immediately confronted Knight after the meeting, "Don, you told me that the cost would be five hundred thousand dollars—not millions." Knight, believing that Harrington would support him, replied, "We've found a virgin, not-torn-apart wreck, and that changes everything. We can't allow anyone to rape, pillage, and plunder this wreck."

Harvey Harrington, Jim Wadsley, and Donald Knight—then and later—all took the lion's share of the credit for discovering the ship to the exclusion of the others. The facts, however, speak for themselves. David Flohr later commented that he had "given up worrying about that" (who did what in the discovery), as he and the other investors weren't there at the time and didn't know one way or the other. From a financial and legal perspective, this didn't matter as much either.

What mattered was that Knight's statement about the money and time requirements had shaken the confidence of the investors. From conservative business practices, they were concerned about his claims that the amount of gold to be found would be valued in the millions. The investors made a demand for an accounting and alleged that he had been making payments to himself as salary without telling the investors—which Don Knight disputes. They said that they would pay him an hourly fee, presumably given for a reduced equity interest, but which Knight refused. Don Knight disputes this, arguing that whatever payments he received were for reasonable expenditures and on requests known by the responsible individuals.

The investors later consulted legal counsel. They were concerned about the way past money had been raised from various people. Although the funding for the exploration was being marketed as a private exempt offering, the lawyer worried that such investment efforts through public seminars, and without strong disclaimers, would be seen as a public offering. Therefore it would require a securities permit from the State of California. They feared that the operations were being run too "loosey goosey" and that there would be sizeable legal problems, in the event the investors didn't receive their monies back.

To be fair to Don Knight, nearly every salvage operation runs into this problem. Explorers want to raise funds to find a wreck and totally believe that they'll find the treasure. They are driven to meet this goal, but at the same time they also need money to pay their bills. On the other hand, the investors who have invested their hard-earned money want more controls, planning, and stretching of cash. Whether an operation is successful or not, the conflict between investors and operators is a built-in problem.

WEEKS LATER the prime investors and directors, other than Don Knight, called a shareholders meeting for February 8, 1994. Faxes under the apparent signature of Jim Wadsley were sent out calling for a special meeting to vote on the board of directors. One day before this meeting, Don Knight held his own board of directors special meeting with basically himself, Deborah Brazeal, and the company's accountant attending, whereby they terminated Jim Wadsley from the operations.

The following day Mark Hemstreet, the president and owner of Shilo Inns, presided over the first-called meeting held at the Palm Springs Shilo Inn in California. Although Mark wasn't a shareholder per se, he held "points" (or the right to profit interests) from his investment, and the investors believed that his neutrality and business experience would be helpful in this explosive situation. Also in attendance were three attorneys to argue over procedures, one representing the investors, another for DSR, and the third representing Don Knight.

At the time the only three shareholders of DSR were Harvey Harrington, Jim Wadsley, and Don Knight, each owning 320 shares. Sherman Harris owned 40 shares for a total of 1000 outstanding shares of stock. According to Don Knight:

> I paid $10,000 for my 320 shares, and Sherman Harris had paid for his 40 shares. Now, Harvey Harrington and Jim Wadsley had been issued 320 shares each, but I didn't think that they had paid their full money in yet. When the vote was taken, the vote was 680 to 320 and I was out. Basically, Harrington and Wadsley voted me out as shareholders, and the other attorneys argued that my prior board action was not effective.

In between arguments made by the various attorneys, the shareholders then voted out the old slate of Donald Knight, Deborah Brazeal, the accountant, and anyone else associated with Don Knight. They voted in Sherman Harris as president, Harvey Harrington as the director of offshore operations, James Wadsley as secretary, and David Flohr as treasurer. During the voting, Flohr said that Knight reportedly asked the others, "Is there any room for me?" They replied, "Not as a director, but you're still a shareholder." Afterward, Don Knight approached David Flohr and asked if he could stay on the board, to which Flohr replied in the negative.

Knight's later complaints didn't rest as much with David Flohr and Sherman Harris, as they did with Jim Wadsley and Harvey Harrington. They were the ones who voted him out. They differed over the salvage procedures, and Don Knight wanted to take all possible steps to fully preserve the ship for posterity and with all due respect for the dead. He said:

> Jim Wadsley and Harvey Harrington worked to kick me out of Deep Sea Research, and I should have done something about that when I heard about Wadsley's first meeting with the investors in late September. But the investors went just nuts when I told them about the "five million dollars and five years" for the complete exploration and recovery of the ship.
>
> I understood later that Wadsley and Harrington had gone to the investors and said that "he," being Don Knight, was only interested in preserving the history of the *Brother Jonathan,* whereas they would recover the gold for $175,000. If you're an investor and faced with five years or $5,000,000 versus $175,000, and sooner, who are you going to go with?*

Mark Hemstreet worked to mediate between the factions that day. Given what transpired later, it is possible that had Don Knight been able to obtain the five million dollars—a big "if"—that everything on board or around the *Brother Jonathan* would have been discovered. On the other hand, he was asking others to finance a very expensive and long plan. As Mark Hemstreet stated later, "Donald Knight is a very colorful personality. The people split because of 'irreconcilable differences'; their personalities and management styles simply clashed."

Although the reasons why the split happened are understandable, one can also see both sides. For years, Don Knight had poured out his heart and soul to find the *Brother Jonathan,* and when he did, he was then denied the opportunity to continue the search for the gold. In a conflict between ideas and personalities, Knight was the

*As it turned out with all the expenses, including legal fees, Don Knight was closer to the ultimate expense number than anyone else.

one who lost. On the other hand, those who were left would have to endure the frustrations of dealing with a recalcitrant State of California, conflicts within and outside the exploration group, and the problem of never having enough money to adequately fund their operations.

LAWYERS FOR BOTH SIDES quickly swung into action. Don Knight argued that he had been illegally voted out of office, while DSR's attorney responded that the change in officers had been according to the law. Knight, after a long negotiation, finally agreed to accept $40,000 to be paid over twelve months plus a boat (the 28-foot, twin-engine Tolley Craft supply vessel) in return for his stock. The boat was signed over to him. Owing to poor cash flow and more disputes between the parties, however, Don ultimately had to accept $30,000 instead of this and paid haltingly over a two-year period.

The ex-officer and head was to turn over all of his corporate and salvage records, and, according to DSR, he was to keep "in the strictest confidence all information he had learned concerning the wreck of the Brother *Jonathan.*" There was no controversy over the records he turned over to the company, but Knight had a different interpretation over what he could or couldn't say to the press. As he hadn't signed a non-compete clause with DSR, Knight decided to head off in a different direction away from this group.

Deep Sea Research soon heard about Knight's radio and newspaper interviews about his having located the sunken ship. On February 24, 1994, for example, on Crescent City radio station KPOD he announced on behalf of DSR the finding of the *Brother Jonathan.* Don said:

> The finding was historically and archeologically extremely valuable. We have found a maritime graveyard, the last resting place of 225 lives. You can see the hub of the paddle wheel on the port side, part of the steam boiler, and part of the engine. It reads "Morgan Iron Works."

He produced pictures of the china plates, a spike from the hull, and the medicine bottle that had come from the wreck. He also showed Don Siverts's underwater video of the ship. Although he didn't give the ship's approximate location, Knight said that Wadsley called the radio station during the interview and angrily demanded that the radio station "pull the plug on the Knight interview." The station declined.

Larry Holcomb also heard about the upcoming interview and showed up at the radio station. When questioned about the ship by the announcer, Holcomb said that there was nothing more to say, because "Don Knight was the one who had discovered the sunken ship." In response, Knight stated over the air that Holcomb had helped every salvor by finding out where the *Jonathan* didn't rest—and saving everyone else that time and expense. Larry Holcomb was also obviously pleased that the ship had finally been discovered.

The next day, the *San Francisco Chronicle* ran a lead story, "1865 Shipwreck Discovered Off North Coast; Legend Says Steamer Sank with Gold, Booze, and Camels." The paper quoted Donald Knight as having found the "maritime graveyard," and he called the vessel, "The Queen Elizabeth II of her day with food fit for the palate of a king."

From DSR's perspective, people were understandably upset. The company had removed Knight as an officer and director, and it was now negotiating to buy back his interest. At the same time, Knight was telling the world about the discovery, and anyone could check the court records and see that DSR hadn't yet perfected its legal claim to the wreck. From Don Knight's perspective, he had given up twenty years of his life to find the ship from which his beloved father had pulled up a piece of the hull. Knight had been kicked out before anything of value had been discovered—and if he sold his interest back, he would be denied that participation if they discovered the gold.

The battle between the ex-partners heated up when DSR's officers watched Knight in a Mail Boxes Etc. television commercial where he was described as being the "renowned undersea discoverer." The advertisement showed him building his *Sea Probe,* one-man mini-sub, and Mail Boxes Etc. delivered the sub's large outer yellow shell from the East Coast to his Southern California facility. The company aired the TV ad during the 1995 World Series, which had a large viewing audience as two networks televised the series between the Atlanta Braves and Cleveland Indians (which the Braves won).

DSR's officers accused Don Knight's sister of following them around Crescent City in her Cadillac "Spymobile," then jumping out to take pictures of everyone and their activities. DSR also accused Knight of "poisoning the waters" in Crescent City by telling everyone they had robbed him of his investment and would rob the undersea graves of the dead. The salvors argued that DSR had hired its own archaeologist and was conducting everything as legally as possible.

Knight told his side of the story through the press to a very interested public. Newspaper reporters quoted him as saying, "What we have down there is a shipwreck that is a graveyard and extremely valuable from an archeological and historical standpoint. I put twenty years of my life into this, and I feel like I'm the real loser." Newspapers quoted Sherman Harris's response that Knight was voted off the board due to differences over the recovery efforts. "Knight's partners felt the project could be done faster and cheaper than the five years and five million dollars that he estimated," Harris said.

The public accusations became ugly. Showing the pictures of the artifacts discovered in September 1993, the press quoted Knight as saying, "Treasure hunters would destroy all of this. Deep Sea Research will pillage history, pillage heritage, and we will all sit back and watch the desecration of a graveyard." DSR denied these allegations. "No way," replied Sherman Harris on behalf of the salvors. "We have an archaeologist on board and we are going about everything by the book. No way are we going to destroy anything."

Despite the bricks being thrown back and forth, DSR was able to accomplish several things that year. David Flohr recommended that since they had discovered the *Brother Jonathan,* the salvors should acquire the insurance interests in the wreck. If insurance companies had paid off claims on the wreck in 1865, then these companies or their successors would still have some ownership rights to the ship. Purchasing these interests also would show that the sunken ship had not been abandoned, which would be important to DSR's legal claims. It would be better to acquire these interests now before anything of value was discovered—which would dramatically increase the cost. Deep Sea Research and its officers had made the decision to fly on a "wing and a prayer" that they would find the long-missing gold.

In its August 2, 1865 issue, the *San Francisco Bulletin* wrote that the insurance coverage on the *Brother Jonathan* and its cargo included: the California Insurance Company, $20,000; California Lloyd's, $13,690; Merchant's Mutual, $10,000; Bigelow and Brothers, $2,500; and Falkner, Taylor, and Company, $2,300, for a grand total of $46,490. The report stated that "probably two-thirds of the cargo was uninsured." The newspaper total was incorrect, and the U.S. District Court in its decisions used the corrected total of $48,490.

The difficulty now was tracking down who owned those insurance companies or had the rights to their assets. Unfortunately, the 1906 earthquake destroyed many San Francisco records, including the actual insurance polices on that ship and its cargo. A specific manifest listing the cargo on board also had disappeared. David Flohr and others consulted various sources, including the *New York Times* and *Alta California,* to determine the cargo and insurers. The problem became how to find the insurance companies that had paid claims and their successors.

For example, Bigelow and Brothers represented the Phoenix Insurance Company of New York, which in turn merged with Fidelity Fire Insurance in 1910. This entity then finally merged in 1959 into the Continental Insurance Company. When the smoke cleared from DSR's contacts and negotiations, Commercial Union Insurance Company and Continental agreed to accept 10 percent of any gold discovered on a prorata basis. The company also continued searching for other insurers and their successors.

Having received legal advice that one of Major Hensley's descendants had a potential legal interest in the *Brother Jonathan,* David Flohr flew to Vancouver, British Columbia, to meet with the representative. Deep Sea Research eventually reached an agreement, whereby the family provided certain genealogical information to the salvors. If this data proved helpful, then a contract for additional compensation would be worked out. As events turned out, no compensation was paid—other than a $250 initial payment for her time.

As the personal battles escalated privately and publicly between Knight, Wadsley, and DSR, the court battles also heated up. In 1991 prior to its locating the ship, DSR filed a lawsuit in federal court under its admiralty jurisdiction seeking the rights to the *Brother Jonathan.* When the State of California intervened and asserted an interest in the action, the salvors decided to wait until they had actually discovered the vessel before fighting this battle. Their attorneys dismissed this initial action without prejudice, which allowed the legal action to be prosecuted later.

While he was running DSR, Don Knight took the six artifacts found by the wreck on October 1, 1993, to San Francisco. The law firm of Gordon & Rees refiled the "in rem" proceeding (a claim over a "thing," such as the wreck at the ocean's bottom) to declare that DSR was the legal possessor of the *Brother Jonathan* under established maritime law. The State of California immediately countersued.

This was the beginning of DSR's long legal nightmare. After DSR's jubilation in finally discovering the *Brother Jonathan,* the State of California took the position that it had total control over all of the operations and the right to one-half of all proceeds and recoveries. Although the wreck settled to the bottom 5.1 miles offshore the California coast, or the closest point jutting off Point St. George, the state took the position that the wreck was still within three miles of its mean high-tide line. It claimed that the three-mile state right was measured from the closest "permanent" offshore reef—not from its coastline, regardless of how far away that outcropping was.

The wreck hit the ocean's bottom within three miles of Whale Rock by a short 600 yards, or another fifteen minutes if the ship could have stayed afloat. When hearing of this "nonsense," one of the salvors said that they could dynamite the reef to below the ocean's level overnight, but the rest of the officers laughed this comment away.

The legal issue was over a basic difference of philosophies. These concepts vary widely among the various state governments. The State of California, and particularly its State Land Commission, really felt that it owned the right to any wreck that was close to its shores, regardless of the technicalities or then applicable federal law. David Flohr said it best:

> The California State Lands Commission said that they had 1,200 to 1,500 shipwrecks off their coastline, and to us that "We think all of them belong to the state." California also gave the message that it would rather have all of these shipwrecks rot on the ocean floor than have any salvors rewarded for discovering the gold.

These great philosophical differences would be argued out in legal technicalities before numbers of judges and courts. Before the great legal battles were underway, DSR conducted further surveying on the site in June 1994, using the *Cavalier* and the mini-sub *Delta*. The purpose of this exploration was to develop a salvage plan for the ship and to ensure the wreck's security.

David Flohr submerged in the *Delta* on this expedition to see the wreck for himself. After all the months and months of hard work meeting with investors, helping to raise money, investing his own money, and concerned about DSR's financial affairs, he wanted to see everything. An experienced diver and seafarer himself, Flohr was flat on his stomach when he spotted the wreck and the distinguishing paddle wheel hub. A moment later, the mini-sub's pilot told him to look out at nine-o'clock (a nautical direction). Looking around through the porthole, he saw "the biggest damn octopus ever." Flohr commented:

> It was at least twenty feet from tip to tip. It slithered about the hull and had a skin on it that was pinkish-red and

> ghastly looking. The beast's texture looked like Kentucky Fried Chicken, original recipe. And instead of scooting away and shooting a cloud of ink, it looked at us. Then the octopus came right at the mini-sub, right at us. It rose against the sub and with a huge, ugly eye, looked directly at me for one moment. It then shot under the bow of the submarine and came out on the other side. The octopus had suckers the size of coffee cups, and it stirred up the silt so badly that we couldn't see as well as we had before. This cloud of dust took time to settle down, as there was a little current moving through then. I thought that I should at least warn the divers about this one small fact—which I did.

AT THE TIME of the June 1994 explorations, a "high-speed spy boat" was monitoring DSR's operations. The craft circled the mother ship with "numerous flashes emanating from the boat" that indicated someone was taking flash pictures. When the *Cavalier* turned to confront the boat, the craft took off with great speed and disappeared. The day after DSR completed those operations, Peter Pelkofer, the senior legal counsel for the California State Lands Commission, sent a letter to DSR threatening legal action to keep it away from the wreck site, until it had the "required" permit.

The State of California subsequently made a motion in U.S. District Federal Court in September 1994 to prevent the recovery of the *Brother Jonathan* by DSR. Fetcher C. Alford of the San Francisco law firm of Gordon & Rees was the legal representative for DSR in these proceedings. He made presentations in court before Federal District Court Judge Louis C. Bechtle, who would end up ruling on all of the major legal and operational decisions for DSR's explorations.

Alford earned his undergraduate degree from the University of Puget Sound in Tacoma, Washington, where he graduated magna cum laude and was the editor of the school's newspaper. He obtained his J.D. law degree from the University of California, Hastings, where he also graduated magna cum laude. After graduating from law school, Mr. Alford clerked for a U.S. District Federal Court judge in Georgia.

He already had extensive trial experience with a cool, factual approach and demeanor in court. According to David Flohr, "Fletcher was six feet, three inches, or so, and a large beefy man. He was a really nice guy and cordial person, who kept his cool in all of the proceedings, when the rest of us could become angry, upset, or simply disbelieve what we were hearing. (His peers voted him in 2005 and 2006 as one of Northern California's "Super Lawyers" in the field of civil litigation.)

As the lawyers and divers worked on land and sea, the former and present partners of DSR waged their attacks in the media, primarily between Don Knight and Jim Wadsley. Knight continued to tell the press that he had been forced out due to his archaeological and conservation views and that any salvaging should wait until a team of marine archaeologists could scrutinize the wreck. Harvey Harrington told reporters that he believed the treasure was there and estimated its value at "$25 million to $50 million—more than enough to finance the treasure hunt and pay for the salvage of relics." A worried Knight told the reporters about his continuing concerns that "Deep Sea Research will pillage history." His statements had to have solidified the State of California's view of this group after he left.

In September 1996, Knight claimed to reporters that DSR personnel "had taken two truckloads of artifacts," implying also that they had destroyed some. Jim Wadsley argued back that they had only removed fifteen pieces of china for conservation purposes and had taken more than one-hundred hours of underwater video to document this fact. Knight alleged he had information that there had been a serious diver's accident; Wadsley's published reply was, "We didn't require a Band-Aid."

They couldn't even agree on who had discovered the wreck. Knight said that his father's experience had inspired his interest and that he was the one who had found the ship. Wadsley said, "I had a target that [Knight had] steadfastly refused to go look at. And we went down with super-high-resolution sonar, and it was the *Brother Jonathan.* We needed only seven and a half minutes to locate what Knight had tried for almost two decades to find."

Don Knight was understandably upset and bitter over what had happened. He was the one who had brought Wadsley, Harrington, and the others into the exploration, not to mention the years Knight had spent in the search. After directing and being part of the team that had discovered the fabled ghost ship, the group ousted him from the hunt for its treasures.

Knight kept telling Pelkofer and the media, "These guys are pirates" and that the salvors would desecrate the site. Wadsley and DSR sued Knight with "three frivolous lawsuits designed to muzzle me," according to Knight—or over "his false remarks that we would pilfer the site," according to DSR. The suits were filed in Los Angeles County where Knight resided.

These basic differences between Wadsley, Harrington, and Knight reached a climax with Knight suing for defamation, breach of contractual relationships, and other causes of actions. Deep Sea Research and the other individuals sued and countersued for defamation and other actions. The attorneys for all of the parties took depositions, or questioning under oath by the lawyers in front of a court reporter. Knight's attorney took the depositions of "Wadsley, Deborah Brazeal, and others, including subpoenaing everyone from David Flohr to Sherman Harris." Giving an idea of how heated these hearings were, the attorneys for both sides became so argumentative and personal toward each other, one observer later said that even the lawyers' conduct shocked him.

In one lawsuit, DSR's attorney missed a filing deadline, and Knight's attorney took a default judgment. When DSR learned about this action, their lawyer filed a motion on appeal to set aside the judgment. This case was settled eventually due to the high legal costs being incurred by all sides. Although none of the lawsuits went to trial, the cost of Donald Knight's legal representation alone, not to mention DSR's bill, was $42,000 by itself.

Lawsuits also flared up between Don Knight's sister, Mary Knight Barnes, and brother-in-law, George Barnes. They filed harassment charges against DSR and alleged that its people had threatened them. DSR answered that the charges weren't true: It couldn't have harassed them when the couple was shadowing DSR's activities by "driving their 'spymobile' while eating chips and drinking coke." These lawsuits didn't go to trial either. Knight then lost a motion and court hearing to reimburse his legal costs, so his out-of-pocket cash and profit losses over his ouster were substantial.

Although suspected as much by DSR, Knight worked afterward with the State of California. His lack of trust in Harrington's and Wadsley's intentions to safeguard the artifacts was a reason why the State of California fought DSR so hard. Pelkofer called Don Knight up one day and said that he couldn't see any details about the wreck from the "fuzzy video shots provided by DSR." Knight gave the commission a clear copy of Larry Patin's edited version of the discovery, as Patin had been retained for his professional editing services. Don Knight was still so enraged by what had happened that he tried to contact Judge Bechtle, who couldn't and didn't return those telephone calls.

By June 12, 1994, Don Knight learned that the salvors with the large *Cavalier* were exploring the wreck site without the knowledge or permit from the state. He telephoned the California State Lands Commission and told them what was happening. When Knight asked if the CSLC knew the location, the official replied, "Of course we do," and wouldn't listen to Knight's arguments that the ship wasn't where they thought it was.

At the time Knight was even talking with the helicopter service that California had quickly authorized at its expense to investigate. The only problem was that the CSLC directed the pilots to nearby Pelican Bay and not two miles south of Jonathan Rock, as Knight had told them. The pilots found no evidence of the warned-about explorations; a cloud cover then blanketed the area and prohibited further flying. Knight later said, "The arrogance of the state's personnel was unbelievable. In this case, only they felt that they knew where the ship was, and they didn't have a clue."

During the public slandering of one another, the newspapers and media ran wild with their stories, running leads such as "Squabbling over a Shipwreck," "Treasure Hunters are Empty Handed; Former Partner Says Gold Isn't There," "Sea Squabble," "Brother Jonathan Saga Continues," and story after story. Don Knight then established Trans-oceanic Research Group, another underwater exploration company.

Given his knowledge and contacts, DSR's concern over his heading back to compete for the *Brother Jonathan* was the reason it put into place land-based security systems and accelerated its on-site investigations. For his part, Don Knight had his own complement of friends and family in Crescent City who were keeping watch on Deep Sea Research's activities from shore and reporting back.

Friends of Knight in June 1994 were the ones who sped out to the *Cavalier* in the fast speedboat and reported back on DSR's activities. They were the ones who took the flash pictures. Two others gave him a report on when DSR was diving on Jonathan Rock on June 12, 1994. The mother ship kept turning its bow toward them, as it did with the speedboat, and the captain in a mega-phone also loudly told them that they had to immediately leave. With this information in his hands, Knight contacted the State of California.

One time Knight's sister, Mary, was at the harbor buying fish. She happened to spot a DSR ship tie up at the dock and watched as one of the men took a radio-telephone call. She overheard him say that he had to leave because there had been an "incident" onboard the mother ship. As the supply ship motored back, Mary told Don who immediately called the Coast Guard. The service then contacted DSR's mother ship and asked if they were having any problems. The surprised person who took the contact call said "No" and hung up—on the Coast Guard. There were no facts discovered, one way or the other, to substantiate what this "incident" was about.

Don Knight then stated publicly that he looked forward to searching and exploring for more shipwrecks. When he had the chance, this would also include the *Brother Jonathan*.

CHAPTER 14

Finding the Gold and the Courtroom

Despite the internal turmoil at Deep Sea Research, the officers tried to keep their operations moving forward. With the ship discovered, the salvors felt confident in securing more investment funds and continued their seminars and search for potential investors. They had conducted further surveying of the site, even as Don Knight's friends were shadowing them on land and sea. They were letting contracts and securing men and equipment for an exploration to search for the gold. Their success in acquiring the insurer's interest would be helpful in their legal filings. The glamour of searching for lost treasure these days, as seen, is balanced by the administrative, financial, and operational business realities that must be met.

The legal side was bad enough when Don Knight and the others were battling each other. It was only a matter of time before the State of California entered the picture. When DSR began its legal proceedings to be appointed the official salvor of the wreck, the state filed a motion in the Northern Federal District Court in San Francisco before Judge Bechtle to dismiss DSR's application to secure the wreck of the *Brother Jonathan*. It argued that the federal court didn't have the jurisdiction, or power, to hear those proceedings. California wanted all of the actions to be heard in the friendly confines of its state courts and favorable laws. No matter how this was to be done, the state wanted it to be declared the sole owner of the *Jonathan*—even though it hadn't found it and didn't know where the ship was.

In March 1995 the court rewarded the salvors with a legal win. The California State Lands Commission (CSLC) motion in the federal district court was denied on March 15, 1995, by the judge. In April, Judge Bechtle awarded DSR a preliminary injunction appointing it as the "exclusive salvor" over the wreck of the *Brother Jonathan.*

The judge granted DSR the warrant for arrest on the wreck for eighteen months as the custodian and exclusive salvor of the *Brother Jonathan,* subject to one-year extensions, until the "salvage operations are completed." The reserved area was set at "about four and one-half miles offshore from the coastline and about nine miles by ship from Crescent City harbor." The prohibited area was a circle with a zone of one mile in diameter from that point. No vessel other than those belonging to or authorized by DSR and law enforcement agencies were from that point on allowed within the area.

Pursuant to established maritime law, a diver took a copy of the federal arrest warrant in waterproof plastic and attached it to the *Brother Jonathan* on the bottom. By District Court order, a notice was to be sent out each month in which salvage operations were conducted. The notice of the court order and its provisions were posted at Crescent City Harbor, its post office, the County Sheriff's Department, and other places, as well as published in *The Triplicate* in Crescent City and two San Francisco newspapers. The notice specifically described the prohibited area, including the provision that "Anyone violating the order is subject to arrest and civil or criminal penalties."

Although the District Court had awarded the salvage rights to DSR, Judge Bechtle also ruled that all salvaging operations would be conducted under the inspection of a qualified archaeologist. It also stipulated that the disposition of all artifacts would be under the court's jurisdiction. One month later, DSR placed a mobile radar system into operation that monitored the movements of unauthorized craft and people into and out of the prohibited wreck area.

With the court's authorization as the exclusive salvor, Flohr and the others felt confident about their chances. The raising of the needed capital, however, wasn't going as fast as they had anticipated. The public differences between Don Knight and the present partners wasn't the publicity they wanted. The group's optimism hit another dent when the State of California filed a motion in July to stay (or overturn) the judge's appointment of DSR as the exclusive salvor. However, the court shortly denied that motion. The investors could only hope that the State of California's legal battles wouldn't continue, as their operations were already based on a tight budget.

Another unanticipated problem then surfaced. Crescent City and its residents had lost a tourist attraction when DSR discovered the wreck. Before then, curious tourists and divers would travel to the area and look for the wreck of the *Brother Jonathan.* Now it was found—and the curiosity attraction was gone. To make matters worse, one of their own had been removed from the operations, and Don Knight's friends and relatives, including his sister and brother-in-law, were not happy about that and made this fact known.

In a small town like Crescent City, DSR, with its "outsiders," had a growing public-relations problem on their hands. Crescent City folks had pulled together regarding their lumbering industry (environmental restrictions), fishing economy (strict regulations and enforced tribal rights on salmon), and tsunami destruction (where the city never completely recovered). Pelican Bay Prison hadn't helped the city much either because prison officials transferred people in from the state system rather than hiring the numbers of locals as first promised. These problems caused the residents to pull together, and people in small towns can basically act as a group—quickly opposing or supporting activities.

The residents were not very receptive to DSR's explorations. A few were even upset that the group had discovered the vessel. "We received a grilling at a Historical Society meeting," said David Flohr. At a later dinner with community leaders, including the director of the Del Norte County Historical Society, the police chief, port district head, and others, the salvors worked to smooth the ruffled relationships. They told those present that someone would eventually find the gold of the *Brother Jonathan,* and that those people wouldn't be as legally oriented and protective of the artifacts. "We have an archaeologist on board, are under continual court supervision, need the court's okay on everything, have to file environmental reports, and more, and we are doing this," the officers argued.

After a fact-finding trip to the city, the negative environment became so evident to Judge Bechtle that he told the salvors they had better start repairing their standing within the community and "mend some fences," especially if they wanted to continue their search with the community's support. Since this also made sense from a civic standpoint, the explorers made plans to work with the city and Historical Society to refurbish artifacts, help in designing a conservation center, and donate artifacts that could be used for an exhibit on the lost ship.

To mark the 130-year anniversary of the ship's sinking, a special ceremony was held in Crescent City on Sunday, July 30, 1995. On behalf of DSR, Harvey Harrington presented a medicine bottle, black wine bottle, and porcelain plate from the wreck to the Del Norte County Historical Society. He told residents that DSR would donate more artifacts to the Society as they were discovered for an exhibit memorializing the tragedy and those who had died. Crescent City could look forward to a new tourist attraction to replace what it had lost. The services were held at the new Brother Jonathan Cemetery and Memorial Landmark at Ninth Street and Pebble Beach Drive, where the grave markers still remained. Julie McArthur, a descendant of Dr. Anson G. Henry, attended along with 125 other persons.

Meanwhile, operations continued under the sea. In September Jim Wadsley and Harvey Harrington used side-scan sonar, a magnetometer, and GPS work to determine what wreckage led from Jonathan Rock to the wreck site. Their hope was to find the much sought-after safe. Although they didn't find anything resembling the valuable item, they did locate a pile of railroad iron in the path leading to the wreck; the *Jonathan* reportedly had a cargo of rails on board.

It soon became obvious, however, that California was not about to give up. The CSLC turned aside all offers by DSR to work out reasonable conditions for the permit's issuance. In 1995, the state's Historical Resources Commission unanimously recommended to the

Historic Preservation Office that it should make a formal application on the vessel to the National Park Service. They wanted the ship to be listed on the National Register of Historic Places. Based on legal advice from California's in-house attorney, placement on the National Historic Register would indicate the ship's historical value and meet one of the federal law's conditions for state ownership. The question was whether accomplishing this act would be viewed as meeting the law after the court's decision. Most legal experts felt that it would not.

During this time, Peter Pelkofer contacted Don Knight about supporting California's position. According to Knight, Pelkofer asked, "Can you help us?" and Don replied, "I've been trying to for some time." The CSLC senior counsel then criticized DSR for not providing an adequate description of the wreck. Given the adversarial stance that California had taken in the courts, the question asked most frequently was, "Why would they?" People understood that the state wanted this information for its National Register nomination on its mission to own the vessel. In response to Pelkofer's request, Knight turned over to the CSLC a much better copy of the underwater video pictures of the ship taken by Siverts. The well-known marine archaeological expert, Jim Delgado, relied on this video and other information to complete his report that accompanied the National Register's application.

After California completed its last required step to nominate the wreck for listing on the National Historic Register, it filed a motion in District Court for Judge Bechtle to take "judicial notice" of this fact. (This legal concept allows a court to take notice and rely on a known fact.) Since California took these steps *after* the lower court's ruling, Judge Bechtle ruled that this evidence couldn't be considered in the court's decision. Attorney Pelkhofer then confirmed the state's hope that the ship's inclusion in the National Historic Register would make a difference in a planned Court of Appeals proceeding. The U.S. National Park Service approved California's application of the *Brother Jonathan,* thanks to Jim Delgado's expert work, and placed the ship on the National Historic Register on October 12, 1995. It listed the wreck site as being "about 4.5 miles west of Point St. George, Crescent City."

Along the way, the State of California made motions for hearings and injunctions at every possible step to halt the salvage efforts already underway as approved by the District Court's ruling. The media gave these legal filings, hearings, and decisions great play, as California's public-relations campaign aimed to convince the public that it only had their interest at heart in such actions.

Peter Pelkofer announced to the press: "If it really is a historic vessel, then it belongs to all of us. They knew before they went looking for it that it was a historic vessel and the State of California had claimed it." California focused on the *Brother Jonathan*'s historical value and the "gold motivation" of the salvors. It also saw that the wreckage represented a "watery gravesite" for those who died in the wreck. The State of California had adopted Don Knight's sensitivities for the dead.

These adversarial tactics quite upset David Flohr, Harvey Harrington, Jim Wadsley, Sherman Harris, and the other salvors. Already subject to the District Court's close supervision of all recovery efforts, their scarce funds had to be diverted to fend off the state's legal attacks and its unlimited taxpayer funding. Newspaper editorials began to support DSR, however, especially the *Triplicate.* Seeing the "David versus Goliath" situation, people felt uncomfortable with a huge state like California trying to eviscerate existing laws and private-property rights to claim state ownership.

The legal attacks continued. In October 1995, the State of California filed a motion to the Federal Ninth Circuit Court of Appeals for an injunction to prevent DSR from proceeding with its recovery efforts. This new court unanimously denied the motion. As the state's legal volleys rocketed in, DSR's officers would become distracted, then win that particular round, turn back to its recovery planning, and then be sidelined by this state's next round of litigation. Judge Bechtle's decision was final that DSR was the exclusive salvor and could accomplish its recovery efforts—subject to the court's supervision—until California somehow managed to overturn that holding at a higher court or proceeding.

ANOTHER YEAR CAME and DSR was fortunate in its fundraising. After the discovery of the ship, the officers raised an investment total of $105,000 in 1994, $120,000 in 1995, and then doubled that to $255,000 in 1996. These were still budget-limiting amounts, given the legal battles being fought and the explorations needed to be funded. Although the ex- and present partners continued to trade barbs in the press, the business-like approach of Mark Hemstreet, David Flohr, and Sherman Harris with their contacts brought results. Strong financial controls were placed on the venture and investor relations were good. Although the average investment was no more than $5,000, the officers continued to find interest with individuals from all walks of life. The large institutional investors that could make a difference, however, were not to be found. Moreover, fighting off the State of California's predatory legal practices was taking an ever-higher percentage of whatever money was being raised.

Any planning or implementation of exploration activities, meanwhile, was subject to the weather. Heavy winds and seas forced the cancellation of exploration efforts planned on site for June. A fierce storm caught a ship carrying a mini-sub with winds, stormy seas, and thirty-foot waves after leaving San Francisco. The forty-foot boat, *Mother Goose,* was hauling Don Siverts's mini-sub, but the storm forced the captain to run for cover north of the city. When Chicken Pox infected one of the crew members, and Siverts's son, Curt, wasn't vaccinated against the disease, they decided to reset the expedition date.

Moreover, the State of California in July 1996 filed an appeal to the Ninth Circuit Court of Appeals to reverse the Northern District Court's decision. The justices unanimously denied that application in mid-July. A few weeks later, it appealed to the Ninth Circuit for a rehearing on the appellate court's decision. This motion was denied unanimously. Legal experts were shocked at the continued appeals by the California State Lands Commission on what seemed to be very shaky grounds. Despite the financial bleeding, DSR set its exploration plans for late August. The objective of this operation was further site exploration, mapping, and recovery work.

As the District Court judge retained jurisdiction over everything discovered, DSR had to apply to court for anything to do with recovered objects—from how they would be conserved to the conditions under which they were to be displayed. In fact, Judge Bechtle had to sign an order allowing the artifacts to be shown at the Del Norte County Historical Society in its public memorial ceremony, including also any long-term loan for display.

California's motions to stop the salvaging required a ten-day response by DSR. If the company didn't answer the filing in that time period, then the state could move for a default judgment and win. After the answer, the applicable court typically had twenty-one days, or another short period, within which to make its decision. These actions initiated by California simply created a climate of uncertainty and increased DSR's costs. Whether that was its intention or not, the explorers nevertheless continued on.

The newspapers ran headlines such as "Sunken Ship Legal Fight Deepens," "State Asks Court to Stop Wreck Salvage," "State Makes New Effort to Claim Wreck," "State Fights for Rights to Historic Ship," "High Court Declines to Halt Ship Salvaging," and so on. When the U.S. Supreme Court loomed into the picture, the stories increased in their national coverage. Up until then, DSR officially declined comment in most cases, as it didn't want to draw even more attention to its recovery efforts. These stories didn't help their fund-raising efforts, however, and the officers believed that California and its officials were intentionally trying to put them out of business and claim the wreck by default.

Despite this, it was business as usual on August 27, 1996, when DSR started its exploration activities with a targeted end of September 6. DSR contracted again for the *Cavalier,* to piggy-back the one-man *Snooper,* and the two-man submersible *Delta.*

* * *

THE *BROTHER JONATHAN'S* first-class staterooms were located on the main deck, behind the engine room and toward the ship's stern. They conveniently surrounded the elongated dining saloon. When stevedores loaded the passengers' baggage onboard, they pulled up the plush carpeting in the lounge, pushed the long eating table aside, opened a hidden hatch, loaded the baggage in the storage area below, locked the hatch, put everything back in place, and rolled the carpet back. People's baggage were kept quite safe this way, although everyone had to take what they needed with them, as getting back into that storage room was quite difficult.

The second-class passenger rooms were built toward the vessel's stern, with the steerage quarters housed in the noisy bow and located underneath the main deck of first- and second-class staterooms. The purser's office was located between the smokestack and the bridge on the main deck on the starboard (right-hand) side of the ship. Underneath the second deck was the "Orlop deck," or where the coal bunker was situated; it was above the bilge, keel, and ribs of the ship but towards its middle and stern. The cargo holds were to the vessel's bow and above steerage with decks being eight-feet high.

Don Knight maintained later that given the extensive damage to the ship's front, the vessel sunk by its bow quickly at a forty-five degree angle with its stern up. Once under the ocean's surface, the ship floated in the currents for some distance. The vessel sailed inside those moving columns of water, hitting 180 feet, and then 220 feet down. As trapped air held its stern off the bottom, the ship bounced along the sandy depths before finally hitting a bump that swung the vessel around. The depths of the final resting place ranges from 270- to 285-feet deep, depending on the underwater currents and tides.

He and others believe that the stern could still contain trapped air. In the 1993 expedition, Knight said the mini-sub accidentally bumped the ship's stern and "pockets of 1865 air bubbled away." His theory is that the ore crusher didn't immediately crash through the ship's bottom until its downward journey. The exact duplicate of this ore crusher is in the Douglas House Museum in Jerome, Arizona. When the manufacturer sent another crusher to San Francisco to replace the one lost, it ended up staying on the docks for months. Wagon trains brought the replacement crusher back to Jerome.

As with the ore crusher, Don Knight and others researched the history of the lost and recovered artifacts. For example, attention centered on the first-discovered champagne bottle. Research determined later that these bottles were to be placed in the first-class cabins. The champagne was shipped from France to Galveston, Texas, then by freight wagon overland to San Francisco, and taken on board the *Brother Jonathan.* Understandably, this transportation was done slowly and carefully, as if the champagne was encased in boxes of gun powder.

The salvors spent Tuesday, August 27, 1996, meeting with the reporters and Sheriff. That evening, they stowed their personal effects in their quarters on the *Cavalier* and shipped out. By eight o'clock the next morning, the *Cavalier* was over the wreck site. The *Delta* was lowered into the ocean with Harvey Harrington on board. Don Siverts's one-man *Snooper* followed the *Delta* down. A shuttle boat brought the lead diver, Wings Stock, and his crew aboard later that morning.

The *Delta* dropped down lines on the paddle wheel shaft, and divers descended to secure the ropes. These lines provided a location reference for subsequent dives. Another weighted rope dropped from the surface and was for the sub-safety divers, in case one of the minisubs ran into trouble and needed help from on top.

Seven large commercial fishing nets floated from the wreck with shadowy, surrealistic effects. Draped around the vessel, the floats on the nets still buoyed them and the effect looked like trees with spreading branches in a forest. Some nets wrapped around the engine and walking beam, but these usually fell apart when touched. No fish, seals, sea lions, or other sealife were found entangled in them.

Due to the lost rigs and nets, commercial fishermen generally tried to avoid this area. The shipwreck proved to be a very hospitable place for numbers of fish to live and multiply, and the area was known as a fishing paradise. Some fishermen took the chance and rigged up their old, worn-out rigs: sometimes this worked and other times they lost them on what they believed was "some underwater reef."

The nets created a risk, however, to the mini-subs. Stories abounded how underwater fishing rigs or nets trapped submersibles underneath the ocean with dangerous consequences. Accordingly, DSR set in place various diving rules. One was that the submarines could never venture close to the nets, until the divers descended and could cut them away if needed. The Coast Guard told the men that if divers "got into the nets," they would have to take the time to carefully cut the netting away, bring them to the surface, dry them on land, and roll them up to be preserved. This made no sense at all, because the rigs weren't artifacts—only beaten nets that commercial fishermen had lost. Instead, DSR's divers cut the floats from the nets, allowed the buoys to pop to the surface, and then pulled the nets away.

"There were a lot of regulations," observed David Flohr. "Harrington, Wadsley, and the divers were unsure about what to do with the concretized sand that had formed around the ship." Whether hull strapping, boilers, furnaces, or other parts of the ship, the *Brother Jonathan* carried so much iron on board that it oxidized in the saltwater and caused hard bottom accretions. The sand around the vessel became so hard, in fact, that the men couldn't excavate anything. "Unlike other salvage operations in soft-sand areas, such as Florida, we had to use equipment such as pry bars to break up the concreted sand," said Flohr. "This was why we didn't find anything between the 1993 discovery and the 1995 activities, as the concreted surface covered everything."

There wasn't much left of the ship. Corroded away by saltwater and eaten by sea organisms, the upper wooden structure of the *Brother Jonathan* had vanished. Only portions of the copper sheathing on the ship's side and hull defined its outline. Most of the bow had sheared off or floated to shore, including the forty feet of the top deck, the ship's bell, and the carved eagle. Above the copper sheathing, all of the wood had virtually disappeared. The horizontal driveshaft for the paddle wheels lay at an angle across the ship with three hubs at one end. The inscription of "Morgan Iron Works/New York" was still visible, and this notation identified this engine as being that of the *Brother Jonathan.*

According to California's application for a national historical registration, an "estimated two-thirds" of the steamer's original length survived to a level below the original waterline. Some ceiling planking and the exposed ends of floors and frames were still present. The hull's line of separation appeared to be close to the bilge in some places, with some frames and the upper hull resting at an angle where they had separated from the floors.

Portions of the ship's diagonal iron strapping were still seen, and a layer of oxidized iron concretion covered several exposed timbers. Caused by the saltwater's effect on the iron, the iron oxides mix with the sand particles, even broken glass, and minerals to form an actual light-weight concrete. Marine organisms had consumed the upper hull, and a layer of silt covered a "number of other timbers." As to the machinery, the port paddlewheel shaft and hubs were in place, but the arms were missing. A steam cylinder lay on its side, and the boilers were still in place, although the enclosing jacket of one had corroded and exposed rows of the boiler tubes.

The divers and mini-subs never discovered any evidence of human bodies or skeletons. Although a high majority of the passengers and crew were already in the ocean when it went down, the marine life around the sunken vessel would have eaten anything left. Various ceramic artifacts lay scattered outside and inside the hull. Rows of plates, bowls, and a chamber pot were on the site, some of them lying atop exposed floor and ceiling timbers and on frame ends.

As quoted in California's application for a National Historic Register listing: "The appearance of the wreck is that of a vessel that sank more or less intact and has slowly disintegrated through organic activity, leaving a number of artifacts in relative position to their original placement in the vessel." However, the extent of how "slow" the disintegration was and the "relative" position of the artifacts is open to debate.

David Flohr commented:

> The sea organisms and corrosive effects of saltwater had eaten up the *Brother Jonathan* by the time we discovered her, and we couldn't even tell whether we were on the bow or its stern. There were no paddles, only where the spikes went out from the main shaft. No hull wood remained and only the copper plating of the hull—which extended to about five feet from the vessel's waterline—gave the ship its look of an "elongated sausage."
>
> When they built the ship, they completely tarred the hull with hot black tar, then crisscrossed horsehair around the hull, and nailed on the copper plating. The thought was that this would keep the sea worms and corrosion down. It worked for the copper, but where the copper plating had pulled away, the sea and worms had eaten everything else away.

Wings Stocks was the head diver on this expedition. A veteran of diving's "technical revolution," Wings was an accomplished exploration diver with a passion for his profession. He was a stocky, strong-looking man with tattoos all over his body and a heavy beard at the time. As Flohr commented, "He was heavily tattooed then and all hair." The Marines apparently wouldn't let him keep a beard when he was in Vietnam, so he vowed to grow a really big one after he became discharged. And he did, all six inches of it. Raised on Lake Michigan in northern Indiana, he joined the U.S. Marine Corps at age seventeen and served in Vietnam before being transferred to Okinawa where he learned scuba diving in a Special Forces program. As a Vietnam veteran, he got along well with David Flohr's son, who had also served in Vietnam.

DSR hired and brought in five divers: three bottom divers and two support or safety divers. Recommended by Jim Wadsley, Wings

Stocks was on this exploratory expedition team as the head of the diving division. His group included another diver, Kendall Raine, nicknamed "The Banker" because he was an investment banker in Los Angeles during his off hours.

Raine's love for diving started at age nine. When he was young, the television series *Sea Hunt* and the shark movie *Blue Water, White Death* mesmerized him. After learning how to dive, he trained for two years to dive on the wreck of the *Andrea Doria*. Sunk in the Atlantic Ocean off the Massachusetts coast, the vessel lies at a depth that varies to 235 feet and is sometimes called the "Mount Everest of Diving." A resident of Malibu, Raine had a youthful, "fresh-scrubbed" look and worked on dives because he loved to, certainly not because he needed the money.

Raine and Stocks were the lead divers, the exact opposite in looks and physique, but had the same love of deep underwater adventure. Their mission was twofold: the recovery of gold treasure and sub support. The divers relied on the mini-subs for their "big lights" and backup safety, but unquestionably these men were the prime recovery vehicles.

"There were no close calls in our diving efforts. Wings Stocks and 'The Banker' were the best," said Flohr later. DSR utilized its mini-subs to spot the artifacts and coins, then used the divers to collect them. Kendall and Wings Stocks stayed on Wings's boat with their wet suits peeled off. Protected by an overhead canopy from the sun, the men drank bottled water and waited for the radio command to get into the water when the mini-subs found "something interesting."

Once they received the instructions, the men suited up and slipped over the side. It took time to slide down the tie line to the bottom of the wreck, locate the rope that led to the quadrant they needed to work, and then find their site of interest. Lights were turned on at the location, and they swam to where they would work. With only fifteen minutes of allowed time to search and collect items, a crewman in the hovering mini-sub banged on its inside hull to let the divers know that their time was up. The men then needed to get back to the lines leading to the surface and start their ascent. They had to stay at various, calculated levels for a total of up to one and a half hours to allow the nitrogen to finish getting out of their blood.

Diving to these depths meant that the divers had to be ever watchful to avoid the "bends". When a diver ascends to the surface too fast, the nitrogen levels compressed into his body by the high pressures below can't slowly work out of the blood. The nitrogen forms into painful bubbles inside the spine, joints, and nerve centers, akin to uncorking a bottle of soda which then releases trapped gas. Not only was this condition painful, but it can produce debilitating injuries and death.

To avoid the effects of quick decompression, the diver must rise slowly or make intermittent stops on the way to the surface (called "decompression stops"). By doing this, the gas is able to safely work out of the diver's blood. If one rises too fast, then the only alternative is to enter quickly a pressurized chamber, where the air pressure matches the high pressure at those depths and then is slowly decreased.

The water pressure was so intense at 280 feet that it was said if a man's air tube were cut, the water pressure would squish him due solely to the pressure differential. Some mini-sub operators couldn't believe how badly the divers' faces had shrunk when they swam by. This pressure was near 140 pounds per square inch, and such intensity made working the claw of the two-man sub very difficult when trying to pick up a plate or other artifact. In fact, some salvors had to push their entire body against the apparatus just to move the outside arm to a desired object.

The waters were "colder than hell" and less than forty degrees at the bottom. Waiting at different low depths for the bubbles to dissipate meant long immersions in the frigid water, and the divers were quite aware of this fact. People also needed to dress warmly even when on the submersibles, as the temperatures at the hull were also that cold.

"Wings Stocks was a very good diver," said Flohr. "He was very meticulous in his calculations as to how long he could stay down, what mixture to use in his tanks, and so on." Wings and "The Banker" continually took readings as to air temperature, water, humidity, and underwater conditions, then ran these factors through their computer to determine how long they could stay under and get back up, including the wait at different levels to allow the nitrogen in their blood to disperse. They typically would have fifteen to eighteen minutes left to work on the bottom—which didn't leave much time to find gold.

Even with the submarine's lights on, any work in these waters was an experience in darkness. Above the ocean on the *Cavalier,* operators manned a glowing screen with a global positioning system (Trac II) and an antenna that descended into the ocean on the starboard side. The operators monitored how the submersibles moved in relationship to the *Cavalier* and then radioed down course instructions, such as "You [the sub] are five feet west of us" or "You're now ten feet south."

On one trip to the wreck, a mini-sub with its strong lights on motored around the entire ship for over an hour, and the operators didn't even know it. It's no wonder the old divers and previous expeditions couldn't find the *Jonathan.* The submersibles sometimes played an unintentional game of "bumper tag" with the bottom, obstructions, and at times even the wreck. As Flohr observed, "It was so dark that once we had the lights on the wreck and thought it had disappeared. We discovered that we were staring at the copper-plated hull, turned black by the sea's oxidation, and that had blended into the surroundings. We actually bumped into the ship one time when we couldn't see it. The worms had cleanly eaten away the wood above that section."

Early each day, the mother ship lowered the mini-submarines into the ocean. They were soon circling slowly around the wreck in their designated areas, looking for anything of interest. When the men spotted an object, the sub radioed up the location for the divers' later inspection and pickup. Anything heavy was wrapped with lines, and a hydraulic wench hauled it up; otherwise, the items were placed in plastic bags and attached to a mini-sub for transportation. The salvors really wanted to find the safe, the Holy Grail of the *Brother Jonathan*. Unfortunately, neither it nor any gold had been found.

Given the constantly changing currents, particulate density, swirling sands, and undersea flotsam, the sub operators usually needed to "feel" their way towards the remains of the *Jonathan*. The wreck would then appear suddenly from the depths, even with the "amazing amount" of luggage and boxes scattered around the site. Don Siverts sometimes dragged a chain behind his mini-sub, so he could follow the drag-marks when making his predetermined passes around the wreck. At other times, he followed the shallow marks made by his propeller screws in the sand. The spinning prop also whipped up the sand particles and floating flotsam, however, which decreased visibility as the currents swept the tiny particles around.

As *Snooper* continued its runs, Siverts became acquainted with the sea life. In addition to the octopuses and small and large denizens, he became used to the continued presence of one particularly large rockfish that was a bright orange, over two feet long, and lived inside the wreck. This particular fish swam around the smokestack base as the mini-sub crept around, and then dove down into the wreck to hide or forage.

Any recovery efforts were difficult, however, given the currents, lack of visibility, limited time that the divers could stay underwater, the ever-present nets, and the sheer coldness of these waters. The currents, in fact, swept the *Delta* several times into the old nets, but the operators were able to extradite the mini-sub. The divers and submersibles did find and carry up old artifacts during their first three days of operations—but still no gold had been discovered.

At the time, David Flohr kept a detailed diary of the expedition. Early that morning on the third day of sea operations, he spotted a beautiful rainbow reaching over the wreck site and hoped that it was a favorable omen. The *Cavalier* maneuvered itself over the site, set its anchor, and prepared to drop the first mini-sub. Harvey Harrington and David Slater submerged in the *Delta* to the wreck and looked around. The mini-sub resurfaced midmorning. As Flohr recalled:

"When Harvey Harrington first spotted a coin that morning, all he said over the radio was: 'Son of a bitch, I saw a coin.' That was it. He came to the surface and reboarded the mother ship."

When Harrington stepped on the deck, he acted as if nothing had happened. Men crowded around him and said loudly, "What did you see? Just what was down there?" Harvey was silent. Being a heavy smoker, he took his time and shook out a cigarette. Lighting it, Harrington took a heavy drag and exhaled the smoke slowly.

The men yelled this time, "What did you see?" After the cigarette's tip glowed red once more, he responded quietly, "I saw gold coins, but I don't know where they are. We lost track of the spot." He said this like asking someone politely to please pass the bread and butter.

The men stood there silently, thinking about what Harrington had just told them. Knowing that Harvey was an affable kidder with a sense of humor, David Flohr asked, "Harvey, are you putting me on?" Harrington responded that he wasn't and had indeed spotted gold coins.

The ocean lapped quietly at the ship's side, as the *Cavalier* slowly rocked in the swells. One crewman disappeared into the *Delta* and quickly emerged, holding the videotape into the air. He quickly walked to the operations room, as everyone sprang into action and raced with him to the video player. As they crowded around to watch the tape in the darkened room, the men were quiet—"deathly" quiet.

Harrington then froze the tape. People stared at a dark area near some "barrel-like objects," as Harvey decided that the mini-sub had been crossing over the wreck towards the iron wheel. No gold coins were visible, but he was sure that the spotted coins were between the *Delta* and those barrel-like objects.

The sub was quickly put back in operation and disappeared into the depths. The new exploration effort, however, didn't find anything after one hour and resurfaced. Harrington and David Slater reported that the bottom currents had whipped up and greatly decreased visibility, stirring up what was called "sea dust" or swirling sand particles. The day before, the undersea currents increased to such a point that they had swept the *Delta* into the ship and its nets, but the two-man sub was finally able to pull away and continue on its mission. The men were now quite disappointed.

The *Delta* submerged a third time in the midafternoon and motored to where Harrington had thought he had been. This time Doug Privitt was the operator. The submersible circled at 1 to 1½ knots. Minutes slowly ticked away; time seemed to stop. The *Delta* searched the area for another hour, but the men didn't see anything interesting, although they were cruising around the specific point seen before.

As the sub worked its way over the site, its propeller continued to wash sand away and the stronger currents swept the sand particles around like milky dust. Multicolored fish swam outside the port windows, and the whites of dishes and other porcelain ware lay around the ship's dark outline. The submersible again approached the area, and the shadows of the *Jonathan* blended into darkness with undefined shapes and swirling silt. Harvey peered through the front port, as the mini-sub slowly turned to cross over the ship in the other direction. He thought he saw something "glittering ahead by the dark spot" and told Privitt to go slow.

As the submersible motored slowly over the sunken ship toward its bow, pointing away from land, Harrington saw a "flash" from the sub's high-intensity lights, very much like what he had seen that morning. As the propeller swept away more of the swirling particles from the ship, Harvey saw the gold coins. There were stacks of them.

He reported they could see the gold coins "mere feet" in front, and the sub tried to hover close to the location. Topside monitors calculated the sub's GPS position and alerted the diving team. Wings was ready to go. He and "The Banker" had watched every underwater videotape taken from the mini-subs so far. This familiarity with the wreck would allow the divers to quickly descend to any area and start immediately working.

Wings Stocks and Kendall Raine jumped into the deep at four o'clock in the afternoon on Friday, August 30, 1996. As they held onto the guiding line, they dropped the 280 feet to the bottom in seven minutes. Their tanks used "trimix" or a mixture of gases, primarily nitrox and oxygen for decompression. Their plan called for spending twenty minutes at the bottom. Wings worked his way over to the paddle wheel hub and gave the hovering mini-sub an "okay" sign that everything was working right. He started his time-watch and within "five seconds" was on top of the site. Despite the dark shadows of the waters and the sweeping underwater currents, the divers held to the area and started their exploration.

Wings Stocks then noticed a "little piece, maybe a half-inch curve" underneath the silt on the ship in the assigned area, and he knew from past experience that this had to be a gold coin. He gently brushed the loose particles away and exposed another gold coin, then saw stacks of the glittering gold an arm-length away. He and Kendall began loading their bag, trying to work fast but not damage their precious finds. The currents kicked up more from the motion, and their visibility rapidly deteriorated.

Before he knew it, Wings heard the knock signals from the nearby mini-sub that hovered above them. The time had come for them to start their ascent and decompress at different depths as they surfaced. He estimated that he had strapped about fifty pounds of gold coins into the two bags. The men attached them to the submersible, and the *Delta* quickly surfaced with its "carry-out" boxes and the filled bags.

On board the *Cavalier*, the mini-sub rose out of the ocean and Harrington yelled out that the underwater visibility had been terrible. "We couldn't see a thing down there," he shouted. The divers meanwhile were still very slowly ascending toward the surface.

Once the mini-sub was on board, Doug Privitt stretched his legs and Harvey Harrington lit a cigarette. No one knew what Wings had first discovered. Bungee cords tightly wrapped a net sack to the sub's top, and two yellow-green plastic bags were inside that black sack. David Flohr said later that, "The bags looked like the saddlebags on a horse."

In charge of security, Barry Sutton then said, "Gee, I'll take a look in the bags." He reached up and grabbed the two yellow plastic bags from their tied place on the *Delta*'s bow. When he dropped one of the bags, however, everyone within earshot heard the distinct metallic clink of the coins.

Sutton released the hook that kept the bag closed. As he stretched open the bag's sides, a mass of gold coins appeared. The men counted 564 mint-condition U.S. twenty-dollar Double Eagles. Minted in 1865, these coins had not even been circulated. They were in clusters of ten to thirty in a group, and they looked to Wings Stocks "as though they'd just come off the press." In just fifteen minutes on one dive, the expedition had discovered hundreds of uncirculated valuable gold coins.

The salvors inspected the gold coins and rinsed them in fresh water. Any erosion from the decades spent in saltwater was almost nonexistent. The near fifty pounds of gold coins were placed in small plastic bags on trays and locked in a nearby cabinet. The men started photographing the gold coins. Early the following morning, the actual inventory count came to be 561 coins—three less than what was initially thought to have been discovered. No one really knew why the count was less. David Flohr later confirmed that "Wings received three points as his fee, each point being a percent of the gross before expenses."

Sherman Harris, David Flohr, Harvey Harrington, and Jim Wadsley celebrated as they identified and counted each coin in the presence of one another. They then locked all of the gold coins in a cabinet. The four left the room as a group with Barry Sutton guarding it, his responsibility being to not let anyone back in.

THE NEXT DAY, Saturday, August 31, Don Siverts submerged his oneman *Snooper* down to the site. While running his hand-held video camera, he very slowly glided the sub around the area. Arriving in their own ship, the *Xanadu*, Stocks, Raine, and the other divers began to check their equipment and work into their wet suits, as the winds began to rise. Over the next hour, the men aboard the *Cavalier* watched nervously as the waves became rougher and the green seas pitched higher.

From the divers' report, the salvors knew that more stacks of gold coins were still there. The elements, however, weren't cooperating. The seas increased in height from the winds and the *Cavalier* rolled violently. The officers reluctantly canceled any exploration that day. They directed Siverts to resurface. When he did, the surprised operator found his mini-sub pitching roughly on top of hissing waves with whitecaps.

Getting the mini-sub back on the ship would be risky. The *Cavalier* was rolling close to the rocking mini-sub in the angry waves, and its crewmen had to lower cables to the sub, catch the eye-hooks, and quickly winch the submersible back up. The first attempts didn't connect. When the mini-sub and mother ship pitched and came too close to a disastrous collision, the ship had to back off. Trying again as the large *Cavalier* approached again, the men were finally able to attach the cables to *Snooper* and winch it aboard.

Turning their attention to the videotape, the men stepped to the operations room to watch Siverts's tape. As the winds howled outside and the ship rolled and creaked, the silent videotape was played in front of the crowded group. Mouths dropped when the sub motored close to the "dark hole." As David Flohr said later, "We saw literally stacks and clusters of gold coins, all from the remains of a larger than expected box that was probably made of wrought iron. Some of the coins nestled inside the remnants of the box, while other coins poised precariously right on the edge of a metal surface with a sharp drop-off into the dark depths below."

The tape corroborated the divers' reports that the discovery area was around the purser's office. Over time, the marine life and saltwater had nearly destroyed the strongbox. The remnants with its gold coins lay at the base of the smokestack on a ledge beneath the purser's room, balanced over a dark hole that dropped to the stacks of coal stored on the last deck. Mining equipment seemed to lie at the stack's base. The collision had forced the smokestack to shift back, not forward as first thought. Located below the pilot's cabin, the purser's office was between the smokestack and bridge where Wells Fargo messenger Joseph Lord, purser John Benton, and engineer Mott were last seen alive. Other boxes about the size of the one already discovered appeared to lie to one side—but the tape wasn't clear as to what the containers were for.

The men were spellbound. They were this close but the weather and wreck seemed to be telling them, "Leave us alone." As a storm raged around them, the long-sought-after gold perched hundreds of feet down on a ledge by a sharp drop-off. A safe was spotted "right in the middle of everything." The men speculated out loud as to what it held and debated on how best to bring up the estimated one-ton object. However, the weather first had to clear.

The *Cavalier* cruised back to Crescent City Harbor to wait out the storm. On the following day, Sunday, September 1, the weather improved on land. Optimistically, the salvors headed out to the wreck site. Once there, however, they discovered high winds and heavy seas. This storm was even stronger now with waves fifteen feet and higher. Whipped up by winds that ripped into the ship at upwards of forty miles per hour, there was no doubt that the wreck, once more, would not be explored. After the discovery of the *Brother Jonathan*'s gold began whetting everyone's appetites, the seas seemed to want to deny them entry again. The *Cavalier* turned back to port, followed by the divers in the *Xanadu*.

That Monday, the hopeful salvors headed again to the wreck site with the *Cavalier* and the *Xanadu*. Surely, they thought, David Flohr's rainbow had been a good omen, but what were these conditions telling them? Once more the weather made recovery efforts too risky, so the ships and their men anxiously headed back to port. The officers—Harrington, Wadsley, Flohr, and Harris—spent their free time packing the coins already discovered for transport to more secure facilities.

Although difficult to make, the decisions to forgo further exploration were wise ones. The 1996 Labor Day storm was one of the worst to hit during any of the expeditions. Its terrifying winds and seas had caught several unwary boats and fishermen outside the safety of the protective harbor. The shrieking weather capsized and sank that Monday a 72-foot long commercial fishing boat and a 53-foot vessel. Again, underestimating the strength of storms cost people their lives.

On Tuesday, September 3, the support ships and divers returned to the spot and discovered better conditions. The seas had calmed to five-foot waves with ten-mile-per-hour winds. In most cases, these would still be difficult conditions, although not that risky, and the exploration activities commenced again. Wings Stocks and Kendall Raine immediately descended to the black bottom and worked their way over the ship to the purser's office. The environment below was also difficult, as the visibility was bad and underwater currents strong.

As before, the bags arrived on the surface with the submersible before the divers did, but the crewmen this time rushed for the mini-sub and its saddlebags. Working the area pictured by Siverts's camera, the divers picked that treasure trove and filled their bags with more twenty-dollar Double Eagles. As more coins were brought to the surface, even the mini-sub *Delta* got into the act with its claw arm picking up thirteen more gold coins. Every time gold was discovered, the four officers sat down together to go over the finds. They identified and catalogued each piece, then turned the cabinet with its locked gold over for Barry Sutton's guard.

The easy access to the gold lessened over time. Once the divers brought up the iron box's treasure, the "easy pickings" seemed to end. The salvors still tried to figure out the best way to bring up the small safe. They agreed that the *Cavalier*'s winch could safely haul the object up, but the question was how best to attach the cable. Two days later, DSR readied its plan to bring up another object of "great interest." At the bottom of the ocean, the divers wrapped steel cable around the safe. They also positioned two inflatable air bags, one tied to the safe and the other positioned under the cable. A nylon rope was attached to the cable. Air lines from the *Delta* then inflated the airbags, as the divers released a buoy with a long nylon line that was knotted to the safe.

David Flohr and David Slater were below on the *Delta* overseeing the work being done. One hour elapsed before they spotted the small safe. Despite the mini-sub's bright lights, the poor visibility made work difficult. The showering of sand and silt from the currents and divers' work mingled with the ever-present, multicolored fish, whites of lost crockery, and the shadows of the wreck's outline, paddle wheel, and boilers in creating what seemed to be a fantasy painting.

As the men on the mini-sub watched, the heavy nylon line, carried up to the surface with the buoy, stretched into the darkness. With everything seemingly in order, the *Delta* left for topside. Meanwhile, the crewmen on the *Cavalier* grabbed the one-half-inch line and started to pull it on board. To their surprise, the nylon rope swept away from them, as the underwater currents pushed the safe and its airbag away from the vessel. Disaster then struck. As the crew tugged mightily on the rope, the line suddenly went slack. It had snapped. The men pulled up the rope and nothing was at its end.

Time seemed to stop. The ocean seemed to be protecting the ship and its contents once more. Men scanned the surface, as others walked away. David Flohr then noticed a rising white shape underneath the ocean's surface. One white airbag was floating upwards but very slowly. This float was the one attached to the safe, and their precautionary back-up had seemed to work. Jubilation replaced the feelings of frustration and despair. Crewmen quickly brought the object to the ship and winched it aboard. The safe was packed away to be opened by specialists later on land, and David Flohr called it, "the most beautiful, rust-covered box that I have ever seen."

When all of the gold coins on this expedition were counted and identified, a total of 875 gold coins had been brought to the surface. Contrary to several published accounts, most of the 875 gold coins weren't discovered scattered around the ocean's floor. Instead, every one was found in or next to that one rusted-open iron box, measuring a small twenty inches by thirty inches. The coins were still wrapped in oil paper, twenty-five coins to a wrap, although some of the protective covering had given way with coins scattered inside. When men peeled the wrapping away, trays inside still held the coins, while other gold coins lay inside, "jumbled around." Divers discovered two intact stacks of twenty-five coins not in their wrappers, but with a surrounding "shell-like growth" that protected the coins from the highly corrosive effects of their long years in saltwater. The oil-paper wrapping and marine encrustations protected the coins well: These coins would eventually be evaluated at nearly the highest numismatic quality grade of all coins, being the "beautiful MS 65, 66, and 67." (This grading is discussed in a later chapter.)

The risks and dangers of explorations like this one were noteworthy. The high seas, strong currents, and bad winds were an unpredictable presence. Sea life abounded. Divers spotted huge octopuses nearby, including one that grabbed a diver's leg, but he was able to shake the tentacles away. The mini-sub was videotaping a gold coin as a crab scuttled over the piece. The arm of a large octopus suddenly snaked over the gold, grabbed the crab, and pulled the crustacean away as a snack in front of the startled cameraman.

There were other practical realities. One of the observers on the *Delta* took his place inside the mini-sub, after eating a big breakfast with lots of coffee. However, he had forgotten to head to the bathroom to relieve himself before getting into the sub for what was planned to be a three-hour dive. Once down on the bottom, the man had to pee and there was nowhere to do it. He grabbed the plastic bag wrapped around snack candies and started to urinate into the bag. The man then felt the urine trickling down his leg. Back on the surface and obviously having wet his pants, he noticed his son starting to film him. The father deadpanned, "Unless you want to be disinherited, kid, I wouldn't take my picture now." His son put down the camera.

Precautions always needed to be taken to ensure confidentiality, as the courts hadn't confirmed that DSR owned what it had already discovered. From boats and cars Don Knight's friends and relatives were trying to garner whatever information was of value, and this could end up in hostile hands, whether the state's or another salvage group.

The explorers, however, looked forward to finding out what was in the small safe. With the press on hand, the safe was finally opened. Everyone waited to see what was inside. To their dismay, they didn't find anything of value. No gold, silver, or jewelry was inside—just clothing. Mark Hemstreet observed:

> Deep Sea Research immersed the purser's safe in saltwater to keep the air oxidation to a minimum and stored it securely at a sea life museum near San Francisco. When the people opened the safe, however, they only found a wool blanket, one coat, and a purser's hammer inside. This was odd to only find these items in a safe in the purser's office. It was as if the panicked passengers had taken everything else out of that safe before the ship sank. They probably took it on one of the lifeboats."

Despite the disappointment over the purser's safe, the 1996 operations were an outstanding success. DSR discovered 875 gold coins in basic mint condition and worth millions—it found the ghost ship's golden treasure, which had been speculated about for years. The question now was how the State of California would react to the good news.

DESPITE THE OPTIMISM of the officers and investors, the discovery of the valuable gold didn't alleviate their monetary pressures. Judge Bechtle refused to let DSR sell the coins or borrow against them until all of the legal issues, California's claims, and court battles were resolved. Chronically under-funded for years, more investors needed to be secured to fund any further exploration—and stand up to the State of California's continual war beats.

With the news about the discoveries, however, it understandably became easier to raise more investment capital. Having already found hundreds of beautiful gold coins, the exploration company even had investors approaching it. They used a brochure created in Don Knight's time with a cover that depicted a gold bar next to gold coins "waiting to be found." They gave detailed slide presentations about the *Brother Jonathan* and its gold. They also told the story of

Mrs. Keenan and her seven "soiled doves," which always seemed to gain the attention of potential investors.

In 1997, the company raised over $600,000 for that year's explorations—double what had been raised in previous years. Deciding to spend one month at the site to map the wreck, the salvors looked over the videotapes for other areas of interest, and decided how to make the site as archaeologically secure as possible. Highly scrutinized by the onboard archaeologist representing the State of California (at DSR's expense) and DSR's own consultant, Judge Bechtle was able to oversee every aspect of the operations. In fact, Bechtle had direct control over all of their activities, operations, and procedures.

Deep Sea Research decided to change its recovery technique to "saturation diving." This utilized a large diving bell, which allowed divers to live inside it for weeks. The bell and living quarters would be housed on a mother ship, from which cranes would lower and raise the bell from the ocean floor. This new approach would greatly increase the time available to search through the wreckage and ocean floor; in place of divers limited to fifteen minutes at a time, explorers could now spend hours without any need to slowly decompress when surfacing. The new operation was a great improvement—although much more expensive—as the salvors fretted over what their implacable, well-funded adversary would do next.

The group arranged for the large 213-foot, multiple-decked mother ship, *American Salvor,* owned by the Crowley Marine Services in Seattle, to be their prime vessel. They designed a "four-point" mooring system that enabled the ship to stay centered over the wreck site, continually making positioning adjustments to cables attached to four-ton anchors. Another GPS tracking system was put in place. Because the safe storage of the coins was a problem the first time, DSR even had a secure coin room placed on board. Don and Curt Siverts with the ever-present *Snooper* complemented the personnel. Indicating the increase in their operational scope, the expense of the successful 1996 gold discoveries was set at "$50,000 to $60,000," while the next explorations in the following year were budgeted at $400,000.

Under the saturation diving approach, divers lived aboard the mother ship in a sealed "hyperbaric" chamber that reproduced the same air pressure encountered at the bottom of the sea. When the diving operations started, a crane lowered the bell over the side to the ocean floor. From there, the divers headed outside and conducted their work assignments as long as necessary. After completing their tasks, they reentered the diving bell, which the *American Salvor*'s crew then winched back to the deck.

The bell connected to an on-board recompression chamber where the divers lived until their next assignment. By continuously staying inside the bell and its connecting "living room," these men could breathe mixed gases and didn't have to continually endure the long, risky decompression procedures on their ascent, as Wings Stocks and his crew did the year before. Breathing these mixed gasses also greatly reduce the problems that occurred from the narcotic effects of the higher nitrogen levels at those levels.

As DSR finalized the numerous details required to operate this more complex exploration, the State of California gave them their answer as to what was next: the United States Supreme Court. In June 1997, the State of California filed a motion with the nation's highest court for an injunction to prevent DSR's continued recovery work. This was after the group not only found the ship but also discovered its valuable gold. Given that the court completely monitored DSR's operations with two archaeologists aboard at their expense, it is hard to believe that the state's motivation was not monetary and control oriented from the start.

Owing to their financial problems, DSR approached suppliers and operators to see if, instead of cash, they would accept receiving a "point" (one point equals a 1 percent share of the eventual profits) or a fraction of a point. From a video director to the ship's captain, personnel were paid in points or fractions, depending on the value of their service. The only problem was that this reduced what everyone else received. The company was even behind in what it owed to the law firm that was to argue its position at the Supreme Court. Gordon & Rees put pressures on DSR for some payment on the arrearages prior to that hearing, and the company's officials scraped together a $50,000 payment as David Flohr, Sherman Harris, and others made a combination of loans and invested capital.

The relentless legal and financial onslaughts by the State of California, however, had taken its toll. As the exploration date approached, DSR was forced to reduce the time that the company planned for its divers to be under the sea. At first this was reduced incrementally until the exploration period eventually was cut in half to two weeks.

Under a District Court approved agreement, the Del Norte County Historical Society agreed to undertake the preservation of the artifacts that the divers found. That summer, DSR established its artifact conservation laboratory at the Flynn House in Crescent City with the Historical Society.

As Flohr said:

> I and others bought the lumber, electrical wiring, metal flashing, and other materials, then converted an old garage into an artifact conservation laboratory. We actually helped build that "community room" over one weekend. This was a double-car garage in which we constructed shelving around the walls, installed holding trays for extracting salts, and provided electronic equipment to conserve and stabilize the metal artifacts. DSR also hired a marine conservator from Florida to travel to Crescent City to train the museum's volunteer staff in the art of marine conservation—and we paid for all of this work. This operation then restored over one hundred and twenty artifacts, including two badly corroded portholes. The volunteers were able to work on the artifacts that the Del Norte County Historical Society now has on exhibit.

After the salvors established the conservation lab, DSR delivered more than seventeen large buckets and plastic bags full of artifacts to the laboratory. Volunteers worked to conserve items that included tools, shaving mugs, a metal strongbox, chamber pot, cigar-box lids, many plates and bottles, and even shoes. The conservation of one chest was particularly difficult. Appearing to be a commercial shipment fully loaded with doorknobs and keys, the chest was packed in something that looked like "grass" but that had now solidified. Workers had to take each layer apart—one by one—and the work proved to be a long process.

From bow to stern, the salvors carved the wreck site on paper into numbered grid sections. When the mini-sub brought up an object, its particular location or grid number was noted onboard, and then the artifact was logged into a master book with a description. DSR personnel then immersed the item in seawater to preserve it from oxidation and prepared the object for transportation to the conservation lab. Once there, the items were transferred to large plastic trays filled with distilled water. Currents of low-voltage electricity ran through this pure water to free up and discharge the accumulated rust and barnacles. The volunteers from the Del Norte County Historical Society then gently scrubbed the artifact every four weeks with a soft-bristle brush to remove whatever was still attached. Log book records were made each time the water was changed or an item cleaned. This was a lengthy process, as some items took eighteen months or more to be restored. If Judge Bechtle believed anyone was stealing California's heritage, it was not DSR.

On August 20, the 1997 explorations began on the *American Salvor.* Able to directly locate herself over the wreck and stay positioned through the onboard, four-point mooring system, the ship lowered the diving bell back and forth into the ocean by its ten-ton hydraulic crane. The twenty-eight-foot, aluminum-hulled *Negotiator,* owned by John Nesbit, supported the *Salvor* by transporting personnel back and forth from Crescent City, as well as bringing fresh food and supplies. It then became a garbage barge on its return trip by carrying away the accumulated trash.

The divers lived in their compartment for the entire month of the dive. "You couldn't understand them, as it sounded like they had been inhaling nitrogen. The captain had to translate what they were saying," said one crewman. The facilities included a toilet, television, and radio, and crew members transferred food and drink to the men through a pressurized lock. The divers submerged to the ocean's bottom inside the detachable bell, worked their shifts on the wreck site, and then returned when the bell was raised back to the mother ship.

Two divers were in the bell: one ventured out, while the other stayed inside in case there were problems. Although the operations were risky, living inside the bell for long time periods became an isolated and boring experience. One observer said that all of the people inside the living compartment and bell were "young and healthy"—and had to be—as he didn't believe that "older people" could live this way.

The daily routine consisted of waking the saturation (SAT) diving team up and serving them breakfast at about 0730 (7:30 A.M.). The diving bell was then locked to the recompression chamber and pressurized. By 0830, the SAT team was dressed, out, and en route to the bottom. Each diver worked a five-and-one-half hour shift, while his partner in the bell acted as back up and the equipment tender. Owing to the limited range of the divers' air hoses, the men were restricted to working in an area that was approximately eighteen by thirty feet. On completion of each shift, the duty diver returned to the bell and switched out with his partner for the remaining five and one-half hours. At the end of the eleven-hour period, both divers were now aboard, the lower hatch sealed, the bell retrieved, brought aboard the *American Salvor,* and locked to the recompression chamber.

Once the pressure was equalized, the divers could remove their diving suits, wash up, and have their evening meal "blown down" to them through the pressurized transfer lock. After they had eaten, the operations people debriefed the divers. With only two interruptions due to rough weather, this routine continued from August 20 to August 31. The SAT team then commenced a two-and-one-half-day period of decompression that brought them back to surface air pressure.

A diver occasionally needed to descend directly from the recovery vessel, either to assist the SAT team or perform a task outside their limited travel range. These explorers had a maximum bottom time of forty minutes, measured from the time they left the surface to when they started their ascent.

A cradle on the *American Salvor's* starboard side housed the one-man *Snooper.* This submersible conducted eleven dives during the operation with a total of 26.5 hours spent at the bottom. The mini-sub collected information on the wreck's layout, assisted the divers by lighting up their work areas, and mapped and videotaped as much of the wreck as possible, including examining parts of the site beyond the limits of the SAT team and surface divers.

DSR confined its recovery operations to a small portion of the wreck in an eighteen- by thirty-foot place, on the port side of the vessel just aft of the smokestack's base. This was the area in which the salvors had successfully located the coins recovered in the previous year's operation. All of the recovered artifacts, items, and gold coins came from this one site, and divers installed polypropylene rope over the work areas in ten-foot sections to match its grid system.

All artifacts recovered from the site were retrieved by hand. The divers placed the majority of the items in specially constructed lift-baskets for transportation to the surface. Occasionally they put small durable items in a diver's net bag, which was attached to the outside of the diving bell. Once raised to the surface, all of the artifacts were taken to the archaeologist for initial identification and cataloging. Crewmen took the coins to be reviewed separately and then stored in the specially designated coin room.

The archaeologist or deck supervisor could direct a diver to recover a specific item visible from the diver's head camera. He put the object in plastic milk-crates lined with shock-absorbing rubber sheeting to prevent damage. The divers then placed the crates inside specifically constructed steel-mesh baskets that were approximately four-feet square. Equipped with its own set of lifting slings, each basket was attached to the hooks of the ship-mounted hydraulic crane, which then lifted everything up.

Crewmen washed each item (including coins) with clean seawater to remove the mud and loosen any marine growth. The operators also removed additional material with running water and a soft brush. Once processed, the men sealed the item into a plastic Ziploc bag with clean seawater to keep it completely saturated. The supervisor then marked each object with an "artifact field number." Copies of these field sheets accompanied the artifacts, as they were then transported ashore to the Del Norte County Historical Society.

During these operations, the diving teams discovered more gold coins. The consulting archaeologists examined and counted each coin before it was taken to a secure storage area—which the judge also approved in advance. Any access to this area required the approval of two DSR principals, each of whom was required to perform part of the unlocking and locking process. Any one single individual could not gain access to the coin room.

The 1996 expedition found a treasure trove of oil-wrapped coins that were kept from the invasive effects of the saltwater. Now, however, the divers were excavating under the surface where the coins were concreted. As numbers of the coins now found were encrusted with concretion or in clumps of concreted coins, only the coin's size could be identified. Any determination of features such as dates and mintmarks were left for another time. To avoid the possible risk of damage, the salvors didn't remove the encrustations on board the vessel, leaving this for professional numismatic processing on land. The initial cataloging on the ship consisted of recording the denominations and counting the approximate number of coins. Retained numismatists conducted later the detailed cataloging and evaluation after the coins were properly restored.

The *Negotiator* transported the artifacts and coins from the mother ship to Crescent City's small-boat docks. Overseen by Barry Sutton, a waiting car then drove the artifacts to the Flynn House for conservation. Armed DSR security personnel guarded the gold coins from the mother ship to a waiting Brinks security truck and its armed guards, including two Del Norte County sheriff's deputies. The Brinks truck then drove the coins to its vault in Eureka, California, to the south of Crescent City.

The operations recovered a total of 220 artifacts, exclusive of coins, during the 1997 field activities. The final total was higher, as some of the objects included boxes with numerous individual items such as locks, keys, doorknobs, rasps, and wooden handles. By far the most numerous items recovered were ceramics, comprised of plates, platters, saucers, cups, mugs, bowls, and sugar bowls. A portion of the cargo appeared to have been English stoneware and ironstone china. Divers recovered a variety of glass items, and these included champagne and spirit bottles, medicine and condiment bottles, pitchers and cruets, and drinking glasses. The salvors also found three bottles of light green glass, embossed with the legend "Lea & Perrins Worcestershire Sauce." These items were also of modern interest.

Numerous ceramic artifacts still lie scattered around and inside the hull, including rows of plates, bowls, and other ceramics, some lying atop exposed floor and ceiling timbers. Divers were able to excavate ceramic bottles, dark glass wine bottles, and ceramic plates with "New York" written on them.

Conservation procedures differed depending on the item. Each artifact was initially subjected to a lengthy period of desalinization and cleaning. For some, this meant soaking in freshwater for weeks with periodic brushings to remove the encrustations. Others received more complicated treatments, such as electrolytic reduction and airbrush cleaning. Metal objects usually underwent electrolysis treatment in different chemical baths that included corrosion-resistant coatings—and this could take years. Conservators treated glass and ceramics with a solution of ammonium citrate and acetone, followed at times by an acrylic coating. Organic materials such as wood, rope, and leather were treated with varying strengths of polyethylene glycol (a type of wax) and then freeze-drying. After conservation, the artifacts were stored at the Flynn House.

The District Court also ordered the hiring of a well-known marine historian, Gary Gentile (the author of *Shipwrecks of Delaware and Maryland)*, to visit the site and submit his observations. Although his expenses were paid by DSR, Gentile was independent in his duties.

He concluded that DSR was performing its explorations in a "professional and appropriate manner" and Gary Gentile reported this directly to Judge Bechtle.

During all of this, Willard Bascom's presence was very helpful to the salvors and in what they were trying to accomplish. Although his diving days were behind him, he watched the operations and made helpful suggestions to the men. His impressive experience and resume as a marine archaeologist lent legitimacy. Bascom was an observer, a mature presence, and a framer of the environmental practices of DSR while in its explorations and recovery operations. In the courtroom, he testified about the built-in safeguards and the high level and efficacy of DSR's conservation practices.

Pat Wilson, the skipper of the supply ship *Sea Chicken,* was brought into Deep Sea Research's activities through his friendship with Barry Sutton. He also taxied men, supplies, and provisions to the mother ship, taking back broken equipment and tired men. On one bad stormy day with seas nearly twenty-feet high, Pat was ferrying investors and Willard Bascom to the mother ship. Even though Bascom at the time was "seventy-something", he was still energetic and Wilson, like the others, considered Bascom to be the "father of oceanography."

Pat maneuvered his ship in the frothy ocean swells toward the anchor wells on the *American Salvor*. Cut to just above the waterline, port and starboard, higher aft but deeper towards the bow, these entry points were inundated by the ocean's whitecaps. With only a "knotted halyard and a sturdy Barry Sutton" to haul up and catch the passengers and freight, this was a frightening ride for most. As the tiny supply vessel slammed up and down against the much-larger *Salvor* in the pitching waves, the men were able to offload their passengers, including the spry "Doc" Bascom, who was the only one that clambered up on his own with a grin.

Wilson also remembered the stories of the divers, such as the six-foot ling cod that attacked one man under water and swallowed his arm to the diver's armpit; but for receiving the scare of his life and a shredded wetsuit, the man survived without injury. During the operations, octopuses seemed always to be present, including a huge one that took up residence inside the wreck and snaked at times towards the men, one time grabbing a surprised diver by the ankle—who shook and ripped the arm away. This happened on nearly every expedition.

At final count, a total of 332 gold coins, again mainly twenty-dollar Double Eagles, were recovered from the 1997 explorations of the *Brother Jonathan*. Coupled with the 875 coins discovered in 1996, the total recovery so far came to 1,207 extraordinarily valuable gold coins. The total cost of the 1997 recovery was $600,000—or more than ten times the cost of the first successful exploration—even though this operation yielded one-third of what the first one discovered. Despite this, the second exploration was still a very good outing. At a reasonable $5,000 valuation per coin, the 1997 expedition would have generated gross revenues of $1,685,000—or a surplus of over $1,000,000 over the exploration costs.

All of the 1,207 coins came from the same quadrant and box. According to Flohr, "This box was perched on a metal shelf that we found out later was part of the base of the smokestack. The box had come from the purser's office and left positioned on the metal base."

Flohr saw the divers continually focusing on that same spot, which he felt was a mistake. They also weren't keeping a record of the date, water, and air conditions, currents, where each worked, and what grid was hit. In fact, it appeared that these explorations were not following the grid system. This observation meant that even with the successful explorations completed so far, many areas hadn't been searched or results recorded.

Given the estimates of what was on board the *Jonathan*, it became clear that much more gold was waiting to be found. The salvors hadn't yet discovered the three Wells Fargo boxes for Crescent City (outbound), Portland, and Vancouver—the smaller coin box with its gold wasn't part of those shipments. Nevertheless, these wood boxes could still be in existence, as they were saturated with linseed oil, which the sea worms and organisms hate. Also DSR still hadn't located Major Eddy's iron strongbox with its $200,000 Army payroll, nor the huge Doblier safe with all of its valuables. Some salvors believed that the huge safe "blew forward," but it probably would have still been anchored to the wall and deck. As to the large payroll disintegrating over time, federal monetary agencies had confirmed that even "a muddy sludge of dissolved currency"—subject to proof of the strongbox—was redeemable.

DSR by this time had expended $1.8 million dollars for its research, exploration, and discovery activities. However, they had to keep raising money to pay for California's continuing legal fights over who owned the gold they had recovered. DSR discovered the *Brother Jonathan*'s gold, but the State of California refused to agree that the adventurers owned one dime. The lawyers for each side finally had their chance to argue the case before the U.S. Supreme Court—and that day was December 1, 1997.

CHAPTER 15

The U.S. Supreme Court and Treasure

The H.M.S. *DeBraak* remained an elusive target until 1984, when Harvey Harrington used side-scan sonar and different assumptions to locate it. The salvage effort never recovered extensive amounts of gold and silver, but it did yield an archaeological treasure. The ship, which sank in 1798, produced everything from leather shoes, wool hats, and quill pens to pottery, a silver trophy cup, and delicate glass-condiment bottles.

From an archaeological point of view, these finds are a treasure trove of information. Scientists had never found a double-frog waist belt (used to carry a cutlass and bayonet together) at sea before—until the *DeBraak* was investigated. Buttons recovered from the ship indicated that officers wore them to show rank, well before these were authorized as being part of their uniform. By analyzing the ship's remains afterward, experts decided that the officers, who had separate quarters and dining area, enjoyed relative luxuries. This was confirmed by the discovery of salt cellars, a black basalt tea set, glass decanters, silver meat skewers, and wine bottles, two of which were found corked although full of seawater.

Dutch sailors rarely ate fish. Superstitiously, they believed that this act would upset a "vengeful" sea. When archaeologists discovered corn, peas, and coffee beans inside the hull, along with rice, salted beef, and salted pork, they learned about the crew's food. Finding a bottle marked "Ketchup"—then made with strong ingredients such as spices, cloves, and even stale beer, the scientists concluded that food on board wasn't typically very good. The marine experts came upon the tools of a surgeon, including bottles that held "essence of spruce" (used to prevent scurvy), a bone saw, and equipment to remove bad teeth.

The most poignant objects discovered were human remains, which were interred in 1998 in Delaware's Zwaanendael Museum. Captain James Drew's mourning ring, whose inscription reads "In memory of a beloved brother Captain John Drew," is touching: It memorializes a brother who had drowned just five months before he did. The archaeologists came upon different objects ranging from bone dice, razors, and toothbrushes to an eighteenth century alarm clock and a tiny cannon complete with a firing mechanism. By analyzing the shoes, the experts determined that the sailors were somewhat fashion-oriented, at least when they cut off their shoe buckles and punched holes for "trendier" shoe laces.

By looking closely at the hull and rigging, the scientists decided why these ships capsized as fast as they did. To make the small boats sail faster, the designers put more riggings on board. This made the vessels less stable and more vulnerable to strong gusts of winds during a bad storm.

Despite all of this information, however, some people criticize whether the reclamation of these wrecks is that important, especially in states that have financial problems. Workers moved the *DeBraak*'s hull to a specially built structure in Lewes, Delaware, where for years they have rinsed the hull three times daily to keep the wood moist. Maintaining the hull in this condition has been expensive. In fact, unless a way can be found to preserve the hull economically, they may need to put it back into the bay and "cover it up" until that process can be discovered. The boat has been in storage since being raised, which includes nearly all of the reclaimed artifacts. State officials talk about a maritime museum built for this ship, but that remains to be seen.

Most salvors and the public agree that a state has rights in overseeing the excavation of a sunken ship to preserve the history that's contained. Overzealous officials seem to look at this process, however, as their private fiefdom to decide what the public wants or doesn't. Then the people never see what the administrators decree to be "public property." If a state doesn't put up any money to help in the search and recovery, as the argument goes, then how can it demand 50 percent of everything found?

Worried over not receiving "their fair share" and controlling what they see as explorers who are "more concerned about profit than antiquities," the states have intervened in numerous high-profile treasure explorations. The first highly publicized treasure-trove case came with Mel Fisher and his Treasure Salvors' discovery of the Spanish galleon *Atocha,* which sank off the Florida Keys. The federal courts ruled that the former owner of the treasure, the Spanish Crown, had abandoned any claims of title to the gold, silver, gems, and artifacts the galleons carried over 350 years ago. The United States and State of Florida also had no real claim to these wrecks: They sunk outside Florida waters and no law gave the United States the right to claim such ownership of ships found in international waters. However, the state and federal governments filed lawsuits to be declared owners.

The U.S. Supreme Court declared Treasure Salvors to be the sole owner of the wreck and its treasures, ruling against the claims of ownership by the United States, Florida, and other entities. After many years in litigation and over a hundred federal court hearings, in 1982, the Supreme Court agreed with Mel Fisher's position. In *Florida Department of State v. Treasure Salvors* (458 U.S. 670), the nation's highest court ruled:

> Let no agency of government stand in the way of what our forefathers created. A free enterprise society in a democracy will flourish. A nation that doesn't understand these basic truths will take its place behind other nations and they will wither.

To establish jurisdiction for the court, the Columbus-America Discovery Group brought into court several artifacts and pieces of coal from its discovered ship, the S.S. *Central America,* which sank in 1857 in a hurricane about 160 miles east of Cape Hatteras, North Carolina. Although the court's jurisdiction did not extend beyond the three-mile limit, it granted exclusive salvage rights to Columbus-America and issued an injunction against everyone else. To establish its right to the salvaging and recovery of the riches, Columbus-America had to prove to the court's satisfaction that it had the financial resources, organizational ability, and archeological skills to properly recover the ship's treasure. Several insurance underwriters then intervened. They claimed ownership of the gold based on paying off insurance claims after the disaster. Because the underwriters had done nothing for more than one hundred years, the court awarded Columbus-America 92.5 percent of the recovered treasure.*

The State of Delaware and others litigated the wreck and exploration of the H.M.S. *DeBraak.* Legal fights similarly erupted over the title to the exploration and recovery of items from the *Titanic* and *Lusitania.* However, established maritime law is basically simple. The finder of a sunken wreck files an "in rem" (a lawsuit against the "thing" or the ship) admiralty action in the U.S. District Court that has jurisdiction. It then seeks to be declared the sole owner under the Law of Finds. This long-established legal concept holds that if the true owner has abandoned a wreck and treasure, then the salvor is to receive full title. Alternatively, in the event that the wreck has not been abandoned, then the salvors petition for the court to award them a portion of its value. To establish this right, the vessel or sunken object must be within the federal court's jurisdiction, which extends a marine league, or three nautical miles offshore. This distance can be extended as seen in the previously discussed *Columbus-America* dispute.

The finder deposits something from the wreck with the court to prove the existence of maritime property within the court's jurisdiction. In the *Brother Jonathan* case, Don Knight deposited the six items

*See further *Columbus-America Discovery Group v. Atlantic Mutual Insurance Company,* 203 F. 3d 291, 2000.

that he discovered among the debris, but California immediately objected. Judge Bechtle in March 1995 turned down the California State Lands Commission motion to dismiss DSR's action for title to the *Brother Jonathan* for lack of jurisdiction. This dispute, however, was much more than what court had the power to make a binding decision on the matter. It was about control and money. The CSLC basically didn't want the action to be heard in the federal courts, arguing that state courts—where more favorable laws applied—were the proper forum. The battle continued from there.

BEGINNING IN THE LATE 1980S, CSLC officials insisted, by administrative fiat, that they would oversee *any* search of the ocean floor in the *Brother Jonathan* case and many others like it. This state had to issue a permit for *any* commercial salvage. Additionally it wanted basically half of all proceeds, regardless that it wasn't taking any risks or fronting any money. The officials seemed to take the position that California owned all of the ships wrecked up and down its coastline, a position that conflicted with long-time established law. For example, when the State of California applied for the *Brother Jonathan* to be placed on the National Register of Historic Places, it stated in the application that it was the owner of the sunken ship—despite the court's ruling to the contrary. What's bizarre is that California was claiming title to the vessel when it didn't know where the *Jonathan* was located.

As seen, when DSR objected that the state had no right to control their work, the whole matter was thrown into the courts—which had to have been CSLC's intention. The "Law of Salvage" basically holds if someone saves property "from a peril at sea," that the salvor is entitled to a "generous reward" from the value of the property, which was so saved or reclaimed. The size of the award depends upon several factors, including the property value and difficulty of the salvage operations. The award is then assessed against the vessel's owner. The court can even order that the ship be sold to produce the funds from which this award is paid.

The explorer who first discovers a wreck petitions the federal court to declare its rights as the exclusive salvor. When this is granted, the discoverer can salvage the wreck without interference from any other treasure hunters. Under the law of salvage, the actual ownership stays with whoever owned the property before that discovery. If the former owners abandon (or give up) their rights to the wreck, then under the Law of Salvage (also called "The Law of Finds") courts can award title of the entire wreck to the salvors. However, just because a ship sinks hundreds of feet to the ocean's bottom does not mean that the rights of the owners are abandoned—and this is a factual issue for a court to determine.

If the owners (whoever they might be) have not abandoned the sunken vessel, then the person recovering either the ship or its contents is entitled to a portion of the value recovered, not the entire find. The difficulty for the courts and salvors lies in establishing factually whether there was abandonment—not to mention that although the general principals are well accepted, applying them can be complicated.

When anyone discovers a sunken ship (or anything for that matter), there is a problem: Companies and heirs connected with the long-lost vessel immediately feel they have a right to the proceeds, whether they legally do or don't. Courts accordingly require proof of abandonment, such as a letter relinquishing any further interest in the lost property. When an insurance company pays money to its insured for that loss of property (whether due to a shipwreck or not), then title to that property passes to the paying insurer.

Dating back to 1953, Congress enacted the Submerged Lands Act (43 U.S.C. 1301). This granted the states title to the natural resources located within three miles of their coastline. Although the legislation didn't include abandoned shipwrecks in its definition of "natural resources," over half of the states decided that the act did and passed laws granting them title to any sunken ships within these limits. The majority of federal courts afterward decided that the states did not have this unilateral power. Undeterred, the states continually lobbied Congress to then grant them this right.

In response to this pressure, in 1987, Congress passed the federal

Abandoned Shipwrecks Act (ASA). This law granted state governments the title to certain historic wrecks that are (1) "abandoned" underneath a state's submerged lands; *and* (2)(a) are either embedded in the sea floor or coralline formations, or (2)(b) are already listed or eligible for listing in the National Register of Historic Places. Before any state gains title to any shipwreck *within* its three-mile limit, all of these conditions must be met. Otherwise, there can be no transfer of title from the federal government under the ASA.

The State of California argued that it had title under the ASA, and regardless of this legislation, that it couldn't be sued under the Eleventh Amendment to the U.S. Constitution. The state's biggest legal problem was proving that the wreck was abandoned *and* that the Eleventh Amendment prohibited admiralty or maritime lawsuits against a state. This amendment prohibits federal courts from hearing a private party's claim against a state government. However, the Constitution specifically grants Congress the exclusive power in admiralty (maritime) actions and courts had emphasized this for years.

The State of California also argued that the ASA couldn't supersede its own state laws passed two years after the federal legislation. This conveniently forgot the "Supremacy" clause of the U.S. Constitution, which prohibits such state acts in the event of a conflict. Passed in order to "preserve and protect the underwater cultural resources of California," the state's law was unique in that it granted the state the rights to *any* shipwreck "older than fifty years" in its three-mile coastal limit. Critics felt that the law was illegal and overreaching, plus that it was really intended to raise revenues despite its "preservation of culture" language. Legal experts felt that California's arguments were "wide stretches" at best.

The ASA granted states the title to certain historic "abandoned" property sunk close to their shores; but for these exceptions, established federal maritime law still controlled. For example, when insurance companies pay the insured claims of the owners of a sunken vessel or its property, then the wreck is not abandoned. In these cases, title to the wrecked vessel passes to the party who paid the owner. Further, a state must prove the rejection of ownership. When owners do not search for a wreck over time, this fact by itself is not considered abandonment.

When a wreck isn't legally abandoned, then the original owners of that property—usually the insurance companies who paid claims off—retain their rights. This precise situation applied in this case when DSR acquired the insurer's rights. Even if all of California's arguments were upheld, existing maritime law held that regardless of who owns title, DSR would be entitled to a "generous" award for its efforts. The State of California's 50 percent assessment didn't meet this test either.

DSR could have argued the shipwreck was not within the three-mile limit, as the state contended that its limits commenced from any reef or rock formation that was not covered by ocean. Despite this, DSR stipulated that the wreck was located on state lands, so that it wouldn't have to disclose the wreck's location—a nice legal gambit by the State of California.

Judge Bechtle's decision was conclusive until an appellate court overruled it. He held that the federal ASA law preempted California's broad law granting title to the state to *any* submerged site lying over fifty years in its three-mile state waters. Judge Bechtle ruled that the *Brother Jonathan* was: (1) not abandoned, as the insurers hadn't abandoned their claims and DSR had purchased those rights; (2) not embedded in the ocean floor, as a substantial portion, or two-thirds, was above the bottom; and (3) wasn't eligible for listing in the National Register, since the State hadn't even made the application during the hearing.

California had not introduced any evidence where *any* of the ASA's requirements were met and its own law was inoperative. The judge granted DSR the warrant for arrest on the wreck for 1½ years as the custodian and exclusive salvor of the ship, and this was extendable for one-year periods until the salvage operations were completed. No one else could conduct salvage operations or collect artifacts within a defined area: "A circle having a radius of 5,200 feet (or one mile), having its center point at the geographic coordinates 41 degrees, 46.29 minutes north, and 124 degrees, 20.50 minutes west." Although very specific as to the area that DSR claimed the wreck to be in, the description didn't precisely identify where the ship was, since the wreck could be anywhere within that two-mile circle.

Although the judge awarded the salvage rights to DSR, he also ruled that any salvaging had to be completed under the watchful eye of a qualified archaeologist and that all discovered artifacts would be under the court's jurisdiction. Thus, DSR had to apply to the court for anything that had to do with the gold and artifacts.

Under the ASA, states were intended to be the protectors of shipwrecks of "historical significance" that fell within their nautical borders—but they generally don't have the funds to oversee these operations. They rely on divers to find the wrecks. They then require them to hire an archaeologist of the state's choice and excavate according to the state's often costly, slow plans. The ever-present concern of the states and CSLC was that, under the salvors' hands, priceless artifacts would be lost and sites scavenged with little regard for archaeological safeguards.

On the other hand, California's rigid rules, such as grabbing half of the "take," requiring expensive environmental studies, and mandating the hiring of underwater archaeologists and artifact conservation at the salvor's expense motivated divers on low budgets to keep their discoveries and salvage efforts to themselves. Other states only took 20 to 25 percent of the profits and were much less restrictive in their approach. Meanwhile, nearly five hundred shipwrecks along the Northern Coast of California continue to disintegrate under the state's tough regulations.

Judge Bechtle's decision was clear, strong, and in accordance with existing law. The state's position was so legally off, that long-time established maritime law would have to be overturned completely for its position to have a chance. However, California's response was to file a motion to stay (or not enforce) the judge's decision. He turned that motion down. California then filed a motion in October 1995 for an injunction to prevent DSR from conducting its salvage operations. The Court of Appeals unanimously turned down that motion.

Then in July, 1996, California appealed the decision to the Ninth

Circuit Court of Appeals. The appellate court affirmed the lower district court decision and ruled that the ship was never legally abandoned, even though it had remained untouched since 1865. When the insurance companies paid the claims, the court said, they took title to at least part of the wreck. The court rejected California's argument that DSR only owned part of the ship, because only one third of the cargo had been insured. It held, "We decline to divide the wreck of the *Brother Jonathan* into abandoned and unabandoned portions."

The State of California immediately filed a motion to the Ninth Court of Appeals for a rehearing on its July 19, 1996, decision. One month later, this court again ruled against California. The U.S. Supreme Court granted rare certiorari, or that it would hear the matter and make the final decision. Deep Sea Research's attorney, Fletcher Alford, said he thought that this case was "significant and unusual and interesting," but that he had no idea this would go all the way to the Supreme Court.

A coalition of insurance firms, salvage companies, and treasure hunters backed DSR's efforts in the Supreme Court hearing. Even the Columbus-American Discovery Group, with its S.S. *Central America* exploration, moved to file an amicus curiae (friend of the court) brief, but the U.S. Supreme Court decided against that—given all the "friendly" briefs already allowed and filed. The National Trust for Historic Preservation, various archaeological conservation groups, and the states of Alabama, Alaska, Florida, Georgia, Hawaii, Idaho, Illinois, Louisiana, Maryland, Massachusetts, Michigan, New York, Nevada, North Carolina, South Carolina, Vermont, and Virginia filed amicus curiae briefs. The State of California had been busy in lining up its support.

The states briefed the court that claims to as many as five thousand shipwrecks in oceans, gulfs, bays, lakes, and rivers were at stake. The states and conservation groups argued that state government had the right to control the fate of historic wrecks, whether off their ocean coastlines or under lakes and rivers, and that this should not be left to private explorers. States worried that if the lower district court's ruling in the *Brother Jonathan* was upheld that this would make it difficult, if not impossible, for a state to assert its determined "ownership rights" over shipwrecks. More than forty states at this time had programs for the recovery of shipwrecks, and at least twenty-seven states had passed laws that claimed the title to shipwrecks within their state waters. By this time, the bottom line was that states wanted the legal authority to deal with every ship that was within their territorial limits. They wanted this regardless of what maritime law provided and without any interference from either the federal government or the salvors.

The State of California battled in the press as well. Radio and television announcers commented on their broadcasts, and newspapers ran the headlines of "Sunken Ship Legal Fight Deepens," "State Asks Court to Stop Wreck Salvage," "State Makes New Effort to Claim Wreck," "State Fights for Rights to Historic Ship," and more. Up until then, DSR declined comment, as it didn't want to draw further attention to its recovery operations. The salvors wanted a fair deal with the State of California to put an end to their financial hemorrhaging. They also wanted to be able to conduct their own recovery and reclamation operations, already subject to extensive court supervision.

California, however, wasn't going to wait until the Supreme Court decided the merits of the case. It immediately filed a motion to stop any salvaging of the ship until the justices decided who owned the salvage rights. The Supreme Court again held that the State of California was wrong in its arguments. In June 1997, the U.S. Supreme Court unanimously held that DSR could again salvage the *Brother Jonathan,* if Judge Bechtle determined that they were following the court-imposed salvage guidelines—and they were. The nation's highest court then set the matter for hearing in its upcoming October term.

Every court and judge by this time had ruled against the State of California's position: The District Court, the Court of Appeals by two-to-zero and three-to-zero votes, and the U.S. Supreme Court by a nine-to-zero vote. One would think that California and its CSLC would have decided the better alternative would be to settle the dispute with the sea explorers. They didn't.

At the time of deciding the *Brother Jonathan* case, the U.S. Supreme Court also agreed to consider the case of the *Lusitania.* A German submarine had torpedoed and sunk this vessel in 1915 off the coast of Ireland in an incident that killed 128 Americans and helped lead the United States into World War I. Although this was also a high-profile case, the justices decided to hold off any ruling until they decided the *Brother Jonathan*'s issues.

At oral argument, Deputy Attorney General Joseph Rusconi told the court that due to the long passage of time, the vessel had clearly been abandoned. "Its original owners are long dead, and the insurers took no steps to find or salvage the ship." Fletcher Alford argued that abandonment had to be a voluntary concept and not something that happens automatically due to the passage of time. He wanted the justices to rule that "a shipwreck is not abandoned unless there was 'some evidence of voluntary relinquishment' by the owners, their heirs, or the insurers"—or the traditional rule of law.

Justice Antonin Scalia scoffed at the notion that a treasure is abandoned just because its owners can't retrieve it, saying, "If I drop a silver dollar down a grate, and I can't get at it with a piece of gum stuck to a stick, I still think that it is still my silver dollar." Justice Stephen Breyer exhibited some sympathy for California's argument when saying, "If a long time passes and nobody does anything, it's not abandoned?" However, Justice John Paul Stevens and other justices pointed out that no insurance company or heir is ever likely to announce that he or she has voluntarily relinquished the rights to their lost property.

The State of California wanted to be automatically entitled to have its ownership claims heard in state court, everything else heard in the federal courts. Justice Ruth Bader Ginsburg said such a policy "would be impractical because this would leave the state as a big player looming out there with an ownership claim even after a federal court had ruled on the case." Justice Stevens said, "Congress thought the 1987 statute would apply to lots of sunken ships. If we take your view, it wouldn't apply to any."

DSR and Fletcher Alford argued:

> The state is arrogant in its conviction that only they can do this right [watching over cultural heritage]. But the state has conceded no funds to recover the wreck or safeguard it from pillagers. Meanwhile, my clients have not seen a penny return on their investment. They've only seen their money bleeding out.
>
> One hundred and four investors—common, ordinary people—have so far contributed $1.2 million to the recovery of the wreck, with the hope of seeing a return on their investment. Afterwards, they plan to donate artifacts to museums, assisted all the time by archaeologists and supervised by a federal court judge.

Justice Sandra Day O'Connor asked Fletcher C. Alford: "Counsel, now isn't the bottom line that, if we rule in favor of the State of California, your clients will have lost everything—all of that work and effort and time and expense, for nothing?"

"That's exactly right your honor, and that would be fundamentally unfair," replied Alford.

On April 22, 1998, after the oral arguments, the U.S. Supreme Court unanimously held—by another nine-to-zero vote—that federal maritime law and the ASA controlled over the state's stricter law on marine salvage under the Supremacy Clause. The justices unanimously agreed that the Eleventh Amendment did not prohibit a lawsuit brought in federal court over title to a shipwreck.

The justices rejected the argument that any lawsuit to determine title to a sunken ship was a lawsuit against the state. As intended by long-standing maritime law and the ASA, salvors could sue the state in federal court to settle disputes over the ownership of sunken vessels lying in offshore or inland waters. DSR had won with everything at stake. An adverse decision would have meant it would have lost everything. The state would have gained all without doing one thing constructively to assist in the salvage operations (*California v. Deep Sea Research*, 523 U.S. 491, 1998).

The Supreme Court reaffirmed the traditional admiralty definition of abandonment. It said that any ownership of historic derelicts must be determined by a lower federal court sitting as a maritime court as the U.S. Constitution provides. The courts held unanimously the entire way up: California had presented no evidence of abandonment. If the shipwreck was never abandoned, then the ASA didn't apply, and DSR had the full rights and title to salvage the *Brother Jonathan*—just as Judge Bechtle had ruled years earlier.

The justices declined to address the constitutionality of the ASA, whether the ship and its cargo had to be treated as one property for the purposes of abandonment, and whether the passage of time to prove intent to abandon is frozen for the period when the technology to salvage a ship isn't available. If these questions needed to be resolved, the justices left them to be tried, considered, and decided later by the district court.

When the decision was announced, attorney Alford said, "We're obviously pleased. The end is now in sight. This has been a long haul and a lot of people have poured their hearts, souls, and pocketbooks into it."

THE LEGAL CONTESTS were a bitterly contested series of hearings, proceedings, arguments, and decisions. Among other experts brought into its fight to win at all costs, the State of California had retained the highly respected and well-known marine archaeologist, James Delgado. David Flohr later commented:

> Initially, the state tried to negotiate a deal with us. California would allow us to salvage the ship, if the state netted half of the proceeds from the recovery. This didn't leave any room for anyone else, including the insurers who had settled with us. And the state wanted the complete title to the ship. We couldn't do that—and who would? The basic issue was con-

trol and money. In the swing of a door, we went from being partners with California to pillagers.

James Delgado and five other marine archaeologists helped frame the state's arguments, and they continually skewered our operational plans and the environmental report. The state and its experts said that we were pirates, that our operations would be like "strip mining a grave site," and that we would steal. They called us "briggoons" and that our actions threatened the integrity of the industry.

Willard Bascomb came in, however, and saved the day with his reputation, especially when he supported what we were doing. He testified under oath that the criticisms of DSR's environmental report showed that "those people didn't know any more now about marine archaeology than they had when they were my students." Bascomb was very helpful, because with his massive resume, he gave us legitimacy to offset these constant criticisms.

The Supreme Court's decision, however, did not mean an end to the litigation. The case meant that Judge Bechtel's decisions not to dismiss the action for a state court and California's confiscatory laws were proper. A full trial could still take place in his federal courtroom. Then, that separate decision could be appealed again all the way up the appellate ladder. California immediately signaled that it intended to continue the fight. State attorney Joseph C. Rosconi even said, "I'm hopeful. We're going to appear in a federal court and make a showing that we own the vessel. The test for 'abandonment' is still up in the air."

Even the media agreed that this state agency was out of control. One week after the Supreme Court's decision, the *San Francisco Chronicle*'s editorial on the matter concluded:

Deep Sea Research took the risks to find the wreck in 1993 and have been fighting state bureaucrats for ownership ever since. We are rooting for the treasure seekers, whose bold adventures spark the imagination and inspire dreams of diving on the estimated 5,000 wrecks—including gold-laden pirate ships—that still lie undiscovered in U.S. coastal waters.

CSLC attorneys served a subpoena on Don Knight to testify for the state's side in the upcoming trial on the merits. Even after losing eleven straight hearings and court decisions—without one judge casting a vote in its favor—California continued to play hardball with its unlimited funds.

Mark Hemstreet had flown previously to Sacramento to meet with CSLC officials and negotiate a settlement. He tried to reason with them, arguing even before the Supreme Court decision that it wasn't in the best interests of the state to lose. One official responded: "We love to scuba dive on wrecks, and we might want to explore the wreck. You found it, but we have the salvage rights." As he returned to his hometown, Hemstreet fumed about what he thought were typical bureaucrats.

California's officials gave the impression that losing again and again wasn't important to them, because they felt they could bankrupt the much smaller DSR into submission. It was time for DSR's personnel to bring their own political muscle into a dispute that really was never about saving archaeological history.

On May 4, 1998, Mark Hemstreet sent a strongly worded letter to Assemblyman Jim Battin and enclosed copies of letters written by David Flohr to Assemblyman Steve Badwin and California Attorney General Dan Lundgren. Asking for a personal meeting with Lundgren, Hemstreet's letter concluded:

> [The State of California] has appealed its defeats, time and again, at very great cost to the taxpayers, and has lost in every court, most recently in the U.S. Supreme Court, 9–0. Yet, it continues to brag to the media that it intends to litigate and delay, using the taxpayers' money, for as long as possible. If an individual, rather than the State of California, was the

> party in this proceeding, he would have been found to be a vexatious litigant.

On August 6, 1998, Hemstreet sent a strong letter to Assemblyman Howard Kaloogian in which he urged Kaloogian to work with Jim Battin for an immediate intervention by the Governor's Office in the continuing *Brother Jonathan* saga. The CSLC was marching down the road for a full-blown trial—although the factual issues were clearly not in its favor. Among other provisions, Hemstreet's letter stated:

> This high-profile case should be used as a clear example of wasteful bureaucratic harassment, completely out of control, against honest citizens. This type of behavior and attitude by an unelected bureaucrat should be most troubling to anyone who really cherishes and respects the foundations of our democracy.

On August 19, 1998, Assemblyman Jim Battin sent a three-page letter to Mr. Robert C. Hight, the Executive Officer of the CSLC about the ongoing legal warfare being conducted against DSR. Among other provisions, his letter stated:

> With seven consecutive rulings since 1995 in favor of DSR, the State Lands Commission has doggedly continued in its unfounded effort to lay claim to the *Brother Jonathan*. Although the State of California has suggested that it is willing to settle this matter, its settlement demand is essentially a demand that DSR give up everything. The State insists that, as a precondition to any settlement, DSR must acknowledge that the State owns the wreck (despite the contrary rulings of three federal courts), and must apply to the State for a permit to recover the wreck, a permit that may or may not be granted. This appears to us to be nothing less than harassment.

Battin went on to state that DSR had established at its expense an artifact conservation laboratory in Crescent City to treat, study, and preserve the artifacts recovered to date. He mentioned that DSR had retained the "world-renowned" Florida conservation expert, Herbert Bump, to oversee the laboratory a relationship that dated back to the days of Don Knight. Most importantly, he wrote that a federal Trial Status Conference was to be convened soon to see if the parties could settle their differences in the "ten-year-old dispute." He hoped that Hight would show the "leadership necessary to help put a stop to this reckless abuse of taxpayers and their money." He copied Peter Pelkofer, David Flohr, and George Dunn, the chief of staff for Governor Pete Wilson.

Not finished, Mark Hemstreet sent a stronger letter on August 21, 1998, to Ms. Kathleen Connell, the chairperson of the CSLC, imploring her to use her influence to stop the runaway California legal train. This letter stated, among other provisions:

> Government servants should be held accountable for their irresponsible, negligent actions, which have cost California taxpayers a great deal of money, as well as consuming the valuable energy, time, and resources of the Attorney General's Office that should be used for truly legitimate cases, which benefit the general public. On behalf of DSR, which is made up of hundreds of law-abiding taxpaying Californians, I would appreciate your reasoning with the Governor's Office to finally end this injustice.

These letters did not result in an immediate settlement. They were credited, however, with putting sufficient pressure on California to reach a settlement. The state formally agreed to end litigation on March 9, 1999, the day *before* the long trial in federal District Court was to commence.

From DSR's perspective, California, Peter Pelkofer, and its CSLC weren't entitled to anything. They hadn't contributed one dollar or a positive step to the recovery and preservation of the ship, its artifacts, or gold. Fletcher Alford advised the salvors, however, that the expense of another California-threatened court battle—now over the issue of abandonment—would cost "another one million dollars." Again, this was despite the experts' shared conclusion that the state would lose again, unanimously, and at every level.

Judge Louis C. Bechtle convened his court on Wednesday, March 10, 1999, in San Francisco for the trial of *Deep Sea Research, Inc. v. the Brother Jonathan*. The parties were ready to proceed, but there would be no trial. The attorneys for DSR and the CSLC had finally reached an agreement—nearly a year after the U.S. Supreme Court decision. Judge Bechtle accepted the parties' stipulations and concluded the hearing with a moment of silence in memory of those who had perished so many years before.

Under the settlement, DSR retained 1007 coins, while California acquired 200 gold coins for their share. At an estimated value of $5,000 per coin, the value of the two hundred coins equaled the approximate amount of the additional legal costs, which another series of lost California court battles would have equalled: one million dollars. As for California's allotment, attorney Peter Pelkofer of the CSLC picked up the two hundred gold coins at a San Francisco bank and drove them to Sacramento, where they were to be stored for safekeeping. Under the agreement, these coins are not to be sold on the open market until at least fifteen years afterwards.

The settlement provisions not only gave California a share of the *Brother Jonathan*'s gold, it also gave the state the right to supervise future salvage operations. The stipulation provided that California's law allowing the state to supervise and own shipwrecks was valid and applied to artifacts other than gold and money. However, just because DSR stipulated for its own account as to California's law *does not mean* that this law is legal, given the court decisions that already took place.

The settlement provided for two other claimants. Having lost its agent, Joseph A. Lord, and the strong boxes decades ago, Wells Fargo and Company, made a claim for any property that could be proved to be theirs. They settled for a padlock labeled "Wells Fargo and

Company," the right to claim items in the future, and the loan by the State of California of five gold coins (later increased to ten) for its San Francisco museum. The agreement provided that descendants of passengers could file claims for recovered goods. "We will recognize these claims," David Flohr said later. "Any claimant who has proof that the material belongs to them will be given that material, minus our costs in recovering it."

Regina Phelan, a retired teacher and author, made another recognized claim. She was a descendant of Henry C. Lee, who owned the traveling circus and lost his wife, Janette Lee, and infant son on board the ship. Regina Phelan's attorney argued she should be reimbursed for the lost circus payroll that Mrs. Lee was carrying. As part of the settlement, California agreed that if evidence came forward proving that the coins (or other discovered objects) were part of the circus payroll, Regina Phelan could claim up to $100,000 against the State of California. At this time, that proof has not been supplied.

The settlement granted 80 percent of any other future "treasure trove" (defined as gold, silver, jewelry, coins, or money) at the wreck to DSR. The State of California retained the rights to the ship and all artifacts not gold, including the right to oversee the conservation process in all future recovery operations. A CSLC official, or designee, would observe future salvage work to ensure that "objects of historic value were properly cared for."

The agreement gave DSR a "one-shot," one-year permit to search for more treasures. California Lieutenant Governor Cruz Bustamante, who was chairman of the CSLC then, commented when the state announced its part of the agreement:

> The settlement secures the commission's right to supervise and own historically significant property recovered from ships that sank within three nautical miles off the coast. The legal battle is justified because the end result gives the state a clear stake in the future finds of historical or cultural importance in any of the more than 1,500 wrecks embedded in commission territory.

This was not what the U.S. Supreme Court, or any of the other courts, had said or held. When the state transported the coins to Sacramento, both Kathleen Harris and Bustamante boasted that "We have won." When a newspaper reporter questioned Cruz Bustamante as to whether they really had won—given that California had lost eleven straight legal hearings at considerable taxpayer expense—Bustamante looked the other way and took another question. Neither he nor any other California official ever answered that reporter's inquiry.

Peter Pelkofer, senior counsel for the CSLC, is quoted as saying that the state was pleased to have retained the right "to tell them how to do it (the salvaging of the wreck)." This right to control the salvage—and getting a heavy share of the loot—was what the state's position seemed to be all about. Prior to the Supreme Court decision and settlement, California's position was that the ship belonged to the regulators and the salvors would get only "what we're willing to give them for bringing it up," as the officials told DSR.

DSR representatives told the press that "they were weary but thankful for the long-awaited payday." However, Don Knight expressed bitterness and anger at the settlement, stating publicly, "I'm extremely disappointed that the State of California would have the audacity to reward this piracy." DSR responded that Don was "bitter because he will not share in the profits."

Afterwards, Knight was in Peter Pelkofer's office. Pelkofer said he had something to show him and left the office. Upon his return, he had a small cloth bag and handed it to Knight, "You deserve this, but you can't have them." In a bitter-sweet moment, Don Knight held five of the recovered gold coins, and then handed them back to the senior counsel.

As to the insurance companies who paid off claims in 1865, the salvors contacted the insurers and told them about the unanticipated "cut" California had received. Even with the gold coins in its hands, DSR had more bills than it could handle. Given this development, DSR asked for a reduction in the insurer's share from 10 percent to 8 percent, or an overall 20 percent decrease as to their share. The insurance companies agreed, and the salvors and their investors viewed this as a "nice gesture." Commercial Union Insurance Company, which was the largest entity and whose predecessor then paid out $20,000, received $138,000.

Two other insurance companies, however, didn't receive anything. One had moved out of the area without leaving a forwarding address. The second pressed for an indemnity provision that DSR would pay for their defense costs and damages should California also sue them. As the state had acquired a very litigious reputation by now, this issue became a "sticking point." The second insurer didn't press its demands and backed away.

When David Flohr looked back at California's approach, he concluded:

> During the battles, Pelkofer retired; however, he came back from retirement to oversee the *Brother Jonathan* case. In 1999, we gave the two-hundred gold coins to Pelkofer as California's representative. Attorney Mosconi for the state, Judge Bechtel, Dr. Kegan [the state's numismatist], and our officers were at the coin transfer. When Pelkofer received the coins from me, he didn't say anything, not even a "thank you," nothing.
>
> Three times, their lawyers in court said for the record, "We're not after the gold." They certainly were. From day one, California wanted fifty percent of the gold, title to the ship, control over all operations, their archaeological man on board at our expense, nothing brought up without their okay, telling them the ship's precise location, completing extensive EIRs, and there was to be no discussion about this—until after the Supreme Court decision. With Stuart Gordon and Fletcher Alford [DSR's lawyers], I had met with Pelkofer in 1992 and his demands were the same six years later.
>
> In my opinion the California State Lands Commission was out of control with no state oversight. After the Supreme Court decision, California's officials told us they were going to full trial on the issue of abandonment and take that deci-

sion all the way to the Supreme Court, again. This issue was clearly against them. The *Central America* decision had already held that abandonment was not about how long a time had passed, but revolved around the intentions of the people who had owned the property. Not only was the law against the state, but it also didn't have possession of the ship.

California had no shortage of funds. They just kept spending money provided by taxpayers—of which I was one—to thwart operations that were already under the court's complete control. We had to get the judge's permission for everything. In fact, the court watched over us so closely that his ruling on what insurance DSR had to carry cost us $16,000 just for the consultant's fees. We ended up having to take out nine different insurance policies.

Shomette's claims in his book [*The Hunt for the HMS DeBraak,* previously discussed] against Harvey Harrington and the *DeBraak* could have been a "red flag" to the state. Don Knight's accusations didn't help us either. Once we were under the court's supervision, however, with the state-appointed archaeologist on board at our expense, then this should no longer have been an issue—especially with Willard Bascomb's oversight.

The question is continually asked, "Why did California fight for so many years as if its fiscal life depended on putting this salvage company out of business?" Don Knight considered himself to be a friend of Peter Pelkofer, who was subject to the salvors' strongest criticisms. Knight said:

> Pelkofer was just trying to do his job as Senior Counsel to the State Lands Commission. He tried to do the case on a "color" claim that was weak—but he did his job. California's officials kept going after Deep Sea Research, because these state people were supposed to be the "Top Dog," but instead

> they were always losing in court and publicly. They kept making mistakes and their egos got in the way of doing what was the right thing.

Although the prolonged legal battles had forced the salvors to reduce their explorations and cut drastically into their operating funds, the sea explorers had further adventures awaiting them. Another risky exploration and selling the *Jonathan*'s gold awaited them as well.

CHAPTER 16

The Auction

With the settlement in hand, it was time to sell the coins and relieve DSR's tough financial straits. David Flohr's blood pressure had soared during the hard times of getting the State of California to come to a reasonable settlement. His doctor advised him to take time off, which he did, but before he knew it, David was back at it, and he was seventy-four years old.

The next important decision was to decide who would oversee the auctioning of the gold. The salvors hired a numismatic consultant, Gene Seton, who recommended that the company invite six of the most reputable rare-coin auction houses to give presentations. "A big guy who wore big belt buckles and knew coins," Seton drove down from Port Arthur, Washington, in his RV to start the process. Prior to presentation time, some of the best coin houses in the business had investigated DSR's operations and inspected the coins after clearing security.

At the formal coin-group meeting, the salvors gave a presentation on the discovery, salvage, and refurbishing operations. They then listened to the various coin-specialist presentations, and gave them supervised access to the gold coins. Holding the coins up to the light, the representatives inspected them with exclamations of admiration and awe. Afterwards, David Flohr couldn't believe his coin count. He said, "One of the six numismatists that we were interviewing actually stole one of the coins and walked away with it from the meeting. We never found out who that person was."

In 1997 the lead principals of the firm, Bowers and Merena, flew to Crescent City and viewed the site of the *Brother Jonathan*. Q. David Bowers was especially interested in the treasure, and Gene Seton recommended that David and his partner, Ray Merena, be included in the presentations. After considering the proposals, Deep Sea Research decided to select Bowers and Merena as its numismatic auctioneer and representative.

Founded in 1953 with its auction division located in Irvine, California, the firm grew to be a leading rare-coin dealer. It handled the multi-million-dollar sales of prestigious collections ranging from Louis E. Eliasberg Sr. ($45 million) to the Garett Collection for Johns Hopkins University ($25 million). The company's services would include appraising coins, creating the auction catalogue, holding the auction, and post-auction functions.

Along with his partner, Bowers is one of the leading experts in the numismatic world. Born in 1938, he became interested in coins at age fourteen, considering himself to be lucky to find his chosen work at such an early age. In his early years as a coin dealer, he had to rely on public—and even parental—transportation. By his senior year in high school in Pennsylvania, Bowers's business was flourishing. A National Merit Scholarship finalist, he graduated with honors from Penn State University in 1960. While still in school in 1958, Q. David Bowers formed his first coin-dealership partnership. Continuing the profession over the years, David moved to Wolfeboro, New Hampshire, in 1980, where he partnered with Raymond N. Merena. He built the firm of Bowers and Merena into one of the largest coin dealerships in the world.

In addition to authoring dozens of books and writing regular columns in *Coin World* and *The Numismatist*, Bowers found time to serve on the Board of Governors of the American Numismatic Association (ANA) for six years, culminating in a two-year term as its President from 1983 to 1985. He was a recipient of the highest honor bestowed by the ANA (the Farran Zerbe Award), the first ANA member to be named Numismatist of the Year (1995), inducted into the ANA's Numismatic Hall of Fame, and received more "Book of the

Year" awards and "Best Columnist" honors given by the Numismatic Literary Guild than any other writer.

He also agreed to write a book on the *Brother Jonathan* that dealt with its history, the successful recovery, and the numismatic background and implications of the discovered gold coins. He hired archival researchers and after considerable time and expense published *The Treasure Ship S.S. Brother Jonathan: Her Life and Loss, 1850–1865.* This book accompanied the 1999 auction of the ship's gold coins. There was no mention of the gold bars, presumably because the auction only concerned the *Jonathan*'s coins.

With its financial problems caused by the State of California, DSR continued to search for investors and money. Bowers and Merena came to the rescue to help keep their legal fees current. The auctionners loaned Deep Sea Research a total of $300,000 in two loans of $150,000 each. These loans were to be paid back from the auction proceeds.

By this time, the discovered coins had been carefully washed and conserved. Although many of the coins were in near-mint condition—due to the $20 pieces being discovered in cyclindrical piles or stacks—some were still covered with marine growth. DSR's archaeologist, Rob Reedy, reported that the seashells growing around those coins had actually saved their quality. Sand couldn't scratch their surface, preserving their value, as the slightest scratch can downgrade any coin's quality under the ANA's scale. Consequently, nearly all of the gold coins were at high grades, and many were virtually as brilliant as the day they were first struck.

The two year total of 1,207 recovered gold coins had made this venture one of the most successful of all time. Bowers and Merena already estimated that the coins would bring $6 to $8 million dollars alone—and this didn't include the State of California's two hundred coins, nor what might be found in DSR's future recovery operations.

AFTER THE GOLD COINS were discovered, the crewmen transferred them from the mother ship to a waiting Brinks armored truck. On one delivery for security reasons, the salvors ordered the *American*

Salvor to sail to Eureka during the night, a small coastal town located ninety miles south of Crescent City. When David Flohr and other men approached the dock, all of the lights were on the pier. A security man worried about a possible ambush, so the officers quickly ordered all of the lights turned off on the pier to complete the transfer in the dark. Under the protective cover of night, the men quietly and quickly offloaded the valuable coins from the large ship to the truck. From the port, the Brinks truck sped the coins to Alameda, close to San Francisco for safe-keeping, inspection, and eventual conservation.

"As another example of how the judge ruled on everything," observed Flohr, "he said we couldn't take more than fifteen percent of the coins out of Brinks vault at any one time, no matter what the reason, and we were required to have two people on site when any coins were transferred." Once the gold coins were secured in Alameda, Jim Wadsley, David Flohr, and other officers had to make seven trips to San Francisco due to the "fifteen percent rule." They had to move the coins from Brinks over to their inspecting numismatist, whose offices were in San Francisco. Once the initial inspection was completed, the men needed to complete seven trips to transport the coins back to the Brinks facility, The precious coins were then driven south to the Los Angeles area for grading.

A Brinks armored truck with armed guards carried the gold treasure to a "nondescript building in a nondescript office park" in Santa Ana in southern California. Guarded by heavily armed security officers and three locked doors, experts in a basement room scrutinized the gold coins—each about the size of a half dollar, but made of near-pure gold—with magnifying glasses. DSR hired Professional Coin Grading Service (PCGS) in Santa Ana, one of the largest rare-coin grading services in the world to perform this function.

The coins involved were five-dollar Half Eagles, ten-dollar Eagles, and twenty-dollar Double Eagles, dating from 1834 to 1865, with nearly every year covered by the five-dollar Half Eagles and twenty-dollar Double Eagles. The great majority of the coins found by DSR were twenty-dollar Double Eagles with 90 percent bearing the years

1863 to 1865. The State of California primarily chose for its share the 1863 to 1865, twenty-dollar Double Eagles.

Sharing a cramped room in the building's basement, six coin graders continually examined the gold coins. They assessed a number of factors, including each coin's brightness, the presence of any scratches on a face, and any imperfections before assigning a numeric value between 1 and 70. As Q. David Bowers wrote, "Grading coins is more like judging figure skating than timing speed skating." Although this grading has very specific rules, applying them is definitely a subjective art and not a science. A small difference in grade, however, can mean a large difference in value, even with a difference of high-grade coins between MS-60 and MS-65.

Coins are designated in quality, ranging at the low-end from Poor (1), Fair (2), Good (G-4 to G-6), and Very Good (VG-8 to VG-10). The next higher quality is Fine (F-12 to F-15), Very Fine (VF-20 to VF-35), and Extremely Fine (EF-40 to EF-45) toward the upper end of the appraisals. Whether a coin is circulated or not has another strong quality influence. A coin with an "About Uncirculated" designation (AU-50) has traces of light wear on many of the high points, but "at least half of the mint luster" is still present. If there is the "barest" evidence of light wear on only the highest points of the design, then the quality is set at AU-55. As each step goes up in quality, the coin becomes more valuable and worth more in price.

New coins showing no trace of wear receive the highest grade of MS—or "Mint State." A MS-60 coin has no trace of wear, but may show various contact marks, and the surface may be spotted or lack some luster. A MS-65, or "choice uncirculated" coin, is an above-average uncirculated coin, which may be brilliant or lightly toned, but evidences "very few contact marks on the surface or rim." The highest quality designation is the MS-70, or perfect uncirculated coin, with a perfect new condition, showing no trace of wear. This is the finest quality possible with no evidence of scratches, handling, or contact with other coins.

From MS-60 to MS-70, there are different grading standards in between and range from MS-61 up the numismatic ladder to MS-70.

Any grade above 60 is considered to be "Mint State"—or above-average high quality. Experts can differ on the MS and nearly any designations; in fact, one coin dealer told the story of sending the same coin out four times for a quality designation, receiving in turn different appraisals ranging from MS-61 to MS-64.

The value of a coin depends on its rarity (the numbers of the coins known to exist), quality (surface attractiveness, sharpness of striking, and "eye appeal"), the demand (whether many or few buyers are interested), and the romance (the pedigree, history, or how "interesting" the coin's story is). Within this, coins are graded basically by the amount of wear, from how often it was held to the effects of the elements, such as immersion for a long time in saltwater.

The experts confirmed that near one thousand of the 1,006 pieces met or exceeded the MS "Mint State" quality standard of MS-60, despite the decades spent three hundred feet below the ocean's surface. One of them, encrusted in coral, had already been donated to the Crescent City Historical Museum in 1999. These were an extremely valuable set of discovered coins due to their quality, romance, and demand. The difficulty, however, was to determine whether the numbers of coins being sold would cut into their price.

The process of grading the coins and sealing them in a heavy plastic protective envelope went fairly quickly. "After doing a few million coins, it gets easier over time," said Rick Montgomery at the time, president of the grading company, who examined each of the coins. Most of the coin graders were collectors before joining the company, and they were impressed by the coins that they were evaluating. "It's almost unheard of for them to be in this condition and quantity," Montgomery said. "It's unlike anything we've ever seen."

Several hundred of the coins were pristine twenty-dollar Double Eagle coins struck in the San Francisco mint in 1865. Only a handful of such coins previously existed in the world and were worth then about $20,000 each. DSR and its coin consultants needed to decide whether all of the coins should be sold, which ones would be a potential depressant on the market, and whether it would be better to sell everything even at lower prices.

Believing that the coins' quality and condition would provide a support level, the principals decided to sell all of the coins at once. Still concerned that the numbers of previously rare coins would lower pre-auction values, the salvors decided to promote the sale to noncollectors with an interest in the Gold-Rush era, as well as to collectors.

One of the recovered coins was an 1865 ten-dollar coin that mistakenly had its date punched upside down. The error was recognized and a correction had been punched over it. This rare mistake brought this coin's worth up to between $50,000 and $100,000, and bets were taken as to what its eventual sale price would be. Experts considered this gold piece to be the prize of the salvaged collection, as it was one of only thirty-six such coins known to exist, and the only one discovered so far beneath the sea.

After the grading, an armored truck transported the coins to the Los Angeles Airport, where they were in turn flown under guard to the Bowers and Merena Gallery headquarters in New Hampshire for appraisal and cataloging. The auctioneers took pictures of each coin, wrote a description, and placed the information in their one-half-inch-thick catalogue. Afterward, the coins were transported under guard and flown back to Los Angeles for the auction.

One and one-half months before the date, Bowers and Merena published David Bowers' 400-page book on the *Brother Jonathan,* and copies were stocked in the bookstores. DSR knew that even a successful auction wouldn't make anyone wealthy—the proceeds would basically pay the bills, including the rest of their $1 million plus legal bill, and return portions of the invested capital with some profit.

After creating and printing the auction catalogues, Bowers and Merena distributed them worldwide to their clients and potential buyers. Bids started pouring into their offices by telephone, fax, and mail, and their personnel were kept busy answering questions, posting bids, and getting ready for the sale. As the auction date drew closer, the firm set up lot viewing in Los Angeles, where the auction would be held. As all sales to floor bidders are final, potential bidders first inspected the pieces they wished to bid on. They verified each coin's grade, appearance, and other details, as the auction house checked on the bidders' credit references.

The long-awaited auction date of May 29, 1999, finally came, and more then 500 eager bidders crowded into a large meeting room at the Hotel Airport Marriott in Los Angeles. The golden treasure recovered from the wreck of the *S.S. Brother Jonathan* was finally on the auction block. The auctioneer greeted the audience, told about the historic nature of the sale, and laid down the ground rules for the auction.

Flanking the auctioneer who stood behind a podium, Q. David Bowers and his supporting staff sat at an elevated front table. During the bidding, another to his left tracked the mail bids already entered into the book. As each lot came up for sale, the spokesperson called out the starting bid, which was typically an advance over the second highest mail bid. If the two highest mail offers received on a lot were $5,000 and $6,000, the lot would be opened at, let's say, $5,500. Or a lot could be opened at the reserve price, if the owners had set that level.

Two staff members sat on the auctioneer's side, and with the aid of a computer, watched over the "one lot only" and "maximum expenditure" bids. In these bids books, a collector could bid amounts for several of the same kinds of coin, but be sure of winning one—or give offers totaling up to eight times the amount wanting to be spent.

After the spokesperson called out the opening bid of $5,500, the auctioneer cried, "I have a $5,500 bid, do I hear $5,750?" If there is floor competition, the price advances rapidly: $5,750, $6,000, $6,500, $6,750, and up. And then, quickly, "sold to bidder number 456 for $10,250," or whatever the highest bid price was.

If no one in the audience bid higher than the opening call of $5,500, then that coin went to the mail bidders, and the person who bid $6,000 acquired it for less than his top authorization. If a floor bidder bid the same amount as the mail bidder, then the mail bidder, who was the earliest into the competition, took preference.

The staff registered and handed out bidding paddles to those at the auction. Most held their paddles in the air, making it easy for the auctioneer and supporting staff to follow the action. However, some bidders wish to remain anonymous, and systems were prearranged. A bidder attending a sale in person might not want to bid from the audience, and, in that case, made the offers before the auction began. The company then entered the figures into the bid book just before the sale, just as it entered the ones by mail. If the floor bidding exceeded the "mail bid," then the bidder or authorized agent could still step in and bid in person.

The auction proved to be lively and exciting, as the auctioneer shouted out in a staccato, sharply escalating voice the ever-increasing numbers being silently agreed to in the audience, over telephone, or the books. David Bowers said that "four to five times" as many people as usual attended the *Brother Jonathan* gold-coin auction in person, many obviously lured by the romance of sunken treasure and the California Gold Rush.

During the day-long auction, the circulated and lesser-grade uncirculated pieces generally fetched more than their catalog values. Prices of higher-grade coins, however, fell below their catalog levels, as the quantity now available lowered the anticipated values. An MS-65 coin—one that would have sold for $30,000 to $40,000 before the extensive coin recovery—settled to around $22,000, including the buyer's fee. Fourteen MS-65 coins in the sale were bid down to prices ranging from $17,000 to $31,000. One MS-66 coin did bring $72,450, and each of the 142 coins graded MS-64 brought an average sales price of $12,500. The first 150 coins were auctioned for a total of $400,000, and the first 450 coins sold were auctioned for $1.3 million, well above their opening bid prices.

David Bowers observed that the market remained strong throughout the sale. "Nothing went real cheap," he said later. "Some coins fetched more than their catalog values due to their association with the sunken ship." He noted that an 1856-S $20 gold piece (graded MS-62) brought a respectable $8,000, despite the fact that the S.S. *Central America* hoard was known to contain numbers of the same coins. Discovered a decade ago, however, these coins had yet to come on the market. The *Brother Jonathan* sale was the first time that a significant, legally acquired auction of gold coins from the ocean's floor ever happened.

The rare nineteenth century ten-dollar gold coin with the date-stamp strike-mistake sold for $100,000 to a collector who would put it on public display. Applause erupted inside the crowded auction room, when the price was reached after only one minute of spirited bidding. "It's a beautiful coin. I love just looking at it, holding it. I'm glad that I'm able to own it," said Ronald J. Gillio, a San Francisco coin dealer and co-owner of the Treasures of Mandalay Bay Museum in Las Vegas. There, he later exhibited the coin in the Mandalay Bay Casino. Gallio said he was prepared to spend up to $100,000 for the coin—which was worth only $10 when it was first minted all those years ago. His cost was $115,000 with the included auctioneer's fee.

David Flohr recalled:

> The auction was all day and exciting. Men were manning phones as agents for out-of-town bidders. The minimum bid was first set at $1,000, then that was increased to $2,000. The cheapest coin was purchased for $1,200, and coins started going for $40,000 to $50,000. Then the big one set for $75,000 went for a higher amount than we thought.
>
> At one time we were thinking about how we could avoid the complications of an auction to hundreds of buyers. We consulted a expert on how to sell the entire lot to just one buyer. After the state's take, we had 1,000 left. At $1,000 a piece, we would receive one million dollars at a low-wholesale price. However, if the auctioned range on the retailed pieces was generally from $3,000 to a high of $10,000 for each one, with an average of $5,000 for each piece, then he estimated that we would receive closer to five million dollars. And that's just about what we got.

The sale of the 1,006 coins fetched a total of $5.3 million that day, including the 15 percent buyer's fee. Bowers and Merena originally estimated the total of 1,206 coins would bring somewhere between six and eight million dollars. When factoring in California's 200 gold coins, or one million dollars, the total "actual" figure came to $6.3 million, toward the lower end of the initial estimate. Given the amount of coins that were now on the market, this was at the same time still an excellent sale.

David Flohr bought a gold coin at the auction, the only one he received from all of his efforts on the *Brother Jonathan*. The sale was the result of a successful bid on an 1858 $20 gold piece for $1,450. Mark Hemstreet, on the other hand, was a very active bidder and purchased more than thirty coins. Other investors and officers were also present and most were successful in their bidding. Expending great sums of time and money to bring about a successful salvage operation—then having to buy the gold coins individually a second time to help free up funds to pay those bills—doesn't sound quite right.

DSR and Flohr received Bowers and Merena's check for the sales proceeds, per their agreement. It included one-half of the 15 percent "buyer's fee," as well as a deduction for interest, the cost of the books distributed, and $300,000 to repay the loans. The auctioneers sent a check to DSR in a net amount of $4,612,775.

When the principals worked out the numbers after all their expenses, there was not enough money to pay all the outstanding bills, the invested capital (plus a return), and finance another exploration. Echoing the sentiments of each principal, James Wadsley reported to the press that his own take from the find would be "minuscule," considering the amount of time he had invested. "I've figured it out," he said. "I'm making $1.43 an hour. With my earnings I'm going to replace the T-shirt with the hole in it and get a new hubcap for the station wagon."

Given that there wasn't enough money to do both returns and explorations, DSR decided to find one "well-heeled" investor who could fund that venture, even if he wanted a larger share of the gold. The officers began to search for that special investor, as the controversy over the gold bars escalated to volatile levels.

CHAPTER 17

The Bars and the "Great Debate"

The conflict over the *Brother Jonathan*'s gold bars had grown over this time. After the first public auction of the *Jonathan* bar number 2186 in 1974 at Stack's, the NASCA sale of another (2184) from the Hanson Collection took place six years later. The heading with a picture of the gold ingot was: "Excessively Rare *Brother Jonathan* Bar." Among various descriptions, the text stated:

> The *Brother Jonathan* also had on board a series of assay bars from the San Francisco Mint in 1865, apparently as the private property of one of the passengers. A group of eleven of these were recovered, sequentially numbered, from a point between the wreck and the shore, and had probably been in one of the lifeboats that capsized (presumably along with the owner of the bars). They entered numismatic channels in 1970, after having resided in one family for quite a long time.

At the 1982 auction of the impressive Henry H. Clifford "Coinage of the American West" sale, the third public offering occurred of a *Jonathan* gold bar. Clifford was a very wealthy investment banker, a past President of the California Historical Society, and an editor and writer of various Gold Rush historical and coinage articles. The catalogue text detailed the ship's history, its cargo, passengers, and the circumstances of the wreck. The lead paragraph in bold face stated that the "gold bar is believed to have been carried aboard as cargo on the *Brother Jonathan*."

When Ted Buttrey analyzed these accounts in detail, he strongly criticized the changes in the text descriptions over time. (For conciseness, the entirety of these texts is not presented.) For example, the number of lifeboats that were lowered toward or into the water, the different wording of the ways the gold bars were brought on board, who recovered them, and how they were found.

The drumbeats of numismatic war continued in 1984 when the American Numismatic Society (ANS) passed a resolution supporting Mr. Buttrey's assertions that certain Mexican gold bars from the Mexico Mint of Spain in the 1700s were fake. No mention was made about the *Jonathan* gold bars. The next public auction of the vessel's bars was the 1985 Superior Gallery's auction of the same bar number 2184, and the seller was presumably the purchaser at the NASCA sale five years before. The heading after the bar's picture reads, "Excessively Rare United States Mint, San Francisco 1865 Gold Assay Bar, known as the *Brother Jonathan* bar."

This sale auctioned the exquisite coin and ingot collection of Dr. Jerry Buss, the multimillionaire real estate investor who had purchased the NBA Los Angeles Lakers, NHL Los Angeles Kings, and Los Angeles Forum in 1979. He continued the succession of the rich and famous who once had owned these gold bars. Modifying somewhat the first writeup, the description read in part:

> One of the eleven sequentially numbered specimens apparently recovered from the sunken side-wheel steamer *Brother Jonathan*. They entered numismatic channels in 1970, after having resided in the same family for quite a long time. Surfaces of all are slightly granular in pieces from saltwater action. This specimen was acquired from John J. Ford, Jr., in 1973 by Jon Hansen.

In 1996, Mr. Buttrey presented another paper at the American Numismatic Society, arguing strenuously that most of the Western gold bars were fakes. He compared them with bars salvaged from the S.S. *Central America*, which had transported gold from California to the East Coast and was wrecked in the hurricane off the Carolina coast in 1857. Buttrey alleged that the Western bars differed significantly from these gold bars—assuming that the strikings, fineness, and other details of the recovered bars were the only model—and that these characteristics significantly differed from what were seen on the Western gold bars. His controversial conclusion continued: John J. Ford's Western gold bars, including those from his Paul Franklin venture, were modern-day fakes. He left an in-depth critical discussion of the *Jonathan* gold bars for another day.

In 1997, bar number 2184 surfaced once more, this time offered for sale at a Stack's auction. The text stated in the twenty-seven years since their discovery in 1970, only three of the eleven *Brother Jonathan* gold bars had ever been offered for public auction. The remaining eight were still being held presumably in the John J. Ford collection.

The catalogue description noted that the ingot was "believed to be from the wreck of the *Brother Jonathan*" and stated that in the 1860s it was commonplace in San Francisco for local firms, such as G.W. Bell, Rogers & Brown, and others to openly compete with the San Francisco Mint for the public's gold ingot business. This was a convenient way for people to transport their savings, since the bars' stamped values included the "guarantee" of a specific mark or stamp.

The text stated:

> In the spring of 1865, a San Franciscan brought a substantial amount of money to the Mint and asked to have it converted into gold ingots. The Mint obliged and paid over to the owner some eleven gold assay ingots, each of which was stamped with a serial number, the ingot's value in dollars, its weight and fineness, and the Mint's own validation stamp, dated 1865. John J. Ford Jr., who has done more research on this subject than any other man alive today, believes that the original owner of the ingots was a San Francisco madam. Ford states that he has seen the Mint's old records, the Assayer's Register, 1854–1865, and the Register of Bar Warrants Paid, that list the names of depositors, and that there was just one

> owner's name listed for ingots numbered 2178–2188. Further, Ford relates that the same woman's name he saw on the San Francisco Mint's registers also appears on the passenger manifest of the ill-fated side-wheel steamer *Brother Jonathan.*
>
> The text continued:
>
> Other passengers brought their own savings in gold in one form or another, including Mrs. Keenan, who carried eleven gold ingots with her totaling a little less than twenty-one pounds, all made for her at the San Francisco Mint. Mrs. Keenan seems to have survived, but the NASCA cataloguer (the prior auction in 1980) stated that the eleven *Brother Jonathan* ingots were recovered from a site between the wreck and the beach. Presumably, they went overboard from one of the capsized lifeboats.
>
> Attempts at salvage began almost immediately, but without success. An 1894 claim of discovery of the wreck appears to have been a sham. There may have been an attempt in 1916 to salvage gold from the *Brother Jonathan,* and the Gibson sale cataloguer mentioned a Los Angeles based salvage group active about 1936. The *Brother Jonathan* gold bars known today may have been found in 1916, 1936, or even earlier.

The bar sold for $33,000 as against its bullion value of $6000.

Michael Hodder, a Stack's consultant, presented a paper at the next annual meeting of the ANS in 1997. He concluded that Buttrey was "plain wrong," had failed to consult the historical archives of the period, and had "waffled" on the evidence. The *American Journal of Numismatics* (11 1999 A.J.N. 85–149) published Michael Hodder's, "Western American Gold and Unparted Bars; A Review of the Evidence," as a rebuttal to Buttrey's criticisms that openly questioned John Ford's authentication of the Western "assay bars"—and which included the *Jonathan* bars.

Hodder's paper argued that although the Mexican bars had not been fully evaluated, some had been tested, and there was nothing in their metallurgy to disprove that they hadn't come from the 1700s. Contrary to what Mr. Buttrey alleged, he said the design on those bars had been used at that time. Mr. Hodder defended the Western bars, arguing that Buttrey had condemned all of the Western bars, but there was "plenty of historical evidence that such bars did exist at the time they were dated."

The experts basically agreed that the glowing metal bars—only a few inches long and with antique inscriptions—are solid gold except for some silver and trace elements that were mixed into the alloy. What makes these particular bars so special, however, is their background. A bar containing only a few thousand dollars' worth of gold can be worth many times more on the open market due to its particular history or pedigree.

The "legends of royalty, outlaws, and treasure ships" surrounded the Mexican bars—and others. They were housed in the Josiah K. Lilly collection in the National Museum of American History in Washington, the Museum of American Money in San Francisco, and in the hands of private collectors. Clusters of the bars were said to have been minted in Mexico during the 1740s for King Philip V of Spain. Other gold objects were said to have been part of a legendary stash known as the Franklin Hoard that was carted around the Far West and discovered by Paul Franklin and his men. The finds also included the gold ingots identified as belonging to the San Francisco madam, Mrs. Keenan.

The question at the center of one of the longest, greatest feuds between icons of the numismatic world is: Where did these assay bars, gold ingots, and objects come from? The controversy revolves around whether the gold bars were created in the 1950s by the gifted metallurgist Paul Franklin, then camouflaged with these historical treasure stories that multiplied their values numbers of times. Not only were large reputations, egos, valuations, and assets at stake, but also the validity of important items in major collections had fallen under question.

The ANS's *American Journal of Numismatics* published Professor Buttrey's 1997 article, entitled "False Western American Gold Bars." It condemned a group of gold bars as modern forgeries and John Ford in the process. Two years later in March, Michael Hodder delivered the Groves lecture on Western Assay Bars in which he took issue with this view and defended the authenticity of many of the pieces Buttrey attacked. Hodder wrote a paper later published, which included these views. Mere months after the successful auction of the *Brother Jonathan* gold coins, the American Numismatic Association (ANA) organized and brokered a debate between Michael Hodder and Professor Ted Buttrey over this issue. This controversy nearly centered on the *Brother Jonathan* gold bars.

In a rare occurrence, leading numismatic experts—such as John J. Ford, Q. David Bowers, and others joined Michael Hodder in support of the gold bars' validity. Buttrey and later John Kleeberg disputed the conclusion. They squared off in a bitter public squabble that led to more litigation. The ANS and the ANA are the two prime numismatic societies that exist in the United States. As one expert observed, "but for the ANS being a little more into 'ancients' and the ANA a little more into 'U.S. numismatics', both organizations are important."

The "Great Debate"—as the industry describes the event—was between Ted Buttrey and Mike Hodder. It took place at the ANA's annual convention and its 108th anniversary, held at the Rosemont Convention Center in suburban Chicago on August 12, 1999. As the coin industry speculated over what would happen, the E-Sylum (the electronic publication of the Numismatic Bibliomania Society) speculated that "spectators will be asked to check their six-shooters at the door."

ONE HUNDRED AND FIFTY NUMISMATIC EXPERTS attended that Thursday morning debate. Enthusiasts packed a room at the convention to watch the two contestants square off. The conference room was stark and dimly lit and the wall lights gave off a foreboding look, appearing to illuminate the walls better than the occupants. Two tables with microphones dominated a stage with stairways on both sides. A lectern with another microphone was in front of the stage.

The ANA's Director, Edward C. Rochette, was the moderator and made an express disclaimer that the association "would not take sides" in the matter. For several months, ANA officials brokered the debate procedures and terms between the two warring sides. Professor Theodore Buttrey would present his views first for half an hour, followed by Michael Hodder's allotted half-hour. Then each would have fifteen minutes to rebut, followed by seventy minutes of questions from spectators who were to have previously signed up on a "question list." A silence pervaded the audience, usually informal and, at times, raucous in other seminars. Now everyone listened intently to the moderator, clearly waiting for the salvos to start.

The ANA representative gave a brief background biography about each man. An English citizen, Professor Buttrey had taught numismatics at Yale, the University of Michigan, and Cambridge University, where he had been the Keeper of the Department of Coins and Medals at the Fitzweiler Museum. He was also the only person to serve on the "Council" of both the American and Royal numismatic societies, having also served as head of the Royal Numismatic Society from 1989 to 1994. He was "extensively" published on numismatic matters.

Born and educated in England, Michael Hodder came to the United States in 1957. In 1980, he went to work for Sotheby's, the well-respected international antique and auction house. By 1982, he was head of the Numismatic Department at Sotheby's, and one year later he was President of Spink and Son, a respected numismatic firm. From 1984 to 1991, he served as Director of Research for Bowers & Merena, the same house that handled the auction of the *Brother Jonathan* gold coins. He was a freelance researcher at the time, working for Stack's and others, and had also been "widely published". Both men were recognized as numismatic experts in their fields.

Buttery wore wide-rimless glasses, was well-groomed, had short hair, was of average height, and dressed with jacket and tie. Hodder was younger, with a crew-cut, broad-shouldered, also dressed with jacket and tie and wore glasses. Both men started their presentations on the floor podium behind the stage.

The professor strode determinedly up to the podium. If the 150 people in the audience wanted to know where Buttrey stood, they didn't have to wait long. He referred to John J. Ford by name and quickly attacked his authentications of the Western assay bars. "A lot of this material came from John Ford," he soon said. "We need some information and aren't getting it. We can't take Mr. Ford's word for anything. . . . Ford has a vested interest in every one of these [Buttrey's disputed gold bars]." Three examples were brought up: a prior auction sale, the Franklin Hoard, and the question of the "missing" receipts for the *Brother Jonathan* gold bars.

Buttrey's statements were pointed and very personal: "This is part of the fraud. . . . He [Hodder] has cooked the evidence and it is shameful . . . but he studied with a master [Ford]." Near inaudible gasps echoed in the hall as Buttrey argued that the numismatic bars secured by Paul Franklin—although never mentioning him by specific name—were fakes. The professor's argument had much less to do with single pieces as with the "lack of provenance," or documented history of the Western assay bars and that their source centered on one person, who transferred them in turn to John J. Ford.

"The issue is not the material, but where it came from and who has handled it," he said. "Then, you share my judgment or not . . . I don't care." The professor made strong comments but did not seem to be as concerned with the ingots' validity: "I see manipulation . . . I see falsification in the evidence, but that doesn't mean that the bars are bad."

Buttrey ended by attacking the *Jonathan* gold bars, starting with the 1974 Stack's sale. He then showed Stack's 1997 catalog on the same *Jonathan* gold bar by an overhead projector, reading the text out loud in quick, seemingly nervous statements.

His main arguments were: (1) No San Francisco Mint ledgers were discovered after John Ford's inspection evidencing that Mrs. Keenan brought the gold to be melted down, nor that she received the manufactured gold ingots; (2) no evidence existed to support the story that Mrs. Keenan was the one who possessed those bars; and (3) the U.S. Mint in San Francisco was a branch mint up to 1873, so that any ingot stamp with the wording of "S.F. Mint" (as on these bars) could not have been correct, since the stamping would have to use the wording "U.S. Mint Branch," or something to that effect. He concluded, "This bar is a fake," and the audience sat poised in their chairs in stunned silence.

Hodder came up and stood behind the same podium, adjusted his papers, and started his presentation. His manner seemed different from the professor's with less nervous energy and personal asides, but his statements—although less animated—were clear and strong with equal preparedness. The two views couldn't have been more divergent.

Hodder strongly argued that Western assay bars did exist prior to 1950 (or before the time when Buttrey alleged that the disputed bars had been "manufactured"). He maintained Buttrey didn't know what assay bars were and that Buttrey thought, "They were all gold bars." In fact, Hodder argued, the Western assay bars were comprised of gold bars, silver bars, and "unparted bars" (or gold and silver), that created a very large number of numismatic pieces that couldn't have been forged. He argued the professor's position (that all bars coming from one source had to be false) didn't follow due to the magnitude of what would have to occur. Hodder maintained that Buttrey was an expert in ancient coins, but he didn't have "any idea about another country's Western assay bars."

He argued that relying on the S.S. *Central America* to determine the standards for bars was a false assumption: Only the "best and cleanest" bars were brought out for that public display. Actually, numbers of other *Central America* bars had conflicting marks, just like the *Brother Jonathan* bars. During this time, the audience reaction seemed to support his position more and much less Professor Buttrey's.

Hodder next disclosed that he had arranged for "Proton Emission Beam tests to be made at Harvard at the Cambridge Center for

Advanced Studies on eleven bars with the same source." Owing to the high cost of these procedures—$300 per hour for two days of testing plus his time—the tests were limited to these bars. He said that every one of those bars had different metallic compositions of silver, gold, copper, zinc, and other trace minerals. Each bar was a different shape and pattern, moreover, but each proton assay matched the stated gold content (i.e., 94.5 percent) as stamped on the ingot.

Hodder's conclusion was that how could one man (Paul Franklin) forge the eleven different bars—not to mention the hundreds of others—when that would have required "hundreds of different molds, the need to obtain high quantities of gold when prohibited by law, and to combine this gold with bizarre trace elements." Next, he would have had to manufacture all of these bars in a city where the smoke and emissions would be highly visible, affixing a unique stamp on each one (including a different pattern just discovered hundreds of feet down in the ocean on the S.S. *Central America),* and "then hide them in little towns in Arizona, California, and Nevada."

Buttrey on his rebuttal continued to call the Western assay bars, the "1950s bars." He said he was talking about gold bars—not silver or "unparted" (mixed) bars. His major point again was that "the issue is where these come from and by whom." Buttrey then said: "I have shown there is fraud . . . and manipulation of the evidence, but if you think that these bars are good, then fine."

The professor concluded by saying an end should be put to this entire "gold bar scam" and that upon his instruction, his attorney had turned over all of his files to the State Attorney General for New York "to see if criminal charges should be brought against John J. Ford, Michael Hodder, Harvey Stack, and Stack's (as a company). We will be working with that office to see if charges should be brought."

The professor from England had shaken the "gentleman's club" at the ANA to its very foundations. Not only was this an out-in-the-open, "bare-knuckled" brawl, but one in which the most famous and well known now had to choose their legal and public-relations weapons. The exquisite Lilly collection of ancient coins and gold ingots at the Smithsonian, distinguished auction houses, and leading experts might be the subject of a criminal investigation. This state of affairs was unheard of.

Hodder maintained his composure, as he mounted the stage above the podium and stared down at Buttrey. "Well, that's a surprise. This goes beyond what I expected. Maybe I shouldn't have been surprised (owing to the personal attacks made)," he responded. "It is very sad that you back-tracked so much. Go back to Roman coins. You condemned an entire bit of material without seeing one of them."

He soon asked strongly, "I have a few questions for you, sir."

"Where do you want me to be?"

"Anywhere you want to be," retorted Hodder. His manner showed he was definitely irritated, to say the least. After the men bantered back and forth, Buttrey came forward and stopped in front of the podium to peer up at Hodder who sat behind a table on the stage. As the larger man stared down at Buttrey through his glasses, Hodder demanded:

"How many bars did you see at the Smithsonian? Answer me, yes or no." The professor's response was that he had looked at the Smithsonian display "under the glass," or as anyone else did at the exhibit.

"Did you go to the Clifford sale (a sale that involved some of the disputed ingots)? Did you attend the Schumacher, Gibson, or Clifford sales?" The answer was "no."

After deliberating over Buttrey's objections to answering any more questions, the moderator ruled that Hodder had the right to ask them and Buttrey had to answer.

Hodder demanded: "How many (of the disputed items) have you tested?" The answer was none. Buttrey, however, responded further, "I haven't handled a lot of them, but I understand them."

"You should have stayed in your field," snapped Hodder. "To you professor, if it doesn't shine gold, then it isn't gold." And the cross examination continued.

When the rebuttal segment came to an end, one man stood up from the audience in front of everyone. "I'd like to make a statement," he said persistently but evenly. No one in the room said a word. "I have been defamed, and I want to make a statement." Tall, balding, handsome, and well dressed in a white coat and dark tie, the man was Q. David Bowers.

The moderator Ed Rochette calmly responded that Bowers would have to ask what he wanted in the form of a question. Holding the public microphone, Bowers said evenly to Ted Buttery, "You have defamed me (owing to items Buttrey attacked that were in the 1982 Clifford sale and authenticated by Bowers) . . ." Rochette answered that he would have to ask a question. Bowers responded, "I question that Michael Hodder has bad intentions." David Bowers basically said that the professor had used "sparse" research, didn't attend most of the auctions or inspect the bars that he questioned as a group, and that Buttrey had pressed "material personal attacks." After the statement, the moderator deadpanned, "Thank you for your question"—and the audience laughed well in response.

During the question period, nearly every person who came to the microphone asked questions of Buttrey that attacked his allegations of fraud against some of the most well-known numismatic players in the world. One questioner maintained that the 1930s to 1974 federal prohibition against the public's ownership of bullion gold was a key reason for the lack of publicity about the "Franklin hoard." (If you could be arrested, you weren't very likely to go out of your way to tell anyone what you owned.)

When the moderator announced that Harvey Stack was next, there was a stirring in the audience. Mustached, with graying hair and wearing black horn-rimmed glasses, the man in the white shirt, dark tie, and dark-tailored suit had a distinguished air about him. Stack began by saying, "I want to defend myself in the form of a question." As people laughed, he opened another issue. Since both were members of the ANS and it had published Buttrey's paper, he asked, "Why did you have more time than I did?"—intimating that he should have had equal time in the defense of himself, his firm, and reputation. "I was asked to be a reader on your paper, four days before it was to be published. Why were you given these privileges?"

Although Buttrey answered by saying he had no influence in such matters, the issue had been raised.

One questioner seemed supportive of the professor by asking if his disputed ingots contained a majority element of gold—or contained at least 50 percent—to which Buttrey answered "yes." Another concluded that the differences in the bars could have been due to the differences in time of manufacture, a likely proposition.

David Alexander then asked what seemed an excellent "question":

> These items were destined to be destroyed. We weren't making Michelangelo paintings. We were making items to be destroyed. [In the 1850s and on, prospectors and travelers alike would take their gold dust, coins, and metal to private firms or the Mint to be melted down into easier-to-be-transported ingots.] These were assay bars, not pure gold bars. Isn't that why these bars that you question look crude?

Although the professor answered the question in the negative, the point had been made. Another person asked Hodder if the analytical testing could determine where a bar was made. He replied in the negative, stating that the average tested bar had 10 to 16 percent silver, 4 percent copper, and .3 to .4 percent lead, the rest being gold. He said that there were some 400–500 Western assay bars, not including those discovered on the S.S. *Central America.*

Another questioned if Buttrey had taken into account that United States collectors, as distinct from other countries, couldn't own gold for forty years until 1974 when President Nixon signed the legalizing legislation. The professor said he had. (The point was that the ingots in question during that time period would have surfaced only at gun shows, antique stores, and other "discrete" places in the West.)

Another asked whether the purpose of scholarship was enhanced by "personal viciousness"—a feeling that some attendees had. This question was met by applause. Buttrey responded: "I didn't come here to make enemies or to make friends. But when one comes into fraud, then that brought me into the matter."

"Why would the numismatic 'anti-Christ' do this?" questioned one man. "There was nothing to gain? Why would Ford do this?" Buttrey retorted that "People could hold the objects and sell them at premiums . . . I can't read the minds of these people. I think the motives can be complex and without monetary terms." When asked if Ford could have been an innocent participant, Buttrey seemed to avoid the question.

When his time again came up, David Bowers said that he couldn't figure out any motive on Ford's part. Another said that Buttrey should emulate Hodder's style of "less contentiousness," to which most in the audience again applauded.

Professor Buttrey was bright, argumentative, coy, and continued to attack, again and again: "Mr. Ford has falsified the evidence of the Mint. Ford says the documents were destroyed, but how could he have known about them if they were destroyed."

The questions of Buttrey continued. Another told an anecdote about how John Ford had spotted counterfeit coins and quickly reported this to the Secret Service, the questioner concluding that Ford was the "scourge of counterfeiters."

Harvey Stack asked: When the government acquired the Lilly collection, did Buttrey feel that no "due care" had been taken and no experts had checked anything out? "Do you believe that the Smithsonian would have been misled?" he asked.

The professor answered, "I suppose my answer is yes."

David Bowers next focused on the *Brother Jonathan* gold bars. He argued that the San Francisco Mint never called itself by its long, formal name as a branch of the U.S. Mint. Buttrey responded that all of the Mint's "formal" correspondence until 1874 did. However, Bowers's point seemed to be aimed at the informality of what could have been happening then in the "Wild, Wild West."

At the conclusion, another ANA representative quickly hustled up. She proclaimed: "The opinions expressed are those of the presenters and not of the ANA." The controversies, however, hadn't come to an end. As people filed out talking to one another, a tall, gray-haired man—informally dressed in boots and open-necked red Western shirt—approached the microphone and in deep a gravely voice demanded, "Buttrey . . . "

Recognizing the man and voice as John J. Ford, people stopped in their tracks. As Ford glared at Buttrey, everyone else stared at both. The room became absolutely quiet. Ford said angrily:

> Buttrey, twenty-seven years ago [1972] you stayed at my house in Arizona and we had dinner. At the end of the evening, you wanted evidence of certain numismatic objects. Of the ingots we had been discussing. I went to my den and took my only original photographic prints and showed them to you. You said you would like to look at them, and I had my misgivings. You said not to worry and that you would give them back to me three to four weeks later. Twenty-seven years later, I still don't have them. I want my photographs back, Buttrey. . . . Your word isn't worth a damn—you used them to write a scurrilous and malicious article. These are all lies. A pack of lies . . . it just shows that your ethics are as low as you are.

A spokesman for the attorney general's office commented later that as a matter of policy it would not confirm nor deny that an investigation was or had taken place. As far as Mr. Hodder and the others were concerned, Professor Buttrey had gone too far. "He accused us of knowingly distributing these items," Harvey Stack said in a published interview, "And the Stack family has been in the business of precious metals and currency exchange since the nineteenth century." Why would Professor Buttrey spend more than twenty-five years questioning the provenance of gold bars sold to Josiah Lilly and a few rich collectors a half-century ago?" Mr. Stack answered, "I think he thrives internally on controversy."

Stack and Ford filed a $6 million libel suit in federal district court in New York. In their lawsuit, which cites more than a dozen of

Buttrey's accusations of fraud, the plaintiffs said that the statements were "uttered with the malicious purpose of causing injury and damage." Citing lack of personal jurisdiction, the federal judge dismissed the complaint in December 2000. The plaintiffs intended afterwards to cure this problem by having a process server personally deliver the summons and papers to Professor Buttrey, should he ever be in the New York City area again. There were no discovered reports as to this conflict later being settled or tried in court, nor public reports as to the results of any public entity's investigation. The Smithsonian may never figure out who is telling the truth because the museum does not have the resources to test all of the bars in detail.

People at the debate still disagree on whose presentation was best. One spectator concluded:

> To make a long story short, Mr. Buttrey believes that they are fake and Mr. Hodder believes they are real and very quickly the fireworks started and the fur flew. We had everything short of a physical fight as threats of legal actions punctuated the show. Two-and-a-half hours and the morning was shot, but it was entertaining!

Over the months following the public fight, numerous articles on this topic appeared in the numismatic press. A number favored Michael Hodder's analysis, presentation, and approach. The ANS Newsletter published Q. David Bowers's response in its fall 1999 issue, primarily taking on Buttrey's article, "False Western American Gold Bars." Among other issues, Bowers made the argument that Professor Buttrey did "not take the effort to consult contemporary San Francisco business directories, or if he did, he overlooked the numerous advertisements of firms—including some he mentioned—that, in fact, made the manufacturing of gold bars one of their most important business specialties." He argued:

> If a given gold bar was first discovered in 1953, or 1964, or yesterday, that does not mean that it is false or even ques-

> tionable. A great example is provided by the discovery in the late 1980s of the long-submerged S.S. *Central America.* This brought to light an even more dazzling array of gold bars—some of them weighing many pounds—and bearing imprints not earlier known to exist, although such existed at one time per early advertisements.

Professor Buttrey had taken dead aim at the *Brother Jonathan*'s gold bars, given the same connection between John Ford and Paul Franklin as the other bars. He specifically challenged the 1997 Stack's catalogue statements as to the records Ford found. To the contrary, Buttrey argued, he hadn't been able to locate those records. If the San Francisco Mint produced these ingots, Buttrey argued that Mrs. Keenan's name would have to have appeared in three documents: the visitor's book, and the registers, both as to the gold she gave up and the bars she received in return. He concluded, "These records all survive, and there is no trace of her in any of them."

Those supporting Ford retorted that by the time Buttrey went to those records that the National Archives and U.S. Mint had put a document destruction policy into effect; in fact, in 1982, many of the Mint's records had already been destroyed. Of the many documents said to be destroyed were the "Weigh Clerk's Bullion Ledger, June 1854 to March 1873," the "Assayer's Register 1854–1865," and other documents that Ford relied on.

In his writings Buttrey admitted that there was "indeed a disposal" of San Francisco Mint records. He argued that a report existed, however, which listed every item disposed of and that this record didn't list "the subject matter of the dates alleged by Hodder." Those supporting Ford weren't sure that the National Archives could accurately describe what records, in fact, they had destroyed—but important records were destroyed, all after the Ford time period.

The professor further argued several other points with respect to the *Brother Jonathan* ingots: (1) their fineness; (2) lack of tax stamp, as required in 1865; (3) the "assayer's cut" was not genuine; and (4) the S.F. Mint "logo" was inaccurate. As to "fineness," eight of the eleven gold-bar set had stamped fineness: six at .995, one at .998 and one at .999, and he argued that obtaining this fineness was not possible 150 years ago.

The professor's argument regarding the missing tax stamp went that this mark should have been stamped on the ingots as was done other gold bars. Buttrey and Kleeberg argued back that the *Central American* bars showed in detail that the assayer's cuts on those bars were considerably different from what was on the *Brother Jonathan* bars.

The last argument was what Buttrey felt was "perhaps" the most important point. The logo on the *Jonathan* bars contained the date 1865, surrounded by the legend "U.S. Mint San Francisco," when it was actually a branch mint.

Charles S. Tumosa, the Senior Research Chemist for the Smithsonian for many years, observed:

> It is very difficult to determine "genuiness." Regardless of whether the era is 1850 or not, you can make "pretty fine gold." Gold is gold, regardless of when it was manufactured. Also, just how do you measure "fineness." And looking at the surface, just how do you analyze the insides. But for knowing that a metal didn't exist at a particular time—an aluminum cent in 1804 versus one said to be created in 1966—you don't know if that gold was made in 1850 or in 1950, unless you cut it in half, and even then that analysis is not foolproof. Further, you can't cut a valuable gold bar in half and preserve its value. The surface just doesn't reflect what's inside.
>
> Not having a tax stamp, assayer cuts, or a certain logo isn't that determinative, as the assayer could have forgotten that time, it could have been a bad day, human error, and all that. Also, just what were the established procedures at that time? And were they followed? Given this, these are judgment calls and the "experts" can and do differ all over the map—and have many times.

> Any opinion is really based on *connoisseurship.* Does it look right? Do the cuts, markings, metallic composition, and other factors look right? Is this the usual striking for this type of coin or bar? Is the appropriate metal being used for the time period?

What is called the science of numismatics is really an art. Experts have seen what others call forgeries, which they conclude are genuine and vice versa. Determining originality and source with limited evidence—given different opinions—is what this business is all about. Numismatics is not as clear cut as one might think, and it is much easier to brand something a fraud than it is to prove its authenticity.

Various coin specialists believe that most of the disputed gold bars at a minimum are authentic. A few felt that if just one bar at the Smithsonian had been discovered not to be authentic, that Buttrey had won—and this happened later. Other specialists thought "very highly" of Ted Buttrey (in part due to John Kleeberg's support), even though they didn't agree with his conclusions; others felt more highly of John J. Ford, mentioning the support by Michael Hodder and Q. David Bowers. This was a battle between the "highest and mightiest," as one observer recounted.

If an expert felt that Buttrey had an edge in his arguments, then the feeling was still that "J. J. Ford was an honorable man and that Paul Franklin had snuck some Western assay bar past him, given all of the transactions that they had done together." One who knew both concluded that the dispute between Ford and Buttrey dated back to when John Ford was brought in to advise on the coins in a "stolen Yale coin collection," which had been subsequently found. He asked Buttrey to identify some of the coins. However, Professor Buttrey was unable to—as the story goes—because he didn't have the pictures of the coins before the theft. Ford told that to others and "the two have hated each other since."

Harry Forman is a well-known, respected figure in the numismatic world, a friend of John J. Ford, and a scholar who has been awarded numerous honors by the ANS. Forman said:

> There are cliques in this business, as with any other. As to the disputed gold bars, the people weren't even talking the same language: They kept calling them "assay bars" when the term should have been "assayer's bars" or "assayer's ingots."
>
> Reasonable men can and do differ over the authenticity of nearly everything. John J. Ford is honest, as is Q. David Bowers, as is Ted Buttrey, John Kleeberg, and Michael Hodder. And many documents are missing from the archives, because two directors of the U.S. Mint oversaw their destruction from the early seventies on.
>
> John Ford told Ted Buttrey that if Buttrey published his findings about the gold bars in the United States—and didn't just leave it in the Royal Numismatic Society's magazine—that Ford would sue Buttrey. They ended up in that lawsuit. Ford then had bulky papers made up in his defense. But the ANA made up with Ford by naming a room after him—and also it seems with Buttrey.

In August 2003, two scientists reported that one of four different bars on display at the Smithsonian's National Museum of American History was a fake. Investigated with the cooperation of the Smithsonian, these were ingots with a controversial past. A second bar was considered doubtful, and two (one gold ingot and one silver) were declared to be genuine. The nearly five-ounce ingot deemed fraudulent was originally part of the huge Josiah Lilly collection and a Justh & Hunter Company 1857 ingot. The one-ounce bar with the markings of a Colorado dentist and prospector, named John Parsons, was the one deemed "doubtful."

"It is certainly possible that the Justh & Hunter piece is a fraud," said Douglas Mudd, the manager then of the numismatics collection at the Smithsonian. He added:

> I am not expert enough to say on my own. There are pieces of evidence that lead to the conclusion. But these bars were traded and most of them were melted down. There is no way

to be one hundred percent sure on these things. They were not made on a factory floor. The molds are not the same.

Mudd agreed that there were uncertainties with the Parsons piece, but that the findings weren't conclusive. Whatever the final opinion, he emphasized that even though outside experts appraise and authenticate every item donated to the Smithsonian, it wasn't unusual for a fake ingot or gold coin to make its way into any display. "Every museum in the world, every numismatic collection, contains counterfeits and duplicates," he told one reporter.

Forman believes that if one or two of the gold bars in the Lilly Collection were declared to be bad that they weren't one of the bars handled by Ford. His assessment of John J. Ford was that the man was "tough, very successful, and as honest as the day was long." These qualities, especially in a business of superegos, create jealousies. "People got their egos caught in the way," he said.

As to the argument that Franklin could have manufactured the gold bars and the engravings, Forman replied, "There are too many smart guys in this business who would have found out any created imperfections." Further, the gold bars would never have been validated by the people that had passed on their authenticity. He felt that Ford got a bad rap at times, as he was "very aggressive and people thought he had a know-it-all attitude and he probably did."

Bob Julian, another well-respected numismatist, supported Harry Forman's assessment about the man. Ford spoke "four to five languages" and was the "collector of collectors." Interestingly enough, the American Numismatic Society bestowed honors and awards on both of these distinguished men, including its dedication of the John J. Ford Jr. Reading Room in the ANS's Harry W. Bass Jr. Library in New York City on May 13, 2004.

Paul Franklin, the treasure hunter and friend of John J. Ford, died in 2000 in Phoenix, Arizona. For the entire time, he had kept out of the fracas. One of the ironies is that the great mind of John J. Ford dimmed with his diagnosis of suffering from Alzheimer's disease. In

2004, four separate, large auctions of his extensive estate began. Never again to be duplicated, the extensive and diverse collections were broken up, put on the auction block, and sold to different collectors.

ADDING TO THE INTEREST are the different stories on how the *Brother Jonathan* gold bars were discovered. Among these, the U.S. Supreme Court in its landmark decision quoted the fisherman's netting of the ruptured lifeboat that carried Mrs. Keenan. There are at least two others. Dr. Larry Holcomb, one of the last searchers, told the following story to a reporter.

One day in 1970, a man wearing a ten-gallon hat walked up to Holcomb and introduced himself. "Larry," the stranger said, "I have something to show you." Holcomb followed the man out to his car. The man told him to reach into a valise and pull out a "white silk bag." Holcomb did as he was told.

As he pulled out the silk bag, a gold bar from the *Brother Jonathan* fell into his hands. "Oh God! This just brings me chills to think about it," he said, reflecting back later. Holcomb continued:

> The gold was from a 1935 diving expedition, they said. Three men and a woman came up to Crescent City on a fishing boat with a .50-caliber machine gun mounted on the bow. They had been sitting on the gold for more than thirty years, unaware that the law prohibiting private ownership of gold had lapsed. The woman had finally sold the bullion to Las Vegas mobsters.

Holcomb's stranger had bought the gold ingots from the "Vegas people" and, hearing of his interest in the *Brother Jonathan,* came to sell the bars to him. According to Holcomb, the story checked out. He later said that the serial numbers on those gold bars matched the ones John J. Ford placed on display at San Francisco's Bank of California.

Don Knight believes a different story. Years before, the good people of San Francisco informed Mrs. Keenan, the famous or infamous madam of San Francisco, that she had to sell her business and "get out of Dodge." This would confirm why her husband was already living in Victoria, British Columbia, and why she was on her way to join him with her "seven soiled doves." Keenan sold the business for $5,500 and the money, presumably in gold, was melted down into the manufactured eleven gold ingots, which she placed in a small leather case. The value of the eleven gold bars at the time was $5,500.

Mrs. Keenan brought the valise on board the *Brother Jonathan* and, in the panic, placed it in the lifeboat. When the large wave smashed the lifeboat against the steamer's side, Roseanna Keenan was thrown into the seething ocean where she drowned. Knight said that the suitcase of gold and crumpled lifeboat that held Mrs. Keenan were not discovered in the 1931 expeditions to find the *Brother Jonathan.* A storm in the 1930s forced the lifeboat to the surface. Noticing a black object by his bow in Dragger Channel, a fisherman found the boat barely submerged. He pulled the Francis Patent Lifeboat to the beach. Knight maintains that the lifeboat was still attached to the ship when it went down bow first, but when the connecting ropes eventually disintegrated over time, the floatation devices in the boat had enough buoyancy to float the lifeboat back to the surface.

Once the rusted crumpled boat was on shore, the man called the Crescent City Sheriff's Department who sent deputies to inspect it. They found the beaten, soft valise underneath one crushed seat. The sheriff deputies broke open the case, discovered the gold bars, and sent the eleven bars down to the San Francisco Mint, where it kept them until the early 1970s. The San Francisco Mint kept one of the bars, sold one to Clifford Henry and the rest ended with Stack's of New York and J. J. Ford. Knight said that he reached this conclusion from his later conversations with maritime experts, and an observer in Crescent City, who had seen the deputies on the beach with the rusted lifeboat.

In its leading decision involving the *Brother Jonathan,* the U.S. Supreme Court stated:

> The only recovery of cargo (prior to 1993) from the shipwreck may have occurred in the 1930s, when a fisherman found twenty-two pounds of gold bars minted in 1865 and believed to have come from the *Brother Jonathan.* The fisherman died, however, without revealing the source of his treasure.

The court's statement on the gold bars can be accepted as being as good as any other explanation given. However, we may never know conclusively who was right: John J. Ford, Jr. or Professor Ted Buttrey. Or what brought about the discovery of the gold bars. Yet this is what legends are made of.

While the numismatic experts were debating gold coins and bars on land, on the sea the salvors were deciding the best ways to find more gold. DSR still had one last exploration left, and the officers wanted to start that search as soon as they could. However, this depended on raising the necessary funds.

Chapter 18

The Super Agent

Of those who approached Deep Sea Research to invest in the last exploration, one person stood out. Rick Hansen told DSR that he knew someone who was "substantial, understood coins, and had the interest." Harvey Harrington signed a contract with Hansen on behalf of Deep Sea Research, and, according to David Flohr, "didn't tell anyone about that 'finder's fee' agreement until after he had signed it." After signing a contract that promised Hansen a fee if his referral invested, he gave the man's name: Dwight Manley.

Everyone in the field of the high-powered numismatic world knew him. Not only was Manley a multi-millionaire gold-coin dealer and marketer, he was also a high-profile sports agent. Born in 1966, Manley began collecting coins at the age of six after finding 1909 and 1910 Lincoln pennies in a coffee can. He still has the coins. A year later, he visited his first coin store and was told that he needed to study numismatics before he bought more coins. Manley continued collecting and reading over the years and in 1981—at the age of fifteen—he met his idol, Q. David Bowers, along with other coin experts and students at his first American Numismatic Association (ANA) Summer Seminar. A year later, Manley attended his second summer session and then his first ANA convention.

When he was growing up in Brea, in Southern California, he did odd jobs for businesses along Brea Boulevard. He also hung out with his friends who worked at Der Wienerschnitzel on the same street.

Manley regularly rode his bicycle to the city's small downtown coin shop, where as a youth he learned his first lessons in trading rare coins. After graduating from high school, he drove cross-country at the age of seventeen to Massachusetts to work for a person he thought was the best coin dealer in the United States.

He started at $20,000 a year in 1984 at eighteen, and within a year he was making *six figures* as a teenager, quickly earning the reputation as one of the top coin dealers in the world. He became so good at it that Dwight Manley became quite wealthy, even being hired as a paid consultant for the Internal Revenue Service when he was in his twenties. He was a millionaire by the time he was twenty-three, buying and selling rare coins across the country.

Manley is also the most unlikely person to be a player agent. He isn't a lawyer, never went to college, and the only sport he ever seriously played is golf. Until he agreed to represent his friend, Dennis Rodman, he never even thought about being an agent. A mutual friend introduced them at a Las Vegas casino in 1993 and that casual relationship grew. Rodman went to Newport Beach to visit Manley one day and ended up living with him for a while. Their personal relationship was well grounded before Dwight Manley even began representing him.

Dennis "The Worm" Rodman's days with the NBA Detroit Pistons basketball team were relatively uneventful as he became a NBA star. He earned two NBA titles and became one of the best-ever basketball rebounders. He had ended his seventh season with the Pistons when he and Manley hooked up. "We got him started doing some promotions and advertisements, then got the book deal *(Bad As I Wanna Be)*. That was the first big thing," Manley reported. "It kind of launched everything."

Rodman's bizarre one-day marriage to Carmen Electra, the former *Baywatch, Scary Movie,* and *My Boss's Daughter* actress, in 1998, was one of his better capers. Rodman's agent, Manley, said the day after the marriage that Rodman was "drunk out of his gills" at the time and that Electra had taken advantage of him. Nine days after he wed Carmen in a chapel in Las Vegas, Rodman filed a petition in Orange County Superior Court to annul his marriage, alleging that he had not acted out of a "sound mind."

Another basketball star represented by Manley is Karl "The Mailman" Malone, another NBA superstar. Malone didn't even know Manley when he signed a contract for a World Championship Wrestling pay-per-view event featuring him and grappler Diamond Dallas Page against Rodman and Hulk Hogan. He came to know Manley while practicing for the event.

Dwight Manley has also represented Bison Dele (aka Brian Williams) of the Detroit Pistons, Doug Christie of the Toronto Raptors, Khalid Reeves of the Dallas Mavericks, Vernon Maxwell of the Charlotte Hornets, and others. "Manley was very sharp," assessed David Flohr. "On the Moses Malone negotiated contract, I understand he got twenty percent of the contract, or some $14 million of the negotiated $70 million."

By 2000, Manley endured a "painful" split with "Bad Boy" Rodman. By then Manley controlled, however, an even hotter property: the Gold Rush loot from the *S.S. Central America.* This included 7,500 gold coins, 485 assayers' ingots, and dozens of gold bricks. Tommy Thompson discovered and brought up the coins. He incurred fifty-two lawsuits in several courts from others who also wanted a piece of the action. Thompson and his backers ended up with 92 percent of the haul, and the insurers received the rest. In 2005, the investors sued Tommy Thompson and his exploration group over the "lack of details about their investment," among other causes of action.

After flirting with twenty different potential deals, Manley persuaded private investors to lend $50 million to him and his three coin-collector partners as part of a venture-capital agreement with profit participation. The deal was valued at a total $100 million. It took eighteen months of negotiations with Thompson to finally cut the deal. Manley, who is the managing partner of his investment group, was paid back, but the amount of his equity position is kept confidential.

Manley built an exhibit that included pieces of the gold booty, a replica of the ship, and $300,000 worth of Gold Rush photographs purchased from Sotheby's. His road show traveled from Omaha to San Francisco and Las Vegas. The specially built fifty-foot long replica of the ship, complete with portholes to view the genuine 1850s gold coins and assayers' bars, was a public-relations' coup. The exhibit included what was billed as the world's largest Gold Rush ingot, an eighty-pound brick of gold called the "Eureka." Starting his marketing in February 2000, Manley's California Gold Marketing Group of Newport Beach, California, reportedly sold or placed every one of the gold coins, bars, and bricks by early 2004. They sold the pieces through authorized dealers to private collectors and a later auction conducted by Christie's.

Among other acquisitions, Manley purchased the world's most valuable five-cent piece: Valued at $3 million, this was the legendary 1913 Liberty Head nickel and which was also put on public display. Only five of these coins exist and show "Lady Liberty" on the nickel, two being in museums, one in a private collector's hands, Manley's, and a fifth unaccounted for for over fifty years.

The owner of several businesses, including a real estate company, with various holdings and his rare-coin business, Manley guesses that his combined annual revenues are in the "tens of millions." Out of his appreciation for the American Numismatic Association's scholarship program, he contributed $250,000 in 2003 toward the renovation of the ANA's Numismatic Library at its headquarters in Colorado Springs, Colorado. A grateful ANA renamed the facility as the Dwight N. Manley Numismatic Library.

It was natural for Manley to become interested in the *Brother Jonathan.* Through Rick Hansen's intervention, the new investor signed an agreement with DSR to provide the "necessary funds" for its last exploration in return for certain amounts of any gold that was discovered.

According to the salvors, Manley invested $2.1 million in this exploration. Under the agreement's provisions, he didn't turn the two million dollars over to the group: He paid only on submitted invoice, which had been confirmed and verified by his representatives.

There was no doubt this was the last exploration for Deep Sea Research—and more than likely for the *Brother Jonathan* itself. Under the court-approved settlement, DSR and the State of California agreed to one last permitted exploration. However, regardless of what the law provided or the court battles decided, California soon decreed that it would not issue another permit for the ship's exploration. Pelkofer told the media that he doubted the state would salvage the wreck, after DSR discontinued its efforts, but it "may allow a university or archaeological group to conduct studies on it."

This last exploration of the *Brother Jonathan* started on September 1 and came to an end on October 10, 2000. The venture decided to use the 1997 approach with the *American Salvor* deployed as the mother ship, the use of the mini-sub *Snooper,* and divers working from a saturation diving bell and onboard compression chamber. Dwight Manley appointed Bob Evans, a historian and geologist, to represent him on board the salvage operations. With that representation, the salvors came into contact with another salvage expert with ties to both Manley and Tommy Thompson.

In the 1980s, Thompson organized the Columbus-American Discovery Group, based in Columbus, Ohio. It was created to explore the ocean depths off the North Carolina coast to find the long-lost S.S. *Central America.* Bob Evans was a scientist and researcher, a close friend of Tommy Thompson, and a man with a "near photographic" memory for exploration approaches and details. After years of studying and searching, Thompson's group finally located the *Central America,* on the ocean floor 7,200 feet below the surface. Over time Evans supervised the recovery of the gold coins and ingots from that wreck.

When Tommy Thompson's deal with Dwight Manley finally closed, Manley formed the California Gold Marketing Group—and Bob Evans was placed in charge of carefully conserving the pristine treasure pieces plus the security and important details of the S.S.

Central America "road show" exhibit. Bob had other responsibilities, including that of representing Manley's interests on the *Brother Jonathan.* Later, he was one of the scientists concluding that a gold bar at the Smithsonian was a fake by comparing the Justh & Hunter Company 1857 ingot to those discovered on the S.S. *Central America.*

With Manley's backing and Evans on board, the *American Salvor* again anchored into position and continuously centered over the *Jonathan* by its global positioning system. A different "water taxi," named the *Superstar,* conveyed men, equipment, and supplies back and forth. As always, the weather was a key factor in the recovery operations. On some days, no winds blew and the ocean was as "smooth as a pond." With these conditions the *Superstar* easily rendezvoused with the *Salvor* to transfer its cargo. However, the winds could quickly whip up, create frothing waves, and all operations would have to be suspended.

The giant ship was a labyrinth of metal staircases, hallways, and side rooms. A large grid map of the wreck site hung in the galley. "Every square yard" of it was marked off by members of the crew who bet where the gold would be found. In the early morning and later at night, crew members congregated at the stern of the ship by the helicopter pad. The *American Salvor*'s public-address system blared, "Divers on the bell, divers on the bell," and the large, motor-driven winch would lift the diving bell to or from the ocean.

The bell would rear up on the surface, like a strange metal beast staring upward at the ship. The crewmen guided it onto the stern, where it docked into the huge decompression chamber looking like a "space shuttle connecting to the space station Muir." Two divers were inside the bell and had just finished their eleven-hour shift of exploring the murky waters surrounding the sunken *Brother Jonathan.* The divers then ate, slept, and watched television in that chamber-room until their next shift came up.

Once the operations commenced, all of the working divers lived inside the huge tank-like container. They would work their way from the enclosed chamber to the next, then into the diving bell. Soon, on their next diving shift, they were back in the black, pressured depths of the ocean. Coping with what was reality versus their confined physical surroundings became a distinct challenge.

With visuals provided by a small video camera mounted on each diver's helmet, DSR and Evans hoped to see what was actually happening below from the divers' view. An ROV would also be used to work its way over the wreck, searching for more objects of interest. With Evans representing the investors and Harvey Harrington the salvors, the two men worked closely together.

The operation was dogged from the beginning by technical problems with the divers' camera feeds and the State of California's generally hostile approach through its representatives. As Bob Evans oversaw its operation, the ROV worked perfectly and as intended. Owing to the problems with the cameras on the divers' helmets, however, the people on topside couldn't see what any of them were doing below on the bottom. Further, the ROV couldn't hover close enough to pick up the divers' actions in those dark waters.

This state of affairs also troubled the State's representatives, as the California State Lands Commission didn't trust anyone involved in these explorations—whether based on fact or not. Representatives of both DSR and California Gold Marketing (CGM) confirmed that California and the CSLC, still smarting from their massive legal and publicity losses, were looking for anything that could be used to put the operation "out of business." Instead of working to see what was archaeologically significant, the state hovered to see what might have been done differently or not at all. As Bob Evans observed, "Where we wanted to undertake a site 'excavation,' the State of California looked at it as being site 'destruction.' " This poisonous atmosphere wasn't helpful.

Conflicts seemed to develop on this exploration more than others. Any diving operation connects different cultures on board that can bring about conflict. First, there are "ROV people" versus divers: Divers understandably don't feel comfortable with today's sophisticated ROVs that can do many different jobs that were once their sole province. Divers are really "jocks," well-conditioned men who accept risks. The more technically-oriented ROV operators don't emphasize this aspect of their personalities.

A different culture usually exists between the ship's crew and the hiring salvors, who usually don't know one another. In the later *Brother Jonathan* explorations, the boat, crews, and people seemed to change with each operation. This was different from expeditions such as the S.S. *Central America,* which used the same company, ship's crew, ROV operators, and people on most of its operations. Boat crews also are generally salty seadogs, whereas the lead salvors are usually educated, technically trained, and versatile people.

The boat crew on the 2000 expedition started calling the salvors "boat trash." One can image what the salvors thought or said in return. The expedition leaders, however, solved that problem by soon saying, "Okay, today we're boat trash." They even made up T-shirts with the inscription of "boat trash" and over time those cultural clashes lessened. Where there was much camaraderie on the Bob Evans–led S.S. *Central America* expeditions, there wasn't much on this one. The continual pressure of California's trying to find any pretext to shut down the exploration cut into the good mood.

Despite this, the teams were pros, and their work went on. The remote controlled vehicle (ROV) crept over the wreck, its ever-watchful lights and camera eyes sweeping for any sign of gold or anything else that seemed "a little different." Other than the murky shapes of the wreck, sea life also abounded. One day Bob Evans took his ROV closer to inspect an object on the sea floor, when a small shape suddenly darted past his cameras. He worked the ROV around and saw a murre, a diving seabird, not known before to dive to these depths. Prior to this, murres were not believed to dive past two-hundred feet down—and that would have been a very rare occurrence.

At other times, the cameras showed a huge shape sweeping in front of a startled diver, who leaped away in response. These animals turned out to be seals. Like the birds, they were on the hunt for the myriad fish that used the wreck as their home. David Flohr's huge octopus, thankfully, didn't turn up on this exploration.

The diver debriefing sessions became important due to the technical difficulties with the camera. The divers at first sounded comically like Mickey Mouse due to the rarefied air that they were breathing. This took time for the operators to get used to.

The divers described digging around in the muck three-hundred feet below or reaching around a ship's timber to pull out a porcelain plate or medicine bottle—even picking up a gold coin and carefully rinsing it in the sweeping currents. Another time, a diver excitedly described his pulling up an "ironized" box from the silt. A different diver told about pulling up a similar box from inside the wreck.

Once these boxes were brought on board the mother ship, everyone wondered again what they were holding. These containers measured three feet by three feet by two feet, were heavy, and looked to be made of iron. As the boxes were transferred to the supply ship, the salvors once more had that inner rush and excitement of finding something unique.

As crewmen hosed each box down with saltwater, the smaller ship sped toward shore where a waiting car drove the large objects to a conservation lab. Since the CSLC required that every find be documented and conserved, the "ironized" containers headed to laboratories. Due to the CSLC's pressures, DSR sent one trunk at its expense ($30,000) to the Nautical Archaeology Laboratory at Texas A&M University, while the conservation lab at the Flynn House worked on the other two. When a large object needed to be moved from Crescent City, workers quickly immersed the item or box inside a larger plastic container filled with saltwater for the travel. Once the iron-encrusted boxes were safe at their destination, hopeful speculation abounded every day as to what they contained.

In their search for more gold, the salvors centered on digging into the coal inside the bunker, located underneath the purser's office. The coins discovered on past operations were found perched above this hold, and its proximity to the purser's office was too good to resist. The assumption was that when the ship hit the sea floor, whatever was contained in the purser's office had shifted or settled into that area.

From inside the wreck, the operators monitored the ROV and later debriefed the divers. The undersea divers described continually reaching toward the bottom of the coal bins in murky, swirling waters, as occasional school of curious, multicolored rockfish in golds, oranges, and reds swept by. As an ROV or mini-sub hovered nearby, their bright overhead lights shining opaquely like strange moons from another galaxy, the men saw the unrealistic form of dim circles.

A diver's light swept over the heavy coal lumps, as hands rolled another one away. Now and then, the illumination lit up a "glow or flash" of something smaller that became visible, then disappeared into the darkness of black lumps. With the sound of bubbles echoing in the background, the salvors could only hope that this one would lead to another strongbox of wealth. As the days ticked by, all of the coal was moved to preset but different positions.

Once finding artifacts or coins, the divers placed the articles in a bag outside the bell. Later, these were hauled up onto the ship. If the discoveries were small enough, the divers simply brought the articles into the bell for the different representatives to retrieve together.

Curator Bob Evans and CLSC representative Bryant Sturgess removed the artifacts or coins from the diving bell or the bag for transfer to a shipboard vault. The findings were then cataloged and tagged, with both men signing as witnesses. Each possessed one of the two keys required to open the vault together, and any entry by both men was logged into a security book. Evans later brought the recovered coins to his lab where he performed conservation work. Immersing the coins in a neutral solution, workers removed any encrustations from the coins for later grading and encapsulation.

With the land conservation lab up and running, the conservators on board assigned identification numbers, wrote the artifact descriptions, and placed each item in a bag of seawater for transportation to the Crescent City lab. Volunteers there transferred items to large plastic trays filled with distilled water, and ran low-voltage electricity through the water to free up rust. Although the conservation work had started, completing this would take much more time than originally thought.

Dwight Manley visited Crescent City to check on the salvaging operations in late September and from time to time during the operations. Manley was quoted in *The Daily Triplicate:* "I would put money into lifting the whole thing up and making a museum with it for Crescent City." He wondered why the State of California—since its stated objective was to preserve the antiquities for its citizens—wouldn't donate its two hundred gold coins to help fund the construction of Crescent City's *Brother Jonathan* museum.

Once these explorations came to an end on October 10, the undersea miners had excavated a total of fifty-eight coins from the coal. Forty-seven were gold coins of different denominations (thirty-eight were $20 U.S. Double Eagles) and eleven were silver. The value of these coins was estimated at upward of $500,000. All of the gold coins were discovered "loose and scattered" about the site.

Time passed slowly as the expedition anxiously awaited the news about the large iron containers and their contents. With the discouraging coin results they were hopeful that more treasure was there. The scientists placed the rock-encrusted containers in briny water and used a pneumatic air hose to excavate the heavily encrusted objects. As each artifact was removed, they carefully placed it in a separate vat of a specially treated water solution to prevent further corrosion.

The first large crate, unfortunately, didn't contain any gold. It appeared to be a shipment of miscellaneous hardware bound for a British Columbia store. Tin sheeting lined the interior of the box, which workmen years ago had soldered with lead at its junctures. The crate contained shafted axes and hatchets, cast-iron meat grinders, and detached handles with wood hand grips, iron scythes, brass keys, and cast-iron window-sash guides.

Specialists at the Crescent City facility worked on the two other boxes. DSR's marine archaeologist, Rob Reedy, opened one end to find several axe handles layered in the rock-encrusted box. He concluded that these were headed eventually for gold miners in Alaska. The next box similarly didn't contain gold, but contained instead "lots of different kinds" of nails. The iron composition and rock complexion of these one-time wood boxes came from the iron concretions that flowed into the pores of the wood, and which then hardened into an oxidized composition.

Although disappointment reigned as to the limited gold recovery, the artifacts continued coming in. Divers found bottles, the boxes of axe handles and nails, sausage-making machines, and a boot. Including past explorations, the men had located hatchets, hooks, meat grinders, brass plumb bobs, tools, door rails, cast iron pulleys, scythes, spring traps, keys, leather sheaths, augers, small pulleys, brass keys, and door knobs—many in boxes or crates brought up from the deep. In numerous instances it was clear that these commercial items were packed alone in boxes, destined for delivery at the remaining ports of call. The explorers brought up bottles, mineral-water jugs, porcelain plates, glasses, decanters, shaving mugs, a chamber pot, cigar-box lids, and other objects over time.

Notwithstanding the number of artifacts recovered, the vast majority still remains underwater. The salvors recovered seventeen bags of artifacts on the last exploration. Including what was found on previous dives, the amount recovered paled by comparison with most other explorations, including that of the *DeBraak*. The California State Lands Commission stated its clear desire to leave the wreck site "totally intact" until someone was willing to do a "careful" archaeological site investigation. Pelkofer and other CSLC staff worried that "any treasure hunting done on it would damage the site and ruin its historical integrity." A CSLC staff member was always on board to ensure that this expedition—and past ones—left the wreck and its artifacts substantially in place.

Bob Evans, Dwight Manley, David Flohr, and various maritime experts couldn't understand this decision. As Manley told one reporter, "Why don't they want the artifacts up? If a bus wrecked on the side of the road, would they just leave it there?" To many, the decision to leave the artifacts in place for a future underwater excavation by an underfunded state or hired marine archaeologists was not realistic.

Dwight Manley clearly lost money on the exploration. Under the terms of the agreement, Manley received the coins. Later, the Numismatic Guaranty Corporation (NGC) certified 38 twenty-dollar gold Double Eagles of the San Francisco Mint as having come from the final dive on the *Brother Jonathan.* Ranging in dates from 1859 to 1865 the coins were certified by NGC as having grades ranging from AU-53 to MS-64, still high standards of quality. DSR seemed to find everything once more, except the prize that drove it there a decade ago: They didn't find the large Doblier safe or anything comparable to their finds of earlier years.

By the end of the 1997 search, DSR had expended some $1.8 million in its search for the gold. When one adds in the $2.1 million spent on the 2000 search, $3.9 million was expended in its actual, operational search for the gold. This number is calculated before adding in the sizeable $1.0 million California-induced legal fees, among other expenses, but still a shoe-string amount of money for what it was doing for those years. In the final expedition and for recent years, the officers received no salary or compensation for their time. The net result was that neither the officers nor the investors would receive a decent return for their efforts, or a complete return of capital for those who invested later.

The final count on the coins discovered was 1,207 from the 1996 and 1997 explorations plus the fifty-eight found on the 2000 expedition—or 1,265 in total. On October 9, 2000, a DSR representative stated, "We really haven't found enough (in their Sept. 2000 operation) to make it worthwhile to the investors, so I don't know if we'll do it again next year or not." They didn't. The CSLC had already made its intentions clear.

The search for the *Brother Jonathan*'s gold had come to an end, but the controversies didn't. DSR had contracted with Crowley Marine Services of Seattle, Washington, for the use of the *American Salvor.* When the salvage operations were completed, the ship began to raise its four positioning anchors. The starboard bow anchor began "acting weird" with "three-hundred yards of chain played out." It was as if it wasn't at rest in the same substrata. Although its captain had positioned the vessel square between the four points that marked the wreck, the ship had somehow dropped westerly toward the beach, so that when it pulled up its anchor, it also snagged a part of the sunken ship. The *American Salvor* returned to Long Beach harbor with the object suspended in the water from the anchor.

At port, workers discovered that the foreign object was the *Brother Jonathan*'s walking beam—or the large "grasshopper-looking" lever apparatus that transferred motion from the engine to the two paddle wheels. The seamen left the walking beam submerged in Long Beach Harbor to prevent its deterioration. The CSLC staff tried "to convince" Crowley Marine Services, Inc. to return the walking beam to the wreck site or pay for its conservation, but these efforts failed.

Pursuant to CSLC authorization, the Attorney General's Office filed a court proceeding entitled *State of California (State Lands Commission) v. Crowley Marine Services, Inc., et al.*, in Del Norte County Superior Court, alleging violations of the law for Crowley's "unauthorized removal" of the walking beam from the wreck site. DSR believes, as does nearly everyone else, that the ship's snagging of the walking beam's lever was accidental and not intentional. However, this was just another red flag to the state.

Before trial, the parties settled their differences in June 2003. Crowley Marine Services paid the Commission a total of $27,000 for its part in the accident. The money was to be used to move the walking beam to the Del Norte County Historical Society, which according to the CSLC was to "either conserve the beam for public display or place it at an underwater site with appropriate signage for viewing by scuba divers."

As part of the agreement, however, the CSLC needed to check with the California Historic Preservation Officer to ensure that the alternative chosen for the walking beam didn't have a significant adverse environmental effect on the *Brother Jonathan* site. Until this consultation, the walking beam stayed in Long Beach Harbor and could not be moved. After researching the issue, the CSLC concluded that an environmental impact report did not have to be completed, deciding that the settlement was not a "project" under that particular environmental law—which made sense.

The $27,000 sum sounded sufficient to move this item intra-state from Southern California to Northern California, until officials reviewed the expense of transporting an artifact of that size without breaking it. The moving expense alone was later found to consume most of the money. The estimate for preserving the walking beam came to another $25,000, and California looked at the nonprofit Historical Society to assume these costs. Given the difference in the funding abilities between these two entities, this development was a surprise. Despite this, the Del Norte Historical Society notified the state that it would still commit to the lever's preservation.

The CSLC then took another look at the walking beam and gave more bad news to Crescent City. The higher oxygen level and salinity of Long Beach Harbor had chewed up the beam's metal to where it was now in terrible condition. The immersion over time under these different conditions had dissolved sections of the layered metal bands to where the edges became sharp as razor blades and eliminated most of the outlining details of the beam. The artifact was not an appropriate museum exhibit.

The Society instead started working with officials of California and Crescent City to place the walking beam underwater, but near the harbor entrance with onshore signage so that divers could dive on it as part of an underwater archaeological park. More bad news came. As part of the next "latest" review of the walking beam's condition, the California examining archaeologist cut his hand on its sharp bands and soon required emergency medical treatment for a severe infection.

Although California wasn't sure whether the infection was caused by bacteria in the water or from the walking beam, state officials became nervous over the prospective liability by placing the beam in Crescent City Harbor, given their knowledge of its "dangerous" condition. The Historical Society's Board discussed the issues at length and notified California that it was now not interested in pursuing the relocation, a prime consideration being the extensive cost of conservation, reconstruction, and creating a large enough tank to submerge the beam inside.

State officials have kept the walking beam submerged at the end of an undisclosed pier in Long Beach Harbor—and the deterioration continues. Whether the public will ever see what California again worked so hard to "preserve" remains to be seen. It did receive its share of the gold. Meanwhile, the *Brother Jonathan* and all of the artifacts that the CSLC was "saving" for future dives and archaeological explorations continue to rot beneath the sea.

As the *American Salvor* was hauling up its anchors to leave the site, Bob Evans was flying the discovered gold coins with a security guard to his conservation laboratory in Orange County in southern California. He had all of the necessary court papers, including one that designated him the court depository for the coins, and each coin was identified on a receipt signed by both Evans and the State's representative, Bryant Sturgess. With the agreement of Sturgess, Evans took the coins in a flight bag onto a waiting Sky West flight headed to Orange County. Harvey Harrington waited nearby in case there were any questions at the airline gate about the documentation. There weren't. Evans passed straight through security with his coins in the bag and boarded the flight without problems.

Bob Evans said he "knows a thing or two" about the conservation of coins recovered from the bottom of the sea. This is an understatement because he is an expert. Evans was not only in charge of the conservation of the gold coins discovered on the S.S. *Central America,* he was also in charge of the entire traveling exhibit. His research included discovering the use of solutions that are neutral to the coins, but can still remove the iron, saltwater immersion effects, and marine organisms. Evans's facility is a "secure facility with a secure-alarm cage and an enclosed secure-alarm safe inside everything." After a conservation process that took five to six weeks, Bob and his security guard transferred the coins to the independent grading company used before on both the *Brother Jonathan*'s and *Central*

America's gold discoveries. He thought that this would discharge his responsibilities; however, he hadn't reckoned on CSLC's protective posture.

"The State of California went simply nuts about my taking the coins out of the court's jurisdiction," said Evans. "It sent memos to me and Dwight Manley that said that the coins weren't his private stock. I couldn't believe their position." When Evans placed the coins in the grading company's security, he signed for them with the agreed and indicated co-ownership of both the CSLC and California Gold Marketing (CGM). Evans's act of conserving the coins brought another "ballistic" approach from the CSLC. It apparently wanted to tell how and where the coins were to be conserved, even though it wasn't any part of the contract between the two private parties.

All of these incidents show an uncompromising bureaucracy that precipitated conflict and didn't care about resolving it. Bob Evans said that the "State's rules were crazy." Some think he was being kind. Even though California had lost in every court, it still wanted anyone connected with the *Brother Jonathan* to fail. Sending in attorneys to court to resolve inconsequential problems is like "sending in pit bulls to negotiate," said Evans. "This won't happen. The State was always about conflict and not about resolution."

California's insistence on the salvors' leaving the site entirely alone was inconsistent with conservation practices. The site was "seriously degraded." There was no ship's bow and the decades spent underwater had corroded much of it. Yet, the CSLC wanted everything kept at the bottom of the sea. The site had "much disturbance" around it. In fact, part of the bottom around the ship seemed to have been liquefied, as if an earthquake had occurred underneath the wreck.

"There was no cooperation from the State at all. This was six weeks of frustration," concluded Bob Evans. He wouldn't do this again unless there was a complete set of understandable rules with the State that it would follow—as other experts have said. Despite the CSLC painting anyone connected with DSR as the enemy, Evans found his work with Harrington to be "honest, ethical, and professional." Harvey still smoked a "ton of cigarettes," and many of the crew were thankful that they didn't come down with cancer from all those weeks of inhaling his cigarette smoke.

After receiving the discovered gold and silver coins, Dwight Manley's association with the *Brother Jonathan* came to an end. He still owns some of the coins—which have been added to his sizeable and rich collection—although they are apparently available for sale. The matter of Rick Hansen's fee did, however, end up in the hands of the lawyers.

Harvey Harrington's finder's fee agreement with Hansen, according to David Flohr, did not contain a payment clause contingent on the amount of gold discovered or any other type of "escape clause." As DSR didn't have the money to meet Hansen's sizeable demands for payment, this controversy also ended in a lawsuit. Hansen hired an attorney and sued the principals and others for $1.25 million. This was another problem that DSR would have to handle as it wound down its operations.

Epilogue

Salvors search for sunken treasure for the adventure, excitement, risk, and romance. The state of the art today in exploration technology is light-years beyond what existed just twenty years ago. Major explorations are well funded; they aren't working on a "shoestring" the way Deep Sea Research did. No matter how deep, the ROVs are much more precise and reliable with sophisticated video eyes and mechanical arms able to mine objects of the smallest size. In 1999, one robot discovered a previously unknown 2,500-year-old Phoenician trading vessel in the Mediterranean at 3,000 feet.

Locating sunken ships is akin to finding a needle in an underwater haystack. The side-scan sonar and magnetometer equipment in use now is magnitudes more sensitive than what DSR could then afford. Controlled from an advanced onboard ship computer, the undersea vehicles prowl at the deepest levels of the seas. Mounted with powerful halogen lamps with wide-angle and zoom color television lenses, this equipment has remarkable abilities to inspect the smallest of objects.

Extensive monies also must be budgeted for legal expenses. Regardless of what is recovered, many archaeologists and state land commissions shudder at the thought of for-profit companies tinkering with wrecks. Legal fights are common, as state and federal governments enter into the fray. Fortunately, the experiences of Deep Sea Research with a state such as California and its State Lands Commission are not common.

The problem is governments don't underwrite or advance the monies needed to fund underwater explorations and excavations.

However, once salvors, at their expense, discover a sunken ship, the states or foreign countries feel they must take all necessary steps to protect the wreck and claim the artifacts and treasures. Expensive legal fights ensue and no one is happy. States need to recognize that private salvors have to recover their costs and a profit—which is why they are in business—and that they will assume the risks that governments will not.

If no wreck is found, then the salvors have gambled their and their investor money and lost all. If a shipwreck is discovered, salvors are willing to accept that states want archaeological safeguards, protection on those artifacts discovered, and a reasonable share of the finds—provided the treasure is located on state coastal lands and the permitting agreement is reached beforehand. Otherwise, unless governments will invest money in the operation, then they should have no financial interest in that process.

A better rationale for this governmental process is in order: establish a fair, uniform "royalty" for the permit, and, if there is disagreement, then establish an administrative hearing procedure where a neutral evaluator makes fair, quick decisions. If the state or salvor unreasonably appeals that decision, then the court will assess all costs against the losing side.

A fair royalty would be, let's say, to allow the salvor to receive all of his or her costs before there is a split of royalties. This sharing would decrease, as the valuation becomes higher. For example, for the first $100,000 of proceeds, the salvor receives 80% and the state 20%. For each $100,000 from there, the state receives an additional 1%, up to one-third for the state and two-thirds for the salvor. This can only apply in waters, of course, where the state has clear jurisdiction.

After losing court battles over an uncertain process, the State of Florida and its legislature brought about some sanity over this permitting controversy. People may beach comb on the shores and in the surf to their "heart's content," according to Florida. You may also metal detect (with permission of the "land manager") on public lands between the mean high and low water lines. On its own Website, Florida encourages divers to explore the numerous shipwrecks on its rivers, bays, and coasts; of course, disturbing the site or any artifacts is not allowed. The only shipwrecks to which access is restricted are the "select few" determined to be especially fragile within the Florida Keys National Marine Sanctuary and the Federal government's jurisdiction. All wrecks under Florida's jurisdiction, including its Underwater Archaeological Preserves, are for the enjoyment of divers, snorkelers, and fishing enthusiasts. However, these activities are not allowed "to disturb" Florida's shipwrecks, including the collection of artifacts.

To search for a wrecked treasure ship in Florida, the salvor must enter into an "Exploration Contract" with the state. The terms of the contract include listing the particular area where it believes the ship is located and including the results of remote-sensing surveys with a magnetometer. All shipwrecks found are to be registered with the state and a report submitted that details this search.

If the salvor locates a historic shipwreck believed to contain treasure, the entity must enter into a "Salvage Contract" with the state. The expedition hires a maritime archaeologist at its expense, and the expedition must prove that it has sufficient funding to properly excavate and record the wreck, as well being able to conserve all the artifacts and treasure so recovered. A second report is submitted that details the excavation. The State of Florida may keep *"up to 20 percent of the materials* discovered on behalf of the people of Florida on whose property you found the shipwreck."

This approach is straightforward, reasonable, and disclosed, as opposed to Deep Sea Research's experience. Numbers of states and even foreign countries aren't as rigid as California's confrontational approach to the search and recovery of the *Brother Jonathan.*

Some salvors work in a constructive partnership with state officials and archaeologists, while others are given the flexibility to arrange creative approaches. In North Carolina, the state and salvors planned to split the costs of finding the wreck of the *Queen Ann's Re-*

venge, a converted slave ship. It was abandoned by the pirate Blackbeard on a sandbar in 1718, shortly before his death in battle. The state was to retain title to the lost ship and its artifacts, while the salvors secured the book, film, video, and software rights, along with a permit to look for a sunken Spanish treasure ship believed lost nearby.

The Massachusetts Board of Underwater Archaeological Resource, and its state legislature, explored a venture where the state would fund the money for its agency to chart the ocean floor of Boston Harbor. This underwater location contains the wrecks of many historical vessels, from Colonial coaches to British cannons. The board was empowered to cut deals with private salvors to map the ocean bottom, and then explore the discovered wrecks. It also agreed to share the valuable artifacts, jewelry, gold, and silver that might be found.

Nova Scotia's Treasure Trove Act empowers its Department of Natural Resources to issue licenses to people "to search for precious stones or metals in a state other than their natural ones and to recover and retain the same upon the payment to the Minister of a royalty." The royalty is 10 percent of the treasure's value.

The H.M.S. *Sussex* sank in 1694 during a gale in the Mediterranean Sea. This vessel settled half-a-mile down while carrying one million pounds in sterling silver. These gold and silver coins are today worth upward of one billion dollars. Odyssey Marine Exploration is conducting its excavations of the *Sussex*. Odyssey's agreement with the British government provides that the company must keep a team of government-appointed archaeological observers on board. The salvors will keep 80 percent of any treasure proceeds under $45 million, 50 percent of everything between $45 million and $500 million, and 40 percent of any returns above $500 million. This agreement was necessitated, as the Sussex was a large, eighty-gun English warship, and it is generally accepted in maritime law that a sovereign government never abandons its vessels, especially men of war. Notwithstanding this, the British agreement shows the reasoning that needs to be applied.

The Jamaican government granted an exclusive permit to Admiralty Corporation to salvage sunken ships on the Pedro Bank, a 2,000-square-mile atoll, eighty miles south of that island nation. As most of the gold, silver, and antiquities captured by the Spanish conquistadors passed through the Pedro Bank on its way to Spain, hundreds of these galleons and ships sank during the vicious gales in the shallow, coral-encrusted seabeds. The three-year permit allowed the firm to recover its costs, and then divide the profits equally with Jamaica. This was an exclusive exploration contract with set boundaries and contractual expectations.

During this time, however, a controversial United Nations Educational, Scientific, and Cultural Organization (UNESCO) treaty, The UNESCO Convention On Underwater Cultural Heritage, would charge governments with the responsibility for jurisdiction and management protection of any non-military ships that are located within two hundred miles of their shores and are more than a century old. Under this treaty, if a sunken Spanish merchant ship was found within two hundred miles of Miami, Florida, for example, the United States would notify Spain to determine their interest in the site. If it had an interest, the two nations would sign a cooperative agreement about managing and protecting that location. If Spain showed no interest, then the U.S. would still be charged with protecting that site, even if archeologists or salvors had no immediate plans to excavate it.

The proposed UNESCO treaty forbids the sale of any artifacts from historic shipwrecks and extends the zone from twelve miles to two hundred in the case of the United States. Salvors could only recoup their costs by selling replicas of artifacts, book rights, movie rights, and other media rights. Although it appears that this treaty is years away from being accepted worldwide, including by the United States, the court battles over these parameters would be numerous.

A growing question with fiscally tight states is what can they do with the artifacts they do receive. With respect to the H.M.S. *DeBraak*, Delaware has yet to build a museum to house the hull and thousands of artifacts, which are currently stored at considerable cost. Including the purchase, study, conservation, and maintenance of the artifacts, the state has paid more than $2.5 million on the *DeBraak* conservation. And that is just for starters. This sum doesn't include the ongoing conservation needed, the restoration of all the artifacts, and a permanent place so that the taxpaying public—which is funding all of this—can actually view what was acquired.

As part of a $500,000 funded program to restore the *DeBraak*'s sixteen cannons, four cannons (each weighing one ton) were refurbished after a four-year restoration project. These cannons are kept now at a secret Delaware State Museum warehouse, and officials said it would be years before there would be a facility to house them. The size of these objects, weight, and environmental sensitivity are additional cost factors.

Thus, most of the artifacts, the cannons, and hull sit in warehouses. The hull section is stored in the facility at Cape Henlopen State Park, the problem being the living bacteria continues to work at rotting out the wood. Although smaller artifacts are available for public view at the Zwaanendael Museum, it could be years before the public sees any more.

Many government officials believe commercial salvors should play a role in excavating marine treasures. Given the fiscal problems of the states, they will have to. The National Oceanic and Atmospheric Administration, which recently helped protect the H.M.S. *Titanic* site, encourages partnerships between archaeologists and expeditions. These commercial ventures are the future. Enlightened government entities are seeing when and where they can tap the financial and expertise assets of the salvors in return for safeguarding the sites. They can obtain valuable artifacts and receive monies for conservation. The explorers have more certainty about returning the investors' capital; everyone can then share the profits.

Underwater ventures have learned to donate artifacts to public exhibits and state museums, as the resulting publicity makes their gold and silver coins more valuable. Film rights and exhibitions are additional profit-makers. However, the strident arguments between the archaeologists and explorers will continue despite the partnership attempts. Hopefully, they won't be as bad as seen with the *Brother Jonathan.*

THE ST. GEORGE REEF LIGHTHOUSE was deactivated as soon as a special buoy light was designed to replace it. A large 42-foot, self-contained navigation aid with a radio beacon, the buoy was anchored in 220 feet of water off the stormy reef in 1975. The lighthouse stood abandoned and neglected afterward until the 1980s when members of the St. George Reef Lighthouse Preservation Society began working to refurbish the tower. They started by arranging to transport the Fresnel lens back to the Del Norte County Historical Society. Before work could start to move the lens, workers first needed to clear a path through five hundred upset sea lions that had taken residence on the rocks below.

When the first person unlocked the door to the tower after those years, the sight nearly shocked him out of his shoes. The last Coast-guardsman to leave eight years before had left a manikin dangling from a noose inside the tower. It was a reminder of what life had been like on the rock. Workers removed the lens and its prisms piece-by-piece and lowered them to a waiting ship. The vessel transported the parts to Crescent City, where they were refurbished, polished, and re-assembled back into their original shape. The three-ton lens, with its magnificent five-hundred ground-glass prisms and brass frames, is now housed in a two-story room at the back of the Del Norte County Historical Society building in Crescent City.

The St. George Reef Lighthouse Preservation Society was formed in 1986 as a nonprofit corporation to acquire and restore the light-house. The group began working with congressional and state repre-sentatives to gain jurisdiction over the lighthouse in a process that took ten years. Since this federal property could not be given directly to any private group, the government finally donated the site to Del Norte County, which then gave a twenty-five year lease to the non-profit entity.

With the cooperation of the Coast Guard, the Lighthouse Preser-vation Society made a successful application to the National Register of Historic Places, which in 1993 accepted the "St. George Reef Light Station" for the U.S. National Historic Register. The lighthouse's location was cited as being on "Northwest Seal Rock, approximately six nautical miles off the coast from Point St. George, Crescent City."

The lighthouse society has been working diligently to refurbish the site. As part of these efforts, a military helicopter removed the lantern room in early 2000 and carried the suspended structure on a flight to shore. As the helicopter approached land, it unfortunately came in too low, and the lantern room crashed onto the beach. After reconstruction on land, another helicopter flight took the restored lantern room back to the tower. This public-spirited group has raised in excess of one-quarter million dollars to rebuild the lantern room, install a new solar-powered light, rebuild the power grid, restore the diesel generators, replace two hundred feet of handrails, and make numerous other necessary maintenance and repairs.

The St. George Reef Lighthouse was relit as a private aid to navigation in October 2002. As the only safe means of transportation to the lighthouse is by a helicopter landing on a forty-three foot pad, a helicopter shuttled visitors and volunteers to and from the lighthouse in celebration of the station's opening 110 years before.

THERE HAVE BEEN no more permitted explorations of the *Brother Jonathan* since September 2000. According to the State of California, the ship's title reverted to it under their agreement with DSR, and the State Lands Commission certainly looks at this ship as its own property to safeguard.

Some legal experts wonder about this position because although the U.S. Supreme Court decision involved important issues, it did not review the substantive facts (which were clearly in favor of DSR). The question is how can any agreement with DSR as to title affect the rights of future salvors? Neither the facts, nor the law, held that the *Brother Jonathan* was its property. From the very beginning the State of California, however, has claimed the vessel and all of its contents.

Salvors believe there's still underwater treasure to be found around the site, including the long-lost huge safe and Wells Fargo boxes once in the purser's room. They didn't find any material objects or debris trail from Jonathan Rock to where the wreck now lies. Given the low oxygen levels at these depths and with some organic materials surviving at the wreck site, protective leather oil-wrapping, or crusting might still be covering valuables—but the time for recovery decreases each year.

David Flohr and others are convinced that a good portion of the ship was never fully explored during DSR's efforts. The first three explorations centered where the entire haul of gold coins came from. Flohr observed:

> All of the recovered 1,207 coins from the 1996 and 1997 operations came from this one location and box, including the coins from the last exploration. The ship still has the safe, which I believe is underneath the wreckage in the sand towards the bow. The payroll is the most valuable object there, as the greenbacks are redeemable into gold, were wrapped in oil paper, and would still be good. Their value as collector items would be even greater than the market value of the $20 gold coins. We didn't find the Wells Fargo boxes, nor did we find the passengers' baggage that was stored in the compartment underneath the dining hall.

All of the coins discovered in 2000 dropped from the box remains at the smokestack's base into the gaping hole to the coal storage at the bottom. Although the divers poked through and pulled up all of the coal, they apparently didn't venture to the bridge or purser's office. Although some believe that the safe moved forward towards the bridge when the ship sank, they argue that the purser's office couldn't have moved that far. The baggage area under the dining saloon was never touched, and observers saw the divers continually focusing on the same general area, but not moving to inspect ship segments that were further away.

The question remains: Where is the safe? Locating Jonathan Rock and the wreck site is no longer a mystery. The filed court documents shine a clear light on the area. The wreck is clear and visible on side-scan sonar as a linear target with a slightly curved ship shape, and divers frequently travel to the site to see the wreck.

Don Knight maintains that at some point, the safe ripped from the sinking ship and buried itself somewhere between the rock and the vessel's ultimate resting place. Don Siverts argues that DSR has already used sonar investigations and didn't find anything "significant" from Jonathan Rock to the wreck site. He feels that the large safe would be sanded in and very difficult to locate. "There was a safe there," Peter Pelkofer told one reporter. "There's no doubt about it." Where the safe, baggage, and the missing gold coins and bullion remain hidden continues to be a mystery.

Due to quad bi-pass heart surgery, Don Knight retired from teaching in 1997, but later established a machine shop in which he fabricated sophisticated metal parts for U.S. Air Force bombers (from the B-1 and B-2 to F-117). He successfully recovered from a second heart attack in 2004 at the age of sixty-two and is again searching for hidden treasure off the California coast. His wife of twenty-five years, Betsy, has worked for Cal-State Fullerton as a senior evaluator in their Records Department and recently retired.

After the last exploration of the *Brother Jonathan,* members of Deep Sea Research went off to other ventures. Harvey Harrington is searching for more sunken ships even though he is in his seventies. Willard Bascomb, unfortunately, died at the age of eighty-four from multiple fractures and infections sustained in a car accident in June 2000. Wings Stocks is operating his company, Adventure Depth & Technology, in Santa Cruz, California; it specializes in remote imaging, search, and recovery efforts. Sherman Harris is in his eighties, still lives in Palm Springs with his wife, Rosemary, but suffers from Alzheimer's disease. After different explorations for sunken ships and other undersea ventures, Don Siverts turned most of his business operations over to his son, Curt, who also is an underwater marine consultant to Hollywood. Curt consulted with the producers on the Caribbean filming of the *Pirates of the Caribbean* sequels.

Q. David Bowers sold his company to another entity in 1999,

Collectors Universe. For nearly three years, he headed the "Bowers and Merena" division of Collectors, before leaving to start up another rare-coin operation, American Numismatic Rarities. The most prolific coin writer in numismatic history, he is the author of over forty books, hundreds of auction and other catalogs, and several thousand articles. The July 1999 issue of *Coinage Magazine* named Q. David Bowers one of the top "Numismatists of the Century."

As an early investor, Mark Hemstreet received his $20,000 back plus interest. He also had the "personal joy of sharing in finding a ship of history." All in all, this was for him a "very rewarding experience, being a major shipwreck on the West Coast of historical significance with the madam, the Commander of the Pacific, and all the famous personalities."

By his own admission, David Flohr was somewhat embittered by the State of California's "search and destroy" tactics. Although he was seventy years old in 1995, he was very busy and worked on both the *Brother Jonathan* as well as the U.S.S. *Midway* projects. Flohr had to work overtime, as his brother-in-law, Sherman Harris, needed to spend much of his time running his restaurant operations in Palm Springs, and there was "too much to be done." The amount of work he poured into the project was extensive, especially when he only intended to be an investor. Unfortunately, the investments of his friends and relatives—including immediate family members from grown kids to in-laws—were made based on his participation.

He observed:

> I wouldn't do this all over again, if I had the chance. I would never again associate with such scoundrels, big egos, and overzealous bureaucrats. The State's intransigence was unbelievable. We didn't even get a "thank you" from the State of California for all of the work that we did.

Years ago, David Flohr read *Gods, Graves, and Scholars,* which turned him on to the search for sunken treasure. As to the effect of gold, he said:

> You can get gold fever. There is an aura about gold, that gleaming opulence against blackness. But it's only a metal: You can't drink it, eat it, protect yourself with it, or starve off the wolves with it. Yet people die for gold.

As Betsy Knight recently said, "It was all about greed, and greed has no reward."

In 2005, David Flohr turned eighty. For twelve years he worked with others to bring about the historical aircraft carrier U.S.S. *Midway* into a floating museum in San Diego Harbor. At the banquet of recognition for the volunteers, the founder chairman called to the podium various people to give them silver plaques as recognition for their volunteer work. David's name was not called for him to walk to the podium. He was a bit concerned, but thought to himself, "Oh, well. . . . " At the end, the master of ceremonies said, "We have one more plaque to give out." He called David Flohr to the podium and presented him with a gold-plated, eighteen-inch long replica of the *Midway,* which was computer generated and machine-cut to the smallest detail.

He is still very active in community activities, from a Prison Outreach Program and Cub Scouts to Junior Achievement and the U.S.S. *Midway.* With near equal time spent on both the *Brother Jonathan* and *Midway,* each activity gave him "moments of great elation and moments of deep despair." Because of the people, he enjoyed his work on the U.S.S. *Midway* the most.

> These persons became my friends, people I could talk to and trust, which wasn't the case with the *Brother Jonathan.* Money and gold seem to bring out the worst in people. With the *Midway,* we weren't going for the gold, but more for the history and service.

The clash of personalities was not only between Don Knight and the others in DSR over the recovery. There were internal disputes as well. The officers in charge of exploration and diving operations,

Jim Wadsley and Harvey Harrington, were adventurers and flamboyant people. They wouldn't and couldn't have the same concern for budgets, legal technicalities, and financial controls, as did the more business-like approach of Sherman Harris and David Flohr. According to Don Knight, Betsy Knight, and David Flohr, "Jim Wadsley had a temper that easily flared up and likeable Harvey Harrington claimed he didn't have the money at times to pay the obligations others felt he should have assumed."

There was the problem with the finder's fee arrangement with Rick Hansen, for example. When DSR officers agreed to individually pay a total of $50,000, the lawsuit in 2004 was finally settled. David Flohr and Sherman Harris paid their share of the finder's settlement, $30,000. Harrington was to pay the remaining $20,000 and, according to Hansen and Flohr, he still hasn't paid. Harrington also was to pay half of the $32,000 legal bill for Rick Hansen's attorney and he didn't, according to Flohr.

Despite the problems and financial constraints, DSR performed as it promised by: (1) conducting mapping of the wreck; (2) performing at its cost the agreed surveying; (3) donating all of the discovered artifacts to the State of California; (4) working under the federal district court's and State of California's supervision for the recovery operations; and (5) giving California 20 percent of its finds. The salvors had no assurance that they would find gold when California started fighting them; in fact, they hadn't even found the ship when the state first made its unreasonable demands for half of whatever was discovered.

The controversy over the gold bars died down somewhat, if only because John J. Ford is ill with Alzheimer's and Paul Franklin passed away. However, Professor Buttrey still feels as passionately about his conclusions. This controversy itself is so much like everything else associated with the *Brother Jonathan:* If there could be a conflict, there was.

People are struck that DSR's principals had to buy their *Brother Jonathan* gold coins at auction, even though they were the ones who discovered them. Further, neither David Flohr nor Sherman Harris owns any meaningful memorabilia from their long and extensive efforts. Under the agreement with Hansen, the parties agreed individually to turn over to him what they had in their possession from the successful recovery of the *Brother Jonathan.* Sherman Harris sent the pictures he had taken; David Flohr sent his extra copy of the Bowers' book, a recovered porcelain plate artifact, a map, and the pictures he took, as well. Flohr was allowed to keep the one gold coin he had purchased at the auction.

Flohr concluded:

> It doesn't matter that some people cheated me or that I did some things not as well as I wanted. Rather, I tried my best, and if I reach heaven, I hope that despite my faults, God will understand that I really tried to apply the Golden Rule: Do unto others as I would have them do unto me. Just don't ever invite me to join any other undersea treasure hunts.

As people drive toward Crescent City's westerly limits at the ocean, they come across the Brother Jonathan Cemetery at the southeast corner of Ninth Street and Pebble Beach Drive. Called the Brother Jonathan Vista Point, an asphalted turnout is located nearby where one can park by the ocean and walk about. It's a grassy but level area, separated by a few trees from a playground area to the east. A large stone bears the plaque stating the cemetery's dedication to those who lost their lives in the shipwreck. The California State Parks Commission with the Del Norte County Historical Society placed the memorial there on Independence Day in 1961.

The bodies of numerous local residents buried in 1865 at a cemetery close to the memorial site were later removed by family and friends for interment at other places. This actual site was located in a wooded knoll between Eight and Ninth Streets at Pebble Beach Drive. In making the park-like setting, workers removed six feet of dirt from the cemetery site to level the ground, and in the process, numbers of rotten boards and knobs of coffins were unearthed—but no remains were discovered. The aged, bleached-white headstones of Daniel and Polina Rowell were relocated to the memorial site.

Young and old collectors alike buy and sell the dead passengers' gold coins and bars over 140 years after the *Brother Jonathan* sank with its 225 lost souls. Meanwhile, the wreck and its many artifacts lie at the bottom of the ocean. As with the H.M.S. *DeBraak* and the State of Delaware, there is no State of California museum dedicated to the *Brother Jonathan,* its gold, and the discovered Civil-War era artifacts. Divers swim instead over the unprotected wreck to inspect and hold the numerous objects scattered around the site.

Salvors and states still argue over the past and who owns its history. The State of California did its job well in protecting this wreck from any possible degradation. It did such a good job that the substantial artifacts, gold, and ship remains will disintegrate before the public or anyone else will ever see them. There is no funded California-statewide shipwreck conservation program with incentives for private-sector salvors to assume the risk that the state will not accept. The *Daily Triplicate* ran a prophetic story in 2000 with the headline, "Legacy in Question: It's Unclear How History will be Preserved after Gold Seekers Leave."

Some of the *Brother Jonathan*'s porcelain plates, mugs, wine bottles, and other artifacts are on display at the Del Norte County Historical Society in Crescent City. This is the only public place of continual display, but for fifteen items at the Crescent City Lighthouse exhibit. Hundreds and hundreds of other interesting artifacts, however, are in the Historical Society's conservation laboratory at the Flynn House.* With scant funds available for the conservation, the non-profit, volunteer Del Norte County Historical Society is trying to do the job that the State of California and California State Lands Commission should have helped fund, especially given the gold it received.

The Flynn House was named for the original owners who willed

*At the time of publication, there were plans to move them to another location.

their home and two-car garage to the Historical Society. Owing to the disrepair of the house, the society sold the house and grounds. For years, the owner rented the garage to the Historical Society as an in-kind donation at $75 per month. This became the facility where volunteers worked on and stored the *Brother Jonathan* artifacts. When the owner rented the house and the tenants eventually moved out, the garage was left without electricity. Later, the power was turned back on with a new tenant, and the conservation work could be done in the light. The security alarm system was again functioning.

The garage is thirty-feet long by twenty-feet wide at best with no more than six-hundred square feet available to work and store the countless numbers of these precious items. When entering by the front side-door, a long table to the left stretches down one side with plastic containers stored on top and below. The containers are full of small sherry glasses, larger glasses for drinking, porcelain plates, and terracotta containers, while numbers of boxes lay underneath, completely filled to their tops with objects wrapped in newspaper. Numbers of white porcelain plates, glassware, cups, glass containers, beer mugs, multi-faceted cruet bottles, and terracotta long-necked containers lie in wrapped seclusion. At one time, the terracotta bottles held mineral water from Germany.

By a dim window on the far wall, thin metal decorations that once surrounded door-handles lay on newspapers. Other boxes contain glasses, shards of broken plates and pottery, and exquisite glasswork. In the center of the dark room, two twenty-foot-long sections of tables lie side by side with plastic containers stuffed full with artifacts, but a number of these containers are filled with water for objects still in conservation. With water barely covering the artifacts, priceless items crowd the containers: antique-looking wine and champagne bottles; more terracotta mineral-water containers; small cruet bottles; and small bottles of yellow, clear, and opaque glass, some with yellowish, sulfuric looking solutions. The "yellowish" fluid or glass tint is from the disintegrated iron that seeped into the bottles and colored the glass. The same process reduced the contained fluids to a sulfuric or "rotten egg" smell and look.

Some items are molded glass with glass stoppers, which appear to be ladies' dressing table articles. Others contain the embossed words, "Soothing Syrup," which was Mrs. Winslow's patent medicine with its opium base for the ladies. As it wasn't considered to be ladylike to drink whiskey in those times, the women drank this. Volunteer Sean Smith observed, "Apparently life on the frontier needed a lot of soothing."

Although the water feels acidic or very salty to the touch, a few of the water-filled containers hold wine bottles that are complete with their corks intact and wine still inside. Apparently one lab volunteer sampled part of the wine from a bottle years ago and said that it "wasn't bad." Flasks, jugs, small medicinal bottles with the tinctures still inside, and other bottles with yellowish fluids line other plastic containers. To a far-right wall, narrow shelves for artifacts are stacked on one side with more containers filled with recovered items.

The job that the Del Norte County Historical Society is doing is very commendable. Supported by an all-volunteer staff of dedicated, hard-working professionals, only its director is paid and this is a small sum by city standards. Over time, each Historical Society lab "leader" taught the next volunteer how to manage the conservation activities.

Becky and Jerry Young ran the lab last and passed on their experiences to Sean Smith, who teaches both science and history to seventh-grade students at Crescent Elk Middle School. Under his direction, Sean's students in his honor's class work in the conservation; the fifth and final year for Smith's classes to be doing this conservation is intended to come to an end in 2006.

Although the "artifacts are in charge of the timetable," Sean believes that the last of the uncorked glassware will soon be completed. His students never worked on the metal items (iron boxes, metal plates, and straps) due to the potential for burns from the chemicals used in the electrolysis. Sean, however, will work in the lab to finish the process. As the middle school is six blocks away from the museum and laboratory, it is a convenient walk from either location.

The California State Lands Commission has directed the conservation through a retained marine archaeologist. Dr. James Allan, who teaches at St. Mary's College of California in Northern California (eighteen miles east of San Francisco in the City of Moraga), is the retained expert, and Dr. Allan consults for California on a variety of maritime archaeological projects. His college students also work on aspects of the *Jonathan*'s conservation, primarily on the iron and copper artifacts that were once undergoing electrolytic conservation in Crescent City, but were brought here for final treatment. In addition to the Flynn House and Crescent City displays, some fifteen pieces are with Jim Allen's conservation and Texas A&M apparently still has the one large iron container.

The impregnation of saltwater into the artifacts is the prime problem, and the embedded salt in the glass, wood, metal, and other artifacts must be removed during the restoration process. Storing the items in constantly changing freshwater serves two purposes. First, it keeps the bottles, glasses, and plates wet to prevent salt crystals from drying out, which expands and cracks the item apart. Second, wet-brushing the salt crystals away and storing the items in more freshwater eventually brings out all of the salt by a process called osmosis. The "brush and soak" approach is being used until the salinity of the water measures zero.

The problem becomes complicated due to the saltwater's actions in breaking down iron, which can bind with nearby glass, wood, and other materials. The brush and soak approach doesn't seem to work on the iron-colored glass, so other methods may be needed to solve this. Corks and wood items have further problems in that the salt actually replaces the cellulose within wood cells; the water "blanching" approach, according to Sean Smith, also doesn't seem to work with them. To prevent the wood cell walls from collapsing, polyethylene glycol must be used additionally to replace the water in the cells.

Smith has used some of his allotted class preparation time to take five students to the garage a week. Different seventh-graders for several years have moved the containers of artifacts out to the lawn in the daylight, measured the chloride levels, took out the items and washed them off with tap water, tossed out the old brackish water, placed the artifacts back in the containers, and put in fresh tap water. The work of the 1997 artifacts has finished, but he and his students are now finishing up the 2000 finds. Once this is completed, the Historical Society will move the artifacts to a climate-controlled storage unit two miles from the museum.

Other than the retained archaeologist, some required chemicals for electrolysis, and final treatments of metals, California provided no funds or support for the conservation. They haven't even guaranteed that the Del Norte County Historical Society will be able to exhibit what its volunteers have worked on for so long. The Society could have accelerated the conservation process if it could have afforded distilled water, brought about more frequent changes of the salty water, paid for the electricity, and conducted more sophisticated conservation approaches. However, the funding did not come.

All of the *Brother Jonathan*'s artifacts remain the property of the State of California and its State Lands Commission. Given the hard work of the dedicated Del Norte County Historical Society volunteers, board members, and students over the years with those artifacts, the State of California should recognize these efforts. It can do this by funding better conservation facilities with a permanent museum exhibit, as well as giving its formal agreement to let the Historical Society exhibit the artifacts that its people have worked on for so long. If the state had been more cooperative with Don Knight in the very beginning, there is little doubt that the results would have been different.

When walking in the lab past these priceless antiquities and their history, images of a long-ago era capture your imagination. Women in brightly colored, high-necked dresses with bustles and tight bodices hold their umbrellas high. Men with handlebar mustaches and muttonchops wear bowler hats and three-piece suits with wide lapels. The people drink from the now-empty champagne bottles, eat off the gleaming porcelain plates, and pour out their tinctures from the small medicine bottles. From General George Wright, James Nisbet, and Roseanna Keenan to Captain DeWolf, Fireman John Hensley, Quartermaster Yates, and the Rowell family, people lived and died after using these items. To hold or just look at an antique wine or cruet bottle recovered from three hundred feet below the ocean is breathtaking and eerie, all at the same time.

One can hear the voices of laughter and joy—and of desperate terror and fear—still echoing from so many years ago. The hard work of a chronically underfunded Del Norte County Historical Society is all that now protects these priceless artifacts from totally disappearing from public view. Meanwhile, the underwater marine life and saltwater eat away and consume what's left of the ship, its treasures, and undersea artifacts. The corroded, five-ton walking beam still lies in twenty-five feet of water at the end of a pier in Long Beach Harbor.

The CSLC still takes the position that it has the sole rights to the ship and the injunctive zone under its agreement with DSR. The CSLC is clear that for any future applications for salvage, "The hoops are pretty high and probably too high an archaeological standard for salvors," said one official recently. California's share of any treasure would be "up to 50 percent" of whatever was recovered. It would require an "expensive" performance bond and be "very cautious" as to any application. All of this sounds like the same tune from the eighties and nineties. With limited motivation for private salvors to work with the State of California due to its inflexible position, unscrupulous people will continue to surreptitiously dive to take what the state will not protect and the ocean hasn't yet claimed.

Despite the millions of dollars that California expended in its staff time, legal fees, costs, and proceedings to own the ship, the state quietly sits on its gold coins, which are now worth millions. Except for ten gold coins leased to the Wells Fargo Historical Museum in San Francisco under the settlement agreement, all of California's valuable gold coins lie in an "unnamed bank vault that is safety-secured in Sacramento."

One member of the CSLC e-mailed his prophecy: "I have this vision after I retire that the *Brother Jonathan* gold coins will remain in the safe-deposit box, like the Ark in *Indiana Jones,* lost to bureaucracy forever."

The dead of the *Brother Jonathan* and those seeking its history deserve better.

Brother Jonathan Event Timeline

1850 Owned by a New Yorker, Edward Mills, the *Brother Jonathan* is constructed and launched at the well-known shipyard of Perrine, Patterson & Stack in Williamsburg, New York.

1851 Sailing the Atlantic route to Panama under the initial stewardship of Captain Charles Stoddard, the ship begins her career in March ferrying Gold Rush prospectors and fortune seekers.

1852 Seeing the potential for the ship's use on the Pacific route to the California Gold Rush fields, Cornelius Vanderbilt purchases the vessel from Mills and completely refurbishes it. He then orders the crew to sail the vessel around Cape Horn to San Francisco.

1852–56 In October 1852, the ship starts its new career for four years on the run from San Francisco to San Juan del Sur, Nicaragua, ferrying prospectors back home; it then transports new fortune seekers back to San Francisco.

1857 John T. Wright purchases the *Brother Jonathan* for Pacific Northwest runs. The Gold Rush days to and from California have matured and other locations, such as British Columbia, Washington, and Oregon, are opening up for prospectors and merchants alike. Wright renames it the S.S. *Commodore* and presses the vessel into the run between San Francisco (her home base) and Vancouver, British Columbia, with stopovers at Crescent City, Portland, and Seattle at times.

1858 A gale engulfs the ship off California and the vessel barely stays afloat. It is later overhauled and again renamed the *Brother Jonathan.* The ship continues on its U.S. West Coast runs, both north and south from San Francisco, opening up, along with other vessels, commerce and trade.

1859 President Buchanan signs the act granting statehood to Oregon, and the *Brother Jonathan* brings the first news of its admission to the state.

1860 Wright sells the vessel to Major Samuel J. Hensley, whose interests eventually become part of the Pacific Steam Navigation Company, and the new owners later order a complete overhaul of the now 10-year-old ship.

1861 On December 19, 1861, the reconstructed vessel leaves San Francisco Harbor on its run to Vancouver. As business booms in the Pacific Northwest, the *Brother Jonathan* earns large sums of money for its owner. With Captain George W. Staples in command, the vessel carries from 700 to 1000 passengers on its trips.

The Civil War has started, but thanks to General George Wright's decisions, the West escapes relatively unscathed. The *Jonathan* continues on its commercial runs up and down the coast.

1862 In April, the vessel carries a record 1,000 passengers from San Francisco to Portland, Oregon, steaming the 680 nautical miles in nearly 69 hours—also the best time on record at the time.

1864 Hensley transfers title to the California Steam Navigation Company, an entity formed by the steamer owners to reduce competition.

1865 In the late spring, a Confederate sympathizer shoots and kills Captain Staples; a seasoned senior officer, Samuel J. DeWolf, becomes the new captain of the *Brother Jonathan.*

On July 30, 1865, the sidewheeler strikes an uncharted, seething reef in heavy seas off Northern California and sinks in forty-five minutes. In one of the West Coast's worst peacetime maritime accident ever, only 19 people in a battered wooden lifeboat survive of the 244 passengers and crew on board.

1865–66 Newspapers from San Francisco to Chicago and New York City blare the tragic news on front-page headlines and calls go out for an investigation. The completed maritime investigation places blame on the uncharted reef, not Captain's DeWolf's decisions nor the ship's loaded condition.

1866–67 In response to the tragedy, federal legislation is enacted with changes in warning light standards and lifeboat regulations.

1868–92 Owing to the tragedy, Congress authorizes the construction of the most remote, expensive, and dangerous lighthouse ever constructed in the United States: St. George Reef Lighthouse, located scant miles from where so many lives were lost. After a ten-year construction period, the lighthouse is completed in 1891 and operational one year later.

1894 The "World's Champion Deep Sea Diver" and promoter, John F. Ryan, reports that he discovered the ship on one of his dives, but then couldn't find it again.

1865 to 1930s Dozens and dozens of intrepid undersea explorers try to locate the treasure of the *Brother Jonathan.* Some say they've found it, but due to darkness and underwater currents aren't able to locate her again.

1930s First reports surface that a fisherman pulled up gold bars from the *Jonathan,* but the precise location can't be found again.

1950s John J. Ford and Paul Franklin join together to search for and find rare gold coins, currency, and bars throughout the Southwest.

1960s Reports surface that John J. Ford has possession of the *Jonathan*'s gold bars through Franklin's efforts.

1970s In 1973, Ford completes the first public sale of several of the vessel's gold bars, reputedly owned by the San Francisco madam, Mrs. Roseanna Keenan. Dr. Larry Holcomb reports in error that he discovered the ship in 1976. He also comes close to writing a screenplay with Ken Kesey about the ship, and is quite helpful to later expeditions by discovering where the ship is *not* located.

1980s Don Knight concentrates his research and inquiries on where the *Jonathan* might be.

1986–91 Knight forms an underwater research company, Sea-Epics Research, and conducts eight different undersea investigations for the ship prior to 1993. He makes two searches each in 1986, 1987, 1989, and 1991.

1991 In May 1991, Don Knight incorporates these activities into a new entity called Deep Sea Research, Inc. Prior to that, Sherman Harris invests his money in the new venture. He is soon joined by David Flohr and Mark Hemstreet. Experienced divers Harvey Harrington and Jim Wadsley join the firm, and with Don Knight form the three-man board of directors.

1993 On October 1, 1993, Don Siverts locates the long-missing ship in the mini-submarine *Snooper* with Don Knight and others on board the mother ship *Cavalier.*

1993–94 Differences over salvage operations immediately surface between Don Knight, Jim Wadsley, and Harvey Harrington. On February 8, 1994, the shareholders vote Don Knight off the board, and he decides to leave the venture. Litigation commences between Don Knight, DSR, and a few principals.

1995 In March 1995, the State of California files a motion in U.S. District Court to dismiss Deep Sea Research's petition to be the exclusive salvor of the ship. The judge rules in favor of DSR and the litigation proceeds up the appellate ladder.

1996 The two-man mini-sub, *Delta,* scoots pass a suspicious "glint" on the bottom. On August 30, 1996, divers find the first gold coins and on that expedition locate 875 1860s gold coins in near-mint condition.

The war in the courts and press continues between Don Knight and the remaining salvors, along with numbers of motions and legal skirmishes brought by the State of California against DSR.

1997 After recovery operations in August, a total of 332 more gold coins (again mainly $20 Double Eagles) are recovered—the total recovery so far is 1,207 very valuable gold coins.

1998 In April, the U.S. Supreme Court decides unanimously in favor of DSR. California immediately responds it will continue to trial in a lower court over the facts (even though these were clearly against its position).

1999 In March, California settles with DSR. In return for 20 percent of the gold discovered by the salvors, or 200 very valuable gold coins, the state agrees to stop its litigation, among other conditions.

On May 29, 1999, more than 500 bidders crowd into the Airport Marriott Hotel in Los Angeles for the auction of DSR's gold coins. The sale of its 1,006 coins that day fetches a total of $5.3 million.

1999 Although the dispute between John Ford and Professor Buttrey over the validity of the *Jonathan*'s gold bars has been going on for some time, it reaches a peak in the "Great Debate" between Buttrey and Michael Hodder on August 12, 1999, at the American Numismatic Association's annual convention.

2000 A last exploration by DSR takes place with $2 million funding from Dwight Manley, a multimillionaire gold-coin dealer. These operations locate another 58 coins, which Manley retains under the agreement. This brings the total coins discovered to 1,265.

2006 Although California has not agreed yet to give title of the artifacts to the non-profit Del Norte County Historical Society in Northern California, the low-funded society continues working to conserve the hundreds of artifacts found by DSR.

SELECTED REFERENCES

"A Sea Tragedy: The Brother Jonathan Wreck Revived." *Del Norte Record,* February 2, 1892.

Affleck, Edward L. *A Century of Paddlewheelers in the Pacific Northwest, the Yukon and Alaska.* Vancouver, British Columbia: Alexander Nicolls Press, 2000.

"Agreement on Treasure of Lost ship Is Ratified." *New York Times,* March 21, 1999, 1–25.

"Arrival of the Del Norte." *San Francisco Evening Bulletin,* August 9, 1865.

American Numismatic Association, 1999 Convention, Tapes of Michael Hodder and Professor Ted Buttrey's "Great Debate" (1999).

Asseo, Laurie. "Who Owns Shipwrecks? High Court to Decide." *Journal of Commerce,* December 9, 1997, 3B.

Bancroft, Hubert Howe. *History of Central America,* Vol. III. 1801–1887 (*The Works of Hubert Howe Bancroft,* Vol. III). San Francisco, CA: The History Co., 1887.

Banks, Lacy J. "Worm's Gamble Pays Off." *Chicago Sun-Times,* April 7, 1998, 100.

———. "Troublesome Clients Burn Manley." *Chicago Sun-Times,* November 14, 1999, 23.

Barra, Ezekiel I. *Tale of Two Oceans; New Story by an Old Californian.* San Francisco, CA: Press of Eastman & Co., 1893.

Barron, Kelly. "Gold Digger." *Forbes,* May 29, 2000, 170.

Becker, Mary Ann. "Regulating the Business of Culture: The Abandoned Shipwreck Act—Can Preservationists, Salvors, and Divers Sail in Calmer Waters?" *DePaul Law Review,* Winter, 2001, vol. 51, 569.

Bennett, Laura J. "Classic Casualty, Brother Jonathan Sinking." *Professional Mariner,* October/November 2004, 60.

Berthold, Victor M. *The Pioneer Steamer California: 1848–1849.* Boston and New York: Houghton Mifflin Company, 1932.

Bledsoe, A. J. *History of Del Norte County, California, with a Business Directory and Traveler's Guide.* Eureka, California: Humboldt Times Print, Wyman & Company, 1881.

Block, Nina. "Sailing into Oblivion." *The Journal of Earthwatch Institute,* October, 1999, vol. 18, issue 4.

Bowers, Q. David. "The Great Debate: A comment by Q. David Bowers." *American Numismatic Society Newsletter,* Fall, 1999.

———. *The Treasure ship S.S. Brother Jonathan: Her Life and Loss, 1850–1865.* Wolfeboro, New Hampshire: Bowers and Merena Galleries, Inc., 1998.

Bowers and Ruddy Galleries, Inc. *The Henry H. Clifford Collection: Coins of the American West,* public auction catalogue, March 18–20, 1982.

Bowles, Samuel. *Across the Continent: A Summer's Journey.* Springfield, Mass.: Samuel Bowles & Company, 1866.

Boyer, Mary Schmitt. "Some Believe Worm Is Digging into Hole." *The Plain Dealer,* March 19, 1999, 4D.

Broad, William J. "Deep-Sea Joint Venture: Britain and U.S. Company in a Treasure Hunt." *New York Times,* October 6, 2002, 1(1), 14.

"Brother Jonathan Wreck Is Again Believed Found." *Crescent City American,* December 18, 1931.

"Brother Jonathan Story Again Revived." *Crescent City American,* April 14, 1927, 1.

"Brother Jonathan Shipwreck (The)." *The San Francisco Chronicle,* April 27, 1998, A24 (Editorial).

"Brother Jonathan Began Life on East Coast, Sank in 1865." *The Daily Triplicate,* September 16, 2000, 9A.

"Brother Jonathan Wreck Yields Additional Coins." Numismatic Guaranty Corporation (www.ngccoin.com/news/enews/ngc_enews_0311nov.htm, accessed June 1, 2004), eNewsletter, vol. 2, issue 11.

Browne, Lina Fergusson (Editor). *J. Ross Brown: His Letters, Journals and Writings.* Albuquerque, New Mexico: University of New Mexico Press, 1969.

Bureau of Marine Inspection and Navigation (National Archives), Steamboat Inspection Service. *Report of Casualties and Violations of Steamboat Laws, First District,* San Francisco, 1865.

———. Annual Reports of the Steamboat Inspection Service, vol. 1864–1867 (1865), *Proceedings of the Board of Supervising Inspectors of Steam Vessels,* RG 41, Entry 3.

———. *Official Report of the Lighthouse Keeper at Crescent City,* G. W. Emery, Crescent City Light Station, August 1, 1865.

Busch, Briton Cooper (Editor). *Alta California, 1840–1842: The Journal and Observations of William Dane Phelps, Master of the Ship "Alert".* Glendale, California: The Arthur H. Clark Company, 1983.

Buttrey, T. V. "False Western American Gold Bars." *The American Numismatic Society,* Second Series 9, 1997, 89.

———. "Gold Bars on the Brother Jonathan? (I); or, How to Read an Auction Catalogue." (www.fake-gold-bars.co.uk/bro1.html, accessed April 15, 2006.)

———. "Gold Bars on the Brother Jonathan? (II); or, How to Read a Fake Bar." (www.fake-gold-bars.co.uk/bro2.html, accessed April 15, 2006.)

"California Gold Pieces Go on Sale." *The Columbus Dispatch,* June 6, 1999, 6K.

California v. Deep Sea Research (www.gordonrees.com/cites/118sct1464.cfm, Gordon & Rees Website, accessed April 15, 2006.

California and State Lands Commission v. Deep Sea Research, 523 U.S. 491, 118 Sup. Ct. 1464, April 22, 1998.

"CC Salvage Company Locates Wreck of 'Brother Jonathan.' " *The Times-Standard,* September 20, 1970.

CDC.gov, National Center for Environmental Health. "Extreme Cold FAQs." (www.cdc.gov/nceh/hsb/extremecold/faq.htm, accessed April 1, 2006.)

Ceballos, Chris. "Heads or Tails, Newport Agent Wins with Coin." *Los Angeles Times,* August 11, 2000, B3.

Charlebois, Dr. Peter. *Sternwheelers & Sidewheelers: The Romance of Steam-driven Paddleboats in Canada.* Toronto: NC Press Limited, 1978.

Carver, Kaaron. "One Man, One Ship, Many Dead." *The Triplicate,* June 2, 1995.

Chase, Doris. "The Brother Jonathan Shipwreck Spelled an End to 'Coffin Ships.' " *The Humboldt Times,* December 13, 1959, 12.

"Cherished Memories: Major Samuel J. Hensley." (cstern.sphosting.com/major.html, accessed on January 1, 2005.)

Chiang, Harriet. "Finders Keepers; Treasure Hunters will be Able to Keep the Gold Found on a Shipwreck off Crescent City." *The San Francisco Chronicle,* March 19, 1999, A19.

Chun, Clarissa A. "Note: Charting through Protection for Historic Shipwrecks Found in U.S. Territorial Waters." *Virginia Environmental Law Journal,* vol. 19, 87.

Clark, William H. *Ships and Sailors: The Story of Our Merchant Marine.* Clinton, Massachusetts: The Colonial Press, 1938.

Clifford, James O. "Is there Gold in the Deep?: Court Fight Continues over 1865 Shipwreck of Brother Jonathan." *Associated Press,* February 12, 1996.

Coleman, Jennifer. "Volunteers Restoring Historic Lighthouse off California's Coast." *Associated Press,* April 20, 2002.

"Commodore's Disaster (The)." *Crescent City Herald,* July 28, 1858.

Compton, Kathleen. "Sunken Treasure up for Public Auction." *The Daily Triplicate,* May 26, 1999, 1.

Conservation Research Laboratory, Texas A & M. Conservation Research Laboratory Report No. 12.; (nautarch.tamu.edu/CRL/Report12/index.htm, accessed April 2, 2006.)

"Court Refuses Delay in 1865 Ship Salvage." United Press International, July 3, 1997.

Curtis, Greenleaf. *Diary of Greenleaf Curtis,* July to August 1865.

Cutler, Carl C. *Greyhounds of the Sea: The Story of the American Clipper Ship.* New York, New York: Halcyon House, 1930.

DeArmond, Robert N. (Edited by Richard A. Pierce). *The USS Saginaw in Alaska Waters: 1867–1868.* Kingston, Ontario and Fairbanks, Alaska: The Limestone Press, 1997.

DeLong, Jeff. "Treasure Ship Search Continues Next Month." *Del Norte Triplicate,* September 25, 1982.

Del Norte County Historical Society. Numerous in-depth files, clippings, handwritten accounts, and information pertaining to the life, loss, search, discovery, and artifact recovery of the *Brother Jonathan.*

DeWolf, Maria (Travis). Various letters written by Captain DeWolf's widow to family members, 1851 to May 27, 1892.

DeWolf, Maria (Knight). *An Episode of Early Life in San Francisco,* March 5, 1857 (handwritten early biography and stories).

———. *San Francisco,* March 19, 1900 (handwritten biography and stories).

Deep Sea Research, Inc. v. The Brother Jonathan, State of California, State Lands Commission, and United States of America, 883 F. Supp. 1343, March 15, 1995.

Deep Sea Research and R2 Consultants. *Report of Field Activities on the Brother Jonathan, Submerged Cultural Resource Site, Crescent City, California, August 18–31,* 1997. Report submitted to the United States District Court.

Delgado, James P. "The Wreck of the Pacific Mail Steamship *Tennessee.*" *Journal of The West,* October 1994, 14.

Delgado, James P. *To California by Sea: A Maritime History of the California Gold Rush.* Columbia, South Carolina: University of South Carolina Press, 1990.

———. "The Wreck of the Pacific Mail Steamship Tennessee." *Journal of the West,* October, 1994, 14.

Delkin, Fred. "Oregon Entrepreneur Franchises Excellence." *Oregon Magazine,* October 2004.

Denniston, Lyle. "Supreme Court to Consider Ownership of Shipwrecks." *The Baltimore Sun,* June 10, 1997, 4A.

———. "Salvagers May Sue States in Federal Court." *The Baltimore Sun,* April 23, 1998, 3A.

Dicken, Samuel N., and Emily F. *The Making of Oregon: A Study in Historical Geography.* Portland, Oregon: Oregon Historical Society, 1979.

Dickens, Charles. *American Notes.* London: Chapman & Hall, 1842.

Downey, Mike. "A Golden Opportunity to Experience Magic." *Los Angeles Times,* February 9, 2000, A3.

DuPree, David. "Dwight Manley Is No David Falk. He Doesn't Want to be." *USA Today,* December 15, 1998, 1C.

Emeigh, Gary, and Molly Murray. "Cannons from Shipwreck 'HMS De-

Braak' Restored." Delawareonline (accessed December 20, 2005); *The News Journal,* November 25, 2004.

Enkoji, M. S. "Treasure Hunters Get One Year to Probe Ship." *Times-Standard,* April 14, 1999.

"Expedition Off to Raise Sunken Treasure Ship." San Francisco Chronicle, June 12, 1917.

Farrell, John A. "Power Struggle Surfaces on Claims to Shipwreck." *The Boston Globe,* December 28, 1997, A1.

"File Salvage Claim on Sunken Vessel off Crescent City." *Crescent City Triplicate,* December 18, 1931.

Flohr, David. Numerous interviews and discussions with salvor by author on history of ship, search, and recovery.

"Florida Underwater Archaeology FAQ." State of Florida, Office of Cultural and Historical Programs. See dhr.dos.state.fl.us/archaeology/underwater/faq.cfm (accessed March 15, 2006).

"Former Wealthy Woman to Enter Home She Founded." *San Francisco Chronicle,* March 10, 1906.

Franks, Jonathan. "Treasure Hunt." *Boys Life,* June 1996, vol. 86, issue 6, Pg. 38.

"Full Particulars of the Wreck of the Brother Jonathan." *Alta California,* August 10, 1865.

"Further of the Wreck of the Brother Jonathan." *Alta California,* August 3, 1865.

"Further Particulars of the Wreck of the Brother Jonathan." *Alta California,* August 6, 1865.

Gibbs, James A. *Shipwrecks of the Pacific Coast.* Portland, OR: Binford & Mort, 1957.

———. *Disaster Log of Ships.* New York, NY: Bonanza Books, 1971.

———. *Lighthouses of the Pacific.* West Chester, Pennsylvania: Schiffer Publishing Ltd., 1986.

"Government Records Disclose Ill-Fated Jonathan Carried Little Treasure." *Crescent City American,* October 9, 1931.

Griffith, John. "Squabbling Over a Shipwreck." *The Oregonian,* September 27, 1996, D8.

Grimes, Jennifer. "No Gold Yet." The Daily Triplicate, September 16, 2000, 1.

———. "The Search for Jonathan's Sunken Gold." *The Daily Triplicate,* September 28, 2000, 1.

———. "Legacy in Question." *The Daily Triplicate,* September 29, 2000, 1.

Graves, Scott. "Ship's Treasure Coming to Museum." *The Daily Triplicate,* April 9, 1999, 1.

"Harbor News." *Crescent City American,* February 16, 1934, 4.

Heiser, Sherry. "Archaeologist Digs into Mystery of Brother Jonathan." *Del Norte Triplicate,* July 21, 1981.

Heisler, Mark. "Rodman Worms out of his Wedding Vow." *Los Angeles Times,* November 24, 1998, D3.

Hempel, Ruth. "A Philanthropist of the Old School." *Business Week,* February 16, 2004, 77.

Heyl, Erik. *Early American Steamers.* Buffalo, NY: Erik Heyl, 1953.

Hill, Ralph Nading. *Sidewheeler Saga: A Chronicle of Steamboating.* New York: Rinehart & Company, Inc., 1953.

Hinckley, Ted C. "The Hoonah's 1862 Seizure of the Hudson's Bay Company Steamer *Labouchere*—A Mixed Message." *Journal of the West,* October 1994, 22.

History of California, Vol. VI., 1848–1859. San Francisco, CA: The History Co., 1888.

Holding, Reynolds. "State Loses Shipwreck Appeal: 131-year-old Wreckage belongs to Private Salvage Company." *San Francisco Chronicle,* July 18, 1996, A18.

James, Charles (Custom House, San Francisco). Letter to the Honorable Hugh McGulloch, Secretary of the Treasury, August 16, 1865.

Jenkins, F. H. *Journal of a Voyage to San Francisco, 1849.* Northridge, CA: California State University, Northridge Libraries, 1975.

Johnston, James C. "Coins and Stamps Are Fraternal Twins," *Journal of Antiques.com* (www.journalofantiques.com/Mar03/coinsmar03.htm, accessed March 15, 2006.)

Jones, John Paul. "The United States Supreme Court and Treasure Salvage: Issues Remaining after Brother Jonathan." *Journal of Maritime Law & Commerce,* April, 1999, vol. 30, 205.

Kelly, Martin. "Searchers Believe They're Close to Finding Schooner." *The Times-Standard,* November 24, 1985.

Kemble, John Haskell. *The Panama Route: 1848–1869.* Columbia, South Carolina: University of South Carolina Press, 1990.

Kilpatrick, James. "Tragedy at Sea Makes for Meaty Case." *San Antonio Express-News,* December 11, 1997, B7.

———. "That Sinking Feeling." *The Tulsa World,* December 8, 1997, A6.

Knight, Donald. Numerous interviews and discussions with salvor by author on history of ship, search, and recovery.

———, and Eugene D. Wheeler. *Agony and Death of a Gold Rush Steamer: The Disastrous Sinking of the Side-Wheeler Yankee Blade.* Venture, California: Pathfinder Publishing of California, 1990.

Koerner, Brendan I. "The Race for Riches." *U.S. News & World Report,* October 4, 1999, 44.

Kooiman, William. "The Burning of S.S. *Japan.*" *Sea Classics,* January, 1990, 28.

———. "The Mystery of the S.S. *City of Rio De Janeiro.*" *Sea Classics,* February, 1990, 52.

———. "S.S. *Colorado:* Paddlewheeler to China." *Sea Classics,* November, 1996, 20.

Kowalski, Kathian M. "Who Gets the Sunken Treasure?" *Odyssey,* February, 2000, 37.

"Later from the Wreck of the Brother Jonathan." *Alta California,* August 17, 1865.

Langworthy, Franklin (Edited by Paul C. Phillips from the 1855 edition). *Narratives of the Trans-Mississippi Frontier: Scenery of the Plains, Mountains, and Mines.* Princeton, New Jersey: Princeton University Press, 1932.

Lewis, Oscar. *Sea Routes to the Gold Fields.* New York City, NY: Alfred A. Knopf, Inc., 1949.

Lighthousefriends.com. "Saint George Reef Lighthouse, California." (www.lighthousefriends.com/light.asp?ID=26, accessed January 12, 2006).

Lomax, Alfred L. "Brother Jonathan: Pioneer Steamship of the Pacific Coast." *Oregon Historical Society,* Vol. 60, September 1959.

Lore, David. "High Court Handed Sunken Gold Case: Insurers Press their Claim to Treasure." *The Columbus Dispatch,* September 23, 1995, 5C.

———. "Judge Adds to Discovery Group's Share of Gold." *The Columbus Dispatch,* November 9, 1996, 3C.

———. "Investors Hope to Structure Business of Treasure." *The Columbus Dispatch,* August 25, 1998, 5C.

Lorello, D. David, Jr. "The Abandoned Shipwreck Act of 1987: Navigating Through the Fog." *Gonzaga Law Review,* 1999/2000, vol. 35, 75.

"Lost Steamer Brother Jonathan Found." The *Courier,* March 24, 1880.

Luo, Michael. "A Gold Bounty to Shiver the Timbers; Coins: A Santa Ana Company is Grinding the Value of More than 1000 Coins." *Los Angeles Times,* April 10, 1999, B1.

MacMullen, Jerry. *Paddle-Wheel Days in California.* Stanford University, California. Stanford University Press, 1944.

Marshall, Don B. *California Shipwrecks.* Seattle, Washington: Superior Publishing Company, 1978.

———. *Oregon Shipwrecks.* Portland, Oregon: Binford & Mort Publishing, 1984.

McAndrews, Robert J. "Twin Ships Come Home to Die." *The Californians,* May/June 1987, 14–20.

McCabe, James Dabney. *Great Fortunes and How They Were Made.* Cincinnati: E. Hannaford & Co., 1871.

McCoy, Keith. *Melodic Whistles in the Columbia River Gorge.* White Salmon, WA: Pahto Publications, 1995.

McKenzie-Bahr, Mike. "Brother Jonathan Saga Continues." *The Triplicate,* February 25, 1994, 1.

———. "State Makes New Effort to Claim Wreck." *The Triplicate,* August 18, 1995, 1.

———. "State Asks Court to Stop Wreck Salvage." *The Triplicate,* September 12, 1995, 1.

———. "Shipwreck Salvaging May Begin." *The Triplicate,* June 14, 1996, 1.

———. "Shipwreck Artifacts Come to Surface." *The Triplicate,* September 6, 1997.

"Memorial to be Built for Brother Jonathan's Dead." *The Daily Triplicate,* July 9, 1959.

Meredith, John D. (Transcriber). *One-Way Ticket to Kansas, the Autobiography of Frank M. Stahl,* as told and illustrated by Margaret Whittemore. Lawrence Kansas: University of Kansas Press, 1959.

Michelsen, Michael W., Jr. "The Brother Jonathan: A Salvor's Quest Pays Off." *Immersed,* Spring 2002, 28–31.

Morrison, John H. *History of American Steam Navigation.* New York: Stephen Daye Press, 1958 reprint of 1903 work.

National Archives and Records Administration. *Guide to Records in the National Archives—Pacific Sierra Region.* Washington, DC: National Archives and Records Administration, 1995.

Neil, Paul. "California v. Deep Sea Research: Leashing in the Eleventh Amendment to Keep Sinking Shipwreck Claims Afloat." *Pepperdine Law Review,* 2000, vol. 27, 657.

Nolte, Carl. "1865 Shipwreck Discovered Off North Coast: Legend Says Steamer Sank with Gold, Booze, Camels." *San Francisco Chronicle,* February 25, 1994, A-1.

Nye, Lydia Rider (Edited by Doyce B. Nunis Jr.). *The Journal of a Sea Captain's Wife, 1841–1845: During a Passage and Sojourn in Hawaii and of a Trading Voyage to Oregon and California.* Spokane, Washington: The Arthur H. Clark Company, 2004.

Odyssey Marine Exploration Website. (See generally at www.shipwreck.net accessed March 15, 2006.)

"Old Gold Bar at Smithsonian Deemed a Fake." *Associated Press,* August 1, 2003.

PBS.org. "Legendary Lighthouses: St. George Lighthouse." (www.pbs.org/legendarylighthouses/html/calgl.html, accessed March 2, 2006).

———. "Nova Online; "Human Response: Ship." (www.pbs.org/wgbh/nova/escape/respship.html, accessed June 18, 2004).

Paddock, Richard C. "Treasure or Time Capsule?: Ex-Partners Are at Odds." *Los Angeles Times,* March 17, 1996, A-1.

Pomfret, John E (editor). *California Gold Rush Voyages, 1848–1849: Three Original Narratives.* (Authorized facsimile of original book, 1972, University Microfilms, a Xerox Company, Ann Arbor, Michigan.) San Marino, California: The Huntington Library, 1954.

Proskocil, Niz. "Gold Coin a Reason to Rush to Heritage Museum." *Omaha World-Herald,* March 6, 2001, 29.

Rainey, James. "Firm to Keep Most of Shipwreck Coins." *Los Angeles Times,* March 18, 1999, A3.

Reddish v. Brother Jonathan, District Court of the United States proceeding, filed August 8, 1865 (representative of three other proceedings filed previously over moneys owed, including *Mayo v. Brother Jonathan,* July 24, 1865; *Rogers v. Brother Jonathan,* July 27, 1865; and *Young v. Brother Jonathan,* August 8, 1865).

Relyea, Kie. "Appeal Set for Historical Ship." *Times-Standard,* January 22, 1996, A3.

Richardson, Albert D. *Beyond the Mississippi: From the Great River to the Great Ocean, Life and Adventure on the Prairies, Mountains, and Pacific Coast, 1857–1867.* Hartford, Connecticut: American Publishing Company, 1867.

"Rodman Marries, but Agent Cries Foul." *The Toronto Star,* November 17, 1998, E11.

Rousmaniere, John (Editor). *The Luxury Yachts.* Alexandria, Virginia: Time-Life Books, 1981.

Rudyalicelighthouse.net. "St. George Reef Lighthouse, Crescent City, CA." (www.rudyalicelighthouse.net/CalLts/StGeorge/StGeorge.htm, accessed April 12, 2006.)

Russell, Amy Requa, Marcia Russell Good, and Mary Good Lindgren (Editors). *Voyage to California: Written at Sea, 1852: The Journal of Lucy Kendall Herrick.* San Marino, California: Huntington Library, 1998.

"Saint George Reef Lighthouse." Rudy and Alice's Lighthouse Page. (www.rudyalicelighthouse.net/CalLts/StGeorge/StGeorge.htm, accessed on February 2, 2006.)

Salecker, Eric C. "A Tremendous Tumult and Uproar: The Tragic Sinking of Sultan." *America's Civil War,* May 2002, vol. 15, issue 2.

"Salvage Company Formed." *Crescent City American,* February 16, 1934, 4.

Savage, David G. "High Court to Weigh Claims to Steamer Wrecked in 1865." *Los Angeles Times,* June 10, 1997, A3.

———. "Justices Hear Shipwreck Ownership Arguments." *Los Angeles Times,* December 2, 1997, A3.

———. "Court Rejects State's Claim to Historic Ship." *Los Angeles Times,* April 23, 1998, A3.

Schmidt, Steve. "Mystery of the Steamship Brother Jonathan: Where's the Treasure?" *The San Diego Union-Tribune,* October 11, 2000, A1.

———. "Gold-Laden Safe still Eludes Salvage Crews." *Copley News Service,* October 23, 2000.

Schott, Jeana Sciarappa. "Federal Wreck Diving Regulations: A Mass of Confusion and Litigation." *Dive Training,* January 2001, 103.

Shomette, Donald. *The Hunt for the HMS DeBraak: Legend and Legacy.* Durham, North Carolina: Carolina Academic Press, 1993.

Smith, Dinitia. "Gold Bars, Glamorous Stories and a Battle over Authenticity." *The New York Times,* March 3, 2001, B9.

Soule, Frank, John N. Bihon, and James Nisbet. *The Annals of San Francisco.* New York, NY: D. Appleton & Company, 1854.

Southerland, Randy. "Retrieving treasures from the sea; Two worldwide salvage firms based here." *The Atlanta Journal-Constitution,* September 20, 2001.

Stack's. *Sale of the Gibson Collection,* November 11, 1974, 42.

———. *Auction Sale Catalogue,* June 11, 1997.

State of California, State Lands Commission. *Proposed Negative Declaration: Salvage Permit for Steamship Brother Jonathan* (Sea Epics Research), September 2, 1988.

State of California, State Lands Commission. *Consider Approval of a Settlement in State of California v. Crowely Marine Services and Authorizing Appropriate Disposition of the Walking Beam,* June 2, 2003 Calendar Item.

Stebinsky, George. "Treasure Ship's Cargo to Hit Auction Block." *The Columbus Dispatch,* March 28, 1999, 81.

Stein, Loren. "When Deep-Sea Treasure Is Found, Who Owns It?" *The Christian Science Monitor,* July 10, 1997, 4.

Suba.doc. "Hypothermia and Near Drowning." (scuba-doc.com/hypoth.htm, accessed February 11, 2006.)

Superior Galleries, division of Superior Stamp & Coin Co., Inc. *The Dr. Jerry Buss Collection* auction catalogue, January 28–30, 1985.

Tebbin, Gerald. "Salvaged Gold Coins on Market at Last." *The Columbus Dispatch,* January 29, 2000, 1B.

"Terrible Marine Disaster." *San Francisco Evening Bulletin,* August 2, 1865.

Terry, John. "Getting the Message Across Long before the Days of E-Mail." *The Oregonian,* January 25, 1998, C4.

———. "Ledger of Oregon Shipwrecks Lengthy and Likely Incomplete." *The Oregonian,* March 14, 1999, B-4.

"The Brother Jonathan arrived", article that starts with these words. *Crescent City Herald,* March 16, 1859.

"The steamship Ocean Queen," article that starts with these words. *Daily National Intelligencer,* August 26, 1865, 3.

Thompson, Wilbur and Allen Beach. *Steamer to Tacoma.* Bainbridge Island, Washington: Driftwood Press, 1963.

"Told by A Survivor, The Wreck of the Brother Jonathan. Mrs. Mary Altrie's Vivid Recollection." *San Francisco Chronicle,* February 11, 1894.

"Treasure Hunters Return to Search for Sunken Gold." *Crescent City Triplicate,* September 11, 1931.

United States, District and Supreme Courts. Various documents pertaining to lawsuits filed against the *Brother Jonathan,* September 8, 1856 to August 8, 1865.

United States Coast and Geodetic Survey. *Annual Report of the Superintendent (Benjamin Peirce) of the U.S. Coast and Geodetic Survey,* 1869–1870, Ex. Doc. No. 206, 41 Congress, Second Session.

United States Printing Office. *Acts of Congress Relating to Steamboats.* Washington: Government Printing Office, 1867.

United States Mint. *Preliminary Inventory of the Records of the U.S. Mint.* Records of The U.S. Mint, Record Group 104 (October 1995).

Van Winkle, Mark. "An Interview With John J. Ford Jr.-Part I." *Legacy (Heritage Galleries),* April 1990.

———. "An Interview with John J. Ford Jr.-Part II." *Legacy (Heritage Galleries),* June 1990.

Wels, Todd. "Brother Jonathan Booty: Recovered Coin Donated to Del Norte Historical Society." *The Daily Triplicate,* September 21, 1999.

———. "Lighthouse Boom Eyed for Possible Restoration." *The Daily Triplicate,* November 17, 2000.

Wexler, Kathryn. "California Seeks to Salvage its Claim to Possible Treasure in a Sunken Steamer." *The Washington Post,* March 13, 1996, A3.

———. "Ship that Went Down in 1865 Stirs up 1996 Dispute." *The Oregonian,* March 17, 1999, A17.

Wilkinson, F. "Doubloon or Nothin'." *Forbes,* March 18, 1991, 59.

Wiltsee, Ernest A. *Gold Rush Steamers of the Pacific.* San Francisco, California: The Grabhorn Press, 1938.

"Wings Stocks—Treasure Salvor." (e-nekton.com/archive/edition9/profiles .html, accessed April 15, 2006.)

"Wreck of the Brother Jonathan." *Alta California,* August 2, 1865.

"Wreck of Steamship Brother Jonathan." *The Oregon Reporter,* August 5, 1865.

Wright, E. W. (Editor). *Lewis & Dryden's Marine History of the Pacific Northwest.* New York, NY: Antiquarian Press, Ltd., 1961.

INDEX